ISLAM IN THE HINTERLANDS

ISLAM IN THE HINTERLANDS
Exploring Muslim Cultural Politics in Canada

Edited by Jasmin Zine

UBCPress · Vancouver · Toronto

© UBC Press 2012

All rights reserved. No part of this publication may be reproduced, stored in a retrieval system, or transmitted, in any form or by any means, without prior written permission of the publisher, or, in Canada, in the case of photocopying or other reprographic copying, a licence from Access Copyright, www.accesscopyright.ca.

21 20 19 18   5 4 3 2

Printed in Canada on FSC-certified ancient-forest-free paper
(100 percent post-consumer recycled) that is processed chlorine- and acid-free.

Library and Archives Canada Cataloguing in Publication

Islam in the hinterlands : Muslim cultural politics in Canada / edited by Jasmin Zine.

Includes bibliographical references and index.
Also issued in electronic format.
ISBN 978-0-7748-2272-5 (bound); ISBN 978-0-7748-2273-2 (pbk.)

1. Muslims – Canada – Social conditions – 21st century. 2. Muslims – Canada – History – 21st century. 3. Islam – Canada. I. Zine, Jasmin

FC106.M9I85 2012   305.6'970971   C2011-907415-X

Canada

UBC Press gratefully acknowledges the financial support for our publishing program of the Government of Canada (through the Canada Book Fund), the Canada Council for the Arts, and the British Columbia Arts Council.

This book has been published with the help of a grant from the Canadian Federation for the Humanities and Social Sciences, through the Aid to Scholarly Publications Program, using funds provided by the Social Sciences and Humanities Research Council of Canada.

UBC Press
The University of British Columbia
2029 West Mall
Vancouver, BC V6T 1Z2
www.ubcpress.ca

Contents

List of Tables / vii

Acknowledgments / ix

Introduction: Muslim Cultural Politics in the Canadian Hinterlands / 1
JASMIN ZINE

Part 1: Gender and Cultural Politics / 39

1 Unsettling the Nation: Gender, Race, and Muslim Cultural Politics in Canada / 41
JASMIN ZINE

2 The Great Canadian "Shar'ia" Debate / 61
ITRATH SYED

3 Toward a Framework for Investigating Muslim Women and Political Engagement in Canada / 92
KATHERINE BULLOCK

Part 2: Media and Representation / 113

4 Colluding Hegemonies: Constructing the Muslim Other Post-9/11 / 115
YASMIN JIWANI

5 Marketing Islamic Reform: Dissidence and Dissonance in a Canadian Context / 137
MEENA SHARIFY-FUNK

6 Toward Media Reconstruction of the Muslim Imaginary in Canada: The Case of the Canadian Broadcasting Corporation's Sitcom *Little Mosque on the Prairie* / 161
ALIAA DAKROURY

Part 3: Education / 183

7 From Mosques to *Madrassas*: Civic Engagement and the Pedagogy of Islamic Schools / 185
NADEEM MEMON

8 Unveiled Sentiments: Gendered Islamophobia and Experiences of Veiling among Muslim Girls in a Canadian Islamic School / 208
JASMIN ZINE

Part 4: Security / 237

9 The Security Certificate Exception: A Media Analysis of Human Rights and Security Discourses in Canada's *Globe and Mail* and *National Post* / 239
JACQUELINE FLATT

10 The Anti-terrorism Act and National Security: Safeguarding the Nation against Uncivilized Muslims / 272
SHAISTA PATEL

Contributors / 299

Index / 304

List of Tables

4.1 Thematic categories used in the *Globe and Mail* and the *National Post* / 118

4.2 Comparison of headlines in the *Globe and Mail* and the *National Post* / 119

9.1 Count totals by theme for the *Globe and Mail*'s and *National Post*'s coverage of the security certificate debate / 251

Acknowledgments

This book emerged from a desire to map the field of Canadian Muslim studies by bringing together timely and relevant scholarship that helps us to understand the various ways that Muslims have been affected by the post-9/11 era of imperialist wars, draconian domestic-security policies, and media sensationalism, which have led to racial and religious profiling as well as to other challenges that shape their everyday lives. This book is dedicated to Muslims who have brought Islam to the hinterlands and who, despite the hardships they left behind and the new ones they encounter, have claimed a space where the tenacity of their faith and their spiritual resilience have allowed them to enrich this landscape with their presence.

I would like to thank all the contributors to this book for their wonderful scholarship, for their inspiring activism, and for their patience, support, and collaboration during the process of putting together this collection.

I am particularly indebted to Emily Andrew, senior editor at UBC Press, for believing in this project from the outset and for her unwavering support, advice, and professionalism, which were absolutely invaluable in bringing our efforts to fruition.

This book was generously supported by the Aid to Scholarly Publications Program and by the Wilfrid Laurier University Book Preparation Grant. I am grateful for the financial contributions they provided.

Last but not least, I present this work as a legacy for my sons, Usama and Yusuf, who inspire me to do work that is close to my heart.

Wasalam/peace,
Jasmin Zine

ISLAM IN THE HINTERLANDS

Introduction
Muslim Cultural Politics in the Canadian Hinterlands

JASMIN ZINE

This book emerges out of a need to map new understandings of the Canadian Muslim diaspora as a site of struggle, contestation, and change. Muslim communities have become increasingly salient in the social, cultural, and political landscape in Canada. This has been due largely to the aftermath of 9/11 (which is this book's starting point) and the racial politics of the ongoing "war on terror," which has cast Muslims as the new "enemy within." The narratives of citizenship, nationalism, and security have become inextricably linked in public discourse and policy making in ways that disproportionately target Canadian Muslims as potential threats to public safety and compromise their civil liberties. Driven by media sensationalism, narrow and limiting constructions of Muslims are commonly purveyed, reproducing Orientalist archetypes of illiberal and anti-democratic foreigners that test the limits of Canadian multiculturalism. Islam has become a permanent feature in the Canadian hinterlands, and Muslim cultural politics have become prominent flashpoints in the social and political landscape.

Increasingly, Muslims figure prominently in contemporary public debates that shape our national consciousness and public policies, from the Maher Arar case, security certificate detainees, and the arrests of eighteen Muslim males in Toronto on alleged charges of "home-grown terror," to racial and religious profiling, Ontario's debates over *shar'ia* (Islamic law) tribunals, and Quebec's questions of "reasonable accommodation," its banning of Islamic headscarves and face veils, and its xenophobic "citizen's codes."

Although these issues dominate media attention, other experiences that shape and impact the lives of Canadian Muslims rarely make headlines, such as migration, settlement, education, access to jobs and resources, poverty, racism and Islamophobia, institutional and organizational development, social-movement building, political resistance, and negotiations of theological pluralism.

The Canadian Muslim diaspora is a complex, contradictory, and hybrid space filled with a mix of liberatory possibilities and productive tensions occurring within and against certain oppressive social and political conditions that create the terrain for a distinctly "Canadian Islam." Islam in Canada has been a highly generative site for new epistemological and ontological positionings. Beyond sectarian orientations, there are new movements toward "moderate" or "progressive Islam" that have gained currency and have spearheaded controversial moves such as female-led prayers and encouraged the promotion of gender equity within religious sites. More gender-conscious forms of mobilization occurred as secular and faith-based Canadian Muslim feminists organized around the widely debated proposal for shar'ia-based arbitration in Ontario. There are also new cultural drivers shaping the Muslim presence in the Canadian national imaginary. The Canadian Broadcasting Corporation's (CBC) groundbreaking comedy series *Little Mosque on the Prairie*, created by Canadian Muslim filmmaker Zarqa Nawaz, has catapulted Muslims into primetime television and the national consciousness in new and challenging ways.

Despite the widespread interest and dynamic social and political engagements relating to Islam and Muslims in Canada, there has been little attempt to document and address Muslim cultural politics within Canada. This collection provides a space to construct multiple readings of Islam and Muslims in the Canadian diaspora through a variety of empirical and theoretical contributions to this field. As an entry point into these discussions, I want to map some groundwork on which the contributions in this collection must be read by articulating some broad political, cultural, and empirical frames that shape the contours of the Muslim presence in Canada. I want to briefly reflect on the social, political, and cultural foundations of the discussions in this collection, which are anchored in questions of diaspora, nation, citizenship, and multiculturalism. These are increasingly sites of contestation in the social, cultural, and political landscape in Canada and are being shaped by the global dimensions of neo-imperial wars and the ruptures between secular modernity and "postsecular" religious politics, social formations, and insurgent forms of identity.

The Canadian Muslim Diaspora

"Diaspora" is a contested signifier. Although the term is rooted in the often violent historical ruptures that lead to exile, displacement, migration, and reformations of communities outside their places of origin, in its most current and perhaps most common usage, it describes postmodern migrant communities that have resettled outside their ancestral homelands due to a variety of social, economic, and political factors. Many of these forces stem from the imperialist, neoliberal foundations of globalization and the dislocations caused by its upheavals. Moghissi and colleagues (2009, 3) note that the term "diaspora" has come to refer to "populations of refugees, migrants, guest workers, expatriates, and the exiled and self-exiled." This new reality means that there is no longer a single narrative for transnational migration and settlement that result in the re-rooting of migrant communities, cultures, and identities in adopted homelands. However, what remains consistent – whether or not the context of migration is forced or voluntary – is the fraught process of reinventing the narrative of "home" and recapturing feelings of familiarity and belonging, the absence of which creates deep social and psychological tensions that can be difficult to reconcile.

On the other hand, a fact often overlooked when Canada's multiple immigrant diasporas are heralded as a multicultural success story is how this story of the nation serves to obscure the realities faced by Aboriginal peoples, who have been further displaced by their presence. The exclusion, isolation, and geographic marginalization of Aboriginal communities in their own ancestral homelands have created a forced diasporization that is muted by celebratory notions of multiculturalism that conveniently overlook this violent history (see also Moghissi et al. 2009). It is an inconvenient truth in the grand narrative of multicultural pluralism that the diasporas of early white European settlers permanently displaced Aboriginal populations from their homelands in Canada and elsewhere. Postcolonial histories are thus rewritten to exclude the memory of violent conquest and imposition, and the notion of diaspora remains untainted by this history.

As generations adapt and acculturate over time, more hybrid social and cultural formations develop that transform both the diasporic and the dominant culture. Yet this plurality and cultural interpenetration occur within unequal relations of power. The incorporation of immigrant groups occurs through their insertion into hierarchal relations of racial, ethnic, and class-based privilege that relegate most of these groups to positions of subordination and marginality (see also Moghissi et al. 2009). These cleavages mark the fault lines between belonging and disavowal and define the space between citizens and outsiders. Cultural dissonance that occurs from residing within these liminal spaces can result in romantic longings for the homeland, yet these attachments are believed to compromise loyalty and kinship within the adopted society. Diasporic communities are derogatorily labelled "ethnic ghettos" and "insular enclaves" – evidence of the failure of multiculturalism and a justification for reviving more assimilationist models of social integration. The "vertical mosaic" of Canada has been forged on this unequal footing, which continues to privilege the diasporic histories, cultures, and conquests of white settlers, thereby positioning indigenous and immigrant communities as subordinate national subjects through their "exaltation" (Thobani 2007).

Muslims in Canada have a longer history than one might imagine. The genealogy of Muslim migrants can be traced back to the arrival in 1854 of a Scottish family – James and Agnes Love and their newborn son. According to Hamdani (1997), James Love, named after his father, was born in Ontario in 1854. He was the eldest of eight children. The youngest one, Alexander, was born in 1868, one year after the Canadian confederation was formed. Lorenz (1998) tells the story of the arrival of the first Arab immigrants in about 1882. Many of them, mostly young men, came from Ottoman Syria fleeing conscription into the Ottoman army. Most of these early migrants were Christians, but a few were Muslims. Most of these wayfarers settled in the East, but a few headed west and arrived at the most remote outposts of Canada's western frontier. In a rare historical narrative of Muslims during this period, Lorenz (1998, 28) relates the story of early Arab migrants who came as peddlers and pioneers:

> "The Syrian peddler was something of an institution in most Western settlements," wrote Gilbert Johnson. "Sometimes on foot, with a pack on his back and a case of trinkets and smallwares in his hand, but more often with a horse and a light wagon in summer, or with a sleigh in winter, he travelled the prairie trails on more or less regular routes ... His arrival often provided a welcome relief from the monotony of pioneer life."

Such stories narrated by Lorenz shed light on the early foundations of the Muslim presence in Canada. One of the first pioneers with any recorded history was Salim Sha'aban. He was born an Ottoman subject in 1880 and arrived in New York as a twenty-year-old, eventually making his way to Iowa in 1908. He peddled goods on foot and later on horseback until he had earned enough to return to Lebanon to find a bride in 1910. Two years later he returned with the hope of finding greater prosperity in Canada. Leaving his wife and their first child behind, Sha'aban set his sights on Alberta, where he built a homestead. His wife's journey is recounted in the passage below as a story of passion, endurance, and perseverance:

> For the young Arab woman who landed, tired and bewildered, at the port of Montreal, a long train trip across the prairies still lay ahead, followed by more travel by horse and wagon. The railway link to Edmonton had been completed in 1904, and agricultural settlement existed only in a band 50 kilometers (30 miles) wide on each side of the single railway line. Beyond that, the great prairies were still the land of the Cree, Assinaboine [sic] and Blackfoot. The winters could hardly have been less welcoming: One 1907 blizzard drove the mercury down to 48 degrees below zero (−55°F). Yet Larry Shaben, Sha'aban's grandson and a leader of today's Alberta Muslim community, recalls that his grandmother, who lived to be 99, was "fiercely passionate" about Canada, and called it "a wonderful country." (Lorenz 1998, 29)

By 1901 Canada's Muslim community had grown to 47 members, who settled in Alberta and Saskatchewan. By 1911 there were 1,500 Canadian Muslims, most of them Syrian and Turkish migrants, many of whom worked on the construction of the western railways (Abu-Laban 1983, Hamdani 1997). According to Lorenz (1998, 29),

> By the late 1920's, a handful of Muslim families were scattered throughout Alberta, earning their livings as fur traders, mink ranchers and, shopkeepers. Shaben, now in his 60's, recalls that when he was growing up in Endiang there was only one other Muslim family in town, and his grandparents "knew every Muslim in Alberta."

By the early twentieth century, governments were enforcing policies of racial exclusion in order to stem the flow of Asian immigrants. Abu-Laban (1983) reports that when the First World War broke out, many Turkish immigrants were classified as enemy aliens and sent back to their country of origin. As a result of these policies, Canada's Muslim population remained relatively small between 1911 and 1951. The 1931 census recorded only 645 Muslims – a figure that had grown to perhaps 3,000 by 1951 (Abu-Laban 1983, 76). After the Second World War, a time when the economy was shifting from wartime to peacetime production, Muslims began entering Canada as skilled labourers. By the end of the twentieth century, Muslims were the largest non-Christian religious group in Canada, having surpassed the Jewish population in 1996 (Hamdani 1997).

Presently, Islam is the fastest growing religion in Canada. According to an Environics report based on the 2006 census, there are 842,200 Muslims in Canada comprising 2.6 percent of the population. With a steady growth in population size and a diverse ethno-racial mix of cultures from South Asia, the Middle East, Europe, Continental Africa, and the Caribbean, the Canadian Muslim community is a heterogeneous ethno-racial population that is even further distinguished along sectarian lines. Although there is a predominant Sunni Muslim community in Canada, there are prevalent Shia, Ismaili, Druze, and Sufi communities in the larger diasporic makeup. The challenges of pluralism that affect Muslims in Canada are therefore internally as well as externally driven. Ideological differences are often pronounced and create schisms among community groups and representatives that sometimes take oppositional stances in important community debates, such as the shar'ia tribunals (see Chapter 2). The Muslim community in Canada is far from homogeneous demographically and ideologically despite the essentialized representations and narrow conceptions that commonly shape perceptions of who Muslims are, what they believe, and how they behave.

Muslim Social, Cultural, and Economic Politics in Canada in a Post-9/11 Context

Since 9/11 greater attention has been paid to how Muslims are integrating within Canada. Much of this interest is driven by the fear that social and cultural isolationism could lead to possible "sleeper cells" of jihadi extremists threatening public peace and safety. The case of seventeen Muslim youth and one Muslim adult arrested in 2006 on alleged terror charges was a flashpoint for fear of "home-grown" terror (see Chapter 10). The idea that Canadian-born Muslims could be involved in potential threats against the nation was unsettling to many. In trying to make sense of these arrests and the threat of the "enemy within," public discourse often turned to the question of values. A 2006 public opinion poll revealed that 65 percent of Canadians were concerned that too many immigrants were not adopting "Canadian values" (Adams 2007, 94).[1] The reasoning followed, then, that the misguided Toronto youth had been deprived of access to "true Canadian values" that would have bound their allegiance to the state and prevented any other form of identification that had the potential to divide their loyalty.

Adopting "Canadian values" was touted as the antidote to the threat posed by those who manifest more questionable ties to citizenship and the nation. These irreconcilable citizens were constructed as "anti-citizens" who threatened to unsettle the narrative of Canada as a peaceful and benevolent nation (see Chapter 1). Muslims at large were seen as residing outside of the common framework of "discursive citizenship" based on a set of shared national values and were therefore in need of "cultural rehabilitation" through the inculcation of Western values. These troubling narratives persist in the ongoing contestations surrounding Muslim cultural politics in Canada that this book seeks to explore.

Despite public concern over the integration of Canadian Muslims, an Environics survey of 500 adult Canadian Muslims conducted between 2006 and 2007 collected interesting data on how Canadian Muslims view their identity and their sense of belonging and satisfaction within Canada. Reporting on these findings, Adams (2007) notes that although about 90 percent of Canadian Muslims were born outside of the country, a vast majority articulated a strong sense of attachment to Canada. It was reported that 94 percent said they were proud to be Canadian, a figure that matches the national average of 94 percent (161). Of those expressing pride in being Canadian, 73 percent acknowledged they were "very proud." Even more recent newcomers living in Canada fewer than five years expressed a high level of national pride: 73 percent reported being "proud" to be Canadians, and 54 percent were "very proud." Immigrants who had resided in Canada fifteen years or more had the highest expression of pride as Canadians. In this category, 99 percent reported being "proud," and 88 percent were "very proud" (161). Also, according to Adams, Muslims noted that freedom, democracy, and multiculturalism were the sources of their pride, which was consistent with what Canadians at large reported feeling. These findings demonstrate that far from being isolationist, Muslims in Canada feel an allegiance to the nation and a sense of pride as Canadians. This outlook, however, does not preclude their right to be critical of the nation and its policies or to assert claims for the recognition and accommodation of their own values, beliefs, and practices. All too often when immigrant groups express dissent or are critical of the conditions of their adopted homeland, they are met with claims of disloyalty or ungratefulness. When they advocate for inclusion and recognition of their cultural beliefs and practices, they are seen as threatening the cultural integrity of Canada and are confronted with the "when in Rome" argument. Therefore, although a significant number of

Muslims have expressed satisfaction and pride in being Canadian, this does not guarantee that they are regarded by others as having the unconditional right to claim a stake within the nation.

Amid an otherwise positive assessment of being Canadian, the findings also revealed significant concerns about discrimination that unsettle the ideal of a multicultural utopia in Canada that Adams (2007) suggests. The report revealed that 66 percent of Muslims surveyed were concerned about discrimination and that 30 percent were "very concerned" (166). Youth reported higher levels of concern than did their immigrant parents. Adams attributes this to their having grown up in Canada, which he argues gave them a stronger sense of entitlement in comparison to their parents, who likely expected some level of hardship as immigrants to a new country and could "overlook an epithet here or there" provided their lives were otherwise improving (166). Yet economic concerns were as highly rated as concerns over discrimination. These categories are not easily separated given the high number of foreign-born and educated Muslim immigrants and the lack of recognition of foreign credentials, which has led to underemployment. The cab driver with a doctoral degree and the medical doctor working as a security guard represent the reality that many immigrants to Canada face, despite the promise of economic gains and multicultural equality.

My 2002 study on homelessness among Latin Americans and Muslims in Toronto (Zine 2002, 2009) found that in a sample of 300 participants (predominantly newcomers), the higher the level of education they reported, the lower their employment status. For example, of those in the workforce, 57 percent had achieved only a high school education, 26 percent had attended a community college, 10 percent had a graduate degree, 6 percent had no formal schooling whatsoever, and 4 percent had an undergraduate degree. Of those who were foreign-trained professionals, only 4 percent had found work in their field, leaving the rest to be underemployed or out of work (Zine 2002, 30). Environics survey data also show that Muslims in Canada are better educated than the population at large (45 percent hold a university degree as compared with 25 percent of all Canadians); however, with respect to income, Muslims fall behind the national average (Adams 2007, 167). Not only are these findings counterintuitive, given that education is promoted as a gateway to economic success and therefore that a positive correlation between levels of education and employability is expected, but these findings also clearly demonstrate that whereas the doors to professional fields may be closed for newcomers with foreign degrees, the doors to the unskilled, low-paid labour force are wide open. Although Adams (2007,

167) also speaks to these concerns stemming from the Environics study, he is hesitant to label this as "discrimination in its purest form," reserving this category for more conscious acts of refusing to hire on the grounds of religious difference. His analysis, however, fails to account for the structural barriers that limit employment opportunities not on the basis of "in your face" racism and Islamophobia but on the grounds of other often more subtle and less visible forms of exclusion and systemic discrimination.

For example, one Canadian study found that Muslim women who wear the *hijab* (headscarf) suffer from discrimination in the workplace. Persad and Lukas (2002) have identified significant barriers to veiled Muslim women in their efforts to find work. As part of the study, two sets of women were sent "undercover" to apply for the same job. They provided almost identical resumes, ages, and ethnic backgrounds; the only difference was that one of the women wore the hijab. The study found that twenty-nine of the thirty-two Muslim women surveyed said that an employer had referred to their hijab while they were applying for work in the manufacturing, sales, and service sectors. Twenty-one of the participants were asked to remove their head covers; one-third were told at least once that they would have to remove their headscarf if they wanted a job. This study highlights how gendered forms of Islamophobia operate on social, cultural, and ideological levels to deny employment opportunities to Muslim women (see Chapter 8) and at the same time reminds us that the multicultural utopia that Adams (2007) proclaims operates more as a national fiction than as a social reality.

Veiled Differences: The Fashioning of Sartorial Nationalism

The issue of veiling, particularly the highly contested face veil, or *niqab*, has been a major flashpoint in Muslim cultural politics in Canada. This has been the case most notably in Quebec, where legislation is presently being proposed to prevent women who wear the face veil from accessing government services and public institutions. The controversial Bill 94 was recently introduced in the National Assembly by the Quebec Liberals, although this is not the first time the Quebec government has raised the issue of veiling as a significant political concern. According to Khan (2010), "politicians have shamelessly used veiled women as cheap electoral targets":

> In the 2007 Quebec election, complaints forced the chief electoral officer to ban the face veil at the voting booth (even though veiled women never asked for an exemption). In a 2008 by-election, Prime Minister Stephen

Harper seized on Quebec discontent with the face-veil by adding his disapproval. The political stigmatization and ensuing "mob mentality" created a climate of fear for a minority who wished to exercise their democratic right to vote.

These attempts by politicians to ban the face veil and their public proclamations condemning its use have resulted in "niqabophobia" and have created the ideological groundwork for the current anti-niqab legislation. Not only are niqabi[2] women's rights to make reasoned choices about their bodies curtailed as a result of these moves, but it also remains unclear what democratic gains are achieved, particularly when these same women are prevented from exercising their right to vote. Indeed, these are anti-democratic moves based on knee-jerk reactions to religious and cultural difference that ironically undermine the very values politicians claim to uphold.

Similar reactionary politics govern the current attempt to exile women from public services and public space through Bill 94. This latest attempt to legislate Muslim women's dress came into effect after an Egyptian immigrant, Naema Ahmed, was expelled from a French-language class for refusing to remove her niqab. Later, when she attempted to enrol in a different school, the Quebec immigration authorities located her, and she was expelled again. The irony here lies in the fact that she was attempting to learn French in order to better integrate into Quebec society but was expelled from the class and further marginalized by her attempts to learn the language. She has since filed a human rights complaint to contest her treatment at the hands of Quebec immigration authorities. A second woman, a permanent resident from India, was also expelled from her French class for refusing to remove her niqab. A spokesperson for Quebec immigration defended the decisions in these cases on pedagogical grounds, stating that "it is important for the teacher to see the student's mouth to teach good elocution" (Scott 2010a). Yet this pedagogical rationale for the government's actions is not defensible since these isolated incidents do not warrant a province-wide policy regulating women's dress; rather, it signals the failure of school authorities to negotiate a suitable arrangement that would ensure these students feel safe in class and also meet the educational needs of the program. These incidents hardly justify the expulsion of these students or the development of legislation that dangerously compromises civil liberties. This puts the government in the wildly ludicrous position of legislating women's dress as a pretext for mediating cross-cultural difference and fostering "communication." It is evident that in the clear absence of sound social or political reasoning, this legislation is being built on a campaign of racial and religious demonization and fear that, far from facilitating "communication" across cultural difference, will lead only to further xenophobia and racist backlash against Muslims in Canada. Yet there is little to warrant such overblown concern. According to the Muslim Council of Montreal, there are presumed to be about twenty-five women in all of Quebec who actually wear the niqab. Further, out of approximately 118,000 people who accessed Montreal's health board services in 2008 and 2009, only ten asked for accommodation, and out of approximately 28,000 who accessed city services, not one asked for special treatment (Shakir 2010).

Given the implications of this draconian legislation, which would effectively prevent women from accessing healthcare, education, social services, and public transportation based on their attire, Bill 94 has been the topic of heated debate across Canada. Opposition from Muslim groups and broader social justice organizations has been mounting. Amnesty International warned that the ban "would violate the rights to freedom of expression and religion of those women who choose to express their identity or beliefs in this way" (Siddiqui 2010). One grassroots Muslim women's group in Ontario echoed these concerns in a press release:

> The proposed legislation, Bill 94, barring individuals who wear the face veil from accessing government services and public institutions, is in direct violation of Canada's own Charter of Rights and Freedom (Section 2), the Quebec Charter and the United Nations Universal Declaration of Human Rights which guarantees all Canadians the right of freedom of expression and religion. The role of a democratic nation is to protect an individual's pursuit of religion or identity without scrutiny or judgement from their respective government. (Coalition of Concerned Muslim Women of Kitchener-Waterloo 2010)

This statement employs a rights-based framework that has interestingly been used by those arguing both for and against the ban. Those individuals and groups arguing against Bill 94 as in the statement above invoke national and international human rights covenants to support their claims for religious freedom, which would be unduly infringed on if the state became the arbiter of women's religious dress. Broad coalitions of Muslim groups, secular women's organizations, student associations, and anti-racist and social justice organizations have galvanized to contest this legislation as an undue form of state control over women's bodies that would effectively trample on their rights and civil liberties and deny them access to basic necessities of life such as education, healthcare, and social services.

Those in favour of banning the niqab also use the same liberal, rights-based framework to build their case. They argue that because the niqab symbolizes the subjugation of women, it contradicts the liberal, secular values of Canadian society and should be banned. Although with respect to freedom of expression and religion, the ban itself also compromises the same liberal rights of women who choose to cover their face, this consequence becomes a matter of necessary "collateral damage" in a larger battle against illiberal minorities. Proponents of this ban (both state and nonstate actors) unwittingly undermine the very liberal values they claim to be championing under the guise of "rescuing" Muslim women from their illiberal values, their faith, and ultimately their "illiberal" clothing. This enacts what I call a form of "sartorial nationalism" where veiled Muslim women within what Anderson (1983) describes as the "imagined community" of the nation are rendered "unimaginable" as citizens and therefore positioned outside of the nation and political community. Their bodies cannot be coded within the dominant boundaries of national belonging due to their dress, which has been described by Christine St-Pierre, the Quebec minister responsible for the status of women, as "ambulatory prisons" (quoted in Peritz 2010). Ironically, they are politically and socially outcast at the same time by their style of dress and by the state's attempt to regulate it. The niqab therefore operates as a negative signifier included within the state only by virtue of its exclusion. In this move, citizenship and national belonging are determined sartorially, as the nation is not only circumscribed by dominant cultural values and beliefs (that veiling is seen to abrogate) but is also configured through the kinds of dress that signify belonging and allegiance to these same values. Under Bill 94, the niqab is a sartorial signifier of national exclusion that is seen as betraying dominant liberal values and thereby positioning Muslim women as outsiders to the nation and deviants within the law. This debate signals a broader attempt to decide the legitimate cultural, and in this case sartorial, representations of the nation and who has a right to belong to it.

The role of the state in determining the way Muslim women should dress in order to render themselves docile national subjects who dutifully demonstrate their allegiance to dominant liberal norms through their dress code needs to be challenged for its racism and sexism. The paternalistic desire to "unveil" and "liberate" Muslim women on the part of Western, secular states is best articulated in Spivak's (1988) famous terms of "saving brown women from brown men" and is part of the deeper impetus for "rescuing" Muslim women from their backward beliefs and from attire presumably forced on them by misogynistic Muslim men. Their right to choose as agentic subjects and to maintain a sense of bodily integrity is nullified by the state's intervention in deciding for them what lies in their best interest. This authoritarian paternalism of the Canadian state mirrors the religious mandates requiring women to cover themselves that the mullahs of Saudi Arabia, Iran, and Afghanistan use in similar ways to regulate the bodies of Muslim women and to deny them the right to decide how to express their identity and faith.

Interestingly, the proposal for legislation regulating Muslim women's dress was first put forward by a Muslim organization. The impetus for the niqab ban was spearheaded in 2009 by the Muslim Canadian Congress (MCC), which appealed to Ottawa to introduce legislation to ban the wearing of masks, niqabs, and the *burka* (full body cloak) in all public settings. In a press statement, the MCC argued that the ban is necessary to ensure public safety since "not only is the wearing of a face-mask a security hazard and has led to a number of bank heists in Canada and overseas, the *burka* or *niqab* are political symbols of Saudi inspired Islamic extremism."[3] The MCC links the niqab and burka to criminality and terrorism in much the same way as do other openly Islamophobic neoconservative fear mongers.[4] There is perhaps some surprise that this proposal and the troubling arguments underpinning it come from a Muslim organization. This is a prime example of the fact that the Muslim community is not a singular entity and cannot be essentialized. Muslims are ideologically and politically as well as racially and ethnically diverse and hold internally competing views on many issues. Of concern, however, is that Muslim organizations are being oriented around neoconservative and xenophobic views such as those espoused by the MCC and in other cases along more patriarchal and puritan religious lines. The situation of Muslim women hangs in the balance between the competing frames of reference and ideologies being purveyed by Muslim organizations (religious and secular) that position themselves as political vanguards for these women. The narrow views of the MCC, which reflect the "Orientalism of Orientals" and the patriarchal and puritan fundamentalist views purveyed by certain religious sectors of the community, place Muslim women in between equally limiting polemics (see, for example, Zine 2004). Both ideological vantage points produce authorizing discourses that leave little space for Muslim women themselves to articulate their sense of agency, womanhood, faith, and citizenship.

Although Muslim women are increasingly claiming spaces within Islam and within the national narrative, they are left unsupported by some women's groups, such as the Quebec Council for the Status of Women, which instead have taken up a paternalistic mode of feminism in their support of Bill 94 as a means to preserve "gender equality" despite the fact that the bill will allow only *some* women the right to choose how to dress (if they want access to healthcare, education, or social services) and will deny this to others. The Canadian Council of Muslim Women has in response rightly pointed out that Bill 94 is short-sighted since its implications are in fact highly detrimental to women:

> We are concerned that those women who want to wear the face covering will become further isolated and marginalized if they are refused services. Their active role as parents may also be restricted and this will harm their children. This does not bode well for integration and participation for women and their children. (Canadian Council of Muslim Women n.d.)

On the other hand, the MCC and others have made troubling claims that the niqab is a threat to security. These discourses are rooted within a culture of fear that has emerged and framed most debates regarding Muslim cultural politics since 9/11 (see also Chapters 2 and 10 for emergent political and cultural debates). Fear makes such rhetoric an easy sell in a climate of increased militarization abroad that includes Canada's role in Afghanistan, the ongoing "war on terror," and domestic anti-terror legislation and security policies (see, for example, Chapter 9). Fear provides the rationale for many repressive policies and practices that are easily legitimized by the public out of "rational" concerns for safety and security. As Agamben (2005) notes, a "state of exception" has been created where exceptional measures reserved for emergency have become the normative practices of modern governments, leaving civil liberties hanging in the balance. In Canada the geopolitical context of the "war on terror" and its impact on domestic polices have affected the way Muslim women's bodies and dress are being coded and regulated. As in France, Germany, and Turkey, where there are similar bans on the hijab, this proposed legislation has raised critical questions about how religion should be negotiated within a secular society and within the multicultural public sphere. That these contestations are occurring under the backdrop of the "war on terror" and heightened fears regarding public safety has been critical to the way these concerns are now being linked to Muslim women's bodies. The state's role in perpetuating these new Orientalist politics of veiling is evident in the way Quebec premier Jean Charest promoted the necessity of Bill 94 for reasons of "identification, security and communication" (Chung 2010). Contestations over Muslim women's dress have been co-opted into this climate of fear and represent the new battleground on which the nation is forging its identity as the secular, liberal champion of women's rights and values. The results are telling: as Canadians at large weigh in on the debate, public opinion polls already show disturbingly strong support for Bill 94 inside and outside of Quebec. A 2010 poll conducted by Angus Reid for the *Montreal Gazette* newspaper reported that 95 percent of people in Quebec and three out of four people in the rest of Canada supported Bill 94 (Scott 2010b).

Through these debates, productive tensions have led to the negotiation of Islam in the public sphere not only through the accommodation of religious practices but also by way of contesting and challenging the theological veracity of particular claims, such as whether the niqab is a religious requirement. Organizations like the MCC have made the case that the niqab is not a religious requirement (i.e., not mandated by the Qur'an or *hadith*)[5] and that there are thus no legitimate theological grounds on which to argue that banning the niqab is a violation of religious freedom. However, as Khan (2010) notes, "Canada's Supreme Court has ruled that the state is not an 'arbiter of religious dogma' – what matters is the sincerity of the individual's beliefs. If a woman honestly believes it is part of her faith to cover her face in public, the state cannot counter that a different religious opinion carries greater religious legitimacy." Many Canadian Muslims, including scholars and activists, do not accept the niqab as a religious requirement and do not support the practice but nonetheless are supportive of women's rights to make reasoned choices about their bodies and therefore stand in solidarity against Bill 94.

Earlier in the fall of 2009 the Conservative federal government refused to consider the proposal for the niqab ban put forward by the MCC. Prime Minister Stephen Harper acknowledged that "in an open and democratic society like Canada, individuals are free to make their own decisions regarding their personal apparel and to adhere to their own customs or traditions of their faith or beliefs" (in Harris 2010). However, the federal government has since back-peddled from these assurances and has come out in support of Bill 94. Challenges to as well as support for Bill 94 have poured into the Quebec Legislature. This fraught terrain is a complex mix of the legal, political, and discursive gendered politics that mark the contemporary formations of Muslim cultural politics in Canada as spaces of struggle, activism, and negotiated citizenship.

Nation, Citizenship, and Belonging? Muslims and the Canadian Security Regime

On September 26, 2002, Maher Arar was detained by US officials at John F. Kennedy Airport in New York and interrogated about alleged links to al-Qaeda while enroute to Canada from a vacation abroad. After being detained for twelve days, Arar found himself chained, shackled, and on a flight bound for Syria, where he would be held in a small "grave-like" cell for ten months and ten days before being relocated to a different prison. In Syria he was beaten, tortured, and forced to make a false confession. Accused of having links to al-Qaeda, Arar was far from the violent militant extremist the Canadian and US governments had accused him of being. He was a thirty-four-year-old wireless technology consultant who, although born in Syria, had immigrated to Canada with his family at the age of seventeen. He became a Canadian citizen in 1991. He did not have a criminal record and by all accounts was a decent law-abiding citizen. Innocence, however, provides no guarantees in a world governed by the politics of risk and "racial securitization."[6] A new era of "border racism" enacts contemporary regimes of surveillance where race, ethnicity, and religion are markers of risk that demand proof of innocence, loyalty, and citizenship. In collusion with domestic immigration policies such as security certificates and anti-terrorism legislation that allow for acts of extraordinary rendition and the outsourcing of torture such as Arar faced, these measures are regarded as necessary rather than as "states of exception" within the rule of law.

Arar's case is instructive in guiding us to consider specific questions about the politics of citizenship and belonging within the nation, namely who is entitled to claim the right to citizenship and who is subject to having this right forfeited, and to examine how the politics of racial and religious difference secure this divide. Although noncitizens in Canada are subject to the security certificate regime and related practices of holding secret trials and maintaining secret evidence that violate and suspend civil liberties (see Chapter 9), Canadian citizens have increasingly become at risk of being situated as "citizen-outsiders" and potential threats to the nation. In these formulations, the nation is being constituted and reconfigured within the global landscape of neo-imperial war and domestic securitization, which operate as racialized processes, and all of this has incited new constructions of Muslims as "subaltern citizens" in the West (see Chapter 1).

Enloe (1989, 45) describes the nation as "a collection of people who have come to believe that they have been shaped by a common past and are destined to share a common future," and this "belief is usually nurtured by a common language and a sense of otherness from groups around them." Similarly, Hage (2000, 39) contends that "nationalist practices cannot be conceived without an ideal nation being imagined by the nationalist." Defining Otherness as the antithesis of the ideal thus becomes a precondition for imagining the nation. This social and political dialectic shapes the contours of nation building and the myths that sustain national ideologies. The binary construct of nationhood defines and epitomizes the terms and conditions for social citizenship, on the one hand, and identifies potential outliers and threats, on the other. In the post-9/11 political landscape, Islam in the West has become the marker of undesirable citizens and in effect represents "subaltern citizens" (see Chapter 1). Positioned either as threats to national security or as being culturally irreconcilable with Western values and norms, Muslims living in Western societies face social, political, and cultural challenges that have been shaped by the violent contours of the global "war on terror."

I recently heard Tariq Ramadan – a European academic and public intellectual widely heralded as one of the most influential Muslim reformers of our time – speak at a Canadian forum about the situation of Muslims in the West. He instructed Muslims to claim and assert their rights as *citizens*, not just as *Muslims*. I understood his point to be that in positioning ourselves in this way, we claim legitimacy under the auspices of citizenship and a shared stake in the country. By locating ourselves as *Canadians*, not simply as Muslims, we can assert our citizenship rights and status and can then stake our claims as *insiders* of the nation. Although I agree with the political spirit Ramadan calls us to adopt, I have two points of contention to raise here. First, such claims rely on the consent of others in recognizing us as "real citizens" and members of the imagined community of the nation (Anderson 1983). Second, the logic of this position dictates that when we speak only as *Muslims* we are locating ourselves *outside* of the narrative of citizenship and national community. Rather than solidifying our status and rights as citizens, this move seems to further shore up the perceived irreconcilability of "Canadianness" and "Muslimness."

This point was brought home to me when I was part of a Muslim panel on a national radio program in the weeks after 9/11. After my co-panelists and I spent two hours positioning ourselves as peaceful "home-grown Canadians," rather than foreign threats, the final question posed to us by the moderator was, "but where do your loyalties lie?" It was sobering to realize that we were still suspected of having divided loyalties after firmly locating ourselves as Canadians. Our Muslimness was perceived as tainting our allegiance to the nation and positioned us as irreconcilable subjects. Was this question prompted by the fact that the three women on the panel (including myself at the time) wore the hijab? Or was this dissonance created because one of the men wore a *kufi* (traditional hat) and a beard that may have seemed a bit too long? Were these markers of identity perceived as telltale signs of violent fundamentalist tendencies that made us fundamentally irreconcilable with liberal democratic society? One thing became clear to me in this exchange: although racially and religiously marginalized groups may have legal rights and obligations in their relationship with the state as Canadian citizens, this does not guarantee their sense of actually belonging within the nation. Multiculturalism is a contingent form of politics that hinges on the ability of minoritized groups to render themselves "citizenship-worthy" through the performance of dominant ideals, values, and practices.

A more recent example of this contingent form of citizenship and the racial and cultural politics that collude in the perpetuation of this subaltern identity is the new Canadian citizenship guide, released by the Conservative government's minister of citizenship and immigration, Jason Kenney. The guidebook, called *Discover Canada: The Rights and Responsibilities of Canadian Citizenship* (Citizenship and Immigration Canada 2009), contains a special section on "The Equality of Women and Men," which states, "In Canada, men and women are equal under the law. Canada's openness and generosity do not extend to barbaric cultural practices that tolerate spousal abuse, 'honour killings,' female genital mutilation or other gender-based violence. Those guilty of these crimes are severely punished under Canada's criminal laws." This statement disturbingly reinscribes the racist civilizational discourse of colonialism and social Darwinism that branded non-Western cultures as inherently "barbaric." By invoking social-evolution discourse, the Canadian citizenship policy now openly employs colonial ideologies of racial and cultural difference to distinguish between desirable and undesirable citizens. At the same time, Canada is reinforced and produced as a benevolent and gender-just state that must preserve its values against the encroachment of "uncivilized" foreign interlopers. This once again recalls the "saving brown/black women from brown/black men" narrative, as the Canadian state is positioned as rescuing immigrant women from their barbaric societies and cultures.

Conservative commentators in Canada and the United States heralded this move by Canadian immigration authorities as "courageous" and a "banner day for immigrant women" (Kay 2009). The statement does not refer to any specific cultures, but honour killing and female genital mutilation are often associated with Islam (even though neither practice has any specific religious connection to Islam). Thus Muslim women are encoded within this text as the beneficiaries of paternalistic state protection. Raising the issue of honour killings, American neoconservative writer Phyllis Chesler supports the statement as a safeguard against this practice, arguing that "these people are coming from countries where these behaviours are never punished. There are people who bring this mindset when they come to the west" (in Carlson 2009). The derogatory reference to "these people" should be enough to discredit Chesler's comments as racist and xenophobic, but they are instead echoed by the Muslim Canadian Congress, as spokesperson Farzana Hassan also maintains that "we cannot ignore this [honour killing] in the name of multiculturalism" and further argues that the statement did not go far enough and would not on its own be able to counter the "irrational religious zeal" out of which these crimes emanate (in Kay 2009). The neoconservative politics evident in these arguments overdetermine religion and non-Western cultures, particularly Islamic ones, as the cause of violence against women. Locating gender-based violence as a foreign cultural import being brought into the benevolent Canadian state by "barbaric cultures" renders invisible the reality of violence against women in Canada as a domestic concern that affects more than just immigrant women (presumably at the hands of barbaric immigrant men). Jhappan (2010) is quick to dismantle such claims by outlining the ubiquity of violence against women in Canada as a reality that exists apart from such dubious links to immigration:

> Has rape been experienced by many Canadian women, long before immigrants from African and Muslim countries were allowed to immigrate? Check √. Sexual assault? Check √. Spousal abuse? Check √. Other forms of gender-based violence? Check √. So are they "barbaric *Canadian* cultural practices" then? What makes them specifically *cultural* practices when we find rape/sexual violence as well as non-sexual violence and many other forms of discrimination against women in almost every "culture" today? Surely these are *patriarchal* practices, not cultural ones, though they may be expressed, practiced, and resisted in culturally specific ways.

Jhappan rightly points out the false conflation of gendered violence and culture through this illustration and instead focuses our attention on patriarchy and how the various expressions of this form of oppression need to be understood and resisted in culturally specific ways.

Despite the fact that honour killing is rare (especially in comparison to other more generically labelled forms of domestic and sexual violence), it has nonetheless become a highly sensationalized practice in the West (see Chapter 1 for a discussion of the Aqsa Parvez case). This is not to say that it should not be a cause for concern and condemnation. Violence against women is a reality within the Muslim community, and along with other practices such as forced marriage, it must be challenged by men, women, community leaders, and religious authorities alike. Such initiatives are already beginning to take place within Muslim communities in Canada and elsewhere.[7] However, greater gender justice does not come through promoting racism and Islamophobic sentiments and the false civilizational divides that the narrow and reductive neoconservative position produces; rather, what is required is a broader analysis of the interlocking social factors that come into play in the perpetuation of violence against women so that proactive community-based interventions can be forged. That the Canadian citizenship guide has attributed gendered violence to cultural differences emanating from non-Western cultures, more specifically Islamic ones, powerfully illustrates how colonial and Orientalist narratives are deployed to position Muslims as subaltern citizens who run the risk of threatening Canada's "openness and generosity." This presupposes the construction of a "good Canadian citizen" who is culturally shaped by Western values, which are portrayed as a necessary corrective in a project to rehabilitate and uplift non-Western cultures that lack the requirements for modernity and democratic citizenship. All of this is achieved under the guise of multicultural "tolerance" and liberalization.

Brown (2006, 166) describes how the "governmentality of tolerance" relies on the circulation of civilizational discourse to contain the "non-Western, nonliberal Other." She outlines how the dominance of liberal subjects as the bearers of tolerance is constituted while at the same time non-Western subjects are deemed illiberal and therefore both intolerant and intolerable:

> Within contemporary civilization discourse, the liberal individual is uniquely identified with the capacity for tolerance and tolerance itself is identified with civilization. Non Liberal societies and practices, especially

those designated as fundamentalist, are depicted not only as relentlessly and inherently intolerant but as potentially intolerable for their putative rule by culture or religion and their concomitant devaluation of the autonomous individual – in short, their thwarting of individual autonomy with religious or cultural commandments. Out of this equation, liberalism emerges as the only political rationality that can produce the individual, societal and governmental practice of tolerance, and at the same time, liberal societies become the broker of what is tolerable and intolerable. (Brown 2006, 166)

Within the governmentality of tolerance, then, the white liberal subject is produced as the arbiter of civilizational norms and of who and what should be deemed worthy of toleration, which in turn positions the white liberal as ontologically superior and culturally and civilizationally dominant. The reproduction of this process – now enshrined within Canadian citizenship policy – is guaranteed. This is another example of how immigration and citizenship policies and practices are increasingly tied to notions of security, whether the cause for concern is threats that are political or, in this case, cultural. In this context, Muslims represent "cultural terrorists" with premodern values that threaten the heart of enlightened Western values, norms, and society. Immigration and citizenship practices targeting Muslims like the use of immigration videos in the Netherlands and citizenship tests in Germany are other examples of how "cultural eugenics" are being employed to weed out undesirable immigrants and to distinguish "good" from "bad" Muslims, at the same time preserving the multicultural fantasy of Western liberal democracies (see Chapter 1).

Canadian Multiculturalism and Its Discontents

Related to notions of citizenship and security are the ongoing debates about the state of Canadian multiculturalism in a post-9/11 context, which is another salient social, cultural, and political reality that informs the writings within this book. The emergence of multiculturalism as a federal policy in Canada came into effect in 1988 through the Multiculturalism Act, but this legislation was precipitated by a number of social, cultural, and political developments that began decades earlier. Multiculturalism in Canada was born out of tensions with francophone Quebec, struggles over Aboriginal land claims and sovereignty, and the growth of immigrant communities of colour seeking the rights of citizenship and inclusion within the national narrative. Thobani (2007, 150) points out another significant context within which multiculturalism was shaped through the politics of race due to an "international crisis of whiteness." She argues that a crisis of whiteness developed in the postwar period due to the rise of fascism in Europe, due to ideologies of biological racism, white supremacy, and eugenics promoted by the Nazi regime, and due to the Western model of the nation-state, which manifested violence and global war and undermined the European imperial order (Thobani 2007, 150). White supremacy as the basis for scientific and social policies was discredited, and therefore whiteness needed to be recuperated from its ties to racism, fascism, violence, and Aboriginal genocide. A new national narrative needed to be forged in Canada and other Western nations, and multiculturalism became a way to recast whiteness as part of a more benevolent process of national identity formation. According to Thobani (2007, 154),

> As in Australia and Britain, the embrace of multiculturalism allowed Canadians to resolve the crisis of whiteness through its reorganization as tolerant, pluralist and racially innocent, uncontaminated by its previous racist history. Because multicultural whiteness claimed to be tolerant of difference, even when besieged by a bewildering global array of diversity it could not re-cast itself as uniquely committed to pluralism and thereby exalt its basic goodness.

This allowed new narratives of the nation to be constructed around diversity and pluralism that recuperated whiteness as tolerance. However, this creation of a new national identity muted rising global anti-racism movements by focusing on culture (largely through creating ways to manage and contain non-Western cultures) and thereby depoliticizing race.

As race was depoliticized, culture became the centrepiece of the new social formation as something to be celebrated through festivals of song and dance and to be managed and contained if it transgressed the limits of white multicultural tolerance. In this way, multiculturalism operates as a spectacle of cultural diversity that masquerades as a liberalizing social policy that is in fact rooted in deep structures of white Eurocentric power and privilege, which it has failed to disrupt and in fact reinforces. Hage (2000) reminds us that multiculturalism was an offer of tolerance that proceeded from unequal relations of power and thus could always be withdrawn. Speaking of the Australian example, he argues that "White multiculturalism cannot admit to itself that migrants and Aboriginal people are actually eroding the centrality of White people in Australia. This is because the very viability of

White multiculturalism as a governmental ideology resides precisely in its capacity to suppress such a reality" (Hage 2000, 22). Increasing pluralism and the integration of multicultural groups into the political sphere have reconfigured the nation in ways that disrupt the imperialist nostalgia (or longing for a white-settler past that conferred unencumbered dominance) on the part of some nationalists who – to borrow Hage's terms – "recall themselves as masters of a territory in which they have managerial rights over racialised/ethnicised groups or persons which are consequently constructed as manageable objects" (Hage 2000, 48). It is also the memorializing of this past and the need to assert the certainty of this order within the present that create the need to discipline groups that step outside of the bounds of multicultural conformity and become "unmanageable." Muslims are viewed as one of these recalcitrant groups. When cases such as the "Toronto 18" arrests of seventeen Muslim youth and one Muslim adult on alleged terrorism charges emerge, public discourse immediately begins to question the "limits of multiculturalism" and the extent to which wayward illiberal groups with questionable national loyalty are testing and abusing liberal tolerance. Such incidents catalyze calls to reign in an unbridled multiculturalism that allows illiberal minorities to run amok and threaten the sanctity of liberal values and democratic rule.

As religion becomes a more central feature of the multicultural landscape, questions about how to accommodate religious diversity have occupied a new salience in multicultural discourse. Recent debates on "reasonable accommodation" have dominated the political landscape in Quebec, spurred by some highly publicized human rights cases that centred on the clash between religious rights and freedom and the secular nature of society. Headed by Gérard Bouchard and Charles Taylor, a commission on "reasonable accommodation" was forged, called the Consultation Commission on Accommodation Practices Related to Cultural Differences and later dubbed the Bouchard-Taylor Commission. Public hearings were held across the province to address issues such as wearing the hijab in martial arts, accommodation of prayers and provision for halal and kosher food in public and private institutions, and the designation of female staff to cater to Muslim or orthodox Jewish women in healthcare facilities. These and other situations where recognition was sought for religious practices were troubling the balance between upholding the duty to accommodate religious diversity as enshrined in the Canadian Charter of Rights and Freedoms, on the one hand, and preserving the distinct nature and secularism of Quebecois society, on the other. Secularism has deep roots in Quebec that are grounded in the

Quiet Revolution of the 1960s, which shifted the social and political foundations of society toward secularization and separatism. According to the architects of the infamous Citizen's Code in Hérouxville, "Contrary to the rest of Canada, the Quebec Nation long ago abandoned its religious foundations during the 'Quiet Revolution' back in the sixties. The theocracy of the past has been replaced by a consensus bringing Quebecers to define themselves as members of the laity" (Drouin and Thompson 2007). These sentiments situate Quebec as distinct from the multicultural context of Canada through the exile of religion within the public sphere. This has since created tensions with communities of faith that seek inclusion of their religious practices within public and private institutions. Immigrants in particular are seen as "ungrateful guests" who bring their religious and cultural baggage to the door and refuse to adapt to the local norms and customs. The Muslim immigrant in particular is constructed as a disruptive, religiously and culturally overdetermined subject whose ways are fundamentally irreconcilable with the demands of secular modernity.

Bouchard and Taylor (2008b, 19) describe the tensions that emerged during the hearings on reasonable accommodation in Quebec, which began in 2007:

> The so-called wave of accommodation clearly touched a number of emotional chords among French-Canadian Quebecers in such a way that requests for religious adjustments have spawned fears about the most valuable heritage of the Quiet Revolution, in particular gender equality and secularism. The result has been an identity counter-reaction movement that has expressed itself through the rejection of harmonization practices. Among some Quebecers, this counter-reaction targets immigrants, who have become, to some extent, scapegoats.

This statement reads as a polite assessment of the often virulent racism and Islamophobic sentiments expressed at the hearings, on talk radio, and in Internet blogs. Although there was also affirmation of more openness and acceptance, it would be disingenuous to downplay the fact that these forums became the stage for public performances of racism and xenophobia.

In their report, Bouchard and Taylor (2008b, 121) conclude that Canadian multiculturalism "emphasizes diversity at the expense of continuity" and therefore is an unsuitable model for Quebec, a sentiment that they note was expressed by most of the interveners at the public consultations, who preferred the model of "interculturalism." According to Sharify-Funk (2009,

13), Bouchard and Taylor see multiculturalism as leading to "ghettoization," whereas interculturalism "assumes that people of different cultures will interact with, and be transformed by, encounters with each other while maintaining some basic social values," which she notes may be "the middle ground between the 'mosaic' and the 'melting pot.'" The report goes on to argue that "interculturalism fosters the edification of a common identity through interaction between citizens of all origins" (Bouchard and Taylor 2008a, 88). In talking about the "edification of a common identity" through cultural encounters and interactions as a hallmark of interculturalism, the report does not take into account the relations of power between dominant and subaltern communities and identities and thereby assumes there is a level playing field for these encounters to take place. Not situating this process within the histories and legacies of subordination on the basis of race, class, ethnicity, religion, language, and culture denies the real imbalances of power and privilege in Canadian society that are hidden beneath the rhetoric of multicultural inclusion. Along with liberal multiculturalism, the discourse of interculturalism also depoliticizes race through a colour-blind politics of denial. In a 2007 survey on racism in Quebec conducted by Léger Marketing on behalf of three Montreal media sites, 59 percent of Quebecers admitted that they were racist (Granofsky 2009, 12), yet the Bouchard-Taylor Commission's report fails to provide any coherent plans for anti-racist initiatives. A representative of the Canadian Race Relations Foundation (CRRF) raised similar concerns. Ayman Al-Yassini stated that the CRRF "is disappointed with the almost casual dismissal in the Bouchard-Taylor report of the role of racism and discrimination in shaping the views of some Quebecers towards members of racialized communities" (in Sharify-Funk 2009, 31). Yet Bouchard and Taylor (2008b, 239) remain wary of "playing the race card":

> French-Canadian Quebecers are sometimes severely criticized. Caution is in order here. We must always be wary of imputing to racism certain attitudes or remarks that in actual fact stem from collective insecurity or, more precisely, from the exploitation of this insecurity. That being the case, it is true that these two factors, racism and insecurity, are not always easy to untangle.

This statement creates a space of innocence for racist ideologies and sentiments. Moreover, the denial of racism is rationalized by invoking the discourse of "security" and the threat that specific bodies (i.e., Muslims) presumably pose, thereby creating an insecure nation. Discussing the basis for security and nationalism, Hage (2000, 40) draws our attention to the affective nature of "feeling secure" in the context of the nation and reminds us that "security is impossible without familiarity and community, but it also involves the possibility of satisfying one's basic needs and an absence of threatening otherness." For dominant nationalists, the fears of encroaching difference and the disrupted familiarity that comes with cultural pluralism create a greater need for feeling secure. The narratives of familiarity, community, and security have become interrelated in new ways in the present context of protracted imperialist wars and global Islamophobia. That "dangerous foreigners" are being proclaimed and charged with changing the face of the nation and with threatening physical and cultural security feeds into this form of "paranoid nationalism" (Hage 2003) evident in some sectors of Quebec society.

A more recent move that exemplifies this paranoia is the Quebec government's plan to force new immigrants to sign a declaration pledging their respect for "Quebec's common values." This move builds on the paranoid sensibilities that informed the Hérouxville Citizen's Code and manifests them writ large as the foundations for immigration to the province (see Chapter 1). Such xenophobic policies create further divides and contribute to the alienation of already marginalized groups. This threatens the fragile communities of difference that must be accommodated within the multicultural nation. Quebec has been officially defined as a nation within Canada, so it is important to consider how this nation is being imagined and constituted. To further engender inclusion, there needs to be a reshaping of the national imaginary in addition to addressing national policy. Colourblindness and the denial of racism couched in the rhetoric of liberal multiculturalism or a new guise of interculturalism are faulty premises with which to counter the racial myths of nation building, as these bland gestures obscure the relations of power embedded within narratives of nation, citizenship, and belonging.

Challenges to the sanctity of the benevolent multicultural nation sully the international prestige associated with this image of Canada and are likely to be seen by many as "un-Canadian." However, it is by upholding the values of equity and social justice that we keep them from corruption and from being further eroded in a climate of heightened fear and risk. In different ways, the contributions to this collection gesture to current tensions within Canadian multiculturalism. It is by being attentive to these tensions and the formations of power underlying them that we can imagine new ways to navigate through the politics of difference in ways that do not result in fragmentation or alienation and guilt but rather inform new possibilities for social, political, and cultural reform as a collective project. This often tenuous relationship between marginalized identities and the dominant cultural spaces of the nation underscores the tensions with which this book grapples and provides the context within which all the contributors must write.

Mapping the Book

It is significant that all but one of the contributors to this collection self-identify as Muslim. This was in part a conscious decision to highlight the scholarship of Canadian Muslim academics (both established as well as emergent scholars) about Muslims in Canada. This move recognizes the presence of academic forms of colonialism in which the narratives and lived experiences of Muslims have been co-opted by those who do not share in this identity or in the costs and implications of labelling and defining the experiences of others. This book allows for a space where Muslim academics can articulate their research and political concerns about issues that are not only of academic interest to them but also implicated in their lives, work, and families.

As a result, the book presents contributions that are based on empirical research of the Muslim presence in Canada as well as critical essays that open up questions about how contemporary Muslim cultural politics are being shaped and formed in relation to specific debates. Some authors have chosen to weave part of their own identity and narrative into their chapters, whereas others have decided not to take this approach. Both of these choices reflect the style, political engagements, and considerations of the authors. Some of the contributors to this collection write from a more liberal framework, whereas others work from anti-colonial and anti-racist paradigms. All but one of the contributors are also female, and some work from anti-racist feminist standpoints, whereas others do not identify their scholarship in explicitly feminist terms but are advocates for gender justice. These varying analytical commitments reflect the intellectual engagements of contemporary Muslim academics and the kinds of political voice they bring to bear on the issues that engage them as scholars and as Muslims. Therefore, although there is no common voice or analytical framework in Muslim studies, those contributing to this volume all acknowledge the saliency of Muslim cultural politics in Canada and the need to make critical interventions into this field as scholars and activists. Unfortunately, there is an absence of scholarship from Quebec, which limits the range of possible voices in this collection. It is hoped that a future volume will provide analysis of Muslim cultural politics in Quebec and of the distinctive social, political, cultural, and linguistic contexts from which they arise.

The first section of the book begins by critically examining gender and Muslim cultural politics in Canada. Issues relating to Muslim women have, as we have seen, become significant cultural and political flashpoints in Canada. In Chapter 1, I provide an overview of some of the contemporary formations of gendered politics that have revolved around "the Muslim women question," such as the issue of shar'ia-based tribunals in Ontario, the Hérouxville Citizen's Code in Quebec, the sartorial, religious, and cultural politics involved in the banning of headscarves on Quebec soccer fields, and the tragic death of a Pakistani teenage girl dubbed a Canadian "honour killing." In this chapter, I ground my analysis in three specific tropes – disciplining culture, death by culture, and death of culture – in order to problematize how these issues have been discursively constituted and how the racialized and gendered politics in which they are embedded unsettle and reconfigure the nation.

The second contribution to this section picks up on one of these specific issues: the highly contested case for shar'ia-based tribunals in Ontario. Changes to the Ontario Arbitration Act in 1991 opened the door for alternative dispute resolution (ADR) to be applied in civil family matters and allowed for the use of any laws agreed to by the involved parties. This legal permission provided the means to utilize religious laws for binding arbitration in private agreements. Jewish rabbinical courts (or Beis Dein) and Aboriginal healing circles are examples of religious and cultural systems of mediation that are used to adjudicate civil matters in Ontario. However, in 2003 an organization called the Islamic Institute for Civil Justice began to advocate for the use of Muslim law in ADR and sought to develop a Muslim Arbitration Board (Darul Qada) where civil disputes such as divorce, child custody, and inheritance could be settled, invoking *fiqh*, or an Islamic system of jurisprudence. Serious public debates erupted in the media over this proposal, which ignited fear and concern about the implementation of patriarchal and fundamentalist versions of shar'ia in Canada and about how in particular this would impact Muslim women. Public dialogue surrounding this issue was largely framed against a backdrop of rampant Islamophobia generated by the "war on terror" and the pervasive negative images of Islam that support it. The debates positioned various actors within civil society and the public at large as either for or against the proposal. In Chapter 2, Itrath Syed provides a critical analysis of the public debate by focusing on the positions taken by opponents of the proposal and on the implications this opposition held for Muslim women's agency and representation. Syed examines some of the key interlocutors in this debate who stood in opposition to faith-based arbitration being extended to include the integration of Islamic law. Using a discourse-analysis approach, she maps the contours of what was largely a feminist engagement (both secular and faith-based) with these issues and discusses her own involvement as a Muslim scholar-activist within the debates. She also engages media representations and challenges the way Muslim women were constituted within the national imaginary as infantilized and politically immature subjects through these representational practices. Importantly, her discussion delves into the ways these varied discourses "fossilize" Islamic law and render it incapable of changing to accommodate greater gender equity.

Finally, the third contribution to this section moves beyond the narrow and limiting parameters that cast Muslim women as victims in need of national, imperial, and/or feminist rescue and instead focuses on their agency as politically engaged activists. In Chapter 3, Katherine Bullock provides a framework for investigating Muslim women's political engagement within Canadian society. This chapter provides an important intervention by highlighting the long-term political work of Canadian women who self-identify as Muslim and articulate their faith as integral to their political activism. The counter-story Bullock provides serves to rupture the stereotypical notions of Muslim women as voiceless and passive and at the same time draws on both her personal involvement and empirical observations to tell us about the history and trajectory of Muslim women's community work. All three of the chapters in this section make important interventions into the emergent field of Canadian Muslim women's studies.

The second section of the book focuses on the cultural production of Muslims in Canada. The chapters in this section provide critical examinations of media and the representation of Muslims in Canada through print journalism, television, and memoir. In Chapter 4, Yasmin Jiwani helps us to consider the ways that the print media shape our ideas about the imagined community of the nation and how this has played out in terms of the way Muslims have been read into the Canadian national imaginary since 9/11. Her discussion provides an examination of two Canadian newspapers, the *Globe and Mail* and the *National Post*, and what she describes as the "hegemonic affinity" between these dailies, which are otherwise viewed differently by their audiences. This affinity, Jiwani tells us, lies in the way they both produce specific narratives about the nation and similarly situate Muslims within Orientalist tropes as the demonic, fanatical followers of a ruthless faith. Unpacking the context within which these narratives are purveyed, Jiwani provides an important overview of media concentration in Canada and the kind of national storytelling that it produces. The particular story Jiwani delves into in this chapter is the immediate aftermath of 9/11 as narrated through these two national newspapers. She critically maps the representational politics of these dailies and how they collude in producing racialized and gendered accounts of the 9/11 attacks. Jiwani's analysis is critical in unpacking how these representational practices collude with the imperial politics of the ongoing "war on terror."

In Chapter 5, Meena Sharify-Funk examines the explosion of popular literature on Islam and Muslims since 9/11. In particular, the genre of memoir promises the reader an "insider" view that goes "behind the veil" of Islam to provide often sensationalized accounts of "real" Muslims. Sharify-Funk examines two particular texts – *The Trouble with Islam Today*, by Irshad Manji, and *Their Jihad ... Not My Jihad!*, by Raheel Raza – that sell as "tell-all" accounts of Islam authored by Canadian Muslim women. Although these are not traditional memoirs per se, they operate in a similar fashion as "insider accounts" of Islam that are legitimated by virtue of first-person narratives that interweave the personal histories of the authors with the textual material; in the case of Raza's book, this is done using a diary-like format. As a result, these authors perform the role of "native informants" who provide the Western reader with authorized accounts of Islam and the Muslim world that are presented as "truth tales" but ones mediated by their ideological and personal desires and ultimately by the status of these books as sources of personal economic gain, notoriety, and prestige. Sharify-Funk is concerned with reading and understanding these texts through the broader lens of identity negotiation and meaning creation within the Canadian Muslim community. She provides a thematic analysis of these texts to elucidate their relation to larger intra-Muslim debates about reform, Western liberalism, and women's emancipation with a view to challenging some of the stereotypical assumptions these debates often raise.

The final contribution to this section, by Aliaa Dakroury, focuses on a Canadian television phenomenon, the Canadian Broadcasting Corporation's sitcom *Little Mosque on the Prairie*. The brainchild of innovative Canadian filmmaker Zarqa Nawaz, the show has become an unlikely hit in Canada and is now syndicated worldwide. Based in part on Nawaz's own journey from the metropolis of Toronto to the prairies of Saskatchewan, the show – set in the fictional town of Mercy – tells the story of a small-town, mosque-based Muslim community that must negotiate its integration into a largely white, Christian community. As I and a colleague have written elsewhere,

> The themes and plot lines of the show present the multicultural possibilities of Canada as a place for differences to be engaged and negotiated through productive intercultural and interfaith tensions but also show the reality of racism and religious discrimination often obscured by the more celebratory rhetoric of liberal multiculturalism. The show represents Muslim cultural politics in the Canadian diaspora as challenging yet resolvable features of life in a racially and religiously plural society. (Zine and Bala 2009)

The show, therefore, is a unique intervention in Canadian television, and as Dakroury notes in her chapter, it has precipitated a significant shift in the representation of Muslims, countering both the Orientalizing and exoticizing *One Thousand and One Nights* depiction and the more nefarious image of the Muslim terrorist, stereotypes that otherwise inform the standard stock images and narratives through which Muslims are represented in film and television. Dakroury locates this show within the emergent genre of Muslim comedy in North America, which has primarily taken the form of stand-up comedy. She argues that it is important for public broadcasting in Canada to continue to nurture these more subaltern forms of comedic cultural production, which are less likely to be given air time where neoliberal economies have a strong hold and dominate media programming decisions. Despite criticisms of the CBC for not truly developing alternative media frames, Dakroury heralds its support of *Little Mosque on the Prairie* as an example of the democratizing possibilities of public broadcasting.

Along with the media, educational systems are also important institutions within civil society that shape our understanding of the world and our own identities. In the third section of the book, education is the focus of the chapters by Nadeem Memon and me. Both contributions are based on empirical research into Islamic education in Canada. In Chapter 7, Memon provides an important historical mapping of the development of mosques in Canada, which provided the first sites for the development of Islamic educational institutions. He then takes us through the philosophical underpinnings of Islamic education and provides a historical overview of the emergence of Islamic educational sites, including *madrassas* (or weekend religious schools), full-time Islamic schools, and home schooling. In addition to mapping the historical contours of education in the Canadian Muslim diaspora, Memon highlights various sociological, philosophical, and pedagogical challenges and possibilities that emerge through the negotiation of faith, education, and citizenship among Muslims in Canada.

Using a critical ethnographic mode of inquiry, my chapter takes a different approach to examining Islamic schooling in Ontario. Chapter 8 is based on qualitative fieldwork conducted in a gender-segregated Islamic high school and focuses on the experiences of Muslim girls and the politics of veiling. I critically explore how these young women reside at the nexus of dual oppressions, confronting racism and Islamophobia in society at large and at the same time contending with patriarchal forms of religious oppression in their communities. The chapter provides an overview of the historical context for veiling within the Islamic tradition, which is useful in situating contemporary contestations about this practice. I also situate the discussion within attempts to ban the hijab in Europe and in Canada, which provides a political backdrop for the debates that have ensued. It is within the fraught terrain of religious edicts and secular political backlash that young Muslim girls who choose to wear the hijab must negotiate their sense of faith, identity, and citizenship. Through interviews with young Muslim women, the chapter provides an analysis of what I call "gendered Islamophobia," which refers to "specific forms of ethno-religious and racialized discrimination levelled at Muslim women that proceed from historically contextualized negative stereotypes that inform individual and systemic forms of oppression." The narratives of the young women in my study reveal their day-to-day experiences with this form of discrimination in secular public schools. I then examine the situation they confront when they enter the discursive spaces of Islamic schools, where they are socialized to conform to the prevailing religious norms. Islamic schools provide a refuge from gendered Islamophobia but are nonetheless places where conservative religious norms determine specific parameters for their dress, identity, and behaviour. This chapter explores the ways that Muslim girls negotiate their identities within these often polarized spaces. It is interesting to note that even though the fieldwork for this study was completed just prior to 9/11, the narratives related by the interviewed Muslim girls reveal levels of racism and gendered Islamophobia comparable to today. This serves as a reminder that Islamophobia did not begin on September 11, 2001 (Zine 2002).

Some of the most significant shifts since the 9/11 tragedy have been the development of draconian security policies as a response to "home-grown" threats of terror. The final section of the book addresses racialized securitization in Canada through an analysis of policies such as security certificates and Bill C-36, the Anti-terrorism Act. Chapter 9, by Jacqueline Flatt, critically examines the Immigration and Refugee Protection Act (IRPA), which stipulates policies for immigration and refugee regulations as well as terms and conditions of detention and deportation. This policy also provides the means for security certificates to be issued to noncitizens who may be detained and deported if it is alleged that they pose a risk to the security of Canada. This policy has received attention more recently due to the detainment of five Muslim men – Mohamed Zeki Mahjoub, Mahmoud Jaballah, Hassan Almrei, Mohamed Harkat, and Adil Charkaoui – but this provision within the IRPA has existed in Canada's immigration law since 1978. In this chapter, Flatt provides a critical analysis of this policy and its implications and then examines the way the discourse surrounding security certificates has been taken up in Canadian print media through an examination of news articles in the *Globe and Mail* and the *National Post* from 2004 to 2008. Flatt provides a comprehensive view of how both the policy and the negative construction of Muslims were narrated within media and security discourses purveyed through these dailies. The analysis further reveals significant findings on how national belonging is defined and policed and on how this is connected to the dismantling of rights for noncitizens in Canada that has been enabled within the current "state of exception" (Agamben 2005).

Chapter 10 continues the examination of the Canadian security regime with an analysis of Bill C-36 and its deployment in the "Toronto 18" case of alleged domestic terrorism by a group of seventeen Muslim youth and one Muslim adult. In this chapter, Shaista Patel begins by employing an anticolonial and anti-racist feminist analysis to map out the role of law in configuring the colonialist Canadian nation-building project and then uses an anti-Orientalist lens to examine and unpack how Bill C-36 is being used to safeguard the nation from "dangerous Muslims" as a way of preserving what Hage (2000) refers to as the "white nation fantasy." Patel interrogates the way techniques and technologies of surveillance emanating from this policy have led to racial and religious forms of profiling targeting Muslims. This chapter provides an important account of how racial securitization has become an institutionalized practice in Canada that continues to be shaped and legitimated by the imperial politics of the "war on terror." Patel's analysis helps us to understand how policies constitute the formation of dangerous populations that must be policed and regulated by the state and how specific racialized ontologies emerge from this encounter. Her anti-Orientalist reading of Bill C-36 is an important and innovative approach to unpacking the implications of this policy and how it has been applied specifically to

Muslim Canadians. Her analysis further reveals how such policies shore up the image of Canada as a benevolent nation being threatened by "enemies within" and the implications this holds for Muslims who are left out of the national narrative until they are determined to be "good Muslims" rather than "bad Muslims" (Mamdani 2004).

Patel ends her chapter with a query about "how to claim humanity as Muslims of colour in a nation built on colonial and racialized violences." This is a question that is critical to this book and to the future Muslim presence in Canada. This book offers a contribution to this collective struggle for greater understanding, critical awareness, and social justice, as a form of "jihad" (which refers to a struggle but not to a "holy war," as this term is often erroneously reduced to signifying). This is in fact the true spirit of the word "jihad" within Islam, so let us reclaim this meaning here and articulate this project as a struggle for Muslims and other marginalized communities to lay claim to the space of the nation as one of belonging and inclusion. In this sense, this book navigates beyond the hegemonic ideologies that dominate the representation of Islam and Muslims and instead allows subaltern voices in the Canadian Muslim hinterlands to be critical interlocutors within the cultural and political landscape of the nation we all call home.

NOTES

1 Adams (2007) notes that, in 1993, 73 percent of Canadians expressed concerns about the integration of immigrants and their adoption of Canadian values but that these figures declined slowly over time to 58 percent by 2005. However, according to Adams, the surge to 65 percent of Canadians expressing concerns about immigrant integration by 2006 can be attributed to flashpoint issues such as the debate regarding shar'ia tribunals in Ontario (see Chapter 2). This demonstrates the volatile effect of Muslim cultural politics on public opinion and public fears in Canada.
2 *Niqabi* is the term for women who wear the face veil known in Arabic as *niqab*.
3 http://www.muslimcanadiancongress.org/.
4 The case put forward by Tarek Fatah and the MCC against the niqab and burka is the same as that argued by the infamous Islamophobe Daniel Pipes. See, for example, http://www.danielpipes.org/.
5 *Hadith* refers to the sayings and actions of the Prophet Muhammad as recorded and collected by his close companions and later codified into a seminal corpus of knowledge by religious scholars in the ninth century. These serve as a major source of religious knowledge and as a companion to the Qur'an.
6 By "racial securitization," I am referring to sets of regulatory ideological and political policies, strategies, and techniques employed by the state as well as some nonstate actors that are constituted and enacted through conflating the otherwise disparate categories of racial and religious identities with the assessment of risk and public

safety. Here, I am expanding on the notion of a "security industrial complex" (Hayes 2006), which is defined as a process by which "the boundaries between internal and external security, policing and military operations, have been eroded" and new forms of surveillance of "public and private places, of communications and of groups of individuals" have been accelerated by the "war on terror." Racial securitization, therefore, links race to the security-industrial complex as an integral feature of this governing apparatus that provides the basis on which threats to public safety are determined and safeguarded against.

7   In Canada awareness surrounding domestic violence and forced marriages is being raised by Muslim leaders, women's organizations, and activist groups such as the Canadian Council of Muslim Women (CCMW), the South Asian Legal Clinic of Ontario (SALCO), and emergent groups such as *AQSAzine,* a collective of Muslim women and transpeople developed in honour of murdered teen Aqsa Parvez. In addition, these concerns have made their way to the *minbar* (pulpit) of mosques, where some religious leaders are raising greater awareness about these concerns from an Islamic perspective in their sermons.

REFERENCES

Abu-Laban, B. 1983. The Canadian Muslim community: The need for a new survival strategy. In E.H. Waugh, B. Abu-Laban, and R.B. Qureshi, eds. *The Muslim community in North America,* 75-92. Edmonton, AB: University of Alberta Press.

Adams, M. 2007. *Unlikely utopia: The surprising triumph of Canadian pluralism.* Toronto, ON: Viking.

Adams, Michael. 2007. Muslims and Multiculturalism in Canada. A Presentation by Michael Adams, President, Environics. Environics Research Group. http://www.environicsinstitute.org/PDF-MuslimsandMulticulturalisminCanada-LiftingtheVeil.pdf.

Agamben, G. 2005. *State of exception.* Chicago, IL: University of Chicago Press.

Anderson, B. 1983. *Imagined communities: Reflections on the origin and spread of nationalism.* New York: Verso.

Bouchard, G., and C. Taylor. 2008a. *Building the future: A time for reconciliation.* Abridged report. Quebec City: Bibliothèque et Archives nationales du Québec.

–. 2008b. *Building the future: A time for reconciliation.* Full report. Quebec City: Bibliothèque et Archives nationales du Québec.

Brown, W. 2006. *Regulating aversion: Tolerance in the age of identity and empire.* Princeton, NJ: Princeton University Press.

Canadian Council of Muslim Women. N.d. Statement on face covering. http://www.ccmw.com/documents/CCMW_Statement_on_Face_Covering_Niqab.pdf.

Carlson, K.B. 2009. New citizenship guide says no to "barbaric" practices. *National Post,* November 12. http://www.nationalpost.com/.

Chung, A. 2010. Quebec niqab bill would make Muslim women unveil. *Toronto Star,* March 25. http://www.thestar.com/.

Citizenship and Immigration Canada. 2009. *Discover Canada: The rights and responsibilities of Canadian citizenship.* http://www.cic.gc.ca/.

Coalition of Concerned Muslim Women of Kitchener-Waterloo. 2010. Press statement on Bill 94, Kitchener-Waterloo, Ontario, April 26.
Drouin, A., and B. Thompson. 2007. Bouchard-Taylor Commission. http://herouxville-quebec.blogspot.com/.
Enloe, C. 1989. *Bananas, beaches and bases*. Berkeley and Los Angeles: University of California Press.
Granofsky, D.R. 2009. "A time for reconciliation?" The Bouchard-Taylor Commission and evolving democratic practices in identity politics. MA thesis, Department of Political Science, University of British Columbia.
Hage, G. 2000. *White nation: Fantasies of white supremacy in a multicultural society*. New York: Routledge.
—. 2003. *Against paranoid nationalism*. Australia: Pluto.
Hamdani, D.H. 1997. Canada's Muslims. *Hamdard Islamicus* 20, 3: http://muslim-canada.org/.
Harris, K. 2010. Canada to reject burka ban. *Toronto Sun*, January 27. http://www.torontosun.com/.
Hayes, B. 2006. Arming Big Brother: The EU's Security Research Programme. Report for the Transnational Institute. http://www.tni.org/.
Jhappan, R. 2010. The new Canadian citizenship test: No "barbarians" need apply. http://blog.fedcan.ca/.
Kay, B. 2009. "Discover Canada: The Rights and Responsibilities of Citizenship" is a watershed moment for the policy of multiculturalism and a banner day for immigrant women. *National Post*, November 12. http://network.nationalpost.com.
Khan, S. 2010. Let's fashion a made-in-Canada approach to the burka. *Globe and Mail*, February 1. http://www.vigile.net/.
Lorenz, A.W. 1998. Canada's pioneer mosque. *Aramco World* 49: 28-31.
Mamdani, M. 2004. *Good Muslim, bad Muslim: America, the Cold War and the roots of terror*. Toronto: Random House of Canada.
Moghissi, H., S. Rahnema, and M.J. Goodman. 2009. *Diaspora by design*. Toronto: University of Toronto Press.
Peritz, I. 2010. Veil dispute reveals Quebec's hardening line on religious displays: Student barred from class for wearing niqab. *Globe and Mail*, March 10, A1.
Persad, J.V., and S. Lukas. 2002. No hijab is permitted here: A study on the experiences of Muslim women wearing hijab applying for work in the manufacturing, sales and service sectors. http://atwork.settlement.org/downloads/No_Hijab_Is_Permitted_Here.pdf.
Scott, M. 2010a. Quebec integration debate reignited over student's use of niqab. *Montreal Gazette*, March 2. http://www.montrealgazette.com/.
—. 2010b. Most Canadians want niqab restricted. *Montreal Gazette*, March 27. http://www.montrealgazette.com/.
Shakir, U. 2010. George Orwell is alive: Niqabs banned in Quebec. *Rabble*, March 29. http://www.rabble.ca/.
Sharify-Funk, M. 2009. Negotiating identity in a Canadian context: Islam, cultural insecurity, and the Bouchard-Taylor Report. Paper presented at the workshop

"Re-Presenting Canadian Arabs in a Globalized World: Racializiation, Media, and Public Policy." Centre for International Governance and Innovation (CIGI), Waterloo, Ontario, January 23.

Siddiqui, H. 2010. The new war over multiculturalism. *Toronto Star,* April 25. http://www.thestar.com/.

Spivak, G.C. 1988. Can the subaltern speak? In C. Nelson and L. Grossberg, eds., *Marxism and the interpretation of culture,* 271-313. Urbana: University of Illinois Press.

Thobani, S. 2007. *Exalted subjects: Studies in the making of race and nation in Canada.* Toronto: University of Toronto Press.

Zine, J. 2002. Living on the ragged edges: Homelessness among Latin Americans and Muslims in Toronto. Informal Housing Network Project Report, Toronto, Ontario.

–. 2004. Creating a critical-faith-centred space for anti-racist feminism: Reflections of a Muslim scholar-activist. *Journal of Feminist Studies in Religion* 20, 2: 167-88.

–. 2009. Living on the ragged edges: Homelessness among Latin Americans and Muslims in Toronto. In J.D. Hulchanski, P. Campsie, S. Chau, S. Hwang, and E. Paradis, eds., *Finding home: Policy options for addressing homelessness in Canada,* 1-23. Toronto: Cities Centre, University of Toronto. http://www.homelesshub.ca/.

Zine, J., and A. Bala. 2009. Representations: Visual arts: Television: Canada. In S. Joseph, ed., *Encyclopedia of women and Islamic cultures.* Brill Online. http://brillonline.nl/.

PART 1

GENDER AND CULTURAL POLITICS

ISSUES of gender have been central to the sphere of Muslim cultural politics in Canada. From the debates in Ontario over *shar'ia* (Islamic law) tribunals and in Quebec over the Hérouxville Citizen's Code and the proposed bans on headscarves and face veils to issues of "honour killing," these contestations draw on specific constructions of Muslim women as either victims or outlaws. At the same time, they secure the notion of the liberal state and Western feminism as a space of benevolence, redemption, and rescue from the restrictions of the Muslim faith, culture, and community.

The contestations over Muslim women's bodies and lives and the debates over whether shar'ia would make them more vulnerable or whether headscarves promote religious fundamentalism or whether they are more likely than non-Muslim women to experience "honor killing," as well as less sensationalized versions of domestic violence, have been matters of public and feminist concern. This attention has limited the agency of Muslim women to make reasoned choices about their bodies and lives and has cast them as victims of patriarchal violence of a kind that is different from and more pathological than that encountered by other

PART 1 ...   Canadian women. This differential rendering of their lives and religion positions them outside of the domain of common intelligibility and national belonging.

The authors in this section grapple with various yet interrelated concerns about how Muslim women have been discursively constituted in relation to these debates and contestations in very narrow ways but nonetheless are able to claim spaces of civic engagement and political participation as social actors and agents. The chapters by Jasmin Zine and Itrath Syed address the way that Muslim women's identities and subjectivities have been produced within specific controversies, such as the proposal for faith-based arbitration in Ontario, the debates over Islamic dress in Quebec, and the tragic death of a young Canadian Pakistani teen at the hands of her father. Katherine Bullock's chapter follows with a discussion of the role Muslim women have played as activists and community builders, which rarely makes headlines. These chapters allow for an examination of the complexities of how Muslim women are constituted within the nation as victims, outlaws, and outsiders and how they construct their own narratives of political and spiritual engagement as Muslims and as Canadians within the public and political sphere in ways that challenge and disrupt these same archetypes.

1

Unsettling the Nation
Gender, Race, and Muslim Cultural Politics in Canada

JASMIN ZINE

From the Hérouxville Town Charter:

Our immense territory is patrolled by the policemen and women of the "Surete du Québec" ... You may not hide your face as to be able to identify you while you are in public. The only time you may mask or cover your face is during Halloween, this is a religious traditional custom at the end of October celebrating All Saints Day, where children dress up and go door to door begging for candy and treats. All of us accept to have our picture taken and printed on our driver's permit, health care card and passports. A result of democracy. (Municipalité Hérouxville 2007)

When folks in a small, ethnically homogeneous town in rural Quebec decided to draw boundaries between themselves and "undesirable" outsiders, they did not build walls or fences; instead, they constructed a manifesto, a discursive fortress to safeguard their values and way of life. Embedded within the Hérouxville Town Charter (or Citizen's Code) is an invisible line that maps the terrain between the familiar and the strange, insiders and outsiders, belonging and Otherness. Not only are the boundaries invisible, but the objects of the code's negative attention are never explicitly named.

Dangerous foreigners remain encrypted in the subtext – a haunting Otherness lurking in the shadows of the town's imaginary and taking the form of a veiled Muslim woman. The act of a woman covering her head and face is seen not only as undesirable but also as outright threatening to settled notions of self, community, and nation.

That Muslim women are embodied in the subtext of the Hérouxville Citizen's Code is a useful entry point into a broader discussion about how gender, race, and religious identity are discursively constituted within the nation and how, at the same time, negotiating these categories of identity is unsettling and reconfigures the constitution of the nation. I want to engage this dialectic of social and national identity first through a transnational perspective – examining how Muslims have become subaltern citizens in the West – and then through a discussion of gender and Muslim cultural politics in Canada.

In addition to debates over the Hérouxville Citizen's Code, Muslim women have been at the centre of several contemporary controversies in Canada: a proposal for faith-based arbitration using *shar'ia* (Islamic law), the suggested banning of the *hijab* (headscarf) in girls' soccer, and the aftermath of an "honour killing" of a Pakistani Canadian teen. Rather than providing a detailed overview of each of these issues, my aim in this discussion is to examine how Muslim women have become discursively located within the narrative of the nation through these case studies. In the post-9/11 context of Canada, these flashpoints have galvanized debates over the "limits of multiculturalism," the boundaries of nation and citizenship, and "good" versus "bad" immigrants.[1]

I want first to locate myself in this discussion. My insights are shaped by my own subjectivity as a Muslim woman who came to Canada from Pakistan at the age of three. Growing up in white, small-town, suburban Ontario, I came to understand how my identity was racialized and ethnicized in ways that separated me from "real Canadians." However, I also came to learn that I could "perform" national identity by adopting ways of talking, acting, dressing, and behaving that allowed me limited acceptance within the dominant society. Hage (2000) suggests that these acquired traits are a form of "national capital" that can be invested in the social purchase of national belonging. I was able to gain this social currency through cultural conformity and by "performing whiteness," which became the antidote to not actually embodying whiteness. In other words, I learned to "pass" as an assimilated foreigner who had disavowed my ethnic and religious identity in favour of performing Canadianness (i.e., the part of "the good immigrant"). But despite my efforts, I found I could never really own or claim national identity; I could only "borrow" it from its rightful owners (i.e., white Anglo-Canadians) so long as I acted in ways that conformed to the status quo culture. When stepping outside of the bounds of the master narrative of Canadianness, one risks the dissolution of ties to the imagined community (Anderson 1983). National identity then remains "borrowed" from those who are the keepers of the meanings and myths of nation building.

Muslims as Subaltern Citizens in the West

It is important to map a broader context for understanding the negotiations of identity faced by Muslims in Western societies before addressing the gendered implications of these formulations more specifically. First, I want to explore the fact that state citizenship does not guarantee national belonging for those already teetering on the borders of inclusion: Muslims have been cast as subaltern citizens in the West.[2] This positioning is institutionally reinforced through xenophobic state policies, new citizenship regimes, and racial and religious profiling – all of which have taken effect since 9/11 and subsequent terrorist attacks. The implications of such policies are both ontological and systemic. Orientalist fears and fantasies of the violent and pathological Muslim are codified and reproduced in the apparatuses of the state and through the relations of ruling. These forms of governmentality produce the subaltern status of Muslim populations in growing Western diasporas. Increasingly positioned as anti-liberal, anti-democratic, and unamenable to the requirements of modernity, Muslims represent the "anti-citizen."

At the root of these ideological and systemic practices of exclusion in Western nations is the global context of the US-led "war on terror." In the discursive battlefield of this conflict, Muslims and Islamic culture are pathologized as breeding transnational hatreds and exporting violence against the peaceful and benevolent West. This dominant trope in the Western imaginary is purveyed through media as a means to justify military aggression in Muslim lands as a just and necessary response to Islamic radicalism.

As a result of this "new world order," we have witnessed the emergence of xenophobic state policies regulating immigration in parts of Europe that employ a form of cultural eugenics as part of their disciplinary techniques of governmentality (Foucault 1991). Dutch immigration videos and the German citizenship test are two examples of new measures geared specifically toward Muslims, targeting them as potentially dangerous interlopers unsettling the civility and safety of transnational Europe. Muslims here represent a threat of "cultural contamination" as well as the physical threat of terrorism. These tests have become the new fortresses protecting Europe from further decline into "Eurabia" (see, for example, Carr 2006).

These gate-keeping tools have a corporeal as well as a discursive-political dimension. As Hage (2000, 45) aptly notes, "Nationalism before being an explicit practice or mode of classification is a state of the body. It is a way of imagining one's position within the nation and what one can aspire to as a national." Which bodies are mapped onto this landscape as natural and rightful bearers of nationalist largesse and which bodies are constructed as alien and unsettling to the nation? Who has the right to imagine the nation as a community to which they have unqualified belonging? One thing is clear: although the members of racially and religiously marginalized groups may have legal rights and obligations as citizens of Western states, this does not guarantee a sense of actually belonging within the nation.

The Muslim woman's body is the new frontier on which battles for national identity and citizenship are being waged. In France, for example, the ban on the hijab in public schools and universities has positioned veiled Muslim women as threats to *laïcité* (or state secularism). A simple head covering has become a symbol of the corruption and pollution of the nation by foreign values and subaltern forms of identity. Syed (2006, 4) points out that it is in the "act of claiming a right to belong to the nation that the Muslim female body becomes threatening and this fear, while seemingly irrational, has become legitimated as the 'reasonable' basis on which to construct laws of exclusion that push the covered Muslim female body from stranger to outlaw." This creates an interesting paradox: the veiled woman is seen as backward and oppressed by her fidelity to anachronistic religious customs and at the same time is positioned as a cultural renegade unwilling to conform to the standards and codes enforced by the modern state. Through these totalizing discourses, she is constructed as both an oppressed victim of Islamic degeneracy and a recalcitrant immigrant refusing to assimilate to French society. Both of these narratives rely on neocolonial tropes to cast Muslim women as politically immature and in need of cultural rehabilitation by the West.

This leads to a second paradox: not only are the bodies of Muslim women being controlled by patriarchal religious authorities that enforce the practice of veiling (often state-sanctioned, as in Iran and Saudi Arabia), but they are also being regulated in equally limiting and demoralizing ways by the state in countries like France and Turkey, where the hijab has been banned in schools. Both moves deny the agency of Muslim women to make reasoned choices about their bodies. Muslim women lose their agentic capacities and freedom as much through these racist and paternalistic state policies as they do through authoritarian patriarchal religious decrees (see also Zine 2004). In theocratic states, women's bodies are controlled according to "divine sanction," although the scriptural validity of determinations are not without challenge (see, for example, Abou El Fadl 2001, Barlas 2002, and Wadud 1999). In the West, however, secularism masquerades as universalism and provides justification for curtailing religious freedom and choice. Liberal democratic states that claim to be committed to women's autonomy and choice are shown to be highly disingenuous when they choose the same techniques of control as the mullahs they decry.

Muslims in the West must navigate between the spaces that separate belonging to the nation and being exiled from it. These liminal territories fracture the ground on which Muslim identities are constituted and contested. Such identities are encrypted with meanings that are imposed by others and over which we often have no control. Our acceptability for nationhood is decided by fellow citizens who regard themselves as more entitled than we to imagining the nation and deciding who has a right to belong to it.

Muslims and Canadian National Identity

Enloe (1989, 46) writes that "if a state is a vertical creature of authority, a nation is a horizontal creature of identity." But what kind of identities are permitted and enabled within the imagined spaces of the nation in Canada, and what kind of identities are regulated and policed? In the officially multicultural polity of Canada,[3] there are no legal restrictions on wearing the hijab or other forms of religious expression in public schools or at other civic sites. However, racism and Islamophobia persist in the informal disciplinary structures policing subaltern identities within the nation at large.

Increasing pluralism and the integration of multicultural groups into the political sphere are reconfiguring the nation in ways that subvert the imperialist nostalgia on the part of some nationalists who – to borrow Hage's (2000, 48) terms – "recall themselves as masters of a territory in which they have managerial rights over racialised/ethnicised groups or persons which are consequently constructed as manageable objects." Canadian multiculturalism is steeped in these historically determined relations of power. Thobani (2007) furthers this analysis by describing those who fit within the dominant narrative of the nation as "exalted subjects." She writes that in Canada "the historical exaltation of the national subject has enobled this subject's humanity and sanctioned the elevation of its rights over and above that of the Aboriginal and the immigrant" (Thobani 2007, 9). This shores up the positional superiority and racial hierarchy of white nationalism despite the rhetoric of multiculturalism.

I became particularly aware of the precariousness and fragility of the narrative of Canadian national identity for Muslims after the tragic terrorist attacks of 9/11. Muslims tend to talk about life in terms of a critical rupture – "pre-9/11" or "post-9/11" – that created an ontological as well as a temporal shift. In the West, peaceful citizens were transformed overnight into threats to national security. Ten years and the deaths (by some estimates) of almost 1 million Muslims in Iraq and Afghanistan in the US-led war on terror have not changed this perception or assuaged the Western desire to root out the Muslim fanatic maybe disguised as the neighbour next door. Razack's (2007) study of Canadian immigration and anti-terrorism policies toward Muslims in Canada suggests that a "state of exception" (Agamben 2005) has been created where war measures are enacted through policies that sanction tactics such as extraordinary rendition, security certificates, and secret evidence and trials. She contends that these measures support the logic of empire in a world increasingly governed by the state of exception, one in which Muslims are cast out of the national and political community.

Arat-Koc (2005) argues that the post-9/11 Canadian identity has resulted in the reassertion of racial boundaries of belonging and the marginalization of nonwhite minorities.[4] I further contend that Canada has evolved historically from a society of white settlers to a society of "settled whiteness" where white, Christian, Eurocentric norms and ideals are still hegemonic despite projections that by the year 2017 one-fifth of Canadians will belong to a "visible minority." In this context, multicultural difference is often seen as a disruptive rather than a harmonizing feature of society. As subaltern groups gain political voice and leverage, whiteness becomes less settled and more vulnerable, especially as the idealized and desired "how it used to be" nation, with its attendant privileges and entitlements for white nationalists, becomes a more distant memory (Hage 2000, 39).

Muslim Women and Gendered Cultural Politics in Canada

Taking into account the precariousness of national identity and belonging for subaltern Muslim citizens in the West, I want to reflect more specifically on the gendered subject formation of Muslim women in the context of the nation. I present three themes – disciplining culture, death by culture, and death of culture – as tropes through which to discuss the proposal for faith-based arbitration founded on shar'ia in Ontario, the "honour killing" of a

Canadian Pakistani teen, the banning of the hijab in girls' soccer in Quebec, and the Hérouxville Citizen's Code.

Disciplining Culture
"Disciplining culture" refers to the disciplinary technologies used to produce and reproduce the nation as a hegemonic cultural entity. Although multiculturalism is the Canadian social paradigm, not all modalities of cultural practice are encouraged. Indeed, there are many cultural practices affecting women that are considered out of line with what common norms of equity and social justice uphold (e.g., female genital mutilation). Cultural relativism in such instances acts in service to patriarchal violence; however, in this discussion I am more concerned with how the disciplining of Muslim culture – done in the name of safeguarding Muslim women – actually secures the paternalism of the state. This was evident in the "shar'ia tribunal affair" in Toronto. Faith-based arbitration has been allowed in Ontario since 1991.[5] Jewish rabbinical courts (or Beis Dein) and Aboriginal healing circles are examples of religious and cultural systems of mediation that are used to adjudicate civil matters. However, when Muslims began to advocate for the use of *fiqh* (an Islamic system of jurisprudence) in civil disputes such as divorce, child custody, and inheritance, the proposal was met with disproportionately negative reactions. The media, notably talk radio programs, conjured images of stoning and flogging in the public square as Islamophobia became rampant.

More legitimate contestations were raised over how women would fare under a religious arbitration scheme, especially as shar'ia has at times been detrimental to women. I was involved in these debates as a faith-centred Muslim feminist and public intellectual, and in addressing these concerns I argued that, even though Islamic law is not intrinsically unjust to women, the interpretive communities that determined these ordinances in the ninth century did privilege men. Although more gender-just rulings are being developed by contemporary jurists (see, for example, Abou El Fadl 2001) and encouraging family-law reform is taking place in countries like Morocco, I was concerned that these moves had not gained legitimacy in mainstream Muslim orthodoxy in Canada and that these tribunals might be a risky proposition for upholding women's rights.

At the same time, I challenged Islamophobic narratives that were circulating with increasing impunity. Neo-Orientalist fears and fantasies of the "dangerous citizen" posing a subversive threat to liberal ideals and democratic freedoms were widespread. This becomes the challenge for Muslim feminists: when we begin to interrogate issues of sexism within our communities, our efforts become subject to the sensationalized racism outside of the community that feeds off such revelations.

There were several common tropes employed by opponents of faith-based arbitration. The first was the need to "rescue Muslim women" from barbaric laws – as in Spivak's (1988) formulation of "saving brown women from brown men." Former Ontario attorney general Marion Boyd was asked to lead an inquiry into the proposal in order to ensure that "vulnerable persons" were protected. There were questions raised by feminist groups about whether women would truly have freedom of choice in deciding whether or not to use shar'ia-based arbitration since they might be influenced by pressure from religious conservatives.[6] Others worried that the infantilizing nature of feminist "concern" was denying Muslim women their agency and the political maturity to make decisions about their lives. These paternalistic narratives not only constitute Canadian Muslim women as universally oppressed victims of cultural misogyny but also, in turn, reconfigure the construction of the state as the benevolent patron and vanguard of these women. The civilizing and recuperative power of the nation is seen to correct the problem of illiberal minorities misusing multiculturalism to promote their anti-democratic and anti-woman practices.

The move to introduce religious arbitration based on Islamic principles was thus seen as a subversion of Canadian ideals and values as well as a threat to the nature of the country itself. The rhetoric purveyed from this standpoint argued that the nation was at risk of being corrupted by foreign ideologies that were regarded as illiberal, anti-democratic, and outside of the progressive turns of modernity and enlightened political values. In the end, on September 11, 2003, Ontario premier Dalton McGuinty put an end to the debate, announcing the termination of faith-based arbitration in Ontario.[7] This unilateralism not only silenced the public debate but also reproduced the state as the civilizing arbiter. Muslim culture remained cast as a dangerous, static throwback in need of containment and disciplining. The assertion of group rights by recalcitrant minorities was quelled and rendered docile. The paternalism of the state was reinforced through this move in the name of rescuing "imperiled" Muslim women (see also Razack 2004).

Death by Culture
The second trope, "death by culture," speaks to how cultural differences in relation to gender have come to unsettle the multicultural nation. This is

particularly apparent in the case of the tragic death of Aqsa Parvez in December 2007. Aqsa was a sixteen-year-old Pakistani teenager from an immigrant family who was killed by her father in what was widely touted by Canadian media as an "honour killing." The catalyst for this violent confrontation was allegedly Aqsa's refusal to wear the hijab. Prior to her death, she had left home and was living with family friends, according to her school friends, because she did not want to wear the hijab and clashed with her parents. This version of the story conflicts with reports from the family friends with whom she was staying, who stated that her problems with her parents were based on broader desires for autonomy – not unlike what many non-Muslim teens experience (Offman 2007).

Any attempt to insert a more normative frame of reference through which to understand Aqsa's death was overshadowed by the barrage of media sensationalism that framed the issue as a "death by culture." The hegemonic construction of the debate purveyed in the media was such that the death was read as an "honour killing" rather than as a case of tragic domestic violence. As a scholar who has conducted research on Canadian Muslim youth especially in relation to questions of religious identity, I received over fifteen requests for media interviews, including from as far away as CNN in Atlanta. All of the reporters with whom I spoke wanted to explore the angle of how Muslim girls in Canada are constrained by Islam and their ethnic culture. The discussion was never approached through broader issues of violence against women or domestic violence but only through Muslim and Pakistani cultural pathology. Not only was it Aqsa's father who had brutally strangled her: it was her culture that had killed her.

The difference between these two narratives is critical. The notion of "honour killing" locates religion and culture as the central factors in this young girl's death, whereas describing the case as domestic violence helps us to understand the ubiquity of male domination as it occurs in a wide variety of cultural contexts. Razack (1998, 57-58) notes that "in a racist society ... violence in immigrant communities is viewed as a cultural attribute rather than a product of male domination." Indeed, one reason why non-Western cultures are regarded as more sexist is that incidents of sexual violence in the West are seen to be socially deviant as opposed to being a characteristic of Western culture, whereas sexism and violence in Third World or immigrant communities are seen as culturally intrinsic and endemic to these societies (Volpp 2003). For example, an editorial in the *National Post* on Aqsa's murder outlines the connections made between her death and the pathologies that are associated with Islam in the rightwing media and public:

Since 9/11, Western societies have begun to closely scrutinize the toxic cultural practices of unassimilated Muslims in Europe and elsewhere. These practices include not only honour killings, but also anti-Semitism, support for terrorism, misogyny, forced veilings and forced marriages. Several high-profile conservative columnists – some of whom appear on these pages – have been particularly vigorous about highlighting these pathologies. And so when a young Muslim girl gets killed by her father, there is a natural tendency to see it as an indicator that Canadian Muslims are about to follow the radicalized path of militant, unassimilated co-religionists in Paris, London and Stockholm. ("Meaning of Aqsa Parvez" 2007)

These comments were put forward to counter the sensationalist reporting and fear mongering in the coverage of Aqsa's death and to avoid furthering a case that her death was an indicator of violent radicalization. Indeed, the editorial goes on to point out that "in truth, however, Canada's Muslim community is moderate by world standards. The sight of a woman in a full burka is an extraordinary rarity outside of a few small urban pockets. And such horrors as that allegedly visited upon Ms. Parvez remain almost unheard of" ("Meaning of Aqsa Parvez" 2007). This puts in perspective the assymetical relationship between the Islamophobic sentiments that were being purveyed around this tragedy and the facts that mitigate against these facile equations of gender and culture with extremist violence.

In my interviews with reporters, I argued that Aqsa's crisis was not simply a matter of religion and Pakistani culture, as the media portrayed it, but was also a matter of Canadian culture. Yet media analysis failed to address the fact that since this crime occurred in Canada, the circumstances leading up to it were also a product of this national context. Instead, settled notions of a benevolent Canadian nation being corrupted by the infiltration of pathological foreign cultures became the dominant narrative, leaving out any interrogation of how racism and Islamophobia are implicated in this tragedy. For example, the competing cultural standards to which Muslim girls are subject – those of their home and community and those of the dominant culture – require a dialectical analysis. Aqsa's home and community were cited as religiously repressive sites, but there was no interrogation of how Canadian attitudes toward Islam impact young girls who wear the hijab at school or in society at large and how this may have impacted Aqsa's self-perception and her decision not to cover (see also Zine 2006). As a result, ethnicity and culture became the culprits, and patriarchy and misogyny were neatly packaged as foreign cultural imports. It became clear to me that the media were limiting Muslims' rights to be individuals; we were permanently tied to our ethno-cultural and religious contexts. The overdetermination of culture in such cases is a burden that is unequally shouldered by racially marginalized communities, especially by women. What if Aqsa had been white? Would her religion and culture have been at issue? Would "Canadian culture" have been invoked as relevant to her death?

The "death by culture" narrative was also salient in another case of national interest: the banning of the hijab for Muslim girls in Quebec soccer leagues. This decision – ultimately supported by the Fédération Internationale de Football Association (FIFA) – erupted when eleven-year-old Asmahan Mansour was told by a referee to remove her hijab because it violated Québec Soccer Federation (QSF) rules. When she refused, she was told to leave the field and was barred from playing. Her team and four others walked out of the tournament in support, calling the ban racist. QSF officials responded that the Muslim hijab is specifically prohibited in tournaments and games in the name of safety: players risk being "strangled by a loose bit of cloth" (*CBC News* 2007b). Islamic head covers are worn by women in a variety of sports and are adaptable in their design to facilitate these activities. Although the hijab is permitted on soccer fields in other Canadian provinces (and indeed globally), this did not influence the decisions made in Quebec.

The question I want to raise here is whether the QSF's concern was physical safety (since there have yet to be massive hijab-related fatalities reported on soccer fields!) or whether the question of "safety" is a cultural rather than a corporeal issue. In other words, the fear of strangulation may imply something more metaphorical: being "strangled" by her culture. It seems that concern over the likelihood of physical danger (which has yet to be proven) masks the real concern over the "civilizational danger" posed by a veiled Muslim woman. Kahf (1999) identifies ways that the veiled Muslim woman has been historically represented in the Western imaginary as a signifier of fear and difference. The colonial fear of being engulfed by difference and cultural degeneracy still has currency and may well be at the heart of the fears over the hijab in the postcolonial present.

The concerns raised in the dominant media discourses in the cases of Aqsa's death and Asmahan's expulsion echoed the argument made in Moller Okin's famous 1999 book, *Is Multiculturalism Bad for Women?* Her concern is that women's rights are being sacrificed on the altar of multiculturalism. She uses extreme examples (e.g., child marriage, rape victims forced to marry their rapists, clitoridectomy) to make her case that multiculturalism and a privileging of cultural-group rights over the individual rights of women have opened the door to misogynist cultures running amok. This perspective was echoed in Canadian media and is to some extent a reflection of public sentiment:

> Canada prides itself on its multiculturalism and, to varying degrees of success, condemns institutionalized patriarchy. But there is growing concern that recent waves of Muslim immigrants aren't integrating, or embracing our liberal values. Aqsa's death – coming in the wake of debates about the acceptability of shar'ia law, disputes over young girls wearing hijabs at soccer games, and the arrest of the Toronto 18 – stoked fears about religious zealotry in our midst. Is it possible that Toronto has become too tolerant of cultural differences? (Rogan 2008, 2)

This rhetoric – that multiculturalism has gone awry and is testing the tolerance of "civilized" society – is invoked when any negative issue implicating racially and/or religiously marginalized groups is sensationalized. The "death by culture" narrative is a vehicle for rampant Islamophobia, but it represents another fear: that multiculturalism is a slippery slope leading toward the death of the dominant national culture in Canada. Eurocentrism and liberal culture, civility, and values are seen to be at peril due to the recklessness of unbridled multiculturalism and the racial and religious minorities who refuse to embrace them. For anti-racists, multiculturalism has always been a smokescreen that obscures the deep racial inequalities of society and operates as a means to contain and control ethno-racial and religious diversity (Bannerji 2000, Thobani 2007). Yet others fear multiculturalism because of its failure to achieve these same ends.

Death of Culture
French Canada has always sought its own distinctive narrative of linguistic, cultural, and political identity throughout the history of Anglo hegemony in Canada. The rural areas of Quebec remain largely homogeneous (francophone, Catholic) in comparison to the diversity and cosmopolitanism of Montreal, where diasporic communities from francophone nations in Arab North Africa, Continental Africa, and the Caribbean reside. How this homogeneity became perceived as under threat is exemplified by the experience of Hérouxville, Quebec, which openly argued that its culture was imperilled by foreign ways of life.

Ethnically homogeneous Hérouxville is situated far away from the urban melting pot of cultural diversity,[8] yet fear for the cultural integrity and racial purity of its community led the town council to draft a charter preserving the town's values from the corruption of unwelcome outsiders. The Hérouxville Citizen's Code was a manifesto of the town's values and way of life, serving as a warning to potential newcomers. According to the preamble of the code,

> Our goal is to inform the new arrivals to our territory how we live to help them make a clear decision to integrate into our area. We would especially like to inform the new arrivals that the lifestyle that they left behind in their birth country cannot be brought here with them and they would have to adapt to their new social identity. (Municipalité Hérouxville 2007)

Embedded in the subtext of the Hérouxville Citizen's Code is a declaration of the authors' fears and desires for the nation. The charter upholds women's rights to "drive a car, vote, sign checks, dance, decide for herself, speak her peace, dress as she sees fit respecting of course the democratic decency, walk alone in public places, study, have a job, have her own belongings and anything else that a man can do." These declarations supposedly provide the grounds for a preferred form of gendered citizenship but in actuality reveal a tacit construction of the "anti-citizen." The code spells out a negative referent for women's standards of conduct, an archetypical woman who is forbidden to drive, vote, dance, claim agency, or make a decision. The code goes on to outline conduct regarding women: "We consider that killing women in public beatings, or burning them alive are not part of our standards of life" (Municipalité Hérouxville 2007). The stereotypical image of a Third World subaltern woman emerges from the page: the beaten, burnt, oppressed, foreign woman of colour. But the code is also clearly self-referential. In this Manichean formulation, she is the debased, downtrodden victim of cultural degeneracy and Hérouxville is a bastion of civility, freedom, and democracy. Ahmed (2000, 54) warns that such "strange bodies" become "a fetish which both conceals and reveals the body-at-home's reliance on strangers to secure his being – his place – his presence in the world."

The code is a means of articulating and, at the same time, reinforcing this fetishized difference. The woman woven into the code is thus a product of Orientalist fiction, more a phantasm than representative of any real person or tangible threat. In this way, the code represents projection and personification of the town's Islamophobic fears and angst. This fear is manifold. At the core, the code represents the fear of "white decline" and the "death of culture" (Hage 2000, 22). Hage (2000, 40) explains that this fear becomes engulfing: "When the nationalist feels that he or she can no longer operate in, communicate in or recognise the national space in which he or she operates, the nation appears to be losing its homely character." The code is an attempt to preserve the "homeliness" of the nation against the onslaught of estrangement and unfathomable cultural difference personified as the body of a veiled Muslim woman.[9] Muslim women become "imperiled Muslim women imperiling the nation." The difference they embody is an imperilling difference; they are threatened by the barbaric misogyny of their culture and religion and at the same time pose a threat to the sanctity of the nation as a space for dominant liberal, Christian, Eurocentric values to prevail. These contradictory tensions produce ambivalent desires to rescue and liberate Muslim women from their debilitating cultures and at the same time keep them outside the physical and discursive boundaries of the nation.

This form of cultural gate-keeping in Hérouxville is driven by the same eugenicist goals as the Dutch immigration videos and German citizenship tests discussed earlier: keeping "dangerous foreigners" at bay. As the result of the "war on terror," citizenship regimes and security regimes are becoming increasingly interconnected in Western contexts. Muslims have come to personify the threat of insecurity. Goldberg (2006, 347) makes a fascinating connection between the fears of physical and cultural "death" and the representation of Muslims in Europe:

> The figure of the Muslim has thus come to stand for the fear of violent death, the paranoia of Europe's cultural demise, of European integrity. For the fear of the death of Europe itself. The Muslim image in contemporary Europe is one of fanaticism, fundamentalism, female (women and girls') suppression, subjugation, and repression. The Muslim, in this view, foments conflict: violence, war, militancy, terrorism, cultural dissension.

The term "Muslim," therefore, metonymically relates to a kind of death in the European imaginary. Whether it is a corporeal death or the death of culture, either narrative is difficult to displace once it gains epistemological and ontological currency.

This fear operates politically in at least three ways. First, these discourses galvanizing fears over the death of national culture are increasingly tied to terror and physical threat in the Western imaginary. "The figure of the Muslim has thus come to stand for the fear of violent death" (Goldberg 2006, 347) of Western culture and identity. Second, in the same way that the state uses racial and religious profiling at its borders to keep out "dangerous foreigners," citizens such as those in Hérouxville are engaged in forms of profiling. The Citizen's Code is an example of profiling that allows dominant citizens to define Others as subaltern and keep them outside of the guarded boundaries of community and nation. Finally, the fears of encroaching difference and the disrupted familiarity that comes with cultural pluralism create a greater need for feeling secure. The narratives of familiarity, community, and security have become interrelated in new ways in the present context of protracted imperialist wars and global Islamophobia. This feeds into the "paranoid nationalism" (Hage 2003) evident in some sectors of Quebec society.

A more recent move that exemplifies this paranoia is the Quebec government's plan to force new immigrants to sign a declaration pledging their respect for "Quebec's common values." This move builds on the paranoid sensibilities that informed the Hérouxville Citizen's Code and manifests them writ large as foundations for immigration to the province. Immigrants to Quebec must promise to learn French and acknowledge that men and women have equal rights and that political and religious institutions are separate. These values are relayed in seminars for new immigrants to ensure they understand and are willing to accept the terms of citizenship in Quebec. According to Quebec immigration minister Yolande James, anyone who refuses to sign the declaration will not have their application accepted. In an article in the *Montreal Gazette* ("Quebec's new immigrant" 2008), the minister is quoted as saying, "Coming to Quebec is not a right, it is a privilege. If you refuse to sign the declaration, you won't be able to come here." Heralded as a move to better help in the integration of immigrants, this policy instead situates immigrants as being illiberal and anti-democratic and in need of "schooling" to be part of a civilized society. Immigrants are required to declare an acknowledgment of and allegiance to these values because they are not regarded as possessing the necessary prerequisites for becoming citizens, which further situates them as outsiders and interlopers. Rather than fostering integration, this policy furthers xenophobic sentiments calling for the cultural rehabilitation of backward immigrants so that they might conform to the standards of a modern democratic nation. According to Daniel Weinstock, a University of Montreal ethics philosopher and member of the advisory committee to the Bouchard-Taylor Commission, the message it sends is patronizing: "It's saying, 'I, as an immigrant, may be tempted to live by my tribal, benighted ways.' If I were an immigrant, I think I'd be quite insulted" (in Chung 2009). Beyond insult, the policy is steeped in racist and xenophobic assumptions about the beliefs and behaviours of new immigrants that in turn constitute Quebec as the bearer of superior civilized values and culture engaged in an internal "mission civilisatrice."

Such xenophobic policies create further divides, contribute to the alienation of already marginalized groups, and threaten not only the fragile communities of difference that must be accommodated within the multicultural nation but also the existence of a multicultural nation itself. Following recent hearings on "reasonable accommodation" in Quebec, it was concluded that a model of "interculturalism" – focused on commonalities and cohesion rather than multicultural difference – would better suit Quebec society (Bouchard and Taylor 2008). I believe that this liberal notion of "colour-blindness" does not address the real challenges of integration – which involves clearly tackling racism, xenophobia, Islamophobia, and other interlocking forms of oppression. It may also simply be a guise for the return of earlier assimilationist policies. Nonetheless, critiques of bland liberal pluralism usually come from anti-racist scholars and activists like myself, who are designated as "angry brown/black people" and are written off as inconvenient and disruptive to notions of liberal "harmonization."

Conclusion

Jiwani (2005) aptly points out that national mythologies rely on both race and gender in their formulation. In this discussion I have attempted to unpack how contemporary Muslim cultural politics affect the ways that gender, race, and religious identity are discursively constituted within the nation and how at the same time negotiating these categories of identity is unsettling and reconfiguring the constitution of the nation. The imagined community of the nation is continually unsettled and reconstituted through contestations over how racialized, gendered, and religious differences are to be incorporated and/or resisted. The complex negotiations over identity, citizenship, and belonging that I have discussed create new contours in the national landscape that shore up paternalist and white nationalist aims but, at the same time, unsettle and reconfigure the boundaries of belonging to the nation in ways that continually decentre the salience of this same project. Race, religion, and gender remain sites of contestation within the constitution of the multicultural nation and yet provide productive tensions through which new imaginings of community and identity are made possible. As we have seen in Canada, Muslim women's identities are both being shaped by these national imaginings and prompting contestations over the very foundations of the national project.

NOTES

1 A notable example of the construction of the "bad immigrant" archetype is the case of Canadian Muslim feminist scholar Sunera Thobani, who was widely demonized in the days after 9/11 for her speech entitled "War Frenzy," which criticizes US foreign policy and imperialism and its complicity in the attacks. Caught up in the frenzy of jingoistic patriotism, Thobani was branded an "enemy outsider." As she notes, "repeatedly reconstructing my status as a non-White, immigrant woman, the media reiterated – in a highly intensified manner – the historically racialized discourse of who belongs to the Canadian nation, and hence, who has a right to speak to it" (Thobani 2007, 401). The social disciplining of Thobani as an "angry woman of colour" operated to silence any spaces of dissent with the dominant discourse (Zine 2004). This case is an example of how racialized bodies become sanctioned and socially disciplined back into the grid of multicultural conformity for not behaving like the "good immigrant."
2 Other categories of the subaltern citizenry may include undocumented migrants and other people without status who are routinely identified as "illegal" or "alien" in political discourses and in policies that erode the rights of these noncitizens.
3 In 1971 the federal government announced its policy of multiculturalism, which recognizes and promotes the reality of pluralism in Canada while encouraging all cultural groups to participate fully and equally in Canadian society. However, anti-racists criticize Canadian multiculturalism for not delivering on its promises of social, economic, and racial equity (see Bannerji 2000, Thobani 2007).
4 Bannerji (2000, 65) sums up the disjuncture between citizenship and belonging for racialized bodies by problematizing the paradox of simultaneously belonging and nonbelonging, which she argues means that we are part of the economy, laws, and civil society, "yet we are not part of its self definition as 'Canada' because we are not 'Canadians.' We, with our named and ascribed Otherness face an undifferentiated notion of the 'Canadian' as an unwavering beacon of our assimilation."
5 In 2002 a proposal was put forward by the Islamic Institute of Civil Justice that was intended to take advantage of an amendment to the 1991 Arbitration Act in Ontario, which opened the door for alternative dispute resolution (ADR) to be applied in civil family matters. This legal permission allowed for any laws agreed to by the involved parties – including religious laws – to be employed in binding private-arbitration agreements.
6 An online publication from the Islamic Institute for Civil Justice (Ali 2004), the organization that spearheaded the proposal for shar'ia-based arbitration, states: "A Muslim who would choose to opt out at this stage, for reasons of convenience would be guilty of a far greater crime than a mere breach of contract – this could be

tantamount to blasphemy-apostasy." Statements like this are coercive, especially for women who look to religious authorities within the community for guidance on doing the "right thing" and being a "good Muslim."

7 The date of this announcement – a Sunday – is notably an unlikely day for the premier to make such pronouncements. It was also September 11, which may not have been purely a coincidence.

8 According to Macpherson (2007), "Hérouxville introduces itself as a town of 1,323 in the Québec hinterland ... Statistics Canada's 2001 community profile says it was 100 percent French-speaking, and 96 percent Catholic. There were no Muslims, Jews or Sikhs (the nearest mosque, synagogue or temple is nearly 200 kilometres away in Montréal). Only 10 inhabitants were born outside of Canada."

9 A delegation of Muslim women visited Hérouxville to attempt to dispel myths about Islam and renegotiate the terms of the Citizen's Code to make it less offensive to minorities. Eventually, the town council adopted changes, which included removing references to "no stoning of women in public" and "no female circumcision" (see, for example, CBC 2007a).

REFERENCES

Abou El Fadl, K. 2001. *Speaking in God's name: Islamic law, authority and women.* Oxford, UK: Oneworld.

Agamben, G. 2005. *State of exception.* Chicago, IL: University of Chicago Press.

Ahmed, S. 2000. *Strange encounters: Embodied Others in postcoloniality.* New York: Routledge.

Ali, S.M. 2004. Are Muslim women's rights adversely affected by *Shariah* tribunals? http://muslimcanada.org/.

Anderson, B. 1983. *Imagined communities: Reflections on the origin and spread of nationalism.* New York: Verso.

Arat-Koc, S. 2005. The disciplinary boundaries of Canadian identity after September 11: Civilizational identity, multiculturalism, and the challenge of anti-imperialist feminism. *Social Justice* 32, 4: 32-49.

Bannerji, H. 2000. Geography lessons: On being an insider/outsider to the Canadian nation. In H. Bannerji, ed., *The dark side of nation: Essays on multiculturalism, nationalism, and gender,* 63-86. Toronto: Canadian Scholars' Press.

Barlas, A. 2002. *Believing women in Islam: Unreading patriarchal interpretations of the Qur'an.* Austin, TX: University of Texas Press.

Bouchard, G., and C. Taylor. 2008. *Building the future: A time for reconciliation.* Quebec City: Bibliothèque et archives nationales du Québec.

Canadian Broadcasting Corporation News. 2007a. Hérouxville drops some rules from controversial code. http://www.cbc.ca/.

–. 2007b. International soccer body to discuss Québec hijab ban. http://www.cbc.ca/canada/.

Carr, M. 2006. You are now entering Eurabia. *Race and Class* 48, 1: 1-22.

Chung, A. 2009. Quebec culture lessons for immigrants questioned. *Toronto Star,* December 30. http://www.thestar.com/.

Enloe, C. 1989. *Bananas, beaches and bases*. Berkeley and Los Angeles: University of California Press.
Foucault, M. 1991. Governmentality. In G. Burchell, C. Gordon, and P. Miller, eds., *The Foucault effect: Studies in governmentality*, 87-104. Hemel Hempstead, UK: Harvester Wheatsheaf.
Goldberg, D.T. 2006. Racial Europeanization. *Ethnic and Racial Studies* 29, 2: 331-64.
Hage, G. 2000. *White nation: Fantasies of white supremacy in a multicultural society*. New York, NY: Routledge.
–. 2003. *Against paranoid nationalism: Searching for hope in a shirking society*. London, UK: Merlin.
Jiwani, Y. 2005. The Great White North encounters September 11: Race, gender and the nation in Canada's national daily the *Globe and Mail*. *Social Justice* 32, 4: 50-68.
Kahf, M. 1999. *Western representations of the Muslim woman*. Austin, TX: University of Texas Press.
Macpherson, D. 2007. The town of Hérouxville is our own Sault Ste. Marie. *Montreal Gazette*, January 30, n.p.
The meaning of Aqsa Parvez. 2007. Editorial. *National Post*, December 12. http://www.nationalpost.com/.
Moller Okin, S. 1999. *Is multiculturalism bad for women?* Princeton, NJ: Princeton University Press.
Municipalité Hérouxville. 2007. Publication of standards. http://herouxville-quebec.blogspot.com/.
Offman, C. 2007. Aqsa Parvez: Mourned slain teen wanted "to get more out of life," friends say. *Edmonton Journal*, December 16, n.p.
Quebec's new immigrant declaration a political stunt: Critics. 2008. *Montreal Gazette*, October 29. http://www.canada.com/.
Razack, S.H. 1998. *Looking white people in the eye: Gender, race, and culture in courtrooms and classrooms*. Toronto, ON: University of Toronto Press.
–. 2004. Imperiled Muslim women, dangerous Muslim men and civilized Europeans: Legal and social responses to forced marriages. *Feminist Legal Studies* 12, 2: 129-74.
–. 2007. *Casting out: The eviction of Muslims from Western law and politics*. Toronto, ON: University of Toronto Press.
Rogan, M. 2008. Girl interrupted. *Toronto Life Magazine*, December. http://www.torontolife.com/.
Spivak, G.C. 1988. Can the subaltern speak? In C. Nelson and L. Grossberg, eds., *Marxism and the interpretation of culture*, 271-313. Urbana, IL: University of Illinois Press.
Syed, I. 2006. Dispensable citizenship: The Othering of the Muslim community in Canada. Paper presented at the Association of Muslim Social Scientists Annual Conference, Hartford Seminary, Hartford, Connecticut, October.
Thobani, S. 2007. *Exalted subjects: Studies in the making of race and nation in Canada*. Toronto, ON: University of Toronto Press.

Volpp, L. 2003. Feminism versus multiculturalism. In Adrienne Katherine Wing, ed., *Critical race feminism,* 395-405. New York: New York University Press.

Wadud, A. 1999. *Qur'an and woman: Rereading the sacred text from a woman's perspective.* 2nd ed. New York: Oxford University Press.

Zine, J. 2004. Creating a critical-faith-centred space for anti-racist feminism: Reflections of a Muslim scholar-activist. *Journal of Feminist Studies in Religion* 20, 2: 167-88.

—. 2006. Unveiled sentiments: Gendered Islamophobia and experiences of veiling among Muslim girls in a Canadian Islamic school. *Equity and Excellence in Education* 39, 3: 239-52.

2

The Great Canadian "Shar'ia" Debate

ITRATH SYED

The great Canadian "shar'ia" debate began in 2003 when a Toronto-based Muslim organization, the Islamic Institute for Civil Justice (IICJ), led by Syed Mumtaz Ali, applied for standing under the Arbitration Act of Ontario to provide arbitration services for the Muslim community.[1] This could have been a forgettable blip in the national consciousness. Indeed, numerous other organizations, representing other faith-based communities, had applied and received standing to provide the same services without any perceivable public response. However, in this case, the IICJ's application became the centre of a full-scale national melodrama that in time spread beyond Canadian borders to find its place alongside other international moral panics involving Muslim minority populations in "Western"[2] contexts.

In the post-9/11 era, with its deep racializing of Muslim communities in Canada and elsewhere in the "West," it was not possible for the discussion around this proposal to be limited to the specifics of the proposal itself. Very quickly this debate descended into the fervent policing of the "national imaginary," which merged neatly into the larger narrative of "civilizational disciplining" (see also Chapter 1). According to the parameters of the discourse, there were only two, very polarized, sides to the debate. One side was civilized, Canadian, and feminist, and the other was barbaric, medieval, foreign, and misogynist. These dichotomies were erected by invoking familiar tropes in which Muslim women were infantilized, the Muslim community of Canada was denationalized, and Islamic law was fossilized.

I, in turn, do not wish to conflate all of the opponents of the proposal or their arguments. However, despite their nuanced differences, all of the opposition forces anchored their arguments to these three pillars, and the nature of the debate precluded the presence of a third space in which a Muslim feminist perspective on Islamic law could be heard. This is not to say that the opposition forces that identified as such were not feminist or not Muslim but rather that the specific feminist reforms of Islamic law, or even the idea that there could be feminist re-engagements with the canon of Islamic law, were not given voice during the dichotomous debate that ensued.

In this chapter, I explore the discourses that were employed in this debate and deconstruct some of the tropes that were invoked by the opponents of the proposal by placing this debate within the context of how Muslim bodies have been increasingly policed and disciplined within the national imaginaries of the West.

The Trajectory of My Own Responses

I first heard of the proposal for Islamic arbitration in late 2003 as it began to make the rounds of e-mail listservs in the Muslim community. My initial response to the proposal was unreservedly negative. My instinctive feeling at the time was that the practical application of this proposal would work against the interests of Muslim women. Based on my own experiences as a Muslim feminist who has been in a life-long, often contentious, negotiation with my own community, I wondered how the IICJ would be different from the other Muslim community organizations with which I had previously dealt. How would this organization realize the principles of gender justice, which many of us believe are integral to an Islamic paradigm, but which we find a dearth of in the actual lived realities of our communities? In an e-mail I sent out on December 23, 2003, I wrote:

> I fear that this kind of tribunal will make women feel obliged to sign away their custody and settlement rights in divorce to a body that they will feel they can not challenge without seeming to challenge "Islam." And why would this tribunal be more respectful of Muslim women's rights, when no other Muslim organization in Canada is??? How are these Muslims going to escape replicating the kind of inequality that has become institutionalized in all other Muslim organizations??? Be afraid. Be very very afraid. (Syed 2003)

It is important to note that this e-mail was sent out to a local community listserv of young Muslims. This was my view on the arbitration issue prior to a thorough reading of the proposal and prior to the vicious media campaign that would soon begin. My absolutist language here is reflective of the informal internal audience and my own desire to emphasize my point. I quote this e-mail because when I read it now I am astounded by the journey I have taken on this issue. As well, I believe that the way my own responses have shifted in the face of the public debate is likely similar to the experience of many other Muslims in Canada.[3]

For another year, I tried to remain out of the debate as much as possible and hoped that the issue would restrict itself to Ontario. This changed in December 2004 when I was invited by a feminist legal organization, the West Coast Legal Education and Action Fund (West Coast LEAF), to participate in a three-day conference on "Women's Equality and Religious Freedom" (WERF). I had not been following the media on this issue extensively and went into the discussions cold. The organizers had assembled a wide collection of feminist lawyers, academics, activists, and representatives of organizations that had been vocally opposing the arbitration proposal. Among them were members of the Canadian Council of Muslim Women (CCMW), an organization that defines itself as "pro-faith," as well as women associated with Homa Arjomand and the "No to Shar'ia" campaign.

It was my first real introduction to the "shar'ia" debate and it was the catalytic moment for this research.[4] I was greatly distressed by the tone of the discussions, particularly by the way the speakers seemed to say that what was good and Canadian was being threatened by what was dangerous and foreign. Within these discussions, there was a "Muslim woman" who was the object of great concern but who was never present herself. It was repeatedly emphasized that this "Muslim woman" was deeply vulnerable to being persecuted by "shar'ia"-based arbitration and yet was considered unable to voice her own opposition to it. Indeed, if she was supportive of the idea, it was only because she was too deluded in her false consciousness to know better.

As a Muslim woman who has been subject to anti-Muslim racism (or Islamophobia) and as an anti-racist activist, I recognized the tenor of this debate. It sounded eerily familiar to me. There was clearly a line being drawn between "us" and "them." Even the participants who identified themselves as being Muslim seemed to be comfortable in speaking of "those" Muslims who were clearly different and in opposition to "us." I found myself wondering why I was on this side of the line rather than the other side? And who exactly was on the other side? And in another similar room, one in which I physically was not present, would I be considered one of "those" women? One participant summed up the issue with very little room for doubt: "Most

Muslim women want Canadian law, [they have] little choice, afraid to talk" (West Coast LEAF 2004b, 16). "The women who support it, they are the ones who are brain-washed, they feel they have no options, it is the law" (West Coast LEAF 2004a, 15).[5] I walked out of the conference in protest on the morning of the third day, deeply upset but not quite clear in my own analysis about all of the ways that I felt repulsed by the discussions. I was aware that given the self-congratulatory passion play at work, there was no room for me to intervene with any subjectivity that was not limited to the role of eager native informant, pitiful unempowered victim, or brainwashed woman deluded into championing her own oppression. My decision to look at the actual substance of the discourse was in large part due to my desire to give voice and vocabulary to my own instinctive disgust with the way this issue was being discussed in that room.

Methodology

For the next year, I researched the ways this debate was playing out in the public discourse. Primarily, I analyzed print media coverage of the debate in Canada's three largest newspapers – the *Globe and Mail*, *National Post*, and *Toronto Star* – for the period of September 2004 to September 2005 (although I have used some sources from beyond this period and from other newspapers). As well, I looked at the media statements, press releases, and position papers issued by various organizations that identified themselves as stakeholders. I have also examined submissions made to the Marion Boyd Commission[6] and scholarly articles published on this debate. Throughout this period, I have tried to engage in political interventions on this issue in the media, through community networks, and in conversations with other activists (Syed 2005a, 2005b).

This debate was wide and diverse. Not all of the debate was negative. There were many surprises, including the unexpected support for the proposal from the editorial board of the *Globe and Mail*. I have chosen to focus primarily on the opponents of the debate and to look at the dominant arguments made against the proposal. As a result, I do not look at the proposal per se but rather at the discourses surrounding it. I believe that within the opposition arguments a thread can be located connecting the operative tropes with other moral panics over Muslim bodies in other contexts. Therefore, I contextualize these arguments within the dynamics of similar debates in other Western countries. I employ an anti-racist, postcolonial, feminist lens in my analysis and situate this debate in the context of the ways Muslim bodies and other bodies of colour are racialized and policed in the West.

In regard to terminology, I have chosen to place the word "shar'ia" in quote marks so as to denote its contested status. At a later point in the paper I explore why this term was misapplied in the debate. At this stage, it suffices to say that the proposal in question was for the use of Islamic arbitration, not the application of "shar'ia." Although many of the major players tried to distance themselves from the term, for the most part they continued to use it themselves and it remained the dominant marker of the debate in the national and international media.

The Denationalizing of the Muslim Community in Canada

One of the most striking characteristics of the "shar'ia" debate has been the ways that the proponents of the proposal (and by extension any in the Muslim community who were not opposed to it) were constructed as foreigners and invaders.[7] There was a central irony to the debate. The proponents of the proposal, with all their faults, were asking for access to existing provisions of Ontario provincial law. They were most explicitly not asking for the transformation of Canadian laws. Yet they were constructed not as Canadians wanting access to Canadian law but rather as part of a larger plan to destroy Canadian society, constituting a full frontal attack on all that is good and decent in the nation. This attack was supposedly such a substantive threat that all of Canada had to be mobilized to defend against it.

Within this discourse, the Muslim community as a whole was metaphorically denationalized and stripped of its collective citizenship. Muslims were constructed as the perpetual immigrant on probation, for whom there is (at the first sign of dissent with the national imaginary) a public outcry for immediate deportation – the very real expulsion of the polluted Other. This was perhaps best encapsulated by the comments made by Monique Gagnon-Tremblay, Quebec's minister of international relations:

> We must rework the social contract (for immigrants) so that Muslims who want to come to Québec and who do not respect women's rights, or rights, whatever they may be, in our civil code, at that moment, that they stay in their country and not come to Québec, because it's unacceptable ... On the other hand, if people want to come to Québec and accept our way of doing things, and our rights, in that instance they will be welcome and we will help them integrate. (De Souza 2005)

In this construction of the issue, the entire Muslim community is an immigrant community, none of whom have an inherent right to belong to the nation. As well, the nation, be it Quebec and/or Canada, is constructed as essentially pure and untainted – a bastion of equality where women's rights are completely uncontested and universal. The only threat to this utopia of gender equality is the potential of contamination by the Muslim immigrant, who, like any recalcitrant child, must be made to accept the authority of his superiors.

Without any actual reference made to the proposal itself and with no engagement with the questionable logistics of the project, many in opposition to the proposal instead engaged in crude and simplistic "love it or leave it" loyalty tests:

> I've lived in Pakistan and Saudi Arabia, two countries that practice shar'ia law. I love the country of my birth, and the country of my youth, and now Canada, the country of my choice. And with that choice I've agreed to live by the laws of this land ... If shar'ia is the system you want then I challenge you to live in Saudi Arabia. I challenge you to give up all the freedoms you enjoy here. No more freedom of movement, to go and live where you please. No more freedom to read or write or say what you like in public. No right to challenge authority. Yes, Saudi Arabia is an example of shar'ia gone horribly awry but what is the guarantee that it won't happen here? (Fatah 2005b)

What is completely absent from this hyperbolic commentary is that the proposal was not about any of the issues that this commentator lists. The purpose of such commentaries was to instil a wild fear among the public, to remove all discussion of the proposal from the realm of Canadian social policy, and instead to cast the discussion in terms of a national threat constituted by the (foreign) barbarians at the gate. Systematically, the opponents of the proposal linked the debate to the agendas of foreign states and foreign actors:

> Tarek Fatah, one of its [Muslim Canadian Congress's] founding members and a leading voice in Canada for progressive Islam, said were arbitration under Sharia to become law, it would be a "Christmas gift to the Mullahs of Iran and Saudi Arabia who will be rejoicing this decision and using it to validate their own oppressive governments." (Hasan 2004)

"They are concerned at bringing justification for introducing shar'ia, and legitimizing it in Pakistan, in Iran (and) in Saudi Arabia," he [Tarek Fatah] said. (Leslie 2004c)

As well, Muslim Canadians – with the exception of those who were allied in opposition to the proposal – were quite strategically constructed as being unworthy of operating within discourses of minority rights and multiculturalism. This manoeuvre delegitimized Muslim activists in social justice spaces and diminished the restraints that these discourses might have brought to the overtly racialized tone of the "shar'ia" debate. This is particularly problematic given the tenuous alliances being formed between Muslim communities and the left in the context of the post-9/11 attacks on civil rights:

As a woman, a New Democrat, and Secretary of the Muslim Canadian Congress, I am appalled at this development and am appealing to all of you to recognise the enormity of Marion Boyd's blunder. She has succumbed to the manipulation of the Islamist lobby that has found fertile soil in many left-wing organisations around the world. Under the garb of promoting minority rights and multiculturalism, these Islamists are taking advantage of the inherent goodwill of New Democrats and other social justice activists. (Salimi 2005)

"One of the strengths of Islamists is that they know you very well. They know our history, they know our culture, they know our justice system, the Charter of Rights," said Houda-Pepin. "They know how to use the system that is at their disposal." She said the lobbyists are trying to impose a political agenda. "Their objective is not to integrate into Canada, it is to integrate Canada to their values," she said. (De Souza 2005)

The language used here plays on all the familiar stereotypes of racialized minority groups being "cunning" or a "silent threat" to society. These are old racist lines that have been used against various communities at different points in Canadian history. That these tropes were invoked by those who position themselves within the Muslim community does not lessen the problematics. Those Muslims who willingly engaged in this discourse are undeniably themselves subject to the same racialized gaze within which they anchored their arguments.

At the WERF conference, many participants consistently raised the issue of who was properly "civilized" and who was not. One participant consistently referred to herself as "Canadian" and situated her opposition to the proposal as being part of her "Canadian duty":

> How can we as a civilized society argue that there is some basis for these people to have rights to do what they're doing? ... My argument is that it does not have a place in the Arbitration Act, we as Canadians do not want this recognized as part of the Arbitration Act because it was never intended for that purpose. (West Coast LEAF 2004a, 21; 2004b, 6)

The constant repetition reinforces the idea that all those who disagree with the speaker are not "Canadian," nor are they properly "civilized." This reading of the proposal and its proponents is in stark contrast to the actual wording used by the IICJ. Despite many problematic contradictions and convolutions within the public statements made by Syed Mumtaz Ali, it is important to note that he conceived of the proposal as providing an opportunity for Muslims to buy into the mythology of Canadian multiculturalism:

> We believe that among the many beautiful aspects of democracy are its capacities for change, flexibility, fairness and accommodation of a spectrum of possibilities and perspectives ... It is important for non-Muslim Canadians to carry out and act upon their fundamental principles and ideology which is put forward in the Canadian Charter of Rights and Freedoms. (Quoted in Mills 1995, 2)

The proposal for Islamic arbitration was situated within a claim of belonging to the nation through its existing policies and laws. That it was then construed as being an assault on the very fabric of the nation is a reflection of the way that the Muslim community is positioned within the dominant frame of Canada's self-perception.

Canada, like all modern states, is sustained by the force of its particular "national imaginary." As defined by Anderson (1991, 7), this is the creative construction of a "national self-consciousness" that provides the citizens of the state with a "deep, horizontal comradeship." This is a comforting force that both limits and binds the nation together in defiance of any actual realities, such as inequality, that would logically work against national cohesion and solidarity. Integral to this process is a set of constructed values that define and demarcate what is appropriately "Canadian" and, more important, what is not. In immediate succession to this is the interrelated process of defining who does, and who does not, legitimately belong within the nation. This idea *of legitimately belonging* is often conflated with the idea of "citizenship" – which is itself a contested term (Thobani 2007). I do not use it here in the sense of being in possession of a passport. Rather, I use the term "citizenship" to refer to the experience of having the right (which is both personally felt and perceived by others) to be on the inside of the nation. It is about both belonging and being seen to belong.

Periodically, the boundaries of the national imaginary have been policed to guard against the intrusive claims of those wanting to be included in the imaginary. The "shar'ia" debate can be seen as one such moment in which the national imaginary was policed and intruders were roundly weeded out. And as such, it follows within the established pattern of other such recent moments of public outrage in various Western societies:

> The Ontario "shar'ia debate" began life as a moral panic. That is to say, a small event came to stand in for a crisis of giant proportions, one on to which was projected social anxieties about Muslim bodies. Parenthetically, it is noteworthy that such media orchestrated panics are traceable in every Western country since 2001 ... In each of these "panics," Muslim women's bodies become the ground on which nations and citizens are made as civilized and modern, while Muslims and immigrants remain trapped in the pre-modern. (Razack 2007, 7)

Thus the "shar'ia" debate in Canada is not dissimilar to the uproar surrounding the wearing of headscarves by some Muslim women in several European countries, most notably France. Indeed, the Canadian "shar'ia" debate fits neatly between the headscarf controversies in Quebec of the 1990s and the "reasonable accommodation" hearings of this decade. All these crises can be read as moments in which the national imaginary was reanimated as part of a public and media anxiety over perceptions that this imaginary was being troubled by Muslim bodies.

In many regions of the West, the national imaginary has constructed the Muslim body as irretrievably strange, alien, and Other. This is a construction in which the Muslim body, male or female, is recognized as being dangerous and in a constant state of trespassing in the West (see also Chapter 1). This notion of the West as a safe, familiar, civilized, non-Muslim space is affirmed and legitimated through its rejection of the Muslim stranger. This process was well underway prior to the tragedy of 9/11. It has, however, received a renewed moral legitimacy and urgency in the post-9/11 period. Ahmed (2000) theorizes about how the act of defining who qualifies as a stranger is central to the ways that boundaries are demarcated and community is produced. She argues that it is through the act of reading certain bodies as "strangers" and others as "neighbours" that we define the "we" in any given polity:

> The definition and enforcement of the good "we" operates through the recognition of Others as strangers: by seeing those who do not belong simply as "strangers" (that is, by not naming *who* are the ones who do not belong in the community), forms of social exclusion are both concealed and revealed (what is concealed is the brute fact of the matter – only some Others are recognisable as "the stranger," the one who is out of place). In this sense, the policing of valued spaces allows the legitimation of social exclusion by being tied to a heroic "we" who takes shape against the figure of the unspecified stranger. (Ahmed 2000, 29-30)

Here, Ahmed is not specifically talking about Muslims, but rather she is discussing the theoretical underpinnings of anti-crime initiatives like Neighbourhood Watch. This theory, however, can easily be taken forward to post-9/11 calls by the heads of state in the West for their citizenry to be vigilant against all "suspicious activity":

> A terrorism alert is not a signal to stop your life. It is a call to be vigilant – to know that your government is on high alert, and to add your eyes and ears to our efforts to find and stop those who want to do us harm.
> After September the 11th, our government assumed new responsibilities to strengthen security at home and track down our enemies abroad. And the American people are accepting new responsibilities, as well. (Whitehouse 2001)

Despite a few rote mentions of Islam as a "peaceful religion" that the terrorists were hiding behind, it is clear that the enemy of the nation, against which vigilance is needed, is the Muslim. This is further concretized by the legislated dismantling of civil rights through the passage of so-called "anti-terrorism" legislation in the United States, Canada, and other regions of the West. This has resulted in the increased surveillance and harassment that Muslims living (read "trespassing") in the West have had to endure. These include the daily indignities of racial profiling, as seen in the detentions at airports and borders that are carried out by official agents of the state, as well as the climate of fear and suspicion that emanates from the general public.

These acts of policing are meant to calm the fears of those who believe the stranger has "come too close to home." Ahmed (2000, 37) argues that the discourse of "stranger danger ... becomes a mechanism for the justification of violence against those who are already recognised as strangers." Again, this perception of Muslims as strangers exists without relation to their actual status as citizens, immigrants, or travellers. The Muslim body is never accepted as being the body of a fully legitimate citizen. Any superficial "acceptance" of Muslims in the territories of the West occurs through a perpetual process of regulation, surveillance, and suspicion. In the national imaginaries of the West, the Muslim citizen continues to be antithetical.

In the current political climate, the citizenship of Muslims is disposable both in the ways that it is discussed in the media and in the reality created by post-9/11 legislation. Within the parameters of political discourse created by the ideologies of the "war on terror," Muslim communities in the West are constructed as the fifth column in the "clash of civilizations." Muslims are not seen as really belonging to the "nation" and must constantly prove their citizenship. Therefore, if the nation is seen to be at war in a far-reaching "clash of civilizations," as per the analysis of Huntington (1993), the representatives of this "enemy civilization" within the nation's boundaries (i.e., the Muslim community) must necessarily be policed, regulated, and if possible, expelled.

This rejection of the intolerable Other through a process of metaphoric denationalizing was dutifully played out during the course of the "shar'ia" debate in Canada. The repeated construction of Muslims as foreigners and/or supporters of foreign regimes within the "shar'ia" debate effectively accomplished this end. In particular, the debate took pains to construct the acceptable/good Muslim who could conditionally belong in the nation and was distinct from the unacceptable bad Muslim who must *reasonably* be feared and controlled. Although the immediate targets of this rhetoric were the specific proponents of the proposal, the larger Muslim community was subject to this gaze, and the legitimacy of such a lens was upheld and normalized.

The Construction of the Iconic Infantilized Muslim Woman

At the centre of the "shar'ia" debate was the "Muslim woman," around whom all the arguments pivoted. This was a social category, constructed as a static unvarying symbol denoting absolute oppression and seen to be entirely distinct from any other grouping of women in Canada. A cursory review of the editorials published in the days immediately following the release of Marion Boyd's report reveals the ways that this construction became iconic. In many of the editorials, an example was repeated of a seemingly generic "Pakistani woman." This was the only anecdotal reference to a Muslim woman, and it was repeated in multiple papers by various columnists:

> Consider a hypothetical immigrant wife from Pakistan, who speaks little French nor English. She has no money of her own; she has no idea that she has legal rights other than those her husband or imam choose to tell her about; she believes that her legal right to reside in Canada is entirely dependent on her husband ... Taken to a shar'ia court and divorced, she might be left with almost none of the family's assets. There is little or no chance that this woman would know how to complain, or to whom. ("One Law for All" 2004)

> Imagine, for example, an immigrant Pakistani woman who has limited education, speaks no English, and is utterly dependent on her husband. Imagine she and her husband divorce. In Muslim family law, the husband usually gets custody of the kids. He may stop supporting her entirely after a short time and keep nearly all the family assets. He may send her back to Pakistan and keep the kids here. All this is okay under the law, so long as she agrees to it. (Wente 2004)

It should go without saying, but it clearly bears repeating, that not all Muslim women in Canada are immigrants, not all immigrant Muslim women are from Pakistan, not all Pakistani immigrant women are without fluency in English or French, and indeed not all are without agency, intelligence, or the capacity for resistance.

Much of the discourse took pains to inscribe the idea of Muslim women's complete and unvarying lack of social power. To achieve this end, Muslim women necessarily had to be constructed as a category entirely separate and distinct from other communities of women in Canada. In fact, it is precisely this difference that was continually emphasized by media commentators. As well, the experience of sexism in the Muslim community was constructed as being of such a particular nature and magnitude that no comparisons could be made to any other manifestation of patriarchy anywhere else in Canada:

> Marilou McPhedran, counsel for the Canadian Council of Muslim Women, labeled Boyd's report "naive" in its assumptions that Muslim women would have the same choices as other women. (Mallan 2004)

> We had a consultation with Marion Boyd, who spoke of Muslim women having choices and being responsible for those choices. We were scared, because we are working with women who are vulnerable, exploited, beaten, living in shelters, etc. (Tarek Fatah, quoted in Greenberg 2004)

The first quotation above is particularly problematic, as it comes from the legal counsel of an organization that claims to represent Muslim women across the country. The irony is that much of this construction of Muslim women as universally oppressed originated with Muslim women and their representatives, who themselves were not without power. They had access to the public discourse and were not limited by conditions that they claimed were nearly ubiquitous. They were however invested in this construction. Their opposition to the proposal, in part, hinged on keeping the category of "Muslim women" static and closed:

> The campaign argued that while, technically, Muslim women will have access to Canadian laws and courts, and the legal system will undoubtedly reject oppressive decisions, "the reality is that most women (will) be coerced socially, economically or psychologically" into participating in shar'ia tribunals. (Homa Arjomand, quoted in Mallan 2004)

> Ms. Boyd has promised all sorts of safeguards so that a woman can appeal a decision she thinks is unfair. All the woman has to do is overcome the immense social pressure to conform, and withstand the shame and ostracism she will experience if she tries to defy the spiritual leaders of the community and her entire family. (Wente 2004)

Again, the idea being reinforced in these quotations is that the *only* experience of a Muslim woman is that of vulnerability and oppression. Through this "logic," Muslim women could not be given the "burden" of choice that other women in Canada are seemingly capable of bearing. Repeatedly, Muslim women were constructed as being entirely without the ability to think critically. And any Muslim woman who took exception to this construction was easily dismissed as brainwashed, afraid, or unable to even understand what equality means. "I assure you, 99 percent of those women who have no choice under this law, don't want it. If they say they want it, they might not know any better, or they are scared to oppose it" (West Coast LEAF 2004b, 7). And if indeed Muslim women are unlike any other women, then so too are Muslim men and indeed so is the entire Muslim community. Many commentators attempted to combat the exceptionalist arguments of the opponents by reminding them that the Arbitration Act was already being accessed by several faith communities. However, this perspective was easily dismissed by opponents:

> The Arbitration Act has already been used by Jewish, Catholic and Ismaili Muslim courts, without incident. But chances are that women in these groups are more assimilated into Canadian life than your average newcomer from Pakistan. As well, Western religions have accepted the separation of church and state for quite some time now. Islam has never done any such thing. (Wente 2004)

Wente's "logic" rests on the marked difference in the ways that the Jewish community and the Muslim community have been racialized in Canada. Jewish women are not racialized in Canada as infantile, unable to look out for themselves, or unable to know their own best interests. In contrast, Muslim women are racialized as entirely unable to have any agency over their lives. Similarly, Jewish men are not racialized as hyper-oppressive, whereas Muslim men are racialized in this way.[8]

The point here is not to construct the opposite fallacy, in which Muslim women are immune from patriarchy, Muslim men are all egalitarian, and the Muslim community is a misogyny-free zone. This construction would be as meaningless as the constructions present in the "shar'ia" debate. Clearly, there are Muslim women who are in abusive marital and familial relationships. And, indeed, many women would likely have been in an unequal power dynamic *vis*-à-*vis* the decision to use arbitration services or not. However, the point is that this scenario does not describe the *only* experience of Muslim women in Canada. To imply otherwise is to infantilize a large group of women and thereby render any meaningful political contribution by this group ontologically dissonant.

Jasmin Zine (2006a, 1) has coined the term "gendered Islamophobia," which she defines as,

[The] dual oppressions [that have] re-vitalized Orientalist tropes and representations of backward, oppressed, and politically immature women in need of liberation and rescue through imperialist interventions as well as the challenge of religious extremism and puritan discourses that authorize equally limiting narratives of Islamic womanhood and compromise their human rights and liberty.

It is precisely this double-bind, so present in the "shar'ia" debate, that made it nearly impossible to intervene with any kind of nuanced position. The battle lines had been drawn and the debate was polarized. To attempt an intervention was to be slotted into the pre-existing script of the passion play already in motion. To dissent with the discourse was simply to be cast in the role of an unthinking tool of patriarchy.

Although many of the opponents in the "shar'ia" debate relied on the construction of the iconic "Muslim woman," they did not invent her. She has been around a long time and is merely a variation on the woman who appears in many feminist discourses in which "brown women are saved from brown men" (Spivak 1985). In fact, it is the familiarity of this trope that makes it so powerful.

Narayan (1997) and Razack (2003, 2004) have written extensively about the problematics of the cultural reductionist arguments that are frequently employed in relation to women of colour. They write specifically about violence against women and how the arguments offered amount to a "death by culture" thesis (see also Chapter 1). These arguments, therefore, reaffirm for the Western audience a hierarchy of cultures in which the "West" is violence-free (with a few pesky aberrations) and the "non-West" is inherently violent (with the occasional brave survivor or hero). Thus any discussion about how to, for example, end violence against women of colour is reduced to an argument of how to "liberate" women from their culture because the culture itself is irretrievable. This serves the primary purpose of providing a reliable and comforting fantasy, in which the heroes are inevitably the white, Western rescuers of women of colour: "Scenarios had their share of Western rescuers, either White men using all of their power to keep brown men in line, or White women, sometimes feminists, drawing on their own innate civility and missionary expertise, to save brown women and teach them how to survive their own cultures" (Razack 2003, 80). When this broader framing brings Muslim women into its gaze, a similar pattern emerges.

Islam, although a religion in which the adherents come from a vast multiplicity of cultures, is reduced to one homogenized culture. And it is this culture/religion that is inherently the cause of any and all sexism to which a Muslim woman is subject. Completely rejected are material explanations of the kind often invoked in discussions of violence against white women. The only relevant factor in this discussion is that Islam is an inherently misogynistic religion. It follows logically, therefore, that all Muslim men are relentlessly oppressive and all Muslim women are perpetually persecuted.[9]

For this trope to function, Muslim women need to be infantilized and seen to have no agency with which to resist their own oppression – and thus be in constant need of rescue/salvation. The actual histories of Muslim women's activism and resistance (e.g., the vibrant canon of Muslim feminist engagement with Islamic law) are erased in order to create a stable and primordial category – one that is completely distinct from all other categories of white women in any "Western" society. Thus, Muslim women stand in for an "oppression ground zero" of sorts against which "Western" women can measure the distance they have travelled. In this way, the Muslim feminist – or indeed any Muslim woman who is different from the construction of the iconic "Muslim woman" – is rendered not just invisible but also ontologically inconceivable.

In the Canadian "shar'ia" debate, the opponents of the proposal, many of them women of colour and/or Muslim women, relied heavily on this trope. The usage of it here, where the dynamic of "white Western rescuers" was not so easily read, is particularly striking. I argue that the trope remained unchallenged and functioned as it was expected to, despite being invoked by women who could also have themselves been subsumed by it. In this debate, the trope of the iconic "Muslim woman" enabled the opponents to make repeated calls for intervention and protection of a benevolent and merciful nature and to summarily dismiss any voices that disagreed with them as necessarily either misguided or complicit.

The Fossilization of Islamic Law

Throughout this discourse, both the IICJ and its opponents portrayed Islamic law as a closed and fossilized system. There was no serious engagement with the idea that Islamic law is a human and living legal framework that incorporates a wide spectrum of legal theory and like all legal systems is constantly evolving. The incorrect usage of the term "shar'ia" reflects the much deeper misunderstandings that characterized this debate.

The Arabic term *shar'ia* literally means a "path leading to water." In the context of the first community of Islam (which existed in the deserts of the Arabian Peninsula), this symbolized what was sought after, precious, hard to attain, and cherished when found. Within the Islamic theological paradigm, *shar'ia* refers to the path that leads to the ultimate truths of the Divine. Human beings, although in constant pursuit of this path, do not attain certainty of it in this world. Among Muslims, the human, temporal endeavour to seek the truths of the Divine through the establishment of law results in a body of jurisprudence called *fiqh*. Islamic law is thus a very human product – although with a scriptural referent at its core. Islamic law, therefore, is routinely subject to critique and reinterpretation. It is not the unassailable divine law that it is often represented to be. Even the most conservative elements in Muslim legal discourses (which argue against a re-engagement with historical legal precedents) recognize in practice that new legal rulings are unavoidable given the rapidly changing material realities of our world. For example, even those who are unwilling to reopen dialogue on classical issues of women's rights must concede that new laws are daily developed in response to advances in reproductive technologies. Indeed, the bulk of Muslim feminist discourse relies entirely on the fact that the law is open to change.

Within the "shar'ia" debate in Canada, both sides were invested in a simplistic caricature of Islamic law. Each side believed that if the diverse and massive canon of Islamic law was utilized in the arbitration process, it would somehow result in consistent decisions. The proponents of the proposal (and Marion Boyd) seemed to have clarity about what "Muslim principles" were. The opponents also believed that there would be a consistency at work. They, however, believed that arbitration rulings would consistently adhere to the most draconian manifestations of Islamic law that have occurred in other contexts – the unspoken subtext of their argument being that specific socio-political contexts have no bearing on the law. However, the reality is that Islamic law, even when restricted to family law, is diverse and multilayered and has historically resulted in a wide spectrum of legal rulings.

Completely absent from this discourse was the fact that there exists a substantial body of contemporary engagement with Islamic law. Quite contrary to what the opponents of the proposal have relentlessly argued, the field of law has been the site within which many reformers and/or feminists have focused their work (e.g., Khaled Abou El Fadl, Asifa Qureishi, and

Azizah al-Hibri). This history was rendered completely absent from the debate. And, indeed, one of the most problematic aspects of the "shar'ia" debate was that it became a zero-sum game.

If one were to accept the idea that all arbitrations conducted under the ubiquitous "Muslim principles" would result in anti-woman rulings, one would in effect be claiming that those very same anti-woman laws were the *only* legitimate Islamic legal rulings. One would as a result be supporting the idea that egalitarian manifestations of Islamic law were, in fact, impossible. For me, a Muslim feminist, this was simply territory that could not be ceded. There was no possible way that I could participate in fostering the idea that Islamic law was not, and could never be, open to reinterpretation. To do so would have been to surrender the entire theological basis of my life's work and the work of countless other activists, scholars, and jurists. However, I would have readily agreed that the dominant interpretations of Islamic law were not supportive of women's rights. What could have, and should have, logically followed from this point was a more substantive engagement with the actual proposal and the conspicuously missing logistics of it. The Canadian Council of Muslim Women (CCMW) (2004b, 5), in its "Position Statement," specifically asked for "a written public proposal from the proponents of Muslim family law," although this willingness to discuss the proposal was not reflected in its media statements on the issue.

On the Canadian Broadcasting Corporation's show *Counterspin*, on March 10, 2004, a young female Muslim audience member said,

> With regards to how the shar'ia is applied, there seems to be a misunderstanding in what is shar'ia. We are not talking here about taking these examples from foreign countries and applying them into Canada, because their misapplication cannot be applied within Canada. We are Canadian Muslims, living in a Canadian society, with a Canadian education on our religion and our understanding. Our mentality is very different. And our pursuit of shar'ia in Canada will epitomize the justice that we as Canadian Muslims believe exists in the shar'ia. And that is how it will, *inshallah* [God willing], be built.

This earnest young woman clearly felt the need to assert her national identity, perhaps as a response to the deliberate denationalizing of the Muslim community in this debate. Alia Hogben, representing the CCMW on this panel, replied to her thus: "You have to decide which shar'ia you are talking about – it is a centuries old system – which has a different application in every country, if you are talking about creating a whole new system for Canada, well that is a long process, and that is not possible" (CBC 2004). The limited willingness to engage with the possibilities of the proposal was very telling. Any substantive interrogation of the proposal would have rendered the discussion plausible and rational. I maintain that the opponents preferred the debate to remain in the realm of the implausible and the entirely unintelligible. That was the only way to completely demonize the proposal and all those who were willing to engage with it. In contrast, the Canadian Council on American-Islamic Relations (Cair-Can 2004), in its submission to the Boyd Commission, specifically dealt with the logistics of the proposal and suggested several safeguards to improve the accountability of the process and to ensure that the arbiters would have the necessary skills and knowledge of both the Canadian and Islamic family-law systems.

An interesting contrast can be made to the role that Muslim feminists and progressives played in South Africa within that nation's Muslim Personal Law (MPL) debate. Instead of an outright rejection of the idea, there was a sustained engagement with the process. For example, when the ruling African National Congress (ANC) first began considering the idea, its members refused to limit their discussions to a small group of Muslim clergy. Instead, they committed themselves to a larger process in which representatives of various sectors of the Muslim community could participate. According to some, this created the structure for "progressive Muslim intervention and involvement" (Jeenah 2004, 3). The process of discussion, debate, and synthesis took upward of ten years. Although Muslim feminists fought and won many battles, they also lost a few. But at the end of the process, there was an MPL Bill, however imperfect, that could be rightfully claimed by all those who contributed to the process.

In other regions of the world, Islamic law has proven to be sufficiently fluid to be used as a vehicle of reform. There are numerous examples from countries such as Tunisia, Morocco, and Egypt, where laws have been passed within the Islamic legal framework to improve women's rights in various areas of family law. These examples deserve *at least* as much recognition and credence as are given to the misogynist interpretation of Islamic law in other regions. Indeed, even in the most limited arbitration process in Canada, there could be benefits for Muslim women. For example, the presence of a structured process by which Muslim women could have their marriage contracts recognized and through which they could pursue religious divorces would alleviate some of the difficulties Muslim women currently face when divorcing only through civil law. (Some Muslim women may not feel completely divorced unless the civil procedure is accompanied by a religious one, much in the same way that many religious people do not feel fully married with merely a civil ceremony.) The reality is that for the opponents of the arbitration proposal, considering any of these examples seriously would have shifted the discourse from hysterical hyperbole into the realm of reasoned debate – which they seemed unwilling to do.

Not surprisingly, through this process of the demonization of Islamic law, Canadian law became stabilized in the debate as egalitarian, accessible, and ideal. Despite decades of feminist criticism of Canadian family law, within the "shar'ia" debate many feminists became impassioned champions of the law. Much like the way real citizens are ennobled when juxtaposed with "anti-citizens," and Western women and men are ennobled when juxtaposed with the racialized constructions of Muslim women and men, so too did Canadian family law begin to take on a nobility when juxtaposed with the spectre of "shar'ia." The result, as in all such cases, was that the boundaries of "here" were policed against the intrusions of "there."

This was perhaps made most clear in the oft-repeated argument that the private mediations that went on in the Muslim community were fine but that they should not be acknowledged by the Canadian state. This contrasts sharply with the stated concern that the proposal was creating a "ghettoized law" for Muslim women (Atwood et al. 2005). The most compelling argument against the proposal was that the entire Arbitration Act created a privatized sphere of law. This, I agree, goes against the feminist principle that "the personal is political" and that family law should not be a private affair (Diamond 2005). However, if the issue is that privatization and ghettoization are against women's interests, then surely the largely undocumented, unaccountable systems of community mediations are worse for women than an arbitration process, which would have a (comparably) greater means of ensuring transparency and would be more amenable to intervention. The compromise suggested by many opponents – that those interested in Islamic law continue to use it privately (i.e., away from the gaze of the nation) – reveals the real issue at hand: it was not the concern for women's rights that was at the core of this opposition but rather the maintenance of the distinctions between what is and is not acceptable as the public face of Canada.

Conclusion

The Canadian "shar'ia" debate was as intense as it was massive. The sheer volume of material it produced was enough to bury any of us who tried to grapple with it. In fact, one of its particular attributes was how it inspired statements of urgency and concern from so many diverse quarters. It seemed that nearly everyone who heard of the issue felt the need to weigh in on it. Aside from a veritable alphabet soup of Canadian organizations, there were statements from international organizations like Amnesty International, Women Living under Muslim Laws, and the Progressive Muslim Union of North America, among others. A whole gamut of prominent Canadian individuals such as Margaret Atwood and Sheila Copps, as well as international figures like Tariq Ramadan and George Galloway, all had their say on the issue.

The question one needs to ask is why did this issue become such a crisis? When delivering an early draft of this chapter at an academic conference, I was confronted by a white feminist who had been active in opposition to this proposal. She was very offended by my analysis of the debate and acknowledged being defensive. She, however, felt that all of the "errors" of the debate could be forgiven since they were made in the course of responding to such a crisis. But why was this a crisis? The Arbitration Act had been in effect for over a decade, and many communities were using the act. Nothing new was being proposed. Even if the argument is to be believed that the opposition was about all faith-based arbitration, not just Islamic arbitration, it still does not constitute an urgent crisis, as the arbitration had been going on for years.

Through my analysis of this debate, I can conclude only that this crisis, this mad storm of hysteria, was unleashed specifically because the subjects of it were Muslim and because it occurred at this specific moment in time. As a result, it provided all of the makings of the proverbial perfect storm. The issue played on all of the existing fears of the safe and stable West being threatened and disrupted by the irrational, dangerous, foreign (Muslim) stranger. Thus, the debate fits neatly into parallel discourses in other regions of the West, the uniting element being that at the core of each case was the collective fear that what had been constructed so absolutely as unequal, intolerable, and strange would gain a degree of parity and legitimacy with what had been concretized as superior, dominant, and unimpeachable. This is perhaps best evidenced by the fact that this debate effectively came to a close on the fourth anniversary of 9/11. Ontario premier Dalton McGuinty chose that weekend to bring an end to the proposal by suspending all faith-based arbitrations in his province. And thus he calmed the fears of the nation and restored the balance between what is good and rightfully Canadian and what is not.

Although the Canadian "shar'ia" debate had its particularities, it fit securely within the previous and ongoing headscarf controversies of Quebec, France, and the United Kingdom. In time, it became a context for other controversies, such as the United Kingdom's own "shar'ia" debate in 2008 and the passing of legislation to "ban shar'ia" in Oklahoma and other American states in 2010 and 2011. In the Canadian context, the legacy of the "shar'ia" debate can be plainly seen again in the Hérouxville Town Charter and in the public hearings in Quebec on "reasonable accommodation." Although the contexts and logistics shift, the core tropes remain stable and, with every repetition, gain strength.

ACKNOWLEDGMENTS

I owe thanks to my master's supervisor, Dr. Sunera Thobani, for her help in developing this chapter and for her support to me during my graduate program. As well, I want to thank my friend Dr. Rita Dhamoon for her incredible solidarity with me during the WERF conference and for her invaluable support in reading several drafts of this chapter and providing feedback. Sara Koopman also graciously read the chapter and offered detailed feedback. Most of all, I want to thank my parents, whose patience, support, and generous love have made this work possible.

NOTES

1 The Arbitration Act was already being accessed by the Ismaili Muslim community in Ontario and in British Columbia without any public discourse surrounding it. This proposal by the IICJ was specifically in regard to the Sunni Muslim community. The disparity in the public concern over Sunni Muslim women and Ismaili Muslim women provides an intriguing tangent, which I explore later in the chapter.
2 I use the terms "Western" and "West" throughout this paper with an acknowledgment that they are deeply problematic. I do not wish to reify the idea that the West is an entirely separate entity from the "non-West." I acknowledge that these terms imply much more than geography. They also refer to a self-construction in which the West is white, secular, developed, democratic, and stable and the non-West is the inherent opposite of this.
3 It is well established that this proposal did not originate organically in the community. Syed Mumtaz Ali and his small organization first put forth their plan in the early 1990s, and aside from their own website (www.muslim-canada.org) and a few commentaries (Khan 1993), it engendered no perceivable enthusiasm in the various Muslim communities across Canada.
4 Although I remain very critical of the way the discussion took place at this conference, the responsibility for it is not solely that of West Coast LEAF. I believe that the discussion was simply a microcosm of the larger discourse that was taking place across Canada.
5 These quotations are from the transcript of the conference that was sent out to each participant. I have removed the names of the participants. Although there was

one male participant, I have identified them all as female in order to conceal the identities of the speakers.
6 In response to the public opposition to the proposal, Ontario premier Dalton McGuinty commissioned Marion Boyd to study the matter and offer recommendations to his government. Various stakeholders appeared before the commission.
7 I need to stress here that this construction was not limited to the proponents of the proposal and their vocal supporters. The construction was so wide and fluid that it encompassed any who were not willing to align themselves with the opponents of the proposal. I explore the critical absence of a third space within this discourse later in the chapter.
8 Of particular note in this quotation is the way Ismaili Muslims are constructed as "Western" despite being Muslim. I am not certain why Ismaili Muslims, many of whom are also immigrants from Pakistan, were not included in the larger construction of the Muslim community in this debate.
9 Razack (2004) describes these categories as "imperilled Muslim women, dangerous Muslim men and civilised Europeans."

REFERENCES

Activists speak out against sharia: Trio of women under threat: Dutch writer sees dire results ahead. 2005. *Toronto Star,* August 13, A18.

Ahmed, S. 2000. *Strange encounters: Embodied others in postcoloniality.* New York, NY: Routledge.

Alcoba, N. 2005. Ontario rejects sharia law. *National Post,* September 12, A1.

Allemang, J. 2005. The limits of tolerance: Patrick Weil, a scholar involved in the ban on Muslim head scarves in France, looks approvingly at Ontario's rejection of sharia courts. *Globe and Mail,* September 24, F6.

Al-Malky, R. 2004. Tariq Ramadan banned from the US on grounds he has endorsed terrorism, grandson of Muslim Brotherhood founder Hassan Al-Banna speaks out on reform, moderation and faith. *Egypt Today,* October. http://www.egypttoday.com/.

Anderson, B. 1991. *Imagined communities: Reflections on the origin and spread of nationalism.* Revised ed. New York, NY: Verso.

Arat-Koc, S. 2002. Imperial wars or benevolent interventions? Reflections on "global feminism" post September 11th. *Atlantis: A Women's Studies Journal* 26, 2: 53-65.

Arbitration based on faith is working, Muslim group says. 2004. *Globe and Mail,* September 11, A11.

Atwood, M., et al. 2005. Open letter to Ontario premier Dalton McGuinty: Don't ghettoize women's rights. *Globe and Mail,* September 10, A23.

Bahkt, N. 2005. Arbitration, religion and family law: Private justice on the backs of women. www.nawl.ca/ns/en/documents/Pub_Report_ReligArb05_en.rtf.

Bannerji, H. 2000. Geography lessons: On being an insider/outsider to the Canadian nation. In H. Bannerji, ed., *The dark side of nation: Essay on multiculturalism, nationalism, and gender,* 63-86. Toronto, ON: Canadian Scholars' Press.

Benzie, R. 2004. Sharia report to be unveiled: Ex-attorney general wraps up 6-month review of Islamic law: Study looks at possible use in resolving civil disputes in Ontario. *Toronto Star,* December 20, A13.

Bernard, C. 2003. *Rand report on civil and democratic Islam: Partners, resources and struggles.* Santa Monica, CA: Rand Corporation. www.rand.org/pubs/monograph_reports/MR1716/MR1716.pdf.

Bilge, S. 2005. Between a rock and a hard place: Minority women's citizenship in Canada, its intersecting inequalities, and what an intersectional theorizing can offer? In proceedings of the symposium *Muslim Women's Equality Rights in the Justice System: Gender, Religion and Pluralism* (Toronto: Canadian Council of Muslim Women), 71-76.

Boyd, M. 2004. Dispute resolution in family law: Protecting choice, promoting inclusion – executive summary. www.attorneygeneral.jus.gov.on.ca/english/about/pubs/boyd/executivesummary.pdf.

—. 2005. Religiously-based alternate dispute resolution: A challenge to multiculturalism. *Canadian Diversity* 4, 3: 71-74.

Boyd gets it right. 2004. Editorial. *National Post,* December 27, A19.

Brennan, R. 2005. Liberal women "loud voice" on shar'ia: Unanimous opposition from 17 ruling MPPs: McGuinty sped up announcement, source says. *Toronto Star,* September 13, A15.

Brennan, R., and K. Gillespie. 2005. Shar'ia no threat, premier says: Vows women's rights won't be compromised. *Toronto Star,* September 7, A11.

Brewin, A. 2005. Report on women's equality and religious freedom consultation, December 2-4, 2004. http://www.westcoastleaf.org/userfiles/file/Consultation Report.pdf.

British Broadcasting Corporation. 2002. Florida Muslim arrests were mistake. http://news.bbc.co.uk/.

—. 2005. Shot man not connected to bombing. http://news.bbc.co.uk/.

Cair-Can. 2004. Submission to the Boyd Commission. August 11. http://www.caircan.ca/downloads/sst-10082004.pdf.

Canadian Broadcasting Corporation. 2004. Is there room for religion in the justice system? Episode of *CounterSpin,* March 10.

Canadian Council of Muslim Women. 2004a. Letter to Ahmad and Faisal Kutty. March 17. http://www.ccmw.com/.

—. 2004b. Position statement on the proposed implementation of sections of Muslim law [sharia] in Canada. May 25. http://www.ccmw.com/.

—. 2004c. Submission to the Boyd Commission: Submission to Marion Boyd, review of the Ontario Arbitration Act and arbitration processes, specifically in matters of family law. July 30. http://www.ccmw.com/.

—. 2004d. Tribunals will marginalize Canadian Muslim women and increase privatization of family law. September 15. http://www.ccmw.com/.

—. 2004e. CCMW letter to premier Dalton McGuinty regarding Boyd Report on religious arbitration. December 20. http://www.ccmw.com/.

—. 2004f. Initial response to Marion Boyd's report on the Arbitration Act. December 20. http://www.ccmw.com/.

—. 2005a. An open letter to Premier Dalton McGuinty and Attorney General Michael Bryant. January 14. http://www.ccmw.com/.
—. 2005b. CCMW welcomes Quebec motion on shar'ia law. May 27. http://www.ccmw.com/MuslimFamilyLaw/CCMW%20news%20release_May%2027.pdf.
Cardozo, Andrew. 2005. Multiculturalism versus rights. *Toronto Star,* September 15, A26.
Cheadle, B. 2005. Protests set to oppose sharia law: Fear Ontario plan for Islamic tribunals: Marches scheduled in Europe, Canada. *Toronto Star,* September 6, A2.
Controversy in Copenhagen – TV host's headscarf stirs debate. 2006. *Spiegel Online,* April 13. http://service.spiegel.de/.
Cooke, M. 2002. Saving brown women. *Signs: Journal of Women in Culture and Society* 28, 1: 468-70.
Copps, S. 2004. Shar'ia law is a danger to women. *National Post,* December 24, A22.
Coyne, A. 2005. In praise of one law for all. *National Post,* September 17, A20.
The crucial message the imams are sending. 2005. Editorial. *Globe and Mail,* July 30, A14.
Cryer, A. 2005. A lesson from Keighley. *National Post,* August 10, A16.
Csillag, R. 2005a. Marriage by the numbers: Some Canadians fear legalizing same-sex marriage will lead to court challenges over polygamy. *Toronto Star,* February 5, L10.
—. 2005b. Persons of no interest: Prophet Muhammad's prohibition against usury has made home ownership a challenge for Muslims. *Toronto Star,* March 19, M06.
Dabashi, H. 2006. Native informers and the making of the American empire. *Al-Ahram Weekly,* June 1-7. http://weekly.ahram.org.eg/.
Dale, G. 2005. Sharia myths. October 12. http://www.muslimcanadiancongress.org/.
De Souza, M. 2005a. Quebec leaders warn Ontario: Reject Sharia: Minister wants immigrants who support it barred. *National Post,* March 11, A8.
—. 2005b. Quebec minister says province should reject Muslims who support use of shar'ia. *Montreal Gazette,* March 11, n.p.
De Souza, R.J., Father. 2005. The wrong kind of multiculturalism. *National Post,* September 15, A20.
Diamond, B. 2005. Religious arbitration in family law – A challenge to women's equality in contemporary Canadian society. *Canadian Diversity* 4, 3: 80-82.
DiManno, R. 2005. Sharia solution a fair one, and not racist. *Toronto Star,* September 16, A02.
Dougherty, K. 2005. Quebec bans sharia: Blow to proponents of Islamic law in Canada. *National Post,* May 27, A1.
Drummond, S. 2005. Not just Muslim women are exploited by "religious" law. *Globe and Mail,* September 9, A17.
Eisenberg, A. 2006. Identity, multiculturalism and religious arbitration: The debate over shari'a law in Canada. In B. Arniel, M. Deveaux, R. Dhamoon, and A. Eisenberg, eds., *Sexual justice/Cultural justice: Critical perspectives in political theory and practice,* 211-30. New York, NY: Routledge.

Emon, A. 2005a. Shades of grey on sharia: Counterpoint. *National Post,* July 29, A12.
—. 2005b. A mistake to ban sharia. *Globe and Mail,* September 13, A21.
Esack, F. 2004. Reshaping Islam in South Africa. *Mail and Guardian,* August 18. http://www.mg.co.za/.
Fatah, N. 2005a. Tariq Ramadan: Shariah courts are "not necessary": Making these demands reflects "lack of creativity" among Muslims. January 9. http://muslimchronicle.blogspot.com/.
—. 2005b. One law for all. *Viewpoint,* April 1. http://www.cbc.ca/.
—. 2006. A plea from 11 Canadian Muslim academics and activists: Don't be silenced by extremists. *Toronto Star,* February 28, n.p.
Fatah, T. 2005. Don't succumb to imams, rabbis and priests. *Toronto Star,* June 22, A15.
Fear not sharia in Ontario. 2005. Editorial. *National Post,* September 9, A14.
Ferguson, R. 2005. "Same law" for all Ontarians: McGuinty decision to end faith-based arbitration stands Muslim and Jewish groups disappointed with turnaround. *Toronto Star,* September 14, A05.
Fournier, P. 2004. The reception of Muslim family law in Western liberal states. September 30. http://www.ccmw.com/.
Frum, D. 2004. The question of CAIR. *National Post,* November 23, A18.
Fulford, R. 2005. Multiculturalism's eloquent enemy. *National Post,* August 15, A16.
Funston, M. 2005. Muslims vow fight to keep shar'ia law: Group urges Premier to reverse decision: Considering court challenge to change. *Toronto Star,* September 15, A23.
Gagnon, L. 2005. The folly of sharia in Ontario. *Globe and Mail,* September 5, A15.
Gillespie, K. 2005. Sharia protest gets personal: Demonstrators criticize McGuinty: Threat to women's rights feared. *Toronto Star,* September 9, A09.
Goar, C. 2005. One justice system or many? *Toronto Star,* June 8, A22.
Gole, N. 2002. Islam in public: New visibilities and new imaginaries. *Public Culture* 14, 1: 173-91.
Greenberg, L. 2004. Muslim critics outraged as report endorses shar'ia. *National Post,* December 21, A5.
—. 2005a. Opposition to shar'ia courts goes global. *National Post,* September 7, A15.
—. 2005b. Women's rights not at risk. *National Post,* September 7, A11.
—. 2005c. Ontario could face court challenge: End to faith arbitration. *National Post,* September 13, A6.
Gulli, C. 2005. U of T hires leaders of Islamic law. *National Post,* July 22, A8.
Gunter, L. 2004. A Dutch lesson for Canada. *National Post,* November 15, A19.
Hall, S. 1996. The West and the rest: Discourse and power. In S. Hall, D. Held, D. Hubert, and K. Thompson, eds., *Modernity: An introduction to modern societies,* 184-228. Oxford, UK: Blackwell.
Hamdani, H., K. Bhatti, and N. Munawwar. 2005. Is the "war on terrorism" a war on religious pluralism and liberty in Canada? *Canadian Diversity* 4, 3: 83-87.
Hammad, S. 2002. Composites. *Signs: Journal of Women in Culture and Society* 28, 1: 470-71.

Hasan, K. 2004. Controversy rages in Canada over shar'ia. *Daily Times* (Lahore), December 22. http://www.dailytimes.com.pk/.

Hashmi, T. 2004. Shar'ia is neither Islamic, nor Canadian. *Muslim Wake Up*, December 31. http://www.muslimwakeup.com/.

Hogben, A. 2004. The laws of the land must protect all of us, irrespective of gender or religion. *Toronto Star*, June 1, n.p.

Howlett, K., and M. Valpy. 2005. Female MPPs' concerns delay sharia decision: Ontario government urged to go slowly on proposal to allow Islamic tribunals. *Globe and Mail*, September 8, A8.

Huntington, Samuel P. 1993. The clash of civilizations? *Foreign Affairs* 72, 3: 22-49.

Hurst, L. 2004. Sharia opponents fight on: "Faith-based tribunals" evoke fear, women say: Court challenge possible if amendments pass. *Toronto Star*, December 22, A12.

–. 2005a. Shar'ia law out of question, Quebec government insists: "Door is closed and will remain closed," justice minister says: Province remains Canada's only officially secular jurisdiction. *Toronto Star*, March 26, A14.

–. 2005b. Distortions and red herrings. *Toronto Star*, September 17, A6.

Jedwab, J. 2005. Muslims and multicultural futures in Western democracies. *Canadian Diversity* 4, 30: 92-96.

Jeenah, N. 2004. The MPL (Muslim Personal Law) battle in South Africa: Gender equality vs. "shari'ah." July. http://www.naeemjeenah.shams.za.org/MPL%20Battle%20in%20SA.pdf.

Jimenez, M. 2005a. A Muslim woman's shar'ia ordeal. *Globe and Mail*, September 8, A1, A8.

–. 2005b. Ontario urged to spurn shar'ia: Premier will open a dangerous precedent with faith-based arbitration, protestors say. *Globe and Mail*, September 9, A10.

–. 2005c. Decision on shar'ia sparks Jewish protest. *Globe and Mail*, September 13, A1, A7.

Kamlani, T., and N. Keung. 2004. Muslim group opposes shar'ia law. *Toronto Star*, August 28, n.p.

Khalafallah, H. 2006. Muslim women: Public authority, scriptures and "Islamic law." Unpublished paper.

Khan, S. 1993. Canadian Muslim women and shari'a law: A feminist response to "Oh! Canada!" *Canadian Journal of Women and the Law* 6: 52-65.

–. 2005. The shar'ia debate deserves a proper hearing. *Globe and Mail*, September 15, n.p.

Khouri, N. 2004. Keep mosque and state separate. *National Post*, September 21, A17.

Kutty, F. 2005. Religious principles have a role in our legal system. *National Post*, January 4, A11.

Kymlicka, W. 2005. Testing the bounds of liberal multiculturalism? In proceedings of the symposium *Muslim Women's Equality Rights in the Justice System: Gender, Religion and Pluralism* (Toronto: Canadian Council of Muslim Women), 53-68.

LEAF. 2004. Women's Legal Education and Action Fund ["LEAF"]: Submission to Marion Boyd in relation to her review of the Arbitration Act. September 17. http://www.leafottawa.ca.

Leong, M. 2005a. Ontario shar'ia law proposal protested in Europe, Canada. *National Post,* September 9, A5.

—. 2005b. Muslim groups promise Liberals a fight on shar'ia. *National Post,* September 15, A12.

Leslie, K. 2004a. Report says Ontario Muslims have right to use religious law in family disputes. *Maclean's Magazine,* December 20.

—. 2004b. Let Ontario families use Muslim law in disputes, report urges. *Globe and Mail,* December 21, A12.

—. 2004c. Ontario Muslims should have the right to use religious law: Report. *Kingston Whig Standard,* December 21, 11.

Macklin, A. 2005. Multiculturalism in a time of privatization: Faith-based arbitration and gender equality. *Canadian Diversity* 4, 3: 75-79.

Mallan, C. 2004. Shar'ia report called "betrayal" of women: Proposal backs use of Islamic principles in settling disputes: Ontario heading in "dangerous direction," opponents say: Shar'ia report called "naïve." *Toronto Star,* December 21, A01.

Mamdani, M. 2002. Good Muslim, bad Muslim: A political perspective on culture and terrorism. *American Anthropologist* 104, 3: 766-76.

Mansur, S. 2005. Sharia's underclass. *National Post,* July 22, A18.

Mardell, M. 2006. Dutch MPs to decide on burqa ban. *BBC,* January 16. http://news.bbc.co.uk/.

Marriage code urged. 2005. *Toronto Star,* May 2, A08.

McGuinty: No shar'ia law: Move stuns shar'ia foes, supporters. 2005. *Toronto Star,* September 12, A01.

McGuinty's shar'ia call. 2005. Editorial. *Toronto Star,* September 13, A20.

Mills, R. 1995. Interview [with Syed Mumtaz Ali]: A review of the Muslim Personal/Family Law Campaign. http://www.Muslim-Canada.org/.

Mills, S. 2004. *Discourse: The new critical idiom.* New York, NY: Routledge.

Mohanty, C. 1984. Under Western eyes: Feminist scholarship and colonial discourses. *Boundary 2* 12/13, 3/1: 333-58.

—. 2003. "Under Western eyes" revisited: Feminist solidarity through anticapitalist struggles. *Signs: Journal of Women in Culture and Society* 28, 2: 499-536.

—. 2004. Towards an anti-imperialist politics: Reflections of a desi feminist. *South Asian Popular Culture* 2, 1: 69-73.

Morgan, Ed. 2005. Rabbis, imams hold similar views on courts. *Toronto Star,* June 24, A27.

Multiculturalism's limits. 2004. Editorial. *National Post,* November 9, A15.

Muslim Canadian Congress. 2004a. Shariah based arbitration racist and unconstitutional. August 26. http://www.muslimcanadiancongress.org/20040826-2.pdf.

—. 2004b. Why MCC opposes shariah law in Ontario: Submission to the Boyd Commission. August 26. http://www.muslimcanadiancongress.org/20040826.pdf.

Narayan, U. 1997. *Dislocating cultures: Identities, traditions, and Third-World feminism.* New York, NY: Routledge.

—. 2000. Essence of culture and a sense of history: A feminist critique of cultural essentialism. In U. Narayan and S. Harding, eds., *Decentering the center: Philosophy for a multicultural, postcolonial and feminist world,* 80-100. Bloomington, IN: Indiana University Press.

Ogilvie, M. 2005. Canadian Muslims give mixed reviews on moratorium: Debate urged on Islamic penal code. *Toronto Star,* April 1, B4.

One law for all. 2004. Editorial. *Montreal Gazette,* December 19, A22.

Oziewicz, E. 2005. Muslim law cleric doubts shar'ia suitable for Canadian society. *Globe and Mail,* May 14, A17.

Perreaux, L. 2005. Quebec rejects Islamic law. *Toronto Star,* May 27, A8.

Québec's rash censure of Muslim arbitration. 2005. Editorial. *Globe and Mail,* May 28, A24.

Rahnema, S. 2005. Unholy alliance on the right. *Toronto Star,* May 10, A18.

Rand Foundation. 2004. Rand study describes how West can counter radical Islam. March 18. http://www.rand.org/news/.

Raza, Raheel. 2004. Shar'ia: It's about religious freedom. *Toronto Star,* December 22, A25.

Razack, S. 1994. What is to be gained by looking white people in the eye? Culture, race, and gender in cases of sexual violence. *Signs: Journal of Women in Culture and Society* 19, 4: 894-924.

—. 1998. *Looking white people in the eye.* Toronto, ON: University of Toronto Press.

—. 2003. A violent culture or culturalized violence? Feminist narratives of sexual violence against South Asian women. *Studies in Practical Philosophy* 3, 1: 81-104.

—. 2004. Imperilled Muslim women, dangerous Muslim men and civilised Europeans: Legal and social responses to forced marriages. *Feminist Legal Studies* 12, 2: 129-74.

—. 2007. The "sharia law debate" in Ontario: The modernity/premodernity distinction in legal efforts to protect women from culture. *Feminist Legal Studies* 15, 1: 3-32.

Rushdie, S. 2005. Keep religion out of public life: Salman Rushdie warns that West will invite tyranny if faith is given a seat in the political arena. *Toronto Star,* March 13, A17.

Salimi, N. 2005. Open letter to the NDP on behalf of the Muslim Canadian Congress. January 17. Distributed via e-mail.

SAWCC. 2005. South Asian Women's Community Centre position on the recommendation to use the Arbitration Act of Ontario to settle family legal matters based on religious laws. March 17. http://www.sacw.net/.

Seguin, R. 2005. Québec quashes idea of Islamic tribunals. *Globe and Mail,* May 27, A1, A10.

Shar'ia tribunals and human rights. 2005. Editorial. *Toronto Star,* September 8, A22.

Siddiqui, H. 2004. Global issues, agendas colour shar'ia debate. *Toronto Star,* May 30, n.p.

–. 2005a. Muslim reformists reject Western view of change. *Toronto Star,* April 14, A27.
–. 2005b. Sensationalism shrouds the debate on shar'ia: Haroon Siddiqui says hysteria shows lack of faith in Canada. *Toronto Star,* June 12, A17.
–. 2005c. Shar'ia issue trumps media and McGuinty: Haroon Siddiqui says Ontario must strike balance between competing rights. *Toronto Star,* September 11, A17.
–. 2005d. Shar'ia is gone but fear and hostility remain. *Toronto Star,* September 15, A25.
Simpson, J. 2005. There's a lesson for all of us from the shar'ia issue. *Globe and Mail,* September 14, A21.
Spivak, Gayatri. 1985. Can the subaltern speak? Speculations on widow sacrifice. *Wedge,* 7-8: 120-30.
Syed, I. 2003. E-mail to listserv, December 23. http://groups.yahoo.com/.
–. 2004. Reflections on the headscarf ban in France. *Ampersand* 2 (Winter): 63-68.
–. 2005a. Sharia law in Ontario – Podcast interview with Co-Op Radio. *Redeye – Co-op Radio,* September 25. http://www.radio4all.net/.
–. 2005b. The tempest in Canada. *Ihsan-Blog,* September 25. http://ihsan.wordpress.com/.
Syrtash, J.T. 2004. Ontario has nothing to fear. *National Post,* September 21, A17.
Thobani, S. 2002. Saving the West: Reflections on gender, race and the war of terrorism. *Fireweed – A Feminist Quarterly of Writing, Politics, Art and Culture,* Part 2: 9-34.
–. 2007. *Exalted subjects: Studies in the making of race and nation in Canada.* Toronto, ON: University of Toronto Press.
–. 2008. Imperial longings, feminist responses. In D.E. Chunn, S.V. Boyd, and H. Lessard, eds., *Reaction and resistance: Feminism, law and social change,* 98-123. Vancouver, BC: UBC Press.
Todd, D. 2005. Why the shariah debate will be good for everyone. *Vancouver Sun,* September 24, C5.
Trichur, R. 2005. Islamic financial services offer a new way to bank: Canadian Muslims not rushing to embrace companies that operate under shar'ia law. *Globe and Mail,* July 18, B5.
Urquhart, I. 2005. McGuinty faced rebellion in his caucus: Why premier chose to act. *Toronto Star,* September 12, A01.
Walkom, T. 2004. Courts must have final say on arbitration. *Toronto Star,* December 28, A17.
Wente, M. 2004. The state should not give its blessing to Muslim courts. *Globe and Mail,* December 23, n.p.
–. 2005a. The woman who just says no – Courting shar'ia: "I can't look away because I know what goes on in Islamic families." *Globe and Mail,* August 20, A19.
–. 2005b. Whistling shar'ia while we go completely off our rocker. *Globe and Mail,* September 8, A27.
West Coast LEAF. 2004a. Consultation on women's equality and religious freedom. *Conference Proceedings – December 3rd, 2004.*

–. 2004b. Consultation on women's equality and religious freedom. *Conference Proceedings – December 4th, 2004.*
White, S. 2004. Hijab hysteria – France and its Muslims. *Open Democracy,* April 4. http://www.opendemocracy.net/.
Whitehouse. 2001. President discusses war on terrorism. November 8. http://www.whitehouse.gov/.
Wilson, W.G. 2005. Listen to the sheikha. *National Post,* September 14, A19.
Wordsworth, A. 2004. Extramarital sex can be a matter of life or death, literally: Islamic law. *National Post,* September 15, A9.
Zine, J. 2004a. Creating a critical faith-centered space for antiracist feminism. *Journal of Feminist Studies in Religion* 20, 2: 167-87.
–. 2004b. Examining the proposal for shar'ia tribunals in Ontario. Lecture delivered at the conference "God is back with a vengeance: Religion and the secular state." Couchiching Institute on Public Affairs, August 7.
–. 2005. Women's rights and shar'ia tribunals in Ontario – An interview with Jasmin Zine. *Challenging Fundamentalisms – A Web Resource for Women's Human Rights.* www.whrnet.org/fundamentalisms/ docs/perspective-zine-0506.html.
–. 2006a. Between Orientalism and fundamentalism: The politics of Muslim women's feminist engagement. *Muslim World Journal of Human Rights* 3, 1: 1-24.
–. 2006b. Unveiled sentiments: Gendered Islamophobia and experiences of veiling among Muslim girls in a Canadian Islamic school. In *Ethno-religious oppression in schools,* special issue of *Equity and Excellence in Education* 39, 3: 239-52.

3
Toward a Framework for Investigating Muslim Women and Political Engagement in Canada

KATHERINE BULLOCK

Studies of women's participation in Western democracies, including Canada, find that women are less involved than men in traditional mass politics in terms of knowledge of party leaders, issues, voting, and running for office (Newman and White 2006, ch. 4). Women are underrepresented in the Canadian national parliament. "Politics remains very much a man's world in Canada" (Gidengil et al. 2004, 8, 174).[1] But feminist scholars have also determined that although women's involvement in formal politics is significantly lower than their percentage of the general population, this by no means indicates that women are not involved politically in their societies (Abu-Laban 2002, 277; Gidengil et al. 2004, 174-75; Newman and White 2006). Women tend to concentrate their political involvement in the informal sector.

Although ethnic minorities, especially people of colour and people of non-Christian faith, are, like women, also deeply underrepresented (Black 2002, 359), research shows that ethnic minorities are not less involved politically with their societies than those from the dominant groups.[2] A study by Gidengil and colleagues (2004, 175) found that they are "as interested (or not) in politics," use media in similar ways, and are members of a political party in similar numbers. They are less likely to vote, but "are [as] active as other Canadians in women's and environmental groups and more active in religious and ethnic associations." Gidengil and her research team's findings are consistent with other studies refuting the myth that immigrants tend to be less politically active than the native-born. Abu-Laban (2002, 278-79) points out that political scientists, by focusing on behavioural measures of politics, have obscured proper understanding of immigrant minority women's political engagement with society. She cites Agnew's (1996) research indicating that immigrant and minority women are to be found mostly in immigrant and ethno-cultural community women's groups, formed in part as a response to the exclusion created both by mainstream groups not taking into account minority issues and perspectives and by minority organizations subordinating the specific interests of women as women to those of the group.

This chapter aims to develop a framework for investigating Muslim women's political engagement with Canadian society. I am not attempting a survey of currently existing Muslim women's groups in Canada; nor have I done any interviews for this chapter. I simply aim to make steps toward laying a theoretical framework for investigating Muslim women and political participation in Canada in the hope that others will be able to utilize such a framework for their empirical studies of particular individuals or groups. I build on Abu-Laban's (2002) and Agnew's (1996) work to demonstrate that Canadian Muslim women have been engaged politically with Canadian society for decades and in a range of activities other than women's groups. There has also been a growing trend of involvement in formal politics since the 1970s. My primary data come from two main sources: autobiographical or biographical narratives about Muslim women activists in Canada; and my personal experiences with, and observations of, Muslim community activism over the past decade in Canada (Bullock 2005, Zaman 1999). The chapter has three parts. Part 1 provides a brief demographic profile of Muslim women in Canada. This helps to establish whether or not Muslim women have the resources (i.e., time, money, know-how) to be politically engaged. Part 2 discusses some definitions of terms. Although it may seem redundant to define the key terms "Muslim," "political engagement," and "activism," given the range of perspectives at play, it turns out that delineating these key terms is a crucial aspect of investigating Canadian Muslim women's political participation. Part 3 is an attempt to categorize Muslim women's political participation. Together, these three parts make a beginning in laying the framework for investigating Muslim women and political participation in Canada. They enhance our understanding of political participation in general and of Muslim political participation in particular. This discussion also highlights the links between informal-sector activism and political participation in society.

Part 1: Who Are Muslim Women in Canada?

The more disposable income, spare time, and family/community support, the more able is a person to be politically engaged. Thus to understand the relationship of Muslim women to political participation, it is useful to start with a brief snapshot of the demographic profile of Muslim women in Canada.

The largest percentage of Muslims in Canada are either immigrants or the children of immigrants from Muslim countries the world over – Arabia, Asia, Africa, China – who arrived after immigration rules changed from race-based criteria to criteria stressing skills, family reunion, and refugees. In Canada, although Muslims represent only 2 percent of the population, "Islam is now the second largest of the three Abrahamic faiths and the seventh overall among the six dozen faiths listed in the 2001 census" (Hamdani 2004, 4-5).[3]

Canadian Muslims are highly educated. Hamdani (2004, 10) found that whereas one in five Canadian women have postsecondary education, nearly one in three adult Muslim Canadian women do. Based on his figures, Hamdani concluded that "among the Muslim females aged 25 years and over in 2001, there were sufficient number of doctoral and equivalent graduates to supply the entire faculty of a medium-size university, such as the University of Western Ontario which has 29,000 undergraduate and graduate students and 12 faculties and schools (1,164 faculty members)."

Hamdani's (2004, 7) research found that Muslim women live in urban areas and are more likely to be married than the national average. One of the surprising findings of Hamdani's (2004, 16) survey was that, although Muslim women's participation in the labour force was low compared to the national average, 36 percent of those Muslim women who were in the workforce had children who were preschoolers, compared to 29 percent of all working mothers in Canada. This must have an impact on Muslim women's civic engagement since juggling family, work, and activism can be quite a struggle.

Overall, these figures show that Muslim women form part of a highly educated, professional, urban, and culturally diverse group. They are highly likely to possess the skills, finances, and opportunity/time to become activists in both the informal and formal political sectors. And research shows that they have done so; Muslim women are definitely politically engaged in Canadian society.

Part 2: Defining the Terms

Muslim

To set up a framework for investigating "Muslim women's political engagement in Canada," I begin with some general delineation of the key words in, or related to, this phrase: "Muslim," "political engagement," and "activism."[4]

Wiktorowicz (2004), a pioneer in the study of Islamic activism from the approach of social-movement theory, in an edited collection that studies Islamic activism in Muslim-majority countries, defines "Islamic" in a purposely broad way. The collection's authors study those groups who mobilize "Islam" in their activism, and as the range of groups claiming adherence to Islam is wide, they seek, as analysts, not to put forth a particular definition of "Islam" that would exclude any group claiming to be "Islamic."

I follow Wiktorowicz and his authors in this demarcation. Whereas religious scholars delineate belief, social scientists seek to understand society. In Canada there are many different orientations and, sometimes competing, interpretations of Islam. To appreciate the full scope of "Muslim" women's political engagement, then, a broad definition of what would count as "Muslim" is required. Too narrow a definition would obscure, rather than reveal, reality.

What counts for me is the self-identification that one is a "Muslim" woman actively concerned about Islam and being Muslim in a Canadian context. Based in the feminist commitment to honour women's experience, I argue that when a Muslim woman is politically engaged with Canadian society and refers to her "Muslimness" in some way to explain her involvement, her activities must come under the scope of "Muslim women's political engagement with society." This brings "orthodox," "heterodox," traditional, conservative, Islamist, and secular Muslims, and those in between, into the same analytical terrain.

However, in contrast to Wiktorowicz, I prefer the term "Muslim" activist to "Islamic" activist since this allows us to keep a distinction between "Islam" and "Muslim." To my mind, the adjective "Islamic" – of or relating to Islam – ought to be defined more narrowly through the lens of the Qur'an, the *sunnah*,[5] and jurisprudence. The adjective "Muslim" – in its Arabic understanding, "one who submits" – allows for a broader canvas since *how* one submits varies greatly depending both on the various interpretations and orientations of Islam and on the way that the lived experience of being a

Muslim is also inflected by local culture, customs, and socio-economic and political conditions.

What my definition puts outside the scope of investigating "Muslim women's political engagement in Canada" are those politically active women who may be of Muslim parents but who themselves have explicitly renounced their Muslim heritage (such as Ayaan Hirsi Ali, a former Dutch parliamentarian of Somali heritage who has renounced Islam) or those who explain their motivations for involvement in terms that do not relate to their faith (such as Canadian Iranian expatriate Homa Arjomand, who campaigned against the introduction of Islamic family law in faith-based arbitration in Ontario on a secular-humanist platform).[6] Women who leave their faith, or who do not speak as persons of faith, cannot be considered to be politically engaged as "Muslim" women. Any specific woman may traverse back and forth through these categories over the course of her lifetime, but this does not alter the definitions.

Political Engagement
Political scientists, in their theories of political participation, divide participation into two aspects: "formal"- and "informal"-sector participation. The formal sector relates to government and the informal relates to participation in civil society, usually understood as the arena of nongovernmental organizations (NGOs) (Newman and White 2006). Civic education theorists, on the other hand, make no such divisions, as civic education is usually considered to concern preparing individuals for citizenship – and citizenship includes both the formal and informal sectors (Bhabha 2006). Of course, feminists have long challenged such dichotomies, not only that of formal versus informal but also another related dichotomy, that of public versus private, as both government and civic space are part of public, as distinct from private, space. "The personal is political" became an important analytical tool to study the status of women in society.

As mentioned above, Abu-Laban (2002) and other scholars have pointed out that to focus only on formal politics as a measure of political participation especially obscures the political engagement with society of immigrants and ethno-cultural minorities. This is also true, as I explain below, of religious engagement with society.

Given the politically charged and negative atmosphere surrounding Muslims in the West, as Said (1981, 72) has observed, "For almost every Muslim, the mere assertion of an Islamic identity becomes an act of nearly cosmic defiance and a necessity for survival."

This has two consequences. First, one's very foundations – one's worldview and perspective – are politicized, not necessarily due to anything one may have done or may want but due to what others have done and what the society around the individual does to that individual. Wearing a headscarf may simply be an expression of devotion to God and spirituality, but society may decide it is a political statement and move to prevent a woman from wearing it. Muslim political engagement can be imposed on Muslims in Canada without their actively seeking it out.

On the other hand, given the prevalent negative stereotypes of Islam, racism, and the practical, day-to-day indignities of being a Muslim in Canada, political engagement with Canadian society must be connected to every attempt to resist them. Thus, like my understanding of "Muslim," my understanding of "political engagement" is also purposefully broad. A narrower definition that focused only on formal-sector participation would obscure almost all of Muslim women's political activity in Canada, but even a slightly wider understanding that only focused on informal-sector activity would still obscure some of Muslim women's political engagement with Canadian society. The public (including the economic), private, formal, and informal sectors are all arenas in which Canadian Muslims engage politically.

Thus I consider anyone who seeks to challenge, resist, combat, or change the negative stereotypes of Islam or Muslims to be politically engaged. This may take the form of a Muslim civic association raising the issue of Islamophobia at election time. It may take the form of a Muslim civic association, such as a Muslim student association, setting up an information *(dawa)* table about Islam at a university (Haddad, Smith, and Moore 2006, 44) or, as the Federation of Muslim Women (FMW) used to do, setting up information tables in a mall.[7] These tables typically have free flyers for passers-by (such as that produced by Islamic Circle of North America), and for sale there are books, beautiful colour posters (such as in the *Discover Islam* series), and other objects (such as the Qur'an, prayer mats, clothing, ethnic food, and so on). Volunteers sit at the table and answer questions from passers-by. Political engagement may also take a pedagogical form, such as the Canadian Council of Muslim Women's current project to examine the representation of Muslim women and girls in the curriculum of Ontario schools and to develop curricular materials to counter negative stereotypes and present a more rounded picture of Muslim women as prominent figures in history, politics, and cultural production.

Political engagement may further take the form of an individual woman, not connected to any association or group, who tries in her own way to combat the negative stereotype of Islam. Many Muslim women, especially those who stay home while the children are young, engage their child's school in order to promote a positive image of Islam. They speak to the class about the hajj or take sweets to the school during Ramadan. This is a form of political engagement.

Even in a regular job search, Muslim women's political engagement with Canadian society is evident. The following story told to Canadian researchers investigating workplace discrimination for women wearing the *hijab* (headscarf) is striking:

> I did an interview over the phone for a bakery position. The guy told me to come in and fill in an application. When I came in wearing hijab he told me the position was taken. I went home, called the place again and changed my voice and asked if the bakery position was still open and they said yes. I took this to the labour board and ended up getting the job because they were found to be discriminating. I took it so that I could change their views about women who wear hijab. (Persad and Lukas 2002, 24)

This anecdote is noteworthy: by applying for a job, the woman clearly showed her need for an income, yet after her experience of discrimination, she said that she took the job not to pay the rent or whatever but "so that I could change their views about women who wear hijab." This indicates the *political* element of this woman's job-related activity – even in her search for a job, she was thinking about dispelling negative images of Muslim women.

Many of these women may not be conscious of themselves as "political activists" and may even resist this appellation given its negative connotation in popular culture (Hamid 2005, 90). And acts such as taking a box of cookies to a school classroom or getting a job are not normally seen as instances of political engagement. Yet, like the conduct of a Palestinian who plants an apricot tree in land being seized by Israel,[8] such individualized work, because it aims to alter relations of power, counts as political action.

Activism

Political activism by self-professed Muslims is usually understood to be part of "political Islam." Wiktorowicz (2004, 2) and other social movement theorists consider Islamic activism to be "the mobilization of contention to support Muslim causes." The authors in Wiktorowicz's (2004, 2) book conceive of their definition of "Islamic activism" as "purposefully broad" so that what counts as "contention" is anything "that frequently emerges under the banner of 'Islam', including propagation movements, terrorist groups, collective action rooted in Islamic symbols and identities, explicitly political movements that seek to establish an Islamic state, and inward-looking groups that promote Islamic spirituality through collective efforts."

Even though Wiktorowicz does include in his understanding of Islamic activism "propagation movements" and "inward-looking groups that promote Islamic spirituality through collective efforts," I do not believe that this approach translates well to studying Muslim political engagement in Western societies. The sense of "Muslim politics" or "Islamic activism" is usually cast in terms of the politics of "protest." Milton-Edwards (2004, 209) characterizes political Islam as "an alternative [ideology that] inevitably places emphasis on protest, opposition and antagonism to prevailing hegemonic orders." Although she recognizes that some Muslims are part of Western political systems (81) and cautions that not all Muslim activism is anti-Western radicalism, she still frames Muslims' political engagement as part of the language of "protest" (78-79):

> It has been demonstrated that in contemporary times the nature of protest politics in majority Muslim domains is varied and expressed through a variety of means, including the ballot box, street protest, the mosque pulpit, and the act of preaching ... Do such patterns of protest change when we examine the politics of protest in locales where Muslims constitute a minority, and more specifically in political systems deemed liberal-democratic in nature? Are the issues around which protest takes place altered by the degree of political participation available in such societies? (78)

Here, Milton-Edwards, like many scholars, assumes that Muslims' political activity will be less "protest"-based the more that "political participation" is offered to them and concludes that tensions between European countries and Muslim inhabitants has led mostly to alienation and protest politics. Hafez (2003) provides convincing evidence of the linkage in Muslim-majority countries between protest and closed political systems and between participation and open political systems, but my argument in this chapter is that we *cannot know* what the full range of political participation in a Western society is if we consider "Muslim" politics only through the lens of "protest."

This point is recognized by Eickelman and Piscatori in their book *Muslim Politics* (1996), where they conceptualize "Muslim politics" more broadly than does this language of protest based on social-movement theory. They argue that "Muslim politics" needs to be placed into "multiple and shifting contexts ... Increasingly, in the venture of Islam, Muslim politics constitutes the field on which an intricate pattern of cooperation and contest over form, practice, and interpretation takes place" (20-21).

Mandaville (2007) first adopted this insight in his study of "global political Islam." He discusses the difference between investigating "political Islam" and "Muslim politics" – political Islam being only one kind of Muslim politics:

> To say that we are dealing with an instance of political Islam would be to suggest that there are times when Islam is not political (i.e., that it is sometimes "just" religious). The term Muslim politics is useful because it allows us to keep the diversity and pluralism of Islam front and center through an emphasis on Muslims as social actors. To focus on Muslims rather than Islam is to emphasize real people in real settings facing real issues ... To study Muslim politics, then, is to look at the diverse ways in which people who identify themselves as Muslims ... understand, make use of, and mobilize the symbols and language of Islam around issues of social order, power and authority. (20)

I argue in this chapter that it is these conceptions of Muslim politics that are best suited to understanding Muslim political engagement with Canadian society. No doubt, "protest" plays an important role in Muslim political engagement in Canada. Indeed, I have argued above that every act to counter racism is a political act – a protest. But this is to use "protest" in its broadest sense. In social-movement theory, "protest" or "contention," even if defined broadly, à la Wiktorowicz, is still identified with "oppositional," "adversarial" politics.

Canadian Muslims do mobilize around protest issues of foreign policy, racism, and discrimination, but much of what they do, what I want to consider political participation, is not linked to mobilization around "protest" (except perhaps in the broadest sense of dawa that spreads a good message about Islam). In addition, many Muslims (and non-Muslims), especially those not familiar with leftwing politics, view "activism" in a negative light. An "activist" is someone who is bringing about chaos or disrupting the system. When I invited women to contribute their stories of activism to my book, I had to convince many of them that to be called an "activist" was not a bad thing. In that book (Bullock 2005), I sought to rescue the concept of activism from its negative connotations. I defined an activist as "doing something concrete for the sake of a social good" (xv). But even though I used the term "activist," meant in a positive way, I think that the language of "Islamic activism" needs to be broadened and attached to the concept of "Muslim politics" because this concept better enables us to capture Muslim women's political engagement in Canada. There are several advantages.

In the first place, since activism by traditionalist, even "heterodox," Muslims counts as "Muslim" political engagement, a broader concept of "Muslim politics" is needed, one that allows us to see political engagement with Canadian society that is bigger than that revealed by investigating "political Islamists" in Canada. Islamist political engagement is only one type of Muslim political engagement in Canada.

Second, even for understanding activism by those associated with political Islam, the broader concept of "Muslim politics" is better because it allows us to see the ways that the goals can be different here. In most Muslim-majority countries, "political Islam" – or "Islamic activism," to use Wiktorowicz's (2004) term – usually takes the form of mobilization of societal dissent on a large scale, hence its interest for social-movement theorists and the concept of "contention." The aims and methods of these social movements do vary, but the general goal is either to establish an Islamic state (even if in the distant future) or to reintroduce *shar'ia* (Islamic law) more broadly as the legal framework for the state. Islamist social movements appeal to the historical past, authenticity, memory, and conscience. They aim to restore to society something that was lost with Western colonialism. As Wiktorowicz (2004) and others who study Islamist social movements demonstrate, they mobilize expressly Islamic symbols to involve the masses in their political movement (Eickelman and Piscatori 1996, Kurzman 2004).

But the situation in North America is quite different. Leaders do seek to mobilize activists by using Islamic symbols, terminology, and concepts, but the aim is not to establish an Islamic state (hyperbole from the anti-Muslim neoconservatives notwithstanding). When focused outward, the aim above all is to undermine negative Western cultural stereotypes that Islam is backward, anti-civilization, anti-women, and violent.[9] Activism here in Canada is more about getting involved and integration than about expressing wide-scale political dissent (other than dissent over the stereotypical negative image of Muslims as violent and backward). The hope is to demonstrate that Muslims are civilized, tolerant, peaceful, and supportive of human rights and that they can be full citizens of Western countries. Thus the Islamic concepts and terminology that are emphasized are those Qur'anic verses or *hadith*[10] that encourage believers to seek justice, to do good to the poor and the traveller, to show compassion, to work for the good of society, to be supportive of pluralism and interfaith dialogue, and to help their neighbours. A group of young Muslims in Canada connected to *Sound Vision* encouraged its members to give gifts to all of the neighbours on the street at Eid time, and the youth wing of the Muslim Association of Canada highlights interfaith work and has encouraged its members to be a part of the initiatives of the broader anti-racist, social justice, leftwing movements in Toronto – for example, a group was formed, and transport provided, to encourage and enable the youth to attend the fundraiser Walk for the Homeless.[11]

And, importantly, in spite of their different and sometimes hostile relations with each other, this work of promoting a good image of Islam, and of mobilizing Qur'anic verses as proof, is done by all Muslims politically engaged in society – from those connected to or sympathetic with political Islam to those opposed to it. We are able to see these similarities, intersections, and criss-crosses between otherwise antagonistic groups through the "Muslim politics" concept better than through the "contention" concept.

Third, much Muslim political participation is civic engagement, akin to that of other groups in society, around activities not usually seen as linked to the politics of "contention." Helping to build a mosque, running a weekend Sunday Islamic school, a seniors club, or a charity, addressing internal community issues of social justice, and so on are all activities related to civic engagement and thus to political engagement with society. Muslims do not live only inside their houses, going only to work and school. They are involved with a range of activities in the informal sector. Some of these activities focus on social services to Muslims, namely poverty relief, housing assistance, and senior care. Others focus on education, establishing Islamic schools, daycares, and preschools.

Indeed, as Muslim groups overcome the fear of exposing their "dirty laundry" to the wider Canadian society, there is a trend toward addressing issues of social justice within their own communities, especially around women's rights (Aly 2010). National and local Muslim women's groups – such as the Canadian Council of Muslim Women (CCMW), the Federation of Muslim Women (FMW), and *AQSAzine*, a collective of young Muslim women founded in honour of murdered Toronto teen Aqsa Parvez – have multiple objectives, including combating anti-Muslim racism, providing marriage counselling, and addressing domestic violence within the Muslim community, forced marriage, and other issues related to Muslim family law.

Some complain that building Islamic schools, relief NGOs, and the like only ghettoizes themselves.[12] But this is not fair and denies to Muslims what other faith and ethnic groups in Canada consider to be normal and par for the course. Activism in these areas is the staple of civil society, and a vibrant civil society is usually considered a vital part of a functioning democracy. To the extent that Muslims are civically engaged in these areas, they contribute to the enrichment of Canadian civil society and thus to Canadian democracy.

Finally, and closely related to the last point, to think of Muslim political engagement only as activism in "support [of] Muslim causes" is to overlook a whole segment of Muslim activists in North America. What about a woman who self-identifies as a Muslim, who is convinced her faith requires her to work for the betterment of society, and who joins, works for, or volunteers with a mainstream organization, such as Save the Children, UNICEF, and so on? Perhaps the woman herself thinks of her work as "supporting a Muslim cause" (the Qur'anic call to justice), but the organization itself does not define its vision or goals as supporting a "Muslim cause." Under Wiktorowicz's (2004) definition, such a woman would be excluded from a study of Muslim activism (and thus of political engagement). Yet it is this kind of work that thousands of Muslim women do in the United States and Canada. To understand how the Muslim community interacts politically with the wider society, it is vital to investigate this kind of activism.

The broader concept of Muslim politics allows us to see this more clearly because it gives an insight into context. In Muslim-majority countries, charity and poverty relief, the kind of work usually associated with civil society, can be seen as a part of the "mobilization of contention to support Muslim causes" because it is in this field that Islamist activists have outshone the state and attracted thousands to their cause. Setting up a medical clinic can be a direct challenge to the state. Islamist movements have been able effectively to run entire neighbourhoods because of the collapse of state provision of services – for example, the Egyptian government allowed the al-Jama'a al-Islamiyya group to run many social services in parts of Upper Egypt, and only when the group began to expand its power toward Cairo did a massive crackdown ensue (Hafez 2003, 83-84).[13] But setting up a medical clinic in the United States is an expression of something different: Muslim commitment to philanthropy, a desire to dispel negative stereotypes that Muslims are destructive, a need for integration with the wider society, and so on.[14]

One final point about definitions that allow us to see society in all its complexity: Muslim women's engagement in civil society is not without its challenges. This reality is not really explored in this chapter, but Muslim women face internal and external hurdles to their political engagement, from pressures not to "compromise" their modesty by taking on public roles to overcoming racism and discrimination in order to make a contribution to civil society.[15] Recalling the feminist theoretical point that the "personal is political," it is important to note that although much of Muslim women's contribution to civil society is less visible than that of men, it should not be regarded as less.

It took forty years for one of the oldest Muslim associations in the United States and Canada, the Islamic Society of North America (ISNA), to elect its first woman president in 2006, Dr. Ingrid Mattson, a Canadian convert to Islam and a professor at Hartford Seminary in Connecticut, but women have been foundational members of ISNA since its very beginning (Ali 2003, 16-24). This involvement may have been in a more "supporting" role – such as preparing food for their husbands who met to discuss the founding of a group – but as Freda Shamma (in Bullock 2005, 166-67) recounts in her narrative, some women conceived of this activity as their contribution to the work of the Muslim community.

Since ISNA is considered to be a conservative association, the election of a woman as president gives insight into just how much the roles of Muslim women in North America are under renegotiation. Haddad, Smith, and Moore (2006, 66, 99) argue that only a minority of traditionalists from the Indian subcontinent and Salafi leaders are not supportive of women's more public role. Yet even here we must be careful not to make public visibility a criterion of civic engagement since women who are members of the traditionalist and conservative organizations mentioned by Haddad and colleagues are activists in ways (however circumscribed) that are approved of in their communities, notably through participation in sister wings of Islamic associations, women's Qur'anic study circles, and women-only or highly segregated events at *masajid* (mosques) like fashion shows, bazaars, fundraising dinners, conferences, and lectures. Women are usually highly involved in organizing and running these activities because, by definition, the men are not to be present. These activities need to be recognized as part of civic engagement.

So keeping the concepts of Muslim, political engagement, and activism as broad as possible allows us better insight into Muslim women's political engagement with Canadian society.

Part 3: Categorizing Muslim Women's Activism

In *Muslim Women in America: The Challenge of Islamic Identity Today*, Haddad, Smith, and Moore (2006) recognize that there are thousands of Muslim women involved in innumerable associations whose work ranges from promoting a better understanding of Islam to providing social services to disadvantaged groups. They point out that in the United States, Muslim women are increasingly part of a public sphere, whether as employees or as members of Islamic and non-Islamic organizations (Haddad, Smith, and Moore 2006, ch. 8). Their findings resonate with my personal and professional experience in Canada: Muslim women are to be found in every arena of the informal sector and increasingly in the formal sector, whether in the niche area of catering to the needs of the Muslim community, in the NGO sector of the wider society, as operators of one-woman outfits, or as participants in party politics, where they may run for office and even win elections.[16]

So, in trying to grasp the significance and scope of "Muslim women's political engagement" in Canada, as mentioned above, I employ an expansive and context-based understanding of this phrase. In addition, the focus in this section is on civil-society activism, based on scholarly arguments and on my own personal sense that this is where the bulk of Muslim women's political engagement occurs. Although there are isolated examples of Muslim women's involvement at a high level of formal politics (where they have run for or been elected to office), and although this is an increasing trend, empirical studies charting their involvement in the arena of formal politics are lacking. It is known that participation in civil society, itself a form of political engagement, is often a springboard to formal political participation (Abu-Laban 2002, 279).[17] So in this section I consider to be Muslim women activists not only those who work in the more recognized activist fields, such as NGOs (whether Islamic or non-Islamic), but also one-woman outfits working quietly, say, to dispel negative stereotypes of Islam.

A categorization of Muslim women activists as individuals defies attempt. In the first place, absent a detailed survey of all NGOs in the United States and Canada, it is hard to know exactly how many non-Muslim NGOs have Muslim women working with them, either on staff or as volunteers. An assessment would be slightly easier in the case of umbrella Islamic NGOS such as ISNA, Islamic Circle of North America, Muslim American

Society, Muslim Association of Canada, Irfan, Kindhearts USA, Islamic Relief, and so on, but, again, absent a detailed survey, it is impossible to have a comprehensive sense of the range of women's activities, roles, and responsibilities in these groups. This is even true of the hundreds of women-only groups that grow year by year. Furthermore, one woman may wear many hats. Usually, activists do not confine their activity to a single group. They may be present on a range of boards, perhaps for a local Islamic school, a charity, an advocacy group, and a woman's group; they may also be on the boards of volunteer associations for their professions, such as a nurses' or teachers' federation. Sharon Hoosein, a past president of the Federation of Muslim Women, is also the education and membership co-ordinator of the International Nurses Interest Group (INIG), a subgroup of the Registered Nurses Association of Ontario (RNAO).

One possible way to categorize Muslim women's activism is to tag activist work as either internal or external based on whether it is aimed at the Muslim community or aimed at the broader society. But this does not really lead to a proper delineation of Muslim women's activism since a woman might be involved in volunteering both for a Muslim charity like Islamic Relief and for the Red Cross. Using the categories of internal and external would separate her activities. So I prefer a categorization based on type of activity, which may fall across the internal-external divide.

With the understanding that the following is only a rough guide to arenas of activity, listed below are the broad categories of Muslim women's activism. This list also probably presents the categories in descending order of magnitude, although I have no evidence to support this other than my own experience. To provide illustrations of the categories, I refer to women who wrote for my book *Muslim Women Activists in North America: Speaking for Ourselves* (Bullock 2005) because it is a public record, not because there is necessarily anything special about these women – they are of course special as human beings, but their stories are replicated countless times by other women whose accounts are not in any book. Because this chapter is about Canada, I mention only Canadian Muslim women, although the book also contains narratives from US Muslim women. As well, I have not listed them under all the categories, even though many of them could be so listed, as they wear multiple hats.[18] Many women, like Dr. Ekram Beshir, start out as a woman working alone, often at her children's school, and later connect with other women to form (or join) a group.[19]

- One-woman outfits: Dr. Ekram Beshir, author and educator

- Social services: Shahina Siddiqui, marriage counsellor and founder of the Islamic Social Services Association
- Education: Olivia Monem, principal of an Islamic school, curriculum development for Islamic school teachers, Islamic-component lesson plans for public schools
- Umbrella women's groups: Mariam Bhabha, founder of the Federation of Muslim Women; Gul Joya Jafri, Afghan Women's Counselling and Integration Community Support Organization
- Umbrella Islamic associations: Khadija Haffajee, Islamic Society of North America Majlis a Shura (executive board); Dr. Mona Rahman, president of Queen's University Muslim Students Association
- Political advocacy: Nadira Mustapha, co-founder and chairperson of Canadian Muslims for Peace and Justice and vice-president of Students for International Peace and Justice
- Media: Tayyibah Taylor, founder and editor-in-chief of *Azizah Magazine*; Samana Siddiqui, writer for *Sound Vision*

Conclusion

This chapter has argued that, in line with other women, Muslim women are deeply engaged in informal-sector politics. I have made the case that because activism is concerned with bringing about social, political, or economic justice, activism should be seen as a form of political participation alongside activities in the arena of formal politics, such as party work, voting, and running for office. My research shows that, despite hardly any involvement in formal politics (although more empirical research is needed here and women's involvement in party politics is on the rise), Canadian Muslim women are politically engaged with society via their involvement as activists in civil society.

Abu-Laban (2002, 279) argues that a fruitful way to explore minority women's political engagement with society is to "incorporate women's, men's, and minorities' *own definitions of their political engagement*, rather than working from pre-established definitions" (emphasis in original). This chapter is meant to do just that. Based on a broad concept of Muslim politics, I have argued that Muslim women's political engagement with Canadian society is instantiated every time a Muslim woman tries to counter a negative stereotype of Islam. The variety of Muslim women's activism in civil society, and the resultant attempt to categorize this activism, demonstrates that Muslim women are without a doubt politically engaged in Canadian society, from the local community to federal politics.

ACKNOWLEDGMENTS

This chapter is based on a paper on Muslim women activists in North America originally presented at the Fulbright symposium "Muslim citizens in the West: Promoting social inclusion," Centre for Muslim States and Societies, University of Western Australia, August 1-3, 2007. Many thanks for the constructive feedback from Jasmin Zine and other colleagues who read that draft paper.

NOTES

1 In terms of women's election to legislatures, Canada ranks 48th out of 181 countries according to the Geneva-based Inter-Parliamentary Union (data as of May 31, 2007; see http://www.ipu.org/). Somewhat ironically, given the perception that Muslim women are oppressed, Afghanistan, Tunisia, Pakistan, and Sudan all have better representation of women in legislatures than does the United States.
2 For Canada, see Black's (2002, 359) study of the percentage of minorities in Parliament; in the 1997 election, visible minorities comprised 11.2 percent of the population but won only 6.3 percent of the seats.
3 Eighty-six percent of Muslim women in Canada are a member of a "visible minority," defined in the Employment Equity Act (1995) as "persons, other than Aboriginal people, who are non-Caucasian in race or non-White in colour." See Hamdani (2004, 5).
4 Alhough some feminists would also question the signifier "woman," I choose not to problematize this term (Riley 1990). Here, I use "woman" in the conventional sense of "being biologically female." Of course, "woman" as a gender category can include the concepts of socialization.
5 *Sunnah* refers to those sayings and actions of the Prophet Muhammad that are considered exemplary for his followers.
6 Some readers have informed me that Arjomand also said on several occasions that she is no longer a Muslim. I did not hear or read this about her myself. If it is true, it makes very problematic the mass media's presentation of Arjomand as the "Muslim woman" seeking justice for Muslim women in Ontario by denying the introduction of faith-based arbitration (see also Chapter 2).
7 I used to co-ordinate this effort for the FMW in the late 1990s.
8 To witness the Israeli army uprooting apricot trees from Palestinian land, see the documentary *The Shame of Eratz,* http://uk.youtube.com/.
9 This matter needs more empirical study and documentation. I make this claim based on my interaction with groups normally associated with conservative and/or political Islam in Canada over the past decade.
10 *Hadith* refers to the sayings and actions of the Prophet Muhammad.
11 This information was communicated to me by the young women activists in charge of these events.
12 This is a complaint of Tarek Fatah, former president of the Muslim Canadian Congress, which opposes faith-based schools in Ontario. See http://www.muslim-canadiancongress.org/.
13 State reductions of expenditures on social services are also related to international pressure to liberalize economies under "structural adjustment plans" through the International Monetary Fund.

14 An example is the Free Medical Clinic in Santa Clara, California, run by the Muslim Community Association of the San Francisco Bay Area. Its mission is to provide "free, compassionate, quality health care to those who are in need and otherwise unable to access health services"; see http://www.mcabayarea.org/.

15 Khadija Haffajee, who became the first woman elected to the Islamic Society of North America's executive board, recalls that the first time she spoke at a Muslim community meeting, which was in Toronto in 1972, she faced a group of men leaving the auditorium proclaiming that her speaking publicly was "haram" (forbidden) (in Bullock 2005, 83).

16 In 2004 Yasmin Ratansi, from the Toronto riding of Don Valley East, became the first Muslim (Ismaili) woman elected to Parliament. As far as I am aware, only one provincial legislature has had a Muslim woman as a member, Fatima Houda-Pepin, elected in Quebec. In 2001 one Ismaili woman, Mobin Jaffer, was appointed to the federal Senate, a nonelected body in Canada (Bullock 2004).

17 Shaila Kibria, a young Muslim woman, who had been a Muslim and university-community activist for years, was a New Democratic Party candidate in the Ontario provincial election in October 2007. For her speech to accept the NDP nomination, she sported a bright pink hijab and peppered her acceptance with *insha'allah* [God willing]. Kibria followed in the footsteps of community activist Lila Fahlman, the founder of the Canadian Council of Muslim Women, the oldest Muslim women's organization in Canada, who was the first Muslim woman to run for office, seeking the NDP's Winnipeg nomination for the 1971 federal election (Fahlman 1999, 64). She was also preceded by activist Dr. Monia Mazigh, who after coming to prominence in Canada for her efforts to secure the release from Syrian jails of her husband Maher Arar, wrongfully deported by the United States to Syria while en route back to Canada, ran for the NDP in the riding of Ottawa South in the 2004 federal election.

18 In addition, as it is now seven years since they submitted their stories to me, they may no longer be active in the listed fields. The categories are based on their activism at a certain moment in time.

19 Dr. Ekram Beshir started out by volunteering at her children's school for field trips and giving talks to the classes about Ramadan. Later, she was teaching her own children Arabic and the Qur'an and decided to teach other people's children too. This led to her co-founding a weekend Islamic school in Ottawa. Years later, she began giving parenting workshops and then writing books about parenting, and she now teaches parenting at the Islamic American University in Detroit (Bullock 2005, 27-28).

REFERENCES

Abu-Laban, Y. 2002. Challenging the gendered vertical mosaic: Immigrants, ethnic minorities, gender and political participation. In J. Everitt and B. O'Neill, eds., *Citizen politics: Research and theory in Canadian political behaviour*, 268-82. Toronto, ON: Oxford University Press.

Agnew, Vijay. 1996. *Resisting Discrimination: Women from Asia, Africa and the Caribbean and the Women's Movement in Canada*. Toronto, ON: University of Toronto Press.

Ali, S. 2003. Building a women's movement. *Islamic Horizons*, May/June, 16-24.
Aly, H. 2010. Nazia Quazi case encourages Canadian Muslims to speak out. *Christian Science Monitor*, May 7. http://www.csmonitor.com/.
Bhabha, M. 2006. Cultivating civic sensibilities: An approach to enhancing civic education in Palestine. Report for the Teacher Creativity Center, Ramallah, and Oxfam-Quebec, Jerusalem.
Black, J.H. 2002. Representation in the Parliament of Canada: The case of ethno-racial minorities. In J. Everitt and B. O'Neill, eds., *Citizen politics: Research and theory in Canadian political behaviour*, 355-72. Toronto, ON: Oxford University Press.
Bullock, K. 2004. Women, gender and political participation and political parties: Canada. In S. Joseph, ed., *Encyclopedia of women and Islamic cultures*, vol. 2, 268-82. Leiden: Brill.
–, ed. 2005. *Muslim women activists in North America: Speaking for ourselves*. Austin, TX: University of Texas Press.
Eickelman, D.F., and J. Piscatori. 1996. *Muslim politics*. Princeton, NJ: Princeton University Press.
Fahlman, L. 1999. Lila. In S. Zaman, ed., *At my mother's feet: Stories of Muslim women*, 51-70. Kingston, ON: Quarry.
Gidengil, E., A. Blais, N. Nevitte, and R. Nadeau. 2004. *Citizens*. Vancouver, BC: UBC Press.
Haddad, Y.Y., J.I. Smith, and K.M. Moore. 2006. *Muslim women in America: The challenge of Islamic identity today*. New York, NY: Oxford University Press.
Hafez, M.M. 2003. *Why Muslims rebel: Repression and resistance in the Islamic world*. Boulder, CO: Lynne Rienner.
Hamdani, D. 2004. Muslim women: Beyond the perceptions: A demographic profile of Muslim women in Canada. http://www.ccmw.com/publications/Reports/Beyond_the_Perceptions.pdf.
Hamid, R. 2005. Rocking the boat and stirring the pot. In K. Bullock, ed., *Muslim women activists in North America: Speaking for ourselves*, 89-96. Austin, TX: University of Texas Press.
Kurzman, C. 2004. Conclusion: Social movement theory and Islamic studies. In Q. Wiktorowicz, ed., *Islamic activism: A social movement theory approach*, 289-304. Bloomington, IN: Indiana University Press.
Mandaville, P. 2007. *Global political Islam*. London, UK: Routledge.
Milton-Edwards, B. 2004. *Islam and politics in the contemporary world*. Cambridge, UK: Polity Press.
Newman, J., and L.A. White. 2006. *Women, politics, and public policy: The political struggles of Canadian women*. Toronto, ON: Oxford University Press.
Persad, J.V., and S. Lukas. 2002. No hijab is permitted here: A study on the experiences of Muslim women wearing hijab applying for work in the manufacturing, sales and service sectors. http://atwork.settlement.org/downloads/No_Hijab_Is_Permitted_Here.pdf.
Riley, D. 1990. *Am I that name? Feminism and the category of "women" in history*. Minneapolis, MN: University of Minnesota Press.

Said, E. 1981. *Covering Islam: How the media and the experts determine how we see the rest of the world.* New York, NY: Pantheon.

Shamma, F. 2005. Muslim activist: Mother and educator. In K. Bullock, ed., *Muslim women activists in North America: Speaking for ourselves,* 165-76. Austin, TX: University of Texas Press.

Wiktorowicz, Q., ed. 2004. *Islamic activism: A social movement theory approach.* Bloomington, IN: Indiana University Press.

Zaman, S., ed. 1999. *At my mother's feet: Stories of Muslim women.* Kingston, ON: Quarry.

PART 2

MEDIA AND REPRESENTATION

THE MEDIA play a powerful and persuasive role in narrating the nation and framing our view of the world. Media construct rather than reflect reality and do so within a framework of embedded interests and dominant ideals. In this section, the authors address the media representation of Muslims in Canada through various genres such as print media, books, and television. They analyze "insider" accounts by Muslims in memoir-style books such as *The Trouble with Islam Today* and *Their Jihad ... Not My Jihad!*, and the Canadian sitcom *Little Mosque on the Prairie,* as well as examining mainstream national print media's accounts of 9/11. Each chapter provides a unique and much needed inquiry into the political and cultural investments of these representational practices.

Focusing on the *National Post* and the *Globe and Mail,* Yasmin Jiwani paints a striking picture of media reporting of the 9/11 tragedy, revealing the reproduction of Orientalist tropes of fanatical and backward Muslims, and Meena Sharify-Funk examines the "Orientalism of Orientals" through the accounts of Muslim women "native informers" who have written "tell-all" books for popular readership that reveal their discontents with Islam and Muslim politics

PART 2 ... from an "insider" perspective. This genre of sensationalist dissident memoirs has gained widespread popularity in the West as native informers take curious Western readers "behind the veil" to examine the "truth" about Islam and Muslims, eschewing political correctness and "telling it like it is." Both the "outsider" mainstream media reporting as described by Jiwani and the "insider" dissent texts examined by Sharify-Funk purvey sensationalist accounts that reproduce Orientalist constructions and leave little room for counter-narratives to be introduced.

The chapter by Aliaa Dakroury examines the production of such counter-narratives, which aim to dismantle the negative stereotypes of Muslims that are prevalent in the media. Focusing on the Canadian comedy series *Little Mosque on the Prairie*, Dakroury examines the way this "home-grown" comedy creates a new discursive terrain within Canadian primetime television for the representation of Muslims not as terrorists or dangerous foreigners but as regular small-town folk living on the Prairies. Although critics of the series have argued that it also promotes particular stereotypes of Muslims as religiously overdetermined or too mosque-oriented, it has nonetheless garnered wide appeal and ratings. More important, this series, created and written by Zarqa Nawaz, a Muslim Canadian filmmaker, represents the space of an emergent Muslim counter-public. The contestations of static and negative representations of Muslims in mainstream corporate media have led to marginalized Muslim groups forming their own public spheres, where they become interlocutors within a subaltern counter-public. The chapters in this section not only provide insight into the various spaces that Muslims occupy within the broader public sphere with respect to the discursive practices of mainstream media and the rhetoric of Muslim native informers but also delve into the new Muslim counter-publics that provide generative spaces where narrow archetypes of Muslim identities can be challenged and new narratives of the nation can be imagined.

Colluding Hegemonies
Constructing the Muslim Other Post-9/11

YASMIN JIWANI

Colluding Hegemonies and Rude Awakenings: Canadian National Dailies Post-9/11

> *The latest "bad things," such as America's and Britain's bombing of civilian targets with cluster bombs, and use of napalm and depleted uranium, in Iraq and Afghanistan, are not reported as acts of rapacious conquest but as imperfect liberation, justified by the myths of the "good war" and the Cold War. The principal conveyer of these myths is that amorphous extension of the established order known as "the media." (Pilger 2006, x)*

In the above passage, Pilger argues that the media frame events to privilege particular interpretations that favour those in power. Thus what might be genocidal to other people in other lands becomes simply "bad" news to those who may be perpetrating these acts of war. However, what is not reported is also an issue worthy of consideration. Complete erasure of specific bodies – including, for example, Muslim victims of the "war on terror" – constitutes a form of "symbolic annihilation," to use a term coined by Gaye Tuchman (1978). In other words, what is outside the frame of a picture is just as relevant as what is within it; *who* tells the story matters as much as *how* the story is told. The ways that different bodies are represented communicate their position within the racialized hierarchies of power.

As bards of the nation (Hartley 1982), the dailies do more than tell stories: they define the stories of the day, they constitute an archival documentation of what is considered relevant, they lay bare the nuances in interpretation that are required of readers, and they offer explanatory frameworks identifying potential or actual solutions. Ideologically, they define the enemy and advocate to be taken seriously by the state and its accomplices in defusing, neutralizing, and annihilating a threat. They obtain consent and through a deployment of "common sense" produce an analysis that resonates with public understandings (Hall 1990). As Gitlin (1980, 2) has aptly put it, "the media specialize in orchestrating everyday consciousness ... They name the world's parts, they certify reality as reality."

"Islam in the hinterlands" is a marginalized phenomenon in the Canadian landscape, especially within its imagined community as reflected in the national dailies. In this chapter, I focus on the print media's coverage of the collapse of the Twin Towers in New York and the attack on the Pentagon on September 11, 2001 (a.k.a. 9/11), particularly that published in the *Globe and Mail* and the *National Post*. Each of these newspapers represents a particular slant on the world, yet, I argue, each reinforces a hegemonic view of social reality. In titling this chapter "Colluding Hegemonies and Rude Awakenings," I want to draw attention to this hegemonic affinity between the two dailies, both of which are viewed very differently by their respective audiences. At the same time, I want to underline that despite the seemingly apparent differences, the result is the same: both of these dailies represent a particular view of the nation, and within this shared framework Muslims remain on the margins as demonic, abject, threatening, and invasive Others belonging to the mysterious, fanatical, premodern, and somewhat ruthless Islamic faith. These newspapers thus reproduce Orientalism (Said 1978).

I begin with a discussion of the Canadian media monopoly in order to situate these two dailies. Thereafter, I analyze the frameworks that each used in organizing its coverage of 9/11 in the week immediately following the event. Subsequently, I discuss the commonalities and differences in the stories that were published, paying particular attention to how hegemonic interests were served by the media's daily output.

Media Concentration in the Hinterlands

Canada has one of the highest levels of media concentration in the world. Few independent newspapers exist, with most of the print media owned by a handful of conglomerates. Canwest Corporation, for example, owns most of the newspapers across the country, including the *National Post*, BCE Globe Media owns the *Globe and Mail*, and both own numerous television and radio stations (Shade 2006).[1] According to their respective websites, the *Globe* reaches 2,440,300 readers in an average week, whereas the *Post*'s readership is 1,507,800 within the same period. Politically, the former has been described as right of centre, whereas the latter has been regarded as even more conservatively inclined, representing the political right (Henry and Tator 2002).

Winter (1997) suggests that one outcome of such concentration is the homogeneity of media output. Journalists and editors are constrained by what they can write and often have to toe the line if they do not wish to be dismissed from their positions. Nevertheless, as the case of former *Post* reporter Patricia Pearson indicates, journalists often internalize the perspective of their employers through a gradual process (see also Hackett et al. 2000). Recounting her experience, Pearson (2003) states,

> It happened gradually, by increments and subtle turns. But being a liberal columnist at the *Post* grew increasingly unpleasant. A paper that started out as imaginative and vibrantly skeptical began sliding into orthodoxy. A kind of Political Correctness, so excoriated as a disease of the left, began to prevail. When CanWest, controlled by the Asper family, acquired the paper from Conrad Black, I no longer dared to express sympathy for Palestinians. When my editor, of whom I am fond, revealed a deep suspicion of environmentalism, I self-censored in favour of conviviality.

Interestingly, the Aspers, owners of the *Post*, have been critical of other media, accusing them of being anti-Israeli and pro-Palestinian (Block 2002). It is apparent that the lack of autonomous and independent media in the country limits the range of opinions that are available to the public. At the same time, the concentrated nature of media ownership imposes a high degree of corporate control of journalists. This control, combined with the power of advertisers to shape content, leads to a situation wherein mainstream media output utilizes similar frames and explanations despite the availability of numerous channels and publications (see Herman and Chomsky 2002). Such is apparently the case with these two Canadian dailies.

Categories – Organizing Ideology

Drawing from Antonio Gramsci, Hall (1979, 325-26) argues,

You cannot learn, through common sense, *how things are:* you can only discover *where they fit* into the existing scheme of things. In this way, its very taken-for-grantedness is what establishes it as a medium in which its own premises and presuppositions are being rendered invisible by its apparent transparency. (Emphasis in original)

In referring to the categories of thought and the organization of knowledge through which common sense makes itself apparent, Hall offers us a tool by which to decode the everyday stories circulated in the media. He draws attention to the categories that are imposed on social reality to make "sense" of events. At the same time, the particular kind of "sense" that is made reflects where these events fit and how they are interpreted vis-à-vis the "existing scheme" or the dominant ideology.

In his analysis of racist discourse in the press, van Dijk (1991) argues that headlines serve as cognitive organizers; they organize information, making it possible for audiences to apprehend immediately how such information should be read and remembered. Although the following categorical headings used in the *Globe* and the *National Post* (Table 4.1) grouped the actual headlines, they nevertheless served the same kind of ideological function: they organized the information so that the reader could anticipate what was to follow and how it should be read. The way that both of these dailies grouped their stories under these categorical headings is revealing insofar as it outlines the point of departure, or the perspective, from which the papers operated.

It is apparent that the *Post* adopted a more aggressive and direct approach than did the *Globe*. The latter presented its immediate coverage under the heading "Day of Infamy," thereby invoking parallels with Pearl

TABLE 4.1

Thematic categories used in the *Globe and Mail* and the *National Post*

Date	Globe and Mail	National Post
September 12	Day of Infamy	US under Attack
September 13	The Day After	Attack Aftermath
September 14	The Aftermath	Day of Mourning
September 15	The Aftermath	Honouring the Dead
September 17	The Brink of War	Preparing for War

Harbor (an event that signalled the first time the United States was attacked on American soil). The *Post*'s approach in defining the event as "US under Attack" immediately invoked among Canadian audiences a sense of their proximity to the United States and, hence, their potential and immediate endangerment. This approach is also apparent in the *Post*'s heading "Preparing for War," as compared to the *Globe*'s "The Brink of War," both of which focused on the impending US invasion of Afghanistan.

A more detailed breakdown of the stories that were published by each newspaper on September 12, 2001, is similarly revealing (Table 4.2).

Once again, these headlines reveal how the *Globe*'s approach tended to centre on a more emotive, empathetic response. It focused on the US reaction, publishing the entire text of President George W. Bush's speech and providing wide and intensive coverage of the human suffering and physical

TABLE 4.2

Comparison of headlines in the *Globe and Mail* and the *National Post*

Globe and Mail	National Post
Day of Infamy: US will never be the same	US under Attack: World Trade Centre collapse
Day of Infamy: US reaction: Text of president's national address	US under Attack: Reaction in Toronto (2 articles)
Day of Infamy: Wall Street in ruins	US under Attack: Sports and entertainment reaction: In Toronto
Day of Infamy: New York	
Day of Infamy: Canada: Apocalypse now	US under Attack: World reaction: Allies in Toronto, in London
Day of Infamy: Eye witness	US under Attack: Canadians in disbelief, fear
Day of Infamy: Celebrating the misery of "the head of the snake"	US under Attack: Scenes from Ground Zero
Day of Infamy: Communicating horror	US under Attack: World reaction
Column: We are at war, by Thomas Axworthy	US under Attack: Air traffic: Tarmacs clogged: In Toronto, in Vancouver
	Special Report: The suspects (2 articles)
	Special Report: The victims (2 articles)

damage in New York. By contrast, the *Post* emphasized the structural dimensions of the tragedy, reactions from within Toronto, and international reactions. It also privileged stories that underlined Canadian security issues and threats to safety. Both newspapers provided coverage on the innocent dead, weeping women, and heroic men, with the latter receiving extra attention. These men included firefighters and police officers as well as ordinary citizens and denizens of the business district and its surrounding environment.

In the following sections, I detail the commonalities and differences in these stories. As will be apparent, whereas the *Globe* offered a more nuanced analysis, albeit pro-American and pro-Israeli, the *Post*'s articulation of these allegiances was more explicit.

Commonalities and Differences

Both newspapers employed the familiar binaries: modernity versus traditionalism, reason versus emotion, order versus disorder or chaos, and civilization versus barbarism. For example, in her column on September 13, 2001, the *Globe*'s Margaret Wente reiterated these same binaries: "The only border that matters now is the one between our world and the killers' world, the one that separates the rule of law from the rule of blood revenge and sacred jihad. The one that separates a tolerant and peaceable society from one that advocates mass slaughter." The *National Post*, meanwhile, published a chronology detailing all the terrorist incidents that had occurred between 1983 and 2001 (Brean 2001). The chronology included a large number of Muslim names.

Where the *Globe* differed from the *Post* was in its greater reliance on historical and literary tropes to invoke these binaries. This often involved the use of expert voices whose quotations selectively encapsulated the kind of analysis that the columnist/reporter wished to make.[2] For example, the day after the tragedy, the *Globe* ran a column by Marcus Gee referencing Palestinians as celebrating the attacks in New York and Washington. Gee (2001) quoted Yitzhak Sokoloff, an Israeli political analyst, as stating, "We're dealing with a culture that celebrates martyrdom and exults in the death of its perceived enemies." Here, the attribution to a cultural framework was privileged: they are barbaric because of their culture/religion. By comparison, a column referencing the same celebration among the Palestinians by the *Post*'s Mark Steyn (2001) began with the following: "You can understand why they're jumping up and down in the streets of Lebanon and Palestine, jubilant in their victory. They have struck a mighty blow against the Great Satan, mightier than even the producers of far-fetched action thrillers could conceive." Featured on the *Post*'s front page, the column went on to justify and legitimize US imperialism. "They" were celebrating because they had won. Steyn did not consider the terrorists "cowards"; rather, they were "mad." While condemning the Americans for being complacent, Steyn also drew on author Niall Ferguson's book *The Cash Nexus* to argue for imperialism as a form of humanitarianism. Unlike Gee, however, Steyn (2001) did not mince words but was clearly on the side of the United States: "After yesterday America is entitled to ask its allies not for finely crafted U.N. resolutions but a more basic question: Whose side are you on?"

This kind of explicit support for the United States, combined with aggressive, pro-war sentiment, came through most clearly in the newspapers' respective editorials. The *Post*'s editorial, printed on September 13, 2001, was titled "Infiltrate Them." Conversely, the *Globe*'s, published on the same day, was titled "The Battle of Ideas." The former editorial began with the following statement: "US President George W. Bush and his government appear, rightly, to be treating the attacks on the World Trade Center and the Pentagon as a de facto declaration of war by a geographically disembodied but utterly determined enemy force." It ended with this call: "The United States and other Western nations must learn from the Israelis. Terrorism has been a daily fact of life in that country since its birth, and so the country has developed a deep and ruthlessly effective intelligence apparatus that includes professional spies and a network of paid collaborators." It is apparent that the *Post* embraced the perspective of the US government in framing the attack as a call to war. Similarly, the *Post*'s referencing of Israel indicated its admiration of the latter's intelligence apparatus. In contrast, the *Globe* editorial took a more liberal approach, relying on reasoned notions of the Other and a respect for universal values. After first listing the litany of complaints normally lodged against the West, the editor argued that "the values that are known as Western – democracy, freedom, individual liberty – are valid and sacred, not just for those who live in the West but for the rest of the world, too. These values are universal and, by rights, they should apply to every man and woman on Earth."

Thus, in a classic distancing move that invoked the moral high ground and implied that, no matter what, attacks against US actions were unconscionable, the *Globe*'s editors reasoned that

> whatever the sins and mistakes of the United States and its allies, terrorism is not our fault. It does not spring from Western oppression, and it is not justified by Western misdeeds. Because the United States bombed

Cambodia in the 1970s or bombed Kosovo in 1999 does not make it all right to bomb the World Trade Center in return. Two wrongs do not make a right. No grievance, however deep, can excuse a resort to the deliberate slaughter of innocent people. ("Battle of Ideas" 2001)

Again, the contrast between these two editorials, published on the same day, reflected the dominant differences between the papers. Although both embraced a pro-American and pro-Israeli position, they nonetheless differed in their approach: one advocated a "soft" approach through persuasion and moral reasoning; the other encouraged the use of brute force. Nowhere was this more clearly enunciated than in a column in the *Post* by Coyne (2001). Critiquing an article written by Rick Salutin in the *Globe,* which argued for Israel's withdrawal from the West Bank, Coyne asserted,

If we are to preserve ourselves from annihilation, we cannot be confined by the usual rules of evidence. Neither can we wait until after the "crime" has been committed: The scale of the threat is too great. That doesn't mean we dispense with all constitutional safeguards, or give our governments carte blanche for a "dirty war." But it does mean we will have to take much sterner measures – and much greater risks – than we would have been prepared to take prior to September 11. I don't mean longer waits at the airport. I mean killing people, and accepting that some of our own people will be killed.

This blatant call to arms and violence represented the tenor of the *Post's* coverage, in that throughout the week following the events of 9/11, the justification for war was ever present. To its credit, the *Globe* did attempt to stir some discussion and debate – albeit debate that was clearly limited within the circumscribed boundaries of being supportive of the US position and of Israel. That said, there was clearly as much "warmongering" in the *Globe* as in the *Post*. Norman Spector (2001b), a one-time Canadian ambassador to Israel, argued in his *Globe* column that "democratic societies have fought and won wars in the past, often at great cost and using horrific means. In our triumph over Nazism, we did not shy away from bombing Dresden. We used nuclear weapons in bringing Japan to heel." Although both papers were critical of the Canadian government's stance and lack of immediate assistance, the *Post* clearly condemned Canada for being a weak ally of the United States. In an editorial titled "Bashing Our Friend" (2001), the *Post* complained that anti-American sentiments were prevalent throughout Canadian history and especially among the literati in more contemporary times, providing as evidence Margaret Atwood's 1987 submission to a parliamentary committee on free trade:

> Canada as a separate but dominated country has done about as well under the United States as women, worldwide, have done under men; about the only position they've ever adopted toward us, country to country, has been the missionary position, and we were not on the top. I guess that's why the national wisdom vis [sic] Them has so often taken the form of lying still, keeping your mouth shut and pretending you like it.

The interesting aspect of this coverage is that it immediately invokes the metonym of gendered subordination. We – meaning Canadians – are weak and feminine. The United States, by contrast, is the stronger, masculine power. In an effort to rid "ourselves" of this feminine weakness and make ourselves worthy allies, we, according to the *Post*, needed to be stronger, more assertive, and more masculine. The *Post*, it seems, shared the US proclivity toward and manifestation of hypermasculinity – the "Rambo" style, as Mann (2006, 159-60) has described it.[3]

Gendered Coverage

The coverage afforded to Palestinians presumably celebrating the US tragedy en masse was circulated repeatedly in both newspapers being discussed here. In fact, it became a point of departure for several other columns printed in the days following 9/11. In the *Post*, for example, the first mention of the incident included a description of women dancing in the streets: "In Nablus, a town in the West Bank, 3,000 people poured into the streets, including a 48-year-old woman in a long, black dress who cried out in happiness: 'America is the head of the snake, America always stands by Israel in its war against us'" (Jimenez 2001). Likewise, Gee (2001) used the same description in his article published in the *Globe* on the very same day. However, unlike Jimenez in her description, Gee not only named the woman (Nawal Abdel-Fatah) but also sourced her quotation, noting that it was an opinion accessed by a reporter from the Associated Press newswire service (see also Adams 2001). Again, these differences are illustrative of stylistic differences in the two newspapers. Yet both tell the same story.

The theme of jubilant Palestinians acquired yet another textual layer in Spector's (2001b) column in the *Globe*. Drawing parallels to the terror experienced by Israelis on a daily basis, the former Canadian ambassador to Israel wrote, "Then came statements by foreign leaders, including Yasser Arafat, who condemned 'all attacks against civilians,' while Palestinian men and children danced in the streets to the sounds of ululating women." The dancing men and "ululating" women constituted the heartless Palestinians. Although Spector (2001b) used the term "ululating," it seems that he was not quite aware of the meaning of the term. "Ululating" refers to "howling or shrieking" in grief: consequently, if the women really were ululating, then they were clearly reflecting their sense of grief. Yet this is not how it was framed or understood.

More to the point, representations of dancing men and of jubilant and "ululating" women contrasted sharply with those of innocent victims buried in the rubble of the Twin Towers or women who lost their husbands, brothers, fathers, and friends when the towers collapsed. These latter women's stories peppered the accounts presented in both newspapers, most especially in the *Globe* (see York 2001). Commenting on the pervasiveness of these portrayals, Rodgers (2003, 207) observes, "pictures of stunned, weeping women on the streets close to the site were circulated worldwide, one of which was used by the *New York Times* no less than three times over a two week period." In the *Globe* and the *Post*, numerous stories focused on the grief, mourning, and despair of the women who witnessed the event or were direct victims of it. Simultaneously, an equally high number of stories focused on heroic men.

Moreover, against the foil of the abject Afghan female victim fleeing war and famine, the heartless Palestinians, as well as other Muslims, came to represent the "darker" side of the Other world. Once rescued by the West, they would prove themselves to be innocent victims; but ensconced within their own worlds, left alone to defend it, they were otherwise considered to be militant and ruthless. What is most interesting about these representations is that the stories in which they were framed barely, if ever, interrogated the context in which these women lived – their realities and truths; instead, positioning the terrorists as resentful of Israel's success and its US support, anti-modern, and "jealous" of the West and its material wealth, these news accounts, by and large, dismissed any notion of Western involvement and culpability in this situation. Thus any dissenting opinion or perspective was immediately branded as treasonous, if not condemned outright. Even the UK news media were castigated as ignorant when one British media outlet critiqued US foreign policy. The *Post* was most ferocious in its attack on dissent (e.g., see Richler 2001).[4]

Representations of "heartless" Palestinian women also threw into sharp relief the passive, victimized status of Muslim women in North America who were fearful of harassment and told to remain in their homes. Both papers featured articles on the backlash against Muslims, particularly Muslim women. However, an approximate count of Muslim women's voices that were featured in stories printed in the week after 9/11 reveals that the numbers for both the *Post* and the *Globe* are identical: both papers quoted or cited eight Muslim women. By contrast, the *Post* quoted the voices of eighteen Muslim men, with another mentioned in passing, whereas the *Globe* quoted twenty. However, when compared with the male voices, most of the female sources are revealed to be unnamed. In the *Globe*, five women were named and three were unnamed, whereas in the *Post*, four were named and the other four were unnamed. Of the male voices that were directly named, most belonged to leaders of nations and well-known mullahs or imams. Conversely, of the women quoted, not one occupied such an elite position. Rather, the majority were women victims – either fleeing refugees or frightened Muslim women living in the West.

It is noteworthy that neither of the newspapers featured full articles on Muslim women living in the West given that, as the coverage indicated, these women were experiencing the brunt of the backlash violence. Indeed, the *Post* and the *Globe* reported only on a news release issued by major Muslim organizations in Canada and the United States cautioning Muslim women to remain at home (Chipman and Schmidt 2001, Lewington and Peritz 2001, Mitchell et al. 2001, Read 2001). This is somewhat ironic given that the Taliban decreed the very same thing, also under the guise of protecting women. Yet, interestingly, whereas the *Globe* made much of the connection between the Taliban/Islam and women's oppression, the *Post* did not. Similarly, whereas the former focused on Afghan women refugees fleeing war-torn Afghanistan, the latter, in that first week, barely made any mention of the ground-level impact of the war, concentrating instead on "Ground Zero" in New York.

In their analysis of American media coverage of the war in Afghanistan, Stabile and Kumar (2005, 770) highlight the play of a "protection scenario" within which "women, like the penetrable, feminized territory of the nation-state, must be protected from the predatory advances of some real or imaginary enemy." Whereas the *Globe* sought to follow its American counterparts in constructing Afghan women as helpless maidens in need of rescue by the West's chivalrous knights (Jiwani 2009), the *Post*, in this period of analysis, turned its attention toward protecting Canada's own female population –

making much of the necessity to act in a defensive posture and legitimizing the war.[5]

Canadian and American women, unidentified by race or religion, were amply covered by both papers, yet the lens through which these women were articulated or framed tended to be one of sorrow and, often, benevolence. There were numerous stories in both papers about Canadian women taking the initiative in organizing memorials, sending donations, giving blood, or investing in a flagging US stock market. When US airplanes were grounded at various Canadian airports, stories recounted how the local populations in these areas – especially the women – rose to the challenge and demonstrated Canadian hospitality. Those businesses that sought to profit from the stranded travellers were reprimanded. Canadian benevolence thus shone through the debris and aftermath of the events of 9/11.

Whereas Muslim women remained largely in the background or were portrayed as abject victims and ululating celebrants, Muslim men fared even worse. Wente (2001a) penned the following on the day after 9/11:

> Those who are responsible are most likely men from remote desert lands. Men from ancient tribal cultures built on blood and revenge. Men whose unshakable beliefs and implacable hatreds go back many centuries farther than the United States and its young ideas of democracy, pluralism and freedom.
>
> Hard men, who hide out in desert bunkers and turn the instruments of Western technology – its computers and CD-ROMs and videotapes and airplanes – against the West. Men capable of flying Boeing 747s with pinpoint, deadly accuracy, and of giving up their lives for the greater glory of Allah, and of murder on a massive scale.

Muslim leaders quoted in the various articles were often presented as misleading the public or being insincere in their expressions of condolences to the United States. Similarly, those who had committed the attacks were represented not as "mad" but as dangerous and irrational. They were portrayed as fanatics who could and did assume appearances of normalcy but who underneath fostered an intense hatred of the West and its "universal" values. Thus the shadow of suspicion was cast on all those who appeared to be Muslims.

Whereas Muslims outside of North America were portrayed as traditional, polygamous, and hard men, those in North America were portrayed as either timid or "sleepers." For instance, in a column for the *Post*, Goldberg (2001) described Sami ul-Haq, who oversaw a *madrassa* (religious school) in the Northwest Province of Pakistan, as a man in his mid-sixties who had "two wives and eight children." Goldberg went on to recount his introductory exchange with Haq: "'The problem,' [Haq] said through an interpreter, 'is not between us Muslims and Christians. The only enemy Islam and Christianity have is the Jews. It was the Jews who crucified Christ, you know. The Jews are using America to fight Islam.'" At this point, Goldberg identified himself as Jewish. The rest of the article painted a picture of the students at the *madrassa* as unable to listen to reason or argue with reason. Rather, these students kept following Goldberg around, chanting "Osama," and pretending to shoot him with their toys. Goldberg concluded that this *madrassa* was a "jihad factory." There was scarcely any context provided in terms of the rates of poverty in Afghanistan and the lack of food, shelter, and resources for those orphaned through violence, abandoned by their families, or rendered destitute and disabled in the preceding wars, nor was there any mention of who funds these *madrassas* and why poverty-stricken parents leave their children there.

Osama

Suspicion on Osama bin Laden as the figure behind the attacks first surfaced on September 13, 2001, following Bush's speech naming al-Qaeda as the source of the attacks. The *Globe* featured a rare article on "blowback," identifying the al-Qaeda network, stating the grievances that fuelled it, and quoting extracts from previous media interviews with bin Laden. In this report, Knox (2001) also included a quotation from an interview with Taliban foreign minister Wakil Ahmed Mutawakkil: "Osama bin laden has been hated because he is accused of killing innocent people. But what can you say then about the firing of cruise missiles at innocent people in Afghanistan?" However, despite this tantalizing lead, which could have taken the story elsewhere, Knox resorted to offering a more psychological portrayal of bin Laden as being a former heavy drinker and womanizer who had become a purist and fanatic. Knox also neglected to elaborate on the fact that bin Laden and his associates "were supported, funded, trained, and armed by the CIA and several US administrations" (Kellner 2003, 30) and that there were close ties between bin Laden's and Bush's families.

The *Post*'s coverage, on the other hand, took a more colonial tone. Titled "In the Lair of the Terrorist: Hero of Radical Islam," Vincent's (2001) article mentioned the CIA connection. However, in profiling bin Laden, her descriptions deteriorated into a construction of him as a strange combination of traditional patriarch, millionaire, and high-tech savant. He was sinister yet a genius, and he was animal-like in that he lived in a lair, as the following description suggested:

> He lives in a cave, surrounded by high-tech surveillance equipment, and only travels under cover of darkness, in a convoy of 20 black four-wheel drive vehicles with tinted windows. His main security guard is his teenage son, who learned to handle a Kalashnikov assault rifle at the age of 14 to protect his father ...
>
> Bin Laden's main source of protection comes from the Pushtunwali – the dominant code of behaviour of the Pushtun tribes of Pakistan and Afghanistan, largely practised by the ruling Taleban [sic] authorities who control most of Afghanistan and harbour bin Laden ...
>
> Two years ago, in order to ensure the Taleban's complete and utter co-operation, bin Laden married his oldest daughter to Mullah Mohammad Omar, the Taleban's leader. He also took a young Pushtun woman as his fourth wife.

The exchange of women, then, enabled bin Laden's protection under the Pushtuns, the dominant ethnic group in Afghanistan. Reference to the Pushtunwali code invokes notions of a patriarchal, tradition-bound, primitive, and nomadic culture, all of which should raise the question: What does Islam have to do with this? Yet Vincent failed to answer this question. Rather, her construction of bin Laden resonates with what Winch (2005) has described regarding the international media's fascination with him. Winch suggests that the obsession with bin Laden as an "evil genius" has to do with the necessity of constructing an opponent worthy of war. In other words, one needs to have a formidable enemy in order to justify an invasion or an extreme use of force. Furthermore, the construction of the opponent as such serves to pre-empt failure – it explains why the US forces could not find him or quell his movement. Either way, the construction of bin Laden in the above terms reinforces Orientalist notions of Muslim men.

Backlash – Legitimizing Violence

Although both the *Post* and the *Globe* carried stories about the backlash against Muslims, it is the contextualization of this violence that is most interesting. The latter carried five stories and an editorial focusing on the backlash against Muslims and other people of colour in Canada and the United States. The *Post*, meanwhile, carried six stories that referenced the backlash against Muslims; two of these were specific to the Toronto edition of the paper, and two others bore no quotations from or interviews with Muslims.

To its credit, the *Globe* issued an editorial condemning the backlash; however, it did so by suggesting that this was not an appropriate response given that "the terrorists who died in Tuesday's suicide attacks would undoubtedly cheer a misguided retaliation against Muslims in North America" ("What We Stand For" 2001). Thus the motive for this editorial was not really the protection of fellow Canadians but the perceived need to raise fears that those targeted might become future recruits of al-Qaeda. Louw (2003) makes a similar argument in his analysis of the mediated terrorism of 9/11, arguing that al-Qaeda was well aware of how Muslim minorities in the West might be treated following such an event and therefore sought to capitalize on this.

A more troubling aspect of the backlash coverage was that it was consistently twinned with expressions of racism. Such expressions were, notably, used as evidence to document the reality of the backlash. Nonetheless, the coverage afforded to racist statements made them seem like rationalized responses of outrage, as evidenced by the following example:

> For some, shock had changed into anger about as fast as the ambulances and police cars racing down Seventh Avenue. "Any form of warfare will be acceptable after this," seethed Sarah Allender, a college student majoring in politics. "I understand that violence begets violence, but we should do what we did the last time people attacked our land: Drop a nuclear bomb. That would be the ultimate message." (Wallis 2001)

The *Globe* employed a similar strategy. For instance, a column by Saunders (2001) featured one American woman's reaction: "'With the shock over, I just feel angry,' said Becky Direly, 17, of Stoystown, PA. Like many locals, she said her country's attitude to the rest of the world has cooled. 'We go opening doors to every country. That ain't gonna happen any more.'" Yet both papers were careful to differentiate between "good" and "bad" Muslims. One difference that emerged appeared in the *Post*'s local Toronto edition. Although both the national and Toronto editions reported on the backlash, the latter framed its coverage in a more sensitive and inclusive manner, with the reporter actually going to a mosque and talking to local Muslims and their neighbours. In his article titled "Another Type of Terrorism: Ignorance," Fiorito (2001a) included the voices of several Muslim men, such as Amjed Syed, the administrator of the local mosque: "We are concerned but not afraid. You can't live in fear. That's what we came here to get away from. By and large, Canadian people are law-abiding. But we are all blamed for the act of one. We find this hard to swallow." Another Muslim interviewed, Mahmoud Ahmed, said, "I prayed for those people, absolutely. I am Muslim. Islam means peace. I don't accept terrorism." The difference here lies not only in the voices of those interviewed but also in what they said. Unlike many other reports of backlash, the men did not express mere fear and timidity; they expressed compassion and courage.

This difference in approach suggests that national dailies such as the *Globe* and the *Post* could, if they were committed enough, exercise responsible journalistic practices by presenting a more humane portrayal of Muslims. Nevertheless, it should be noted that Fiorti's column ran only in Toronto and, moreover, as with the *Globe*'s pleading editorial, that the explanation offered with regard to the backlash was one grounded in a notion of "ignorance." This is the same argument that Elmasry (2001) put forward in his article – the only one written by a Muslim – in the *Globe*. Printed in the Facts and Arguments section, Elmasry's article went on to describe those who committed the deeds in New York as not representing the true essence of Islam; in other words, they were "bad" Muslims. Again, he rested his case on the idea that the terrorists were ignorant. What is problematic in this and in Fiorti's article is the issue of ignorance; this reasoning suggested that the panacea for the backlash was education. If ignorance were indeed the "root" cause of terrorism and violence, then widespread education would be the correcting agent. However, Timothy McVeigh, who bombed the Murrah Federal Building in Oklahoma City in 1995, was never regarded as a "bad" white person in contrast to other "good" white people (Volpp, in Bahdi 2003, 312), nor were his actions attributed to ignorance, which could then be treated with a requisite amount of education. Mamdani (2004, 24) observes that "good Muslims are modern, secular, and Westernized, but bad Muslims are doctrinal, antimodern, and virulent."

Distancing oneself from the actions of these Others, then, constitutes evidence of being "good" Muslims. Thus it is not surprising to observe that the few articles accessing Muslim voices tended to position those living in the West as differentiating themselves from Other Muslims who lived in other parts of the world and who had undertaken these grievous actions.

This strategy also became a ploy by which columnists and reporters could demonstrate their credentials as non-Islamophobic and liberal. Witness, for example, this insertion in a column by Wente (2001b): "Then I had another call, from a woman I didn't know. 'My name is Shima,' she said. 'I am a Muslim who lives here in Canada. Please let your readers know that we are as disgusted and horrified as everyone else and we want these animals brought to justice.'" This kind of token inclusion provided the dailies with "proof" that they did include the views of Muslims and, moreover, that their reporters and columnists were unbiased.

On Islam

Echoing the various attempts by US president George W. Bush and Canadian prime minister Jean Chrétien to stem the tide of Islamophobia after 9/11, national dailies like the *Globe* and the *Post* offered in-depth analyses of contemporary Islam. The *Post*, for example, ran an article by Rose (2001) that ruptured the notion of a monolithic Islam. However, not only did Rose quote as an expert on Islam, Daniel Pipes, founder of CampusWatch, a website that encourages students to report on pro-Palestinian professors, but he also fell into the trap of dichotomizing the Muslim world as being populated by "bad" and "good" Muslims. As he put it,

> It is often overlooked in the West, but in the Middle East true Muslims loathe the fanatical Islamists who seek to overturn governments and destroy opposition to their fantasies. They look with horror on the Algerian civil war between Islamists and the secular government, which has killed more than 70,000 people since 1992. There are numerous instances there of Islamists mass machine-gunning fellow Muslims. The dreadful examples where Islamists have seized control of government – namely, Sudan, Afghanistan and Iran – present terrifying visions of the future for true Muslims.

There was no interrogation of why these movements had emerged, what they offered to their potential followers, and what grievances they sought to address. Similarly, and more pointedly, there was no examination of the structural conditions that might have favoured the rise of these movements.

What is even more damaging is that Rose's article was accompanied by a picture of the celebrating Palestinian women. Hence, despite any attempt to show the differences between Muslims and their diverse interpretations of Islam, the viewpoint privileged was that of an irrational and fanatical faith whose followers were intent on revenge. In the *Globe*, Elmasry's (2001) article, along with the others discussed here, offered more nuanced interpretations of Islam, yet even so, the overshadowing archetype of Osama bin Laden and his nebulous and insidious al-Qaeda network served to clinch the preferred framework of meaning. Although some voices in both papers mentioned Timothy McVeigh and other kinds of fundamentalism, there was in that first week rarely, if ever, any acknowledgment that Christians would not be tarred in the same way if the Vatican were supportive of wars, nor would the conflict in Ireland have been construed in the same terms – as a fundamentalist Christianity wanting to subsume a moderate and reasoned interpretation of the faith or to terrorize peaceful Christians. Instead, the only parallel to emerge was the continual reference to Israel. Israel represented the nation under siege, and hence America, in being attacked, was akin to Israel and so needed to adopt the latter's stringent security measures. In his *Post* column, Philps (2001) quoted Ehud Sprinzak, an Israeli counterterrorism expert: "The pictures [of 9/11] are terrible, but better than 1,000 ambassadors trying to explain how dangerous Islamic terror is." Israeli actions and retaliatory measures, then, had been naturalized as appropriate responses to the threat of terror.

Conclusion

Among the general public, there is a sense that Canadian dailies offer a range of political perspectives and interpretations. Common "sense" suggests that the *Globe* is more centrist and the *Post* more conservative. However, this analysis suggests otherwise. It appears that both dailies have reproduced Orientalist thought and frameworks of meaning. Further, both have engaged in warmongering, giving expression to racist and vengeful sentiments, while at the same time highlighting the backlash against Muslims. Yet, based on the textual analysis of the week's coverage in both dailies, it appears that the *Globe* employed a "softer" approach, grounded in an appeal to reason and universal values. The *Post*, in contrast, took a more hardline approach, openly justifying the need for war and chastising the Canadian government for not immediately joining the United States in its effort to mobilize an intervention in Afghanistan.

What is more interesting is how both papers failed to provide any insightful analysis of the conditions contributing to the rise of fundamentalism or to the importation of particular interpretations of Islam. In this regard, the connection between the Bush family and the Saudis and their joint business affairs were not interrogated by either newspaper. Similarly, there was no real analysis of the US involvement in fomenting and fostering the emergence of groups such as al-Qaeda. Support for Israel was also not scrutinized, nor were Israeli actions against Palestinians examined in a critical fashion. Rather, the picture of those celebrating alongside the "ululating" women served only to underscore a negative representation of Muslims, Palestinian or otherwise.

It is noteworthy that, despite stories of intense and violent backlash, there was little outrage. At the same time, neither of the newspapers suggested that the Canadian government undertake more stringent actions to stop the violence. Instead, Muslims were left on the margins, as poor victims of an unprecedented – but "justified" – wave of anger. It was not until September 17, 2001, that the *Post* even mentioned the nationalities of the non-Americans who had died in New York ("Victims Were from All Over the World" 2001).

Colluding hegemonies make for rude awakenings. They indicate that there are few options in the public sphere not dominated by the mainstream media. However, the hope is that those in the vibrant communities that exist on the margins can foster their own media and encourage alternative voices and visions among themselves.

ACKNOWLEDGMENTS
The research presented in this chapter was made possible by funding from the Social Sciences and Humanities Research Council of Canada. I wish to acknowledge Alan Wong, Kenza Oumlil, and Meg Leitold for their research assistance.

NOTES
1 In an article published on the Fairness and Accuracy in Reporting (FAIR) website, Canadian scholar James Winter (2002) outlines the extent of the media monopoly: "The telephone company Bell Canada owns the *Globe and Mail* as well as CTV, the largest private television network; it also controls Sympatico, a Web portal and high-speed Internet link. Montréal-based Québecor owns the *Sun* newspaper chain, magazines, cable T.V., the Canoe Internet portal, music and video stores and the private TVA network in Québec. Torstar Corporation, publisher of Harlequin romance novels, also owns the *Toronto Star*, Canada's largest circulation daily, as well as four other dailies and 69 weeklies. Rogers Communications has interests in cable, radio, television, magazines, video stores and wireless telephone."
2 I am not drawing any distinction between journalistic accounts as "hard news" and columns as "soft stories" or "soft news." Both of these types of content (hard and soft) – "chronicles" and "stories," to use Bird and Dardenne's (1988) terms – constitute the mythic nature of news. Both communicate the myths of the nation (Lule 2002).

3 Agathangelou and Ling (2004, 519) argue that such hypermasculinity is reflective of a "reactionary stance. It arises when agents of hegemonic masculinity feel threatened or undermined, thereby needing to inflate, exaggerate, or otherwise distort their traditional masculinity."
4 This trend continued and escalated to a point of "war frenzy," as Thobani (2003) has described. Attacked for her opposition to the war, Thobani was held up as the sign of the ungrateful immigrant Other who, according to some media commentators, needed to be "sent back" (see also Jiwani 2006).
5 Undoubtedly, the *National Post*'s coverage changed after November 17, 2001, when First Lady Laura Bush and the British prime minister's wife, Cherie Blair, made their pleas for continued support for the Afghan war in the name of rescuing Afghan women (see Russo 2006).

REFERENCES

Adams, P. 2001. The aftermath: The world reacts: Palestinians massage their message. *Globe and Mail,* September 14, A17.

Agathangelou, A.M., and L.H.M. Ling. 2004. Power, borders, security, wealth: Lessons of violence and desire from September 11. *International Studies Quarterly* 48, 3: 517-38.

Bahdi, R. 2003. No exit: Racial profiling and Canada's war against terrorism. *Osgoode Hall Law Journal* 41, 2-3: 293-316.

Bashing our friend. 2001. Editorial. *National Post,* September 15, A17.

The battle of ideas. 2001. Editorial. *Globe and Mail,* September 13, A18.

Bird, E.S., and R.W. Dardenne. 1988. Myth, chronicle, and story: Exploring the narrative qualities of news. In J. Carey, ed., *Mass communication as culture: Myth and narrative in television and the press,* 67-87. Beverly Hills, CA: Sage.

Block, I. 2002. CanWest chief attacks "cancer" in the media. *Montreal Gazette,* October 31, A3.

Brean, J. 2001. Terrorist attacks, 1983-2001. *National Post,* September 12, D4.

Chipman, J., and S. Schmidt. 2001. Arab-Canadians feel wrath of their fellow citizens. *National Post,* September 14, A8.

Coyne, A. 2001. Mortal threats and moral options. *National Post,* September 17, A14.

Elmasry, M. 2001. Neighbours as collateral damage. *Globe and Mail,* September 14, A26.

Fiorito, J. 2001a. Another type of terrorism: Ignorance. *National Post,* September 13, A22.

–. 2001b. Neighbours try to build bridges with local mosque. *National Post,* September 17, A17.

Francis, D. 2001. We must hunt and eliminate these monsters: America falls victim to vicious attack over ideology. *National Post,* September 15, C3.

Gee, M. 2001. Celebrating the misery of "the head of the snake." *Globe and Mail,* September 12, N8.

Gitlin, T. 1980. *The whole world is watching: Mass media in the making and unmaking of the new left.* Berkeley, CA: University of California Press.

Goldberg, J. 2001. Hitting the books at Jihad U. *National Post,* September 13, A20.
Hackett, R.A., R. Gruneau, D. Gutstein, T.A. Gibson, and News Watch Canada. 2000. *The missing news: Filters and blind spots in Canada's press.* Ottawa, ON: Canadian Centre for Policy Alternatives and Garamond Press.
Hall, S. 1979. Culture, the media and the "ideological effect." In J. Curran, M. Gurevitch, and J. Woollacott, eds., *Mass communication and society,* 315-48. London, UK: Edward Arnold in association with Open University Press.
–. 1990. The whites of their eyes: Racist ideologies and the media. In M. Alvarado and J.O. Thompson, eds., *The media reader,* 7-23. London, UK: British Film Institute.
Hartley, J. 1982. *Understanding News.* London and New York: Methuen.
Henry, F., and C. Tator. 2002. *Discourses of domination: Racial bias in the Canadian English-language press.* Toronto, ON: University of Toronto Press.
Herman, E.S., and N. Chomsky. 2002. *Manufacturing consent: The political economy of the mass media.* Toronto, ON: Pantheon and Random House.
Infiltrate them. 2001. Editorial. *National Post,* September 13, A19.
Jimenez, M. 2001. Many Arabs celebrate: Leaders decry attack: "Bull's eye." *National Post,* September 12, A6.
Jiwani, Y. 2006. *Discourses of denial: Mediations of race, gender, and violence.* Vancouver, BC: UBC Press.
–. 2009. Covering Canada's role in the "war on terror." In L. Trimble and S. Sampart, eds., *Covering Canada,* 294-316. Toronto, ON: Pearson.
Kellner, D. 2003. *From 9/11 to terror war: The dangers of the Bush legacy.* Lanham, MD: Rowman and Littlefield.
Knox, P. 2001. The day after. *Globe and Mail,* September 13, A3.
Lewington, J., and I. Peritz. 2001. The aftermath: Day of mourning. *Globe and Mail,* September 15, A14.
Louw, E. 2003. The "war against terrorism": A public relations challenge for the Pentagon. *Gazette: The International Journal for Communication Studies* 65, 3: 211-30.
Lule, J. 2002. Myth and terror on the editorial page: The New York Times responds to September 11, 2001. *Journalism and Mass Communication Quarterly* 79, 2: 275-93.
Mamdani, M. 2004. *Good Muslim, bad Muslim: America, the Cold War and the roots of terror.* Toronto, ON: Random House of Canada.
Mann, B. 2006. How America justifies its war: A modern/postmodern aesthetics of masculinity and sovereignty. *Hypatia* 21, 4: 147-63.
Mitchell, A., with reports from Reuters, Associated Press, J. Rusk, S. Fine, and K. Cox. 2001. The aftermath: Arab Canadians duck to avoid harassment. *Globe and Mail,* September 14, A1.
Pearson, P. 2003. See no evil, no more. *Globe and Mail,* April 19, A19.
Philps, A. 2001. Palestinian leaders rush to US side of divide. *National Post,* September 13, A9.
Pilger, J. 2006. Forward. In D. Edwards and D. Cromwell, *Guardians of power: The myth of the liberal media,* ix-xii. London, UK: Pluto.

Read, C. 2001. Stay inside, Muslims warned. *National Post*, September 13, A14.

Richler, N. 2001. UK left's envy discolours some reporting. *National Post*, September 15, B7.

Rodgers, J. 2003. Icons and invisibility: Gender, myth, 9/11. In D.K. Thussu and D. Freedman, eds., *War and the media*, 200-12. London, UK/New Delhi: Thousand Oaks/Sage.

Rose, A. 2001. The Islamist jihad: Radical Muslims who kill in the name of religion. *National Post*, September 13, B1.

Russo, A. 2006. The feminist majority foundation's campaign to stop gender apartheid. *International Feminist Journal of Politics* 8, 4: 557-80.

Said, E.W. 1978. *Orientalism*. New York, NY: Vintage.

Saunders, D. 2001. The day after: Faith, hope and fear. *Globe and Mail*, September 13, N2.

Shade, L.R. 2006. O Canada: Media (de)convergence, concentration, and culture. In P. Attallah and L.R. Shade, eds., *Mediascapes: New patterns in Canadian communication*, 2nd ed., 346-64. Toronto, ON: Thomson and Nelson.

Spector, N. 2001a. Deja vu for Israelis. *Montreal Gazette*, September 12, B3.

—. 2001b. The day after: Goin' down the Israeli road to thwart terror. *Globe and Mail*, September 13, A19.

Stabile, C.A., and D. Kumar. 2005. Unveiling imperialism: Media, gender and the war on Afghanistan. *Media, Culture and Society* 27, 5: 765-82.

Steyn, M. 2001. West's moral failure at root of tragedy. *National Post*, September 12, A3.

Thobani, S. 2003. War and the politics of truth-making in Canada. *Qualitative Studies in Education* 16, 3: 399-414.

Tuchman, G. 1978. The symbolic annihilation of women by the mass media. In G. Tuchman, A.K. Daniels, and J. Benet, eds., *Hearth and home: Images of women in the mass media*, 3-38. New York: Oxford University Press.

van Dijk, T.A. 1991. *Racism and the press*. New York, NY: Routledge.

Victims were from all over the world. 2001. *National Post*, September 17, D6.

Vincent, I. 2001. In the lair of the terrorist. *National Post*, September 13, A8.

Wallis, D. 2001. Changed forever, in an instant. *National Post*, September 12, B12.

Wente, M. 2001a. US will never be the same. *Globe and Mail*, September 12, A1.

—. 2001b. The day after: We're all Americans now. *Globe and Mail*, September 13, N3.

What we stand for. 2001. Editorial. *Globe and Mail*, September 17, A18.

Winch, S. 2005. Constructing an "evil genius": News uses of mythic archetypes to make sense of bin Laden. *Journalism Studies* 6, 3: 285-99.

Winter, J. 1997. *Democracy's oxygen: How corporations control the news*. Montreal, QC: Black Rose.

—. 2002. Canada's media monopoly: One perspective is enough, says CanWest. In Fairness and Accuracy in Reporting (FAIR), *Extra!* May/June. http://www.fair.org/.

York, G. 2001. The brink of war: Afghans run for border. *Globe and Mail*, September 17, A1.

5

Marketing Islamic Reform
Dissidence and Dissonance in a Canadian Context

MEENA SHARIFY-FUNK

Marketing Islamic Reform: Dissidence and Dissonance in a Canadian Context
Although hardly a rigorous way of ascertaining what Canadians are reading about Islam, visits to major bookstore chains such as Chapters can be quite revealing. Content on the shelf (or, on occasion, two shelves) labelled "Islam" varies from week to week and month to month, yet a certain genre almost always appears to be well stocked, prominently displayed with covers facing outward and perhaps even showcased in the "best picks" section by the staff. The titles of the books in this genre grasp the attention of the bookstore patron by invoking themes of alarm or dissidence: examples are *The Trouble with Islam Today*, *Infidel*, *Nomad*, *Their Jihad ... Not My Jihad!* and *Standing Alone in Mecca*.

Intriguingly, the authors of these books are typically women who represent themselves as people who are at odds with their faith-tradition and community. Their message is one of righteous, risk-taking dissent, and the authorial image they project on the back covers is one of boldness in the face of dangerous intolerance: they are women calling for reform "from the margins," ready to "take on" fanatical jihadists or a larger, male-dominated religious establishment. However accurate these self-portraits of defiant marginality may be (the authors' views, after all, are far from popular within Muslim religious communities), the apparent popularity of the books attests to the fact that, at least in mainstream North American society, the authors are far from marginal.[1]

The ubiquity of these self-conscious dissident publications in mainstream Canadian bookstores finds a dramatic counterpoint in their virtually complete absence from shops that are oriented toward Muslim-minority communities. For a variety of reasons, few Muslim book merchants would deem it appropriate to sell them, and many no doubt fear the way that placing such texts on the shelves might be interpreted by their clients. The books contain generalizations about Islam and about the state of contemporary Muslim communities that have hardly been welcomed by traditional voices of authority in Canada or in the wider Muslim world. Moreover, in diaspora communities as well as in Muslim-majority countries, there is a widespread feeling that outsiders are interested only in negative perspectives on Islam, and books like Irshad Manji's *The Trouble with Islam Today* and Ayaan Hirsi Ali's *Infidel* reinforce this perception of living in the glare of intense, unfriendly scrutiny. And it is true that, in stating their claims provocatively, the authors of such books have aroused the ire of radicals.[2]

As I consider the simultaneous attraction and repulsion with which these books are regarded, I am reminded of the adage "Fools rush in where angels fear to tread." Yet the remarkable popularity of these texts (which are among the top sellers on Islam in Canada and many other Western contexts) and the love-hate reactions they engender are parts of a phenomenon that calls for scholarly investigation.

Given recent events, the success of these books is not surprising. It would appear to say something not merely about what booksellers deem worthy of promotion but also about what the North American reading public finds plausible and engaging. The books have been written primarily for non-Muslims who adhere to mainstream Western liberal and conservative political assumptions, and their style and content respond to a market that was created in North America after the events of 9/11.

When I encounter someone who reads about Islam as a layperson, these are the types of texts they are likely to have read. The genre is popular because it claims to offer answers to the questions non-Muslims are asking: Why are Muslims angry at the West? Why do they reject Western solutions to political problems and resist notions such as women's liberation, gay rights, and freedom of choice for the individual? How do we explain phenomena such as al-Qaeda and suicide bombing? The explanations these texts offer are straightforward, palatable to the nonacademic reader, unburdened by footnotes and unfamiliar terms, politically comfortable, and easy to assimilate. Their message is one that resonates with the contemporary reader who feels at least moderately threatened by Islam and who has come to the conclusion that there is a basic conflict between his or her values and those of most Muslims.

Sadly, the popularity of these texts comes at the expense of many other potential sources of knowledge about Islam, some of which manifest considerably greater academic rigour and nuance. Although one would expect simpler, "edgier," and more journalistic books to perform well in the aftermath of terrorist attacks and wars, the inability of a more diverse range of authors to make their voices heard creates problems for majority-minority relations in a multicultural society. To be heard and welcomed in the public sphere, Muslims in Canada and in the wider North American context experience pressure to assume an adversarial posture toward the larger Muslim community and frequently acquire credibility and even accolades[3] to the extent to which they abandon more "mainstream" minority-group strategies of identity negotiation by positioning themselves as Muslim dissidents aligned with the majority culture. Although self-critique is to be welcomed in any national or religious community, the enthusiasm of Canadians and North Americans for "Muslim dissident" literature comes at a price: an inability to more fully understand the daily concerns, "common-sense" perceptions, and existential dilemmas that accompany "being Muslim in Canada" and, indeed, to hear the claims of dissident voices in a larger context.

This chapter aspires to situate the central claims of two popular Canadian texts, Irshad Manji's *The Trouble with Islam Today* (2005) and Raheel Raza's *Their Jihad ... Not My Jihad!* (2005), in a broader context of identity negotiation and meaning creation within the Canadian Muslim community. After beginning with a discussion of the challenges faced by Canadian Muslims seeking to define themselves as members of a culturally diverse yet frequently stereotyped minority group, I analyze themes in these two texts in terms of their relation to larger intra-Muslim debates about reform, Western liberalism, and women's emancipation and consider the extent to which each book encourages readers from the majority culture to question some of their own assumptions about Islam and Muslims. I would like to stress that I am focusing only on these two texts, not on any other works by Manji and Raza.[4]

Negotiating Canadian and Muslim Identities

Controversies surrounding the brisk sale of dissident texts on Islam reveal a great deal about identity negotiation between "majority-culture" Canadians and the Muslim-minority community, as well as within the Muslim-minority community itself.⁵ Whereas many non-Muslims feel that by reading these books they have been liberated from "political correctness," excessive politeness, and other niceties, a solid majority of Muslims regard the same books (and especially Manji's) as fuel for an oppressive environment of fear, misunderstanding, and Islamophobia. The same authors who may be regarded as heroes and exemplars of moral courage by the majority community are regarded as purveyors of hurtful stereotypes by members of a Muslim diaspora community who feel burdened by the intense scrutiny that accompanies the transformation of their religion into a "security threat." Books that strike so many non-Muslim readers as "the truth about Islam" evoke exactly the opposite reaction among many Muslims.

In the majority culture, popular Muslim reactions to dissident texts seem to confirm many of the accusations they contain. Reports of death threats against authors, after all, are profoundly disturbing, and emotional denunciations of the authors incline many spectators to wonder whether perhaps uncomfortable truths are being spoken. The popularity of the authors among readers from the majority culture appears to depend in no small part on the unpopularity of the writers' arguments among members of their "root" communities. Books such as *The Trouble with Islam Today* are read by many Canadians as timely reminders against excessive multicultural tolerance and as affirmations of a need to reassert a more uniform approach to Canadian culture, identity, and values. The implication is that Canadian identity needs to be renegotiated in favour of a past Anglo-Saxon/French/Western synthesis, with stronger pressure for immigrant communities to abandon the values, loyalties, and traditions of their mother countries insofar as they diverge from authentic Canadian norms.

This notion that the majority culture has been too accommodating diverges quite dramatically from commonplace perceptions among members of the Muslim-minority community, who read the message of the dissident texts quite differently. These texts' defiant calls for reform appear to have little appeal not only among "extreme" Muslims but also among the many Muslims in Canada and beyond who genuinely wish for changes in their tradition. The messages of defiant reformers sell to non-Muslims far better than to Muslims, in no small part because these messages appear to have been crafted with non-Muslim or secularist audiences in mind. Among those who feel that Islam has been misunderstood and subjected to unfair attacks, there is great discomfort with the manner in which many authors of the bestselling books about Islam have utilized their lack of "good standing" within the Muslim community as a selling point and have marketed books with a noticeable absence of back-cover blurbs by Muslim scholars.[6] Although this response is not universal, the formulation of a desirable Canadian (or Western) Muslim identity in the dissident texts differs quite dramatically from the types of nonsecular, transnationally networked identities that so many members of the Muslim-minority community value (see Sharify-Funk 2008, Mandaville 2001).

Since September 11, 2001, Muslim Canadian debates about the meaning of "Muslim" and "Canadian" have ceased to be merely "internal" matters and have come to reflect some of the dynamics that are present in American and European contexts. Non-Muslim communities are listening closely to intra-Muslim negotiations about the relationship between Islam and conventional "Western" values such as secularism, gender equality, and national citizenship, and they take particular interest in the views of those Muslims who may be described as dissidents and extremists. Whereas for most Muslims, Islam signifies "peace," "safety," and perhaps even righteous forbearance in the face of persecution, it has become associated with opposite qualities for many non-Muslims. The desire of some Muslims to distance themselves from radical groups has led to the coining of new terms such as "ex-Muslim"[7] and "Muslim refusenik,"[8] and the allergic or prejudicial reaction of some non-Muslims to all things Islamic has led to the deployment of the term "Islamophobia" by members of Muslim-minority communities. Islam has become a symbolically charged topic, and Muslim identities have become increasingly polarized between would-be "Westernizers" and defenders of various formulations of cultural authenticity and religious authority.

One result of the charged atmosphere of identity negotiation is that the issue of dialogue itself has become contested. With which Muslims should a non-Muslim enter into dialogue? Who speaks for and represents Islam? Who has legitimacy as a "reformer" and who does not? Just as there are many Christianities and Judaisms, so too are there many formulations of Islamic piety and politics that contend for the attention of Muslims and that represent themselves as the only "authentic" perspective. We face a fundamental paradox: Islam is one, and it is many. Its meaning for believers transcends history, yet the development of diverse Muslim standpoints and beliefs is an inevitable outcome of historic processes.

Even where there is agreement about symbolic reference points and essential values, collective identities are always works in progress, formulated and reformulated through negotiations among contrasting and competing worldviews. Contemporary Canadian identity differs profoundly from

Canadian identity in the late nineteenth century, and despite the existence of generally agreed reference points – multiculturalism, cultural accommodation, integration, liberal values – their overall meaning is subject to contestation. Canadian identity, then, continues to change and evolve through dialogue as well as through debates about what is "genuinely Canadian" or "Canadian enough." Commentators differ on whether relative newcomers, especially those who hail from Asia, Africa, or Latin America, are subject to un-Canadian discrimination or are failing to demonstrate sufficient "Canadianness."

Similarly, Islamic identity is also a work in progress both in Muslim-majority lands and in countries of immigration. Life in diaspora creates special challenges and pressures, increasing the felt need of many Muslims to simultaneously prove that they are "Muslim enough" and also members of their new, chosen civic community. Although there are inevitably those in Muslim-minority communities who fully embrace or categorically reject the mores of North American culture, complex and eclectic responses are more typical – for example, wearing the *hijab* (headscarf) as well as high heels or becoming a Muslim rap artist articulating Islamic as well as "quintessentially Canadian" themes. The manner in which the "Muslim dissident" literature calls on Muslim minorities to choose between or prioritize one identity over another – that is, to *prove* that they are adequately Canadian or Western – is one of the many reasons for the passionate responses it has evoked.

In Canada, two nationally recognized, self-proclaimed Muslim dissidents – both women – are Irshad Manji and Raheel Raza. Manji, a journalist, activist, and former television broadcaster for *Queer Television*, shifted toward advocacy of Islamic reform in 2003 with the publication of her top-selling and controversial book *The Trouble with Islam.*[9] Raza, a journalist and proponent of interfaith dialogue, published her own views on contemporary Islam two years later in her less popular (and also less controversial) book *Their Jihad ... Not My Jihad!* Both have entered, albeit in different ways, into ongoing debates about "Muslimness" and Canadian identity, and both have spoken with special passion on the highly charged subjects of reform, Western liberalism, and the status of Muslim women. Whereas Manji largely abandons internal Islamic discursive strategies and stakes out a position in which "mainstream Canadian values" are adopted as superior normative standards – a position that has no doubt had much to do with the success of her book – Raza adopts a stance that, if still controversial, is articulated in a manner that is more consistent with internal Muslim negotiations over Islamic meaning and identity.

The Agenda of Reform and Reclaiming Islam: Responding to Terror

After the tragic events of 9/11, Muslims in Canada reacted in a variety of ways. Recognizing the potentially grave implications for Muslim communities in North America as well as for international peace and security, many actively sought to bridge the gap between Muslims and non-Muslims by redoubling their engagement with interfaith dialogue and other forms of advocacy. Whereas some reacted to heightened scrutiny of Muslim communities and institutions by retreating from the public sphere, others sought to either protect Islam from common misperceptions or to initiate new calls for change among Muslims. The dramatic rise of public interest in (and concern about) Islam brought new prominence to some Muslim commentators and spokespersons, some speaking in the name of established organizations and others acting in a more freelance capacity.

Both Manji and Raza fall into the latter category of freelance Muslim commentators, and both have written books responding to the climate of fear and insecurity that followed the events of 9/11. Both regard themselves as protagonists in a larger struggle to reclaim Islam from jihadists or militant Muslims. In doing so, they also aspire to shed light on longstanding problems and "injustices" found in traditional Muslim societies.[10] Despite adopting different rhetorical styles and approaches to activism, both claim to respond to a crisis precipitated by radical Muslims through new calls for critical thinking and Islamic reform. Both insist that a time has come for Muslims to more assertively apply the principle of *ijtihad* (the traditional juristic term for "independent reasoning") and to engage the modern world with less deference to culturally and politically inflected understandings of Islamic values and traditions. Both decry what Raza (2005, 40) describes as "the extremist voices from the pulpit" and celebrate "the freedom to logically research and interpret the Qur'an with reason and intellect."

In staking out these positions, Manji and Raza have clearly and unapologetically associated themselves with modernist approaches to the Islamic tradition and with those in diaspora Muslim communities who argue that there is no necessary contradiction between being Muslim and being a Canadian or a member of another "Western" polity. They argue for delinking Islamic thought in diaspora communities from the politics and religious trends of "homeland countries" and more generally for sweeping changes in the way Muslims read and interpret their sacred texts. The problems facing Muslims, they suggest, are fundamentally epistemological and textual: new criteria for determining essential Islamic values need to be adopted in order to liberate Muslims from oppressive cultural conventions and dangerous political agendas.

Although united by this call for reform, Manji and Raza differ quite profoundly in their understandings of what it is that must be reformed. For Raza (and indeed for most others who describe themselves as "moderate Muslims"), the basic problem is that Islam itself has been "hijacked" by radical forces. Raza (2005, xv), who was born and raised in Pakistan, speaks passionately about her dismay at seeing "the Islam that I love and venerate ... being hijacked with the introduction of a new fundamentalism and the rise of the Taliban." She describes her extensive public speaking in churches, schools, and community centres as "essentially damage control" (38) – that is, as an attempt to counter both misperceptions created by Muslim radicals and misinformation propagated by the Western media and Christian fundamentalists. After 9/11, she says, she took it upon herself to inform non-Muslims about authentic Islam by "teaching Islam 101" (38). She describes her new vocation in the following terms:

> Muslims have been stripped naked by the likes of Christian fundamentalists Jerry Falwell and Pat Robertson and political interviewer Oriana Fallaci. Even some local Muslims made a name for themselves by pointing out the trouble with Islam. In this atmosphere rampant with distrust and fear, people became confused. As a Muslim involved in doing damage control, it was time to go back to the books and read, which is the first message of the Qur'an. (60)

For Raza, Islam itself is *not* implicated in terrorism, political violence, or intolerant thinking. Islam has been misunderstood by Muslims and non-Muslims alike; a proper, reformed understanding of Islam is now necessary to achieve reconciliation between Muslims and the West.

In contrast, Manji (2005) criticizes those who argue that Islam itself is "innocent" with respect to contemporary violence, and she rejects the notion that the Qur'an itself provides an adequate response to the messages of radicals. In her view, Islam is not purely a religion of peace and tolerance; neither Islam nor "moderate Muslims" should be insulated from the harsh questioning of those who have been alarmed by recent developments.

Muslims, she suggests, are complicit in the events of 9/11 insofar as they refuse to adopt a critical view of their religion: "With morose faces, we [Muslims] said that our faith had been 'hijacked' ... As if our religion was an innocent bystander in the violence perpetrated by Muslims. Hijacked. An emotionally charged word that acquits mainstream Muslims of the responsibility to be self-critical" (Manji 2005, 46-47). For Manji, Islam is emphatically not an ideal system of values and contains within itself contradictions that permitted the events of 9/11. Although Manji professes to be a Muslim, Islam itself – not Muslims alone – is the target of her criticisms and the object of her calls for change.

What Needs to Be Reformed?

Although Raza and Manji appear to agree on many substantive issues, this basic difference between reforming Islamic *interpretation and practice* and challenging foundational Islamic *beliefs and doctrines* constitutes a major difference in their respective forms of advocacy. Raza's condemnation of Muslim militants and, even more, her decision to lead an Islamic-ritual prayer service at a venue in Toronto have subjected her to harsh criticism from radical and conservative thinkers, yet her basic style of argumentation (affirming that Islam, authentically understood, has the solutions wayward Muslims need) is compatible with the language of faith utilized by most observant Muslims. Although Raza (2005, 39) may argue that "today, the Muslim world stays dangerously silent," she insists that the problem is Muslims, not Islam. Manji's approach, in contrast, directly challenges the faith that observant Muslims have in the essential goodness, sacred meaning, and spiritual truth of their religious tradition. For Manji (2007), the approach of moderate Muslims (Raza is indirectly included in this) lacks the level of honesty necessary to affect real change because they base their calls for reform on the assumption that it is Muslims, rather than Islam, who are the root of the problem. Manji (2005, 49-50) argues that Islam is not the divinely inspired "straight path" sought by Muslims in their daily prayers and life aspirations; it is an inherently contradictory set of injunctions and proscriptions that bears the marks of its human founders. "Far from being perfect," she states, "the Quran is so profoundly at war with itself." Although Manji alleges that there are "good" as well as "bad" statements in Islamic texts, her writing devotes greater attention to the latter than the former and exhibits reticence with respect to the reasons why the author continues to describe herself as Muslim. Many, if not most, Muslim readers have found this stance, which deconstructs Islamic doctrines and texts with the intent of revealing incoherence rather than consistency, alienating and threatening to their core identity at a time of profound existential vulnerability.

The implications of these divergent approaches to Islamic reform become especially apparent on the "religion of peace" issue. Raza (2005) asserts that Islam is fundamentally a religion of peace that has been misinterpreted and abused by Muslim radicals. Although those who speak out against extremists are few, most Muslims are able to recognize the basic priority Islam gives to peace over war:

> What needs to be done? The solution, I believe, lies with the silent majority in Islam who need to speak up and ensure the hateful rhetoric and actions of people like Osama bin Laden and his supporters die before they take root. They need to ensure the pulpit of a mosque is not used to spew hate, and, most of all, they need to empower other Muslims to take action against injustice, intolerance and violence wherever it is happening ... We must reiterate that Islam was and should remain a message of peace and love. The few of us who speak out will face resistance and criticism. But maybe what we need right now is a renaissance or revival in Islam to clean out the extremist elements that have muddied our clean image. For this to happen, we have to first accept that the enemy is not outside, but within us. (Raza 2005, 28)

Unlike Manji, Raza reads passages of the Qur'an that relate to conflict contextually, as do many Christians and Jews dealing with conflict verses in their own scriptures. She rejects traditional Western stereotypes about Islam "as a religion of force and violence" and proposes that "tolerance is the cornerstone of Islam and has emerged out of the very nature and history of Islam" (Raza 2005, 30). Problems in Islamic practice relate to religious interpretation – which is not absolute – rather than to the religious texts Muslims must strive to understand.

Manji offers a perspective that is more in line with traditional "Western"[11] perceptions of Islam. She rejects the "religion of peace" argument as an "emotionally comforting" fallacy: "While I would have loved to believe this account of things, the more I read and reflected, the less sense it made" (Manji 2005, 49). Believing that Islam is a religion of peace, she argues, absolves Muslims of responsibility for critical thinking about their tradition. In making this argument, she does not qualify her position by proposing that the inherent peacefulness of other religious traditions might also be questioned or by cautioning against a return to religious polemics attributing violence to the "Other."

For Manji, as implied by the title of her book's first edition, *The Trouble with Islam*, there is something inherently flawed in Islam and, in turn, in Muslims (see note 8). Manji makes no attempt to correct traditional misperceptions or stereotypes, nor does she allow for the possibility that problematic historical and political relations between Western and Muslim-majority countries can be invoked as contributing causes of religious militancy. The "trouble" is inherent to Islam and is not circumstantial.

Critics of Manji have argued that her approach lacks balance and attention to the larger context of relations between Islam and the West. There is no mention or disclaimer that a larger history is present in the contemporary struggles. Manji is silent with respect to contemporary scholars who argue that, in historical terms, Islam and Muslims have been predominantly perceived in the Judeo-Christian West as outsiders – that is, that Islam has been unjustly treated as an "exception" to humane or progressive trends in world civilization and that Islamic civilization's many contributions to world civilization have too seldom been acknowledged.[12] It is therefore not surprising that some Muslim and non-Muslim scholars regard Manji's treatment of Islam as more reminiscent of the Orientalist tradition than of recent scholarship in North American universities. Although Khaled Abou El Fadl (2006, ix), a professor of Islamic studies at the University of California at Los Angeles (whom Manji mentions in her book), does not refer to Manji directly, he appears to offer an implied reference in his "Foreword" to Amina Wadud's *Inside the Gender Jihad: Women's Reform in Islam:* "Unlike so much of the sensationalistic, and at times Islamophobic, writings that are published these days, this is not a book about the trouble with Islam, what went wrong with Islam, why Islam is a problem, why Islam is some type of implicitly failed religion."

What sets Manji apart from so many other self-proclaimed Islamic reformists is her insistence on bluntly and directly challenging core Islamic beliefs and her dismissal of those who have staked out more modest reform programs rooted in historical Muslim reform and renewal movements. In her manner of arguing against the absolutizing of essential Islamic precepts or of declaring that Islam cannot be regarded as "a wholly original way of life," Manji (2005, 24) insists on rupture with the past rather than continuity and favours individualism rather than what she describes as a "herd" mentality. The following quotations are illustrative:

> [We must] openly question the perfection of the Quran so that the stampede to reach a correct conclusion about what it "really" says will slow down and, over time, become an exercise in literacy instead of literalism. At this stage, reform isn't about telling ordinary Muslims what not to think, but about giving Islam's billion devotees permission to think. (Manji 2005, 40)

> The Quran's perfection is, ultimately, suspect ... What if the Quran isn't perfect? What if it's not a completely God-authored book? What if it's riddled with human biases? (50)

> The very act of questioning the Quran is a central piece of the reform puzzle because it signals a breach with the herd. (52)

Whereas Raza and most other Islamic reformists advocate change through rereading sacred texts and acknowledging the relativity of human interpretations, Manji argues that the solution lies in a more secular and skeptical attitude toward sacred texts. Whereas Raza (2005, xv) argues that the central challenge is "to separate culture from religion; truth and justice from propaganda, and the ritual from the spiritual," Manji rejects the notion that Islamic reform can come from a renewal of internal Islamic spiritual resources and opts for a direct confrontation with religious certitudes.[13]

Moderate Muslims: Problem or Solution?

The nature of each writer's reform project determines her attitude toward ideas of moderation in Islam. Raza (2005, 35, 50) chooses to label herself as a "pluralist practicing Muslim and a caring Canadian" and as a "moderate Muslim." In the process, she seeks to distinguish herself from "immoderate" (i.e., radical, extremist, or fundamentalist) Muslims who in her view are seeking to hijack Islam and silence a less politically driven majority. "Moderate Muslims like me," she states, who "want to differentiate our faith from extremist Muslims' twisted ideologies are facing increasing resistance" (50).

The appeal of this "moderate" label – and its utility in a Western context – seems obvious in an era of elevated security concerns, in which members of the majority culture tend to be curious about who their Muslim allies may be and anxious about the intensity of patriotism or extent of acculturation among Muslim citizens. It should come as no surprise, then, that designations such as "moderate Muslim" have become commonplace.

Predictably, many Muslims feel frustrated or ambivalent about these labels. Although the connotation of being "against violence" has its appeal, there is an additional undesirable implication: that violence committed by Muslims takes place for primarily ideological (as opposed to political, economic, or historical) reasons. As some scholars have observed, labelling Muslims as either "moderate" or "immoderate" tends to silence a majority of Muslim voices, reinforcing the problematic dichotomy between "good Muslims" and "bad Muslims." In a special issue of the *American Journal of Islamic and Social Sciences* entitled *Debating Moderate Islam,* Barlas (2005, 161), a prominent Muslim feminist, offers a sharp critique:

> The official view of Islam as a pair of good and evil twins conjoined at the hip performs two crucial political functions. On the one hand, by portraying "militant Islam" as the real threat to global security, Washington is able to deflect critiques of the US's role in underwriting injustice and oppression on a global scale. On the other hand, by shifting the burden of "defeat[ing] and eradicat[ing] militant Islam" onto "moderate Islam," the US is absolved of the responsibility to rethink its own injurious policies.

For Barlas, the project of supporting "moderate Muslims" comes, then, at a high cost for both non-Muslims and Muslims. Non-Muslims misread the sources of Muslim resentment, and genuine Muslim voices go unheard.

According to Barlas and other critics, terms such as "moderate Muslim" provide little insight into the actual beliefs and policies of those who bear the label and are primarily used in a strategic manner. At the same time, the "moderate Muslim" label implies (however subtly) that most Muslims are *not* moderate:

> If calling oneself a moderate at a time when there is such pressure to "toe the official line" can thus "easily become too much a badge of mindless loyalty," refusing to call oneself a moderate can just as easily become a sign of disloyalty. Either way, the state's advocacy of "moderate Islam" is a kiss of death for Muslim critics abroad, wary of the US's agendas, and of non-Muslim critics at home who are convinced that a moderate Muslim is merely a militant in denial or in disguise. (Barlas 2005, 162)

As a quick Internet search can reveal, there is a diverse range of Muslims who are being labelled "moderate."[14] Although few would dispute Raza's moderate credentials, it is possible for a Muslim to be regarded as "moderate" by some commentators and as "radical" by others. This raises many questions: Is a consensus definition of "moderation" possible? Is moderation the hallmark of a particular epistemological or interpretive tendency, or can it be found among diverse varieties of Muslims – not only among "ex-Muslims," Muslim secularists, and reformists but also among traditionalists and revivalists? Raza suggests that most Muslims are moderate yet passive but does not draw attention to problems inherent in the "moderate"-"extremist" binary.

Interestingly, Manji rejects use of the "moderate Muslim" label but for reasons that differ quite profoundly from those cited above. Aligning herself more closely with Western critics of Islam, Manji creates a more sweeping and deeply polarizing distinction between "good Muslims" and "bad Muslims" by suggesting that so-called "moderates" are in effect apologists for Islamic extremism: they provide cover for their more radical co-religionists by insisting on superficial rather than penetrating and thoroughgoing reforms. For her, moderates contribute to the risk of failing to address real sources of problems within the Muslim community such as violence because, despite denouncing violence committed in the name of Islam today, they deny that Islam today has anything to do with it. To distinguish herself from moderates, Manji (2005, 24, 3) elects to define herself as a "modern Muslim" and, more pointedly, as a "Muslim refusenik." With the latter label, Manji evokes the ideological competition of the Cold War era and the legacy of Soviet Jews whose "persistent refusal to comply with the [Soviet Unions'] mechanisms of mind-control and soullessness helped end a totalitarian system" (3). Thus does she portray herself as an agent of liberation in a new Cold War between the West and a presumably "totalitarian" Islamic system.

Virtues of Western Liberalism and Secularism

The concept of reform presupposes not only "something that is wrong" and that needs to be changed but also "something that would be better" as a normative standard to guide aspirations. Both Manji and Raza agree that the transformation of Muslims is inextricably connected to the many values of Western liberalism and secularism. They differ, however, in their manner of approaching what they regard as the virtues of liberalism and secularism. For Raza, essential Islamic and Western values are compatible, so the task of reforming Muslims does not require fundamental changes in Islam. For Manji, there are basic contradictions between Islamic and Western values, and the task of Islamic reformation requires a transformative Westernization of religious culture.

In her book, Manji upholds "the West" as a haven for ideal modern values such as critical thinking, individual freedom, and democracy. These values, she suggests, are largely alien to the Muslim experience but nonetheless ought to be embraced and emulated. Reflecting on her cultural formation in Canada, Manji makes repeated references to the Western virtues and goes so far as to entitle her final chapter "Thank God for the West." The following quotations are exemplary:

> I lived in a part of the world that permitted me to explore. Thanks to the freedoms afforded me in the West – to think, search, speak, exchange, discuss, challenge, be challenged, and rethink – I was poised to judge my religion in a light that I couldn't have possibly conceived in the parochial Muslim microcosm of the madressa. (Manji 2005, 21)

> But it wasn't Islam that fostered my belief in the dignity of every individual. It was the democratic environment. (6)

> I look back now and thank God I wound up in a world where the Quran didn't have to be my first and only book, as if it's the lone richness that life offers to believers. (6)

> Lord, I loved this society. I loved that it seemed perpetually unfinished, the final answers not yet known – if ever they would be. I loved that, in a world under constant renovation, the contributions of individuals mattered. (10)

Manji highlights the virtues of secularism over not only religiously directed politics but also religion itself. At a Detroit screening of the film *Faith without Fear* (National Film Board of Canada 2007), she responded to a question about Islam and its compatibility with secularism by stating, "There are very few times when I feel comfortable saying that something is superior to something else. I feel very comfortable saying that secularism is superior to religion on its own because secularism makes room for religion."[15]

Manji's (2005) discourse attributes almost providential significance to Western values and includes direct challenges to Western multiculturalists (220-21) and peace activists (214) who demonstrate excessive tolerance toward Islam and Muslims. The Western value of individuality must not be compromised in efforts to reform and liberalize "tribal" or "desert" Islam (33).

For Manji, the resources to transform the Islamic world are readily available in the Western world. In contrast, most of the Muslim world (with the possible exception of Turkey) is mired in traditions linked to desert, Arab tribalism. Although Manji briefly mentions some Muslim reformists outside of the West (including Zainah Anwar, a Malaysian feminist), her predominant emphasis is on the need for reform to come from Muslims in the West and from Western policies supporting objectives such as the liberation and economic empowerment of women. Muslims in the West, she states, are ideal for reforming Islam since they "have the luxury of exercising civil liberties, especially free expression, to change tribal tendencies" (Manji 2005, 207). She cites the Progressive Muslim Union of North America, a recently formed network of Muslim thinkers and activists, as evidence that "the freedoms of the West can impel a new generation of Muslims to revive ijtihad, Islam's lost tradition of creative thinking" (175).

Although Raza also upholds values that are commonly regarded as "Western," the stated intent of her writing is to defend what she understands as true Islamic values from Muslim distortions (political violence, oppression of women) and Western misunderstandings. She credits her Western experience with deepening and broadening her faith through interfaith dialogue and advocacy, but unlike Manji, she hesitates to evoke an attitude of cultural triumphalism in which the West assumes a virtually providential role vis-à-vis contemporary Islam. The West can support Islamic reformation by providing a context in which Muslims recognize their own universal values, but it does not assume the role of mentor. The fundamental distinction is not between Islam and the West but between authentic values and their abuse or politicization. Raza also practises what some scholars call "multiple critique" by arguing that responsibility for introspection does not lie with Muslims alone. Although she does not delve deeply into the complexities of North American and Western policies toward Muslim countries, she does encourage Westerners to reconsider their attitudes toward Islam, particularly those conveyed by the media. "Thanks to Western media's irresponsible use of jingo-ism instead of journalism," Raza (2005, 43) states, "Muslims today have been made synonymous with terrorism, fundamentalism and militancy."

Although Raza protests Western stereotypes of Muslims, she also calls on Muslims to move beyond their love-hate relationship with the West, especially the tendency to use the West as a scapegoat. It is unfair, she suggests, for Muslims in Pakistan and other countries to evade responsibility for their own internal problems by blaming them on America or the West. She also claims that many Muslims observe double-standards, criticizing the West one moment and then pursuing a Western dream by eating at McDonald's or vacationing in Florida (Raza 2005, 36).

Whereas Manji argues that Western and especially North American democracies exhibit too much tolerance toward Muslim minorities, Raza exhibits more sympathy toward her co-religionists even as she calls on them to become more integrated with the majority culture. She notes that Western Muslims "are under massive pressure since 9/11 and have faced severe backlash" (Raza 2005, 60) and calls for interfaith solidarity against phenomena such as hate-speech and vandalism, whoever their source or target may be (60-61). Moreover, Raza comments that Muslims should not accept extremism in their own community: "In Canada, we must take back the mosques to ensure the voices of reasonable Muslim men and women are heard over the stringent calls for a physical *jihad*" (61).

Overall, both authors demonstrate positive regard for North American models of secularity and articulate arguments that are compatible with what some writers describe as a Judeo-Christian-secular synthesis. Manji portrays contemporary Islamic culture as antithetical to this synthesis, whereas Raza represents Islam as a system of values that is compatible with it.[16] Whereas Manji's approach frames Western superiority in the domain of values as an established fact that should be confronted with "honesty," Raza rejects such comparisons while remaining staunch in what she regards as widespread abuses of Islam. Although both highlight contradictions in Islamic societies, neither grants weight or legitimacy to Islamic counter-critiques of Western contradictions (e.g., excesses of consumerism, commercial objectification of women as sex objects, foreign policy double-standards, social fragmentation, environmentally unsustainable practices, unfair management of the global economy). Manji goes much further in denying the value of engaging and listening to mainstream Muslim voices, but neither book emphasizes the importance of gaining a more nuanced understanding of Muslims' diverse perceptions concerning the West. Manji (2005, 145) is especially curt in dismissing Muslim critiques: "Liberal Muslims have to get vocal about this fact: Washington is the unrealized hope, not the lead criminal." Muslims, her argument suggests, have so many internal problems that their critiques of others need not be taken seriously. Whatever historical contributions they may have made to Western civilization, these contributions are largely irrelevant in the present context.

Women's Emancipation as a Focal Point

Both Manji and Raza view women's emancipation as an issue that is inseparably linked to Islamic reform and the liberalization of Muslim culture. For both writers, the strengthening of women's rights is regarded not merely as an outcome of reform but also as a catalyst.

One of Raza's (2005, 76) chapters bears the title "To Change the Image of Muslims, Let's Begin with the Women." Once again, Raza articulates criticism of Western stereotypes (68), while also calling for honesty about challenges and problems facing Muslim women. Raza believes that it is necessary to educate non-Muslims about the diverse realities experienced by Muslim women, while continuing to engage in advocacy for those women who must wrestle with cultural norms that permit honour killings, domestic violence, inequitable inheritance, and obstacles to divorce. With women's rights, as with liberalism, Raza asserts that there is no inherent contradiction between her positions and the essential values of her faith:

> I was battling a series of questions from a journalist about how I could profess to be Muslim and a feminist! To her, this was contradictory and in order to answer her query satisfactorily, I had to go through practically the entire history of Islam and explain a simple fact that many people forget, even when they study Islam: Islam was sent as a system of social justice and to free women from infanticide, slavery, oppression and bondage ... In theory Islam gives women the basic rights to live, work, marry, vote, have freedom and justice based on the Qur'an. How these rights are being practiced today in culturally male-dominated societies is something the entire community must face and address. (76)

As an activist, Raza admits to facing a "catch-22" scenario: talking about problems facing women tends to reinforce Western stereotypes in the West and to provide fuel for anti-Islam rhetoric. Yet allowing one's agenda to be determined by the possibility of distortions would mean becoming silent about issues that genuinely matter.

Manji's discourse on women's emancipation does not exhibit a similar concern about Western stereotypes. "Muslims," she states categorically, "exhibit a knack for degrading women and religious minorities" (Manji 2005, 176). Placing particular emphasis on her negative personal experiences with Muslim men, especially her father (10), Manji places women's empowerment at the top of her list of prescriptions for Islamic reform, as a means of overcoming traditional male dominance in the economic as well as religious domains:

> The road forward, it seems to me, must try to tackle three challenges at the same time: first, to revitalize Muslim economies by engaging the talents of women; second, to give the desert a run for its money by unleashing varied interpretations of Islam; and third, to work with the West, not against it ... My tentative conclusion: God-conscious, female fueled capitalism might be the way to start Islam's liberal reformation. (175-76)

Manji refers to her program as "Operation Ijtihad" (the title of her seventh chapter) and makes it clear that her primary intended audience is Western. "In each case," she states, "what we're undermining is hoary tribalism" (Manji 2005, 175). Unlike Raza, she makes no effort to inform the reader about profound differences between the life circumstances experienced by Muslim women. Manji's critics have objected to this implied equation of rural Saudi Arabia with the streets of West Beirut and to what they see as an equally problematic silence concerning the progress achieved by Muslim women in recent decades.[17]

Conclusion

Writers such as Manji and Raza have become increasingly influential sources of information about Islam and Muslims for the lay reader in Canada as well as in the United States, Europe, and (in the case of Manji) beyond. Both write in a highly accessible and conversational style, offering critiques that make references to academic literature while ultimately deriving their legitimacy from personal narratives and lived experiences. Their approaches are centred on issues that intrigue the mainstream reading public, and book sales (especially for Manji) appear to indicate that a large number of readers find "Muslim dissident" literature appealing.

Although the boldness of each author arguably merits recognition, some critics note that their writings are constructed in ways that are unlikely to win the confidence of most Muslim readers in Western as well as Muslim-majority countries. This criticism appears especially applicable to Manji, who appears to thrive on the controversy her book has generated and views it as a sign of progress. More cautious Muslim reformists and women's advocates who now go to great lengths to differentiate themselves from Manji may beg to differ. By dismissing as inappropriate or ill-founded virtually all

Muslim complaints vis-à-vis the West and upholding the West as a model for sweeping changes in Islamic religious and gender cultures, Manji constructs arguments that have little traction among all but the most secular of Muslims. Although some may unjustly reject Manji merely for her countercultural identity, her reluctance to articulate what it is that genuinely *inspires* her about Islam renders her critique unpersuasive and unmoving even to worldly and self-critical Muslims. Her stated intent in writing *The Trouble with Islam Today* was to initiate debate and provoke reform, yet many have found her approach to identity renegotiation unnecessarily polarizing at a time when dialogue and active listening might prove more effective for stimulating critical reflection.

Raza's approach, although not necessarily easy reading for many Muslims, is nonetheless couched in a language of faith that establishes a connection of sympathy with co-religionists. Her underlying message that Islam is a "religion of peace" helps to ensure that her book will never become a national bestseller, but many Canadian readers may nonetheless appreciate her willingness to engage sensitive topics. Although some have objected to what they regard as a Westernizing agenda, her book's most controversial content for Muslim readers is not so much in the realm of ideas as in her account of leading a mixed-gender prayer service in Toronto.

Of the two writers, Manji's style and market success have ensured stronger political criticism, particularly among those who fault her for failing to practise multiple critique. Whatever merit there may be in some of her criticisms of contemporary Muslim practices, why does she dismiss peace activists and encourage Western readers to resist multicultural accommodation of differences? Is it truly inappropriate to discuss lingering residues of the colonial era or the impact of power imbalances on Muslim behaviour? That Manji needs bodyguards lends some credibility to her allegations about closed-minded and unreasonable opponents, but political critics are arguably correct to point out larger implications of Manji's cultural and religious arguments.

Other lines of critique should also be noted. Those who assume a postmodernist stance may find that, when written in a "Western" (i.e., predominantly non-Muslim) context, books in the "Muslim dissident" genre tend to say as much about the author's immediate social, cultural, and political context as they say about the Muslim realities to which they refer. Islamic scholars are likely to take another tack, focusing on the journalistic and unsystematic style of both authors and on the need for deeper engagement with historical texts and precedents. Neither author, for example, takes the time to explain to the reader the juridical roots of *ijtihad*, a concept that is central to their reformist arguments and repeatedly invoked. Even a brief discussion of past usage of this concept in juristic reasoning would provide valuable context for considering ways that the principle might be expanded and applied more vigorously within contemporary Muslim communities.

At a time of profound international and intercultural tension, unprecedented numbers of people are seeking quick answers to questions about Islam. One place in which quick answers can be found is the "Muslim dissident" literature. The genre is by no means monolithic, as this comparison of Manji and Raza has demonstrated. It provides an intriguing window into the politics of Muslim identity in Canada and beyond but ultimately (at least for this author) generates more questions than answers. To what extent must the cause of reform in the Muslim world be directly linked to the values associated with Western liberalism and secularism? Are dissident writers wise to invoke Western standards as guiding principles for the renegotiation of Islamic identity and norms, or would they be well advised to imagine "Islamic futures" that would represent less of a rupture with internal Islamic resources, values, and traditions? Is the contemporary encounter of Western liberalism and Islam making each tradition more rigid and exclusive, or is there potential for bridge building, mutual accommodation, and more consciously pluralistic forms of social identity? Contributions from Canada's "Muslim dissident" writers remind us that we do indeed live in interesting times. Let us hope that, in the decades to come, today's heated controversies begin giving way to more enlightening negotiations.

ACKNOWLEDGMENTS
This chapter is a revised and extended version of my article "Dissident Muslims, Dissonant Times," which appeared in *Inroads* 26 (Winter/Spring 2010): 132-42.

NOTES
1. Many of these titles have been on the bestseller list in North America (e.g., *The Trouble with Islam Today* and *Infidel*).
2. As stated in a variety of interviews, several of these authors have received death threats. One author, Raheel Raza, claims on her website to be the sixth name on a "World's Most Hated Muslims" list (see http://www.raheelraza.com).
3. Irshad Manji has held a variety of honorary positions, as stated on her website (http://www.muslim-refusenik.com): she was a senior fellow with the European Foundation for Democracy; she has served as a visiting fellow at Yale University; and she has served as a journalist-in-residence at the University of Toronto. In addition,

the World Economic Forum has selected her as a Young Global Leader; *Ms.* magazine has named her a Feminist for the 21st Century; the *Jakarta Post* in Indonesia has identified her as one of three Muslim women creating positive change in Islam today; and the Government of Canada claims that "she is on a journey around the world to reconcile Islam and freedom."

4 At the time of publication of this chapter, Manji came out with another book, entitled *Allah, Liberty, and Love* (2011). Please know that I am not analyzing this text.

5 Speaking of a Canadian "majority culture" and a singular "Muslim-minority community" is, of course, potentially misleading. Even less diverse societies than Canada are far from monolithic, and Muslims in Canada are sufficiently diverse that some would deny the existence of a coherent "Muslim-minority community." Notions of a "majority culture" and a "Muslim-minority community" do, however, have sufficient symbolic resonance within Canada as a whole and among Muslims to merit the use of this terminology as a point of departure for more nuanced discussion of identity politics.

6 It is interesting to note that there has been no or little support for such dissident literature from Muslim women scholars (e.g., Leila Ahmed and Fatima Mernissi) who have been working on reform for decades.

7 In Germany a group of secularists from Turkish, Iranian, and Arabic backgrounds have formed the Central Committee for Ex-Muslims as a form of protest against being automatically identified as Muslim by the German government. This committee was also formed in opposition to the Central Committee of Muslims, which is Germany's most prominent Muslim organization. For more, see Saunders (2007).

8 Manji (2005, 3) coined the term "Muslim refusenik" and uses it to refer to her way of being Muslim; it implies a Muslim freedom fighter who strives against the oppressive nature of Muslim leadership.

9 The latest edition was published with the new title *The Trouble with Islam Today*. As noted in the "Afterword" of her 2005 edition, Manji was approached by a variety of Muslims who encouraged her to change her title to reflect the trouble is not with Islam but with Muslims. In response, Manji comments that her critics have a point; however, she states that "calling this book *The Trouble with Muslims*, as a lot of my critics have proposed, would invite another distraction: the charge – however politically motivated – that I'm attacking an identifiable group of people. Great for sales; not for sparking sincere conversations" (241). Her compromise would be to change the 2003 title of her book from *The Trouble with Islam* to *The Trouble with Islam Today*. This change in title implicitly acknowledges to a certain extent the possibility that Islam previously had no trouble. But in the book's content, Manji argues that there were problems with Islam even before "today."

10 In *Their Jihad ... Not My Jihad!* (2005), Raza introduces the problems and "injustices" that concern her about Muslims: fundamentalism and the rise of militant Islamic groups, including the Taliban; widespread injustices against women; and the challenges of separating culture from religion, truth and justice from propaganda, and the ritual from the spiritual. Manji, in her book *The Trouble with Islam Today* (2005) and in a documentary entitled *Faith without Fear* (National Film Board of Canada 2007), critiques a variety of problems and "injustices" in Muslim-majority countries,

such as the forcing of the *burqa* (cloak or overcoat) upon women in Yemen, the widespread phenomenon of fanaticism, which led Mohammed Bouyeri to murder filmmaker Theo van Gogh, and the suppression of independent thought regarding religious matters in any non-Western country where Muslims live.

11 I want to acknowledge the limitations in using such terms as "the West" and "Western." However, I try to use them to illustrate the perspectives taken by Manji and Raza. That being said, these labels, ultimately, tend to mask reality as much as reveal it.

12 Examples of such scholars are Karen Armstrong, Richard Bulliett, Norman Daniel, and Maria Rosa Menocal.

13 It is interesting to note that many wonder why Manji continues to label herself a Muslim if she is hanging onto Islam "by her fingernails," as she declares in the first lines of her book. Ayaan Hirsi Ali, another popular dissident writer about Islam, specifically states, "I could not believe she [Manji] was not an atheist" (in Gewen 2008).

14 After the tragic events of September 11, 2001, you find numerous articles, reports, and initiatives supporting the project of "moderate Islam," all of which share a common objective: the prevention of terrorism by Muslim extremists. Other examples of supporting a "moderate Islam" agenda are found in mainstream American institutions, as in the RAND Corporation's project and subsequent report "Civil Democratic Islam: Partners, Resources, and Strategies" (see Haddad 2004). The Carnègie Council on Ethics and International Affairs also sponsored a program entitled "The War for Muslim Minds" (September 2004), in which Gilles Kepel, a French Arabist, argued with Ian Buruma, author of books dealing with radical Islam, that moderate Muslims (especially living in the Muslim diaspora found in Europe) may be more powerful than previously perceived. There are also Muslim organizations, like the Center for the Study of Islam and Democracy (CSID), that advocate the project of "moderate/liberal" Muslims. However, as pointed out by Radwan Masmoudi (executive director of the CSID), to be labelled a "moderate Muslim" may benefit a Muslim in a Western context (i.e., in terms of backing as well as funding from Western political institutions) and simultaneously delegitimize a Muslim in an Islamic context (i.e., insofar as all your projects are seen as Western conspiracies). For more see Masmoudi (2003, 2004).

15 See the "Special Features" section of *Faith without Fear* (National Film Board of Canada 2007).

16 Both use modern Muslims to illustrate their points of critique. One shared resource mentioned by both authors is Khaled Abou El Fadl.

17 Although Muslim women do indeed face many difficulties that are increasingly unfamiliar to the average middle-class North American woman, as stated by many scholars of Muslim societies in most Muslim countries, a majority of university students are now women.

REFERENCES

Abou El Fadl, K. 2006. Foreword. In Amina Wadud, *Inside the gender jihad: Women's reform in Islam,* vii-xiv. Oxford, UK: Oneworld.

Barlas, A. 2005. The excesses of moderation. *American Journal of Islamic and Social Sciences* 22, 3: 158-65.
Gewen, B. 2008. Muslim rebel sisters: At odds with Islam and each other. *New York Times,* April 27, 3.
Haddad, Y. 2004. The quest for a "moderate Islam." *Al-Hewar Magazine* 115, 2: 8-12.
Mandaville, P. 2001. *Transnational Muslim politics: Reimagining the umma.* New York, NY: Routledge.
Manji, I. 2005. *The trouble with Islam today.* Toronto, ON: Random House of Canada.
–. 2007. Moderate Muslims must do more than preach moderation. *Globe and Mail,* July 4, A15.
Masmoudi, R. 2003. The silenced majority. *Journal of Democracy* 14, 2: 40-44.
–. 2004. Why the US should engage moderate Muslims everywhere. *Daily Star* (Beirut, Lebanon), October 26, n.p.
National Film Board of Canada, producer. 2007. *Faith without Fear.* DVD.
Raza, R. 2005. *Their Jihad ... Not my Jihad!* Ingersoll, ON: Basileia Books.
Saunders, D. 2007. Muslims find their voice outside religion: Secular movement stirring controversy across Europe. *Globe and Mail,* March 10, A01, A20.
Sharify-Funk, M. 2008. *Encountering the transnational: Women, Islam and the politics of interpretation.* Burlington, VT: Ashgate.

6 Toward Media Reconstruction of the Muslim Imaginary in Canada
The Case of the Canadian Broadcasting Corporation's Sitcom *Little Mosque on the Prairie*

ALIAA DAKROURY

Keeping up with fast-moving global technological advances, our age arguably leaves no space for the marginalized existence of minority cultures and their presence in their social milieus. According to Bhabha (1998, 33), "Obviously the dismissal of partial cultures, the emphasis on large numbers and long periods, is out of time with the modes of recognition of minority or marginalized cultures." Hence diversity and issues of equity cannot be ignored, especially in a country like Canada, where recent statistics show that in 2017 "roughly one out of every five people ... or between 19 percent and 23 percent of the nation's population ... [will be] a member of a visible minority" (Statistics Canada 2005). Within this context, Muslims, like other marginalized groups, seek to maintain and promote their culture, rituals, and religious rights in the post–September 11 media world.

As media constitute one of the most important means for accessing information, news, education, and entertainment in our lives, questions emerge in this context about whether media represent or *mis*represent Islam and Muslims. Do they enforce the stereotyping of Muslims as extremists, fundamentalists, and terrorists, among a long list of charges? Or alternatively do the media portray Muslims as an integral part of the Canadian multicultural social fabric?

In addressing such debates, this chapter provides a media-policy analysis of the groundbreaking sitcom *Little Mosque on the Prairie*, produced by the Canadian Broadcasting Corporation (CBC). This sitcom has arguably opened a public space for Muslim Canadians to express their traditions, rituals, culture, and religion on primetime Canadian television. *Little Mosque on the Prairie* debuted in the fall of 2007 as what might be called a *"halal"*[1] version of comedy and as an unprecedented intervention into Canadian television and the world of sitcoms. Here, it is argued that this program is an important part of a conscious, progressive, public attempt to reconstruct Muslim representation within Canadian society by shifting it away from the exotic tales of *One Thousand and One Nights*, on the one hand, and from the stereotyping of Muslims as terrorists, on the other. This sitcom has genuinely shifted the post–September 11 Muslim image, replacing the "fundamentalist" with the Canadian *"FUNdamentalist,"*[2] a natural human being who is simply "allowed to laugh."

Drawing on the work of Edward Said, this chapter questions and contests earlier scholarship on cultural-minority groups in Canada, using the case of *Little Mosque on the Prairie* to argue that it is not always true that media portray minority groups only when they "fit prevailing stereotypes of their groups" (Jiwani 1993, 10). In this particular case, one can see that there is a conscious attempt by a public broadcasting service – the CBC – to *reconstruct* the prototype media imaginary of Muslims and develop a new model of representation. The chapter goes on to articulate the role of media in fostering inclusion versus exclusion of minority groups and how the media could be seen as a site of competing agendas and a means of struggle and resistance for some cultural groups. Further, it highlights how publicly owned media have historically sought to create a Canadian national identity and how, through *Little Mosque on the Prairie*, the way that Muslims are perceived is being shaped within the Canadian imaginary.

Media: Our "Windows" to the World

Following the Second World War, media studies became one of the important sites of social research. Among the earliest efforts to theorize the function of media in our society is the research of Rivers and Schramm (1969, 14-15), who explain that media help to transmit cultural and societal values from one generation to another as well as among members of society. Media also play a chief role in creating awareness and reinforcement of opinions and attitudes as well as informing the public about issues of interest.

Marshall McLuhan, one of the most famous Canadian media theorists, envisaged the creation of a *global village* due to the widespread advances in the field of media technologies since the late 1950s. In recent years, contemporary media formations are seen as "'divisively' changing the traditional perspective of older media versions" (Appadurai 1996, 3). Claims have been made to underscore the role of media as one of the pervasive forces in our modern societies and to illustrate our heavy dependence on their different forms (e.g., newspapers, magazines, television, radio) to receive information about communal, national, and international society. According to Brawley (1983, 12), "Our understanding of and attitudes toward people, events, and problems are greatly influenced by the information and views communicated through these media."

Furthermore, the media are not only a means of accessing information but also a tool of cultural domination, struggle, and resistance, as Michèle Martin explains in her book *Communication and Mass Media* (1997). Detailing the process of the social construction of events in the media, Martin (1997, 5) emphasizes that "mass media content is not a simple reflection of society, but a product that is intended to achieve a specific goal." This reminds us that there are diverse and often destructive motives behind different messages transmitted in the media (see also Chapter 4). Adopting a Gramscian perspective, Martin (1997, 72) argues that media messages tend to be dominated by a hegemonic culture that is "powerful enough to impose its norms, values and ideas on the cultural practices of an entire society in terms of both the activities of *everyday life* and artistic creation" (emphasis added). In other words, media help to transfer events or information rather than *produce* a given society's built-in symbolic system of language. Hall (1977, 343) argues strongly in favour of this account:

> Events on their own cannot ... signify: they must be *made intelligible;* and the process of social intelligibility consists precisely in those practices which translate "real" events ... into symbolic form ... [and hence] There are significantly different ways in which events – especially problematic or troubling events ... can be encoded. (Emphasis in original)

In others words, media *selectively* assign a particular meaning (or code, in Hall's understanding) to a given event within a particular context. Media present events in a particular sequence, correlating them to a particular meaning and framing them in terms of selective codes that are often scripted negatively. Lull (2000, 242) confirms that media imagery is key in reconstructing "essential axes of cultural distance – space and time ... [as it] permits new perceptions and uses of cultural time." Today's electronic media, such as films and audio and video productions, have transformed the way that culture is interpreted in society. In other words, media have become our windows to the world, as we depend on their screens, pages, images, and interpretations to know what we can experience and what we *cannot*.

Media in Canada: A Site of Struggle and Contestation

In June 2008 many observers, human rights advocates, journalists, Muslim groups, and media professionals in Canada were carefully following the trial of Mark Steyn (a senior columnist of *Maclean's Magazine* and a strong opponent of the idea of multiculturalism in Canada) for promoting hatred against Islam and Muslims in his 2006 published article "The Future Belongs to Islam." The Canadian Islamic Congress accused Steyn and *Maclean's* of being "flagrantly Islamophobic," asserting that a total of eighteen articles published in *Maclean's* between 2005 and 2007 "subject[ed] Canadian Muslims to hatred and contempt" (Levant 2007). Although the case was dismissed by the Ontario Human Rights Commission (2008), the commission has been clear about the conduct it expects of the media in Canada:

> While freedom of expression must be recognized as a cornerstone of a functioning democracy, the Commission strongly condemns the Islamophobic portrayal of Muslims, Arabs, South Asians and indeed any racialized community in the media, such as the Maclean's article and others like them, as being inconsistent with the values enshrined in our human rights codes. Media has a responsibility to engage in fair and unbiased journalism.

Such a controversial case exemplifies, to a great extent, the debate surrounding the role of media in Canadian society, particularly the question of whether media act as a site of protracted struggle against neoconservative corporate and political interests or whether they are a tool of liberation and a means for gaining discursive authority, especially in the case of Muslims and Islam. Numerous studies have investigated the role of media in this debate, taking several intellectual and philosophical turns. One of these important contributions is the work of Razack (1998, 91), who argues that Western media are producing "a discursive apparatus that entrenches notions of Western superiority and Third World inferiority." In other words, applying this understanding to the case of non-Western cultural communities, there is indeed an ambiguity in viewing cultural forms and backgrounds with suspicion, if not exclusionary narratives. Sassen (2006, 414) underscores the importance of religion and culture as social and political dynamics in the discourse of nationalism, arguing that the use of religion and "culture" rather than citizenship to construct membership may well be a function of the changed relationship of citizens to the state and the insecurities it produces. In this regard, use of religion is not an anachronism but a formation arising out of particular changes in the current age.

Indeed, since September 11, there have been debates over what "being Canadian" means and over the notion of belonging, especially among Canadian Muslims, who have been marginalized by what scholars describe as a "fragile narrative of 'Canadianness'" (Zine 2006, 246). Empirical studies show that media represent one of the important means of constructing identity, especially for immigrant, diasporic, and minority groups. For example, Anderson (1983) asserts that different media forms make possible the construction of "imagined communities," with electronic online media tools facilitating communication between home and a new homeland for many immigrants of minority groups in the world. Gillespie (1995, 16) further argues that communication technologies can melt distances and overcome time, concluding that the use of media "[allows] people to escape from forms of identity forged by the relation between person and the 'symbolic place' identical with geographical locality." Therefore, the main objective of media output, such as news reporting and audio and video productions, is not to convey an "understood" meaning, as van Dijk (1991, 229) asserts, but to build *a system of meanings and representation*. He adds that such social representations are generalized to the "organized clusters of socially shared beliefs ... and so are ideologies" (46). Thus the very nature of ideology, according to van Dijk, manages how certain groups (or group relations) are represented in the media of a given society. He adds that "positive self-presentation and negative other-presentation seems to be a fundamental property of ideologies" (69). Indeed, media do not present a "mirror-image" of society but rather frame relationships between discursively constituted ideologies, generating notions of "us" versus "them." Naturally, the "us" are represented as "good," whereas the "them" are represented as "bad." This is especially true in the portrayal of religious ideologies, which "represent Us as (good) believers and Them as (bad) non-believers (infidels, heathens, etc.)" (68). Members of the public, as consumers of media, are not neutral subjects but rather are "social subjects of a particular class, society or culture, as family members, and therefore their behaviours, including media consumption and interpretation are shaped by this membership" (Harindranath

2000, 154). Ramji (2005) adds that such media narratives are historically evident as early as 1896, when American cinema stereotyped Muslims as the "cultural other" through various racial and religious themes. For instance, Ramji analyzes the depictions of Arab Muslims as "faceless militant terrorists" in the movie *The Siege*, which uses the word "terrorist" eight times to describe Muslims. This finding relates to Muslims living in the West today, who seriously perceive such ongoing representations with "ambivalent feelings of frustration at the colonial attitudes fostered about them and of the fear of Western retaliation based on these racial suppositions" (Ramji 2005).

Islam in the Media Imaginary: A Saidian Lens

> *Islam has been fundamentally misrepresented in the West – the real issue is whether indeed there can be a true representation of anything, or whether any and all representations, because they are representations, are embedded first in the language and then in the culture, institutions, and political ambience of the representer. If the latter alternative is the correct one (as I believe it is), then we must be prepared to accept the fact that a representation is ... implicated, intertwined, embedded, interwoven with a great many other things besides the "truth," which is itself a representation. (Said 1978, 272, emphasis in original)*

Said (1978) has framed the notion of "culture" through a discourse of cultural imperialism, providing an interpretation of culture that is uniquely different from interpretations offered in previous scholarship, which are framed in terms of a critique of modernity, of global capitalism, of political and media imperialism, or of nationalism. Said's work builds on Fanon's (1965) idea of situating culture and media as *tools of struggle*. Fanon legitimized the use of communication media, such as radio and newspapers, in the Algerian struggle for independence from the French colonizer. Similarly, Said argues that culture can be used in two different ways in resistance movements. The first is through creating different communication patterns or practices to defend culture and its existence; an example is the emergence of cultural cinema, theatre, poetry, and literature as an "assembly of cultural expression that has become part of the consolidation and persistence of ...

identity" (in Barsamian 2003, 159). However, he puts a great deal of emphasis on the use of culture as a "critical" discourse that analyzes history and investigates its consequences, not only in the past but with considerations for the future. He asserts, "The power to analyze, to get past cliché and straight out-and-out lies from authority, the questioning of authority, the search for alternatives. These are also part of the arsenal of cultural resistance" (in Barsamian 2003, 159). Undeniably, Said's (1993) understanding of cultural resistance, especially in opposing media *mis*representation – such as the case of Muslims in the West – offers an excellent explanation of the success of *Little Mosque on the Prairie* in Canada. This show has to a great extent resisted the impetus to purvey a particular image of Muslims as "enemies" or the "Other," an image increasingly prevalent since 9/11, and instead actively works to subvert this paradigm.

Said (1978, xiii) also highlights how media constitute the nation: "Culture is a concept that includes a refining and elevating element, each society's reservoir of the best that has been known and thought ... in time, culture comes to be associated ... with the nation or the state; this differentiates 'us' from 'them' almost always with some degree of xenophobia." Outlining the imperialist divide between the "West and the rest of the world" (108), Said describes the "codification of difference" on linguistic and historical levels, where certain codes are used to signify the difference between civilized and primitive peoples/nations. Such categorizations can be easily seen in the dichotomy between "superior or civilized" people and "savage, natural" people. For instance, stories and novels – as examples of cultural productions – are for Said integral to the explorer's imagination, both as a means to know about certain places in the world and as a tool of struggle in places where people defend their existence in the historical sphere. Said (1978, 3) argues that "without examining Orientalism as a discourse one cannot possibly understand the enormously systematic discipline by which European cultur[e] was able to manage – and even produce – the Orient politically, sociologically, militarily, ideologically, scientifically, and imaginatively during the post-Enlightenment period."

For Said, Orientalism is a condition that has had a long history and that is not simply the product of today's problems of representation (such as the current representation of Islam). Rather, he notes that Orientalism can be traced back as far as the eighteenth century and Napoleon's knowledge about Egypt before his expedition to that country. Said (1978, 94) argues that what Napoleon knew about the Orient was written in the tradition of Orientalism, which "made the Orient possible. Such an Orient was silent, available to Europe ... and unable to resist the projects, images, or mere descriptions devised for it." What Said wants to explain here is the profound impact of the Occidental culture on the Oriental culture and traditions, an impact made possible by the belief that power always came from the West to the East.[3] Said adds that even after becoming independent, in the eyes of the Occident, or the West, the Orient is still unable to adopt modern changes in realms such as politics: "Orientalism has taken a further step than that: it views that Orient as something whose existence is not only displayed but has remained fixed in time and place for the West" (108). Thus the West is convinced that the Orient is incompatible with the Occident since the Orient's cultural production cannot by any means be compared favourably to that of the West; consequently, the "Arab and Islamic world[4] [as one example] ... as a whole is hooked into the Western market system" (324).

We can see that Said's work informs this discussion of how media practices, especially since 9/11, have purveyed cultural images that portray the West as the *hero* and the rest of the world as the *villain;* the recent spread of the cultural image of the Muslim as terrorist is undeniable. Within a Canadian context, Ramji (2005) squarely endorses the Saidian explanation for this phenomenon, arguing that the "media in many ways has painted a distorted picture that equates terrorism with all Islam ... Islam has continually been depicted as 'other', separate from values of Western democracy and society: now though, Muslims battle against the label of Islamic terrorist."

This is certainly evident in many Western media productions. Taking the Disney *Aladdin* movie as one example, we can see Islam – its distant Oriental place, its setting in the desert between the caravan and camels, and its practice – depicted as "barbaric," even if framed in a musical format and directed to an audience of children:

> Oh I come from a land, from a faraway place
> Where the caravan camels roam
> Where it's flat and immense
> And the heat is intense
> It's barbaric, but hey, it's home. (Walt Disney Company 1992)

Drawing from Said's work, Karim (2000, 62), in his analysis of a group of Canadian newspapers, confirms that dominant images of Muslims (and Arabs) continue to depict them as "all fabulously wealthy; they are barbaric and uncultured; they are sex maniacs with a penchant for White slavery;

and they revel in acts of terrorism." Northern discourses over the past fourteen centuries, as Karim outlines in his analysis, centre on "the Muslim's depiction as a villain [which] carries a high level of plausibility in cultural entertainment that portrays the struggles of the good against the bad" or simply against the "Other," who is depicted negatively as the enemy, rival, and villain (65).

A timely question here is whether this view of Muslims can be *changed*. And what factors could possibly enforce such a transformation in the Western mainstream media? Scholars maintain that "Muslims in the media have no voice, no platform, so they cannot object or explain" (Akbar 1992, 256). Can we apply the same argument in Canada? In the following section, I give an overview of a Canadian public-media attempt to *reconstruct* this media imaginary of Islam and Muslims through the case study of CBC's *Little Mosque on the Prairie*.

Little Mosque on the Prairie: Toward Media Inclusion of Muslims in Canada

The Canadian Broadcasting Corporation's sitcom *Little Mosque on the Prairie* is a "Canadian-made" attempt to make Muslims more visible in Canadian mainstream media. Since September 11, 2001, Muslims have been sensationalized in media that highlight the inherited clashes between Western and Muslim cultures.[5] Thus, for the first time, this sitcom portrays daily interactions between Muslims and non-Muslims, namely between the residents of the fictional town of Mercy, Saskatchewan. Yet one can wonder why Zarqa Nawaz, the creator and writer of the show, chose to replace the American house of *Little House on the Prairie* with a mosque? Besides being the place of worship for Muslims around the world, mosques have become "the most prominent institutional symbols for Muslims in Canada" (Abu-Laban 1983, 79). For many Muslim Canadians, mosques represent a communicational space and a community forum where they not only pray but also interact with others and engage with social and political concerns as well as sponsor social and educational events.

Nawaz explains that "in Canada, the mosque [as an Islamic institutional symbol] may be the only Muslim space available to women," an observation that opposes the traditional view of the mosque as an "exclusively male space" in many Islamic countries (in Hussain 2006, 125). In her first documentary, *Me and the Mosque* (2005) – distributed by the National Film Board of Canada – she relates her concerns about North American Muslim women's space in mosques. She elaborates on these tensions and relationships in her *Little Mosque* sitcom, which premiered in the fall of 2007 with a viewership of 2 million, the most watched debut of any Canadian television show. For Nawaz, this show is an important corrective to the stereotypes of Muslims and simply shows that they *can* laugh and, importantly, that they *can make* people laugh:

> Anyone who belongs to a faith community can recognise the stereotypes that exist in a mosque because they also exist in their houses of worship. So the primary motive was to make it fun and humourous and to get people to laugh. Ultimately if it's not engaging and entertaining, people won't watch it and we won't get the ratings to get renewed. That, ultimately, was our priority. (In Amanullah 2007)

Adding to the storyline, the mosque is located in a rented basement of the parish hall of the town's Anglican Church, resulting in hilarious inter-religious situations. For instance, when a local citizen visits the church, he is shocked to see Muslims (women in veils and men in turbans) praying and bowing. Instantly, he runs outside to call the "Terrorists Attack Hotline." Later, when he meets the Reverend Magee from the church, he exclaims that he "saw them bowing just like on CNN!" and accuses the reverend of "renting our parish hall to a bunch of fanatics!" (*Little Mosque on the Prairie*, episode 1, January 9, 2007).

Such stereotypes are evoked in order to reveal their fallacy. Nawaz argues that "the Muslim community is dying for a portrayal of Muslims that is more dynamic and more nuanced than the traditional terrorist villain" (in Intini 2006). The stereotype of Muslims as connected with terrorism is clearly projected in one of the sitcom's scenes where an Anglo-Canadian character insists that being a Canadian Muslim *contractor* doesn't refute his confirmed link to terrorism, commenting that "Osama bin Laden runs a construction company too!" (*Little Mosque on the Prairie*, episode 1, January 9, 2007). Interestingly, the issue of connections between Muslim Canadians and bin Laden was one raised in one interview with Nawaz, where she was asked, "How much are you paid by Al Qaida to produce your show to try to soften up the Canadian public for an attack? The idea is to reduce our suspicion of these lovely humourous Moslems so they can do their worst" ("Little Mosque on the Prairie" 2007).[6]

It is important to recognize that this CBC sitcom has garnered widespread media attention not only in Canada but also globally. The English version of the Al Jazeera Network, for instance, has praised the cultural and social effects of the sitcom on Muslim Canadian immigrants, who surprisingly are portrayed in a positive manner:

> They're not terrorists, they're not religious freaks. There's nothing odd or menacing about the Muslim characters on *Little Mosque on the Prairie* – they're just like any other Canadian citizens ... The show tells universal stories about the interactions and relationships between people and familiar topics about immigrants. It is enlightening. People will come away with an understanding of a misrepresented group. (Al Jazeera English 2007)

Little Mosque's tides of success have carried it to many places around the world, where audiences have requested either to see the sitcom, to have it translated into their own language, or to produce their own version of it. For example, in France, the French broadcasting company Canal + has signed an agreement with the production company WestWind Pictures to distribute *Little Mosque* in France, considering it one of the top television hits among popular American series such as *Desperate Housewives*, *Will and Grace*, *Weeds*, and *The Simpsons*. Similar deals have been signed in Switzerland, Israel, the West Bank, Gaza, Finland, and the United Arab Emirates. Recently, Fox Television announced that it will import *Little Mosque* to the United States (Surette 2008). Within Canada, Radio-Canada has also agreed to air *La petite mosquée dans la prairie*, the francophone version of the sitcom.

It is important to underline here that although *Little Mosque* is a unique attempt to integrate a comedic Muslim presence into Canadian television, it builds on the work of other Muslim comedic endeavours in North America, such as the Muslim stand-up comedy of Preacher Moss and Azhar Usman and their first Muslim comedy tour in the United States, *Allah Made Me Funny*. However, *Little Mosque* stands in contrast to a show like *Aliens in America*, a sitcom produced by the CW Network – a joint venture of Warner Bros. Entertainment and CBS Corporation (Ausiello 2008) – that premiered around the same time as *Little Mosque*. Philip Bennett (2008, 11), the managing editor at the *Washington Post*, has admitted that with such a Muslim presence in the American media,

> Muslims in the US are on the march from being "them" to being "us." Journalism plays a role in transforming "Others" into us. This is not necessarily a happy story; it does not mean papering over conflicts or uncomfortable truths. It does mean crossing boundaries – sometimes on a map,

sometimes in your head – to engage honestly with how we are all influencing each other's lives.

As stated in the title, Muslims are assumed to be "aliens" in America, with only one character – Rajaa, the Pakistani exchange student – having visited the United States. In contrast, *Little Mosque* integrates different Muslim characters into the sitcom's plot – a physician, university professor, student, restaurant owner, government employee, lawyer, and contractor, among others – as part of the social fabric of increasingly diversifying small-town Canada. Despite the success of *Aliens in America*,[7] the CW Network cancelled the sitcom's second season at a time when *Little Mosque* was reporting top ratings[8] that even other established Canadian sitcoms had not reached – like the CTV's *Corner Gas* (Macdonald 2007). In the interview cited above, Zarqa Nawaz was asked about the difference between the Canadian and the European portrayals of Muslims in the media, an indication of the show's global popularity:

> I think the reason it wasn't made in Europe was because the Muslim experience in Europe has been very different than the Muslim experience in North America. For the most part, the Muslim community has been far more assimilated and has integrated more successfully in North America. The rates of employment and income are much higher and therefore you have a different population which doesn't have a lot of anger on its shoulder. And I think comedy has to come from a good place, a place where someone is fairly well adjusted and happy with her surroundings. Those combinations together, I think, resulted in the show coming out of Canada first. ("Little Mosque on the Prairie" 2007)

Interestingly, the *Little Mosque* venture has resulted in a desire among some Muslims for a similar media production in Europe. Sardar (2007, 28), for example, notes that although there are ethnic sitcoms in Britain centred on blacks, Indians, and gays, there has been no attempt to broadcast any Muslim sitcoms. He adds that the British broadcaster is more "obsessed" with *shar'ia* (Islamic law) and with conservative Muslims, to the extent that in October 2007 the BBC aired a three-hour episode of the reality show *Shar'ia Street*. Sardar points out that this media focus should be terminated to prevent viewers from adopting a view of Muslims as the "Other": "The ghoulish fanatics, the shar'ia schlock, the ex-Islamist, the burqa-clad evangelical have now become banal and boring. It's time to satirise them out of existence. So, bring on the comedians and the sitcoms" (28).

One can argue that there is a *new* movement in the media in Canada toward a reconstruction of the Muslim imaginary in order to counter the image of Islam as "the deadly enemy of the West and the source of terrorism," an image that "regularly appears in American, British, and Canadian press articles" (Karim 2000, 80). Karim (2002) advocates the idea of promoting ethnic media that serve the minority communities in Canada by preserving their cultures, rituals, and languages. This position is sound and might be productive, yet I argue that it continues to draw a distinction within Canadian society between "we" and "them," *our* media and *their* media, *our* programming and *their* programming. *Little Mosque*, in contrast, has pioneered a new kind of media production that portrays Muslim Canadians as a part of the multicultural mosaic, using close-ups, music, and humour to convey banal, everyday life in small-town Canada.

The Canadian Broadcasting Corporation and the Public Interest

The Canadian Multiculturalism Act of 1985 states a fundamental guiding principle of this act in Article 3g, which regards "promoting the understanding and creativity that arise from the interaction between individuals and communities of different origins" (Department of Justice Canada 1985). The question for media and cultural producers who seek to promote such dialogical encounters is how to actualize these utopian ideals, keeping in mind the relations of power between differently enfranchised groups in this country.

Public-service broadcasting is a key component in establishing and enforcing a democratic dialogue in society. However, others believe that Canada *does not* need a public broadcaster. For marginalized communities such as Muslims, a question remains about the degree to which public broadcasting acts as a means for social inclusion. Raboy and Taras, in "On Life Support: The CBC and the Future of Public Broadcasting in Canada" (2007), pinpoint a crucial problematic in the future premise of the Canadian broadcasting system. They highlight the challenges that surround Canadian broadcasting in an era of globalized cultural productions and their effective dissemination via different media technologies, such as the Internet and satellites. Raboy and Taras explain that due to the multicultural, multi-ethnic, and multilinguistic makeup of Canada, and the resulting divergent tastes of the population, Canadians receive broadcasting signals from around the world, including tempting popular American programming. Still, it is critical to question whether more viewing choices can be produced in Canada. The authors maintain that although it is necessary for Canadians to receive such cultural production via non-Canadian channels, it is equally important that this not be "at the expense of the country's need to communicate *with itself* to keep its own channels of communication open and available" (Raboy and Taras 2007, 85, emphasis added).

This position maintains that democracy is furthered whenever we have open channels of debate, corresponding regulative bodies, and a dynamic public sphere, among other apparatuses. Furthermore, broadcasting – notably television broadcasting – has proven to manipulate its audience, particularly in relation to politics, political images, and the political process. Research argues that public broadcasting has transformed politicians into "actors" and turned political debates into "entertainment." Because of this phenomenon, it has been stated that although it is a "noble argument" to maintain that "public broadcasting [is capable of airing] unconventional, controversial, or challenging materials ... [that] can speak for those who are disenfranchised, marginalized, or ignored by private broadcasting ... [and that can] treat viewers as citizens rather than as consumers," this contention is "unfortunately ... inaccurate" (Raboy and Taras 2007, 102).

Despite how sound the previous position might be, I argue that to some extent it is not practical and does not offer a solid basis for marginalized and minoritized citizens who have the right to self-representation. Whether private or commercial, broadcasting has proven, at least historically, to be driven principally by a consumerist approach. Babe (1995, 75-80) argues that politically it is possible to preserve "sovereignty" by means of communications that grant credence to a group of ideological myths, such as the myth of the *market* as exemplified through neoliberalism (i.e., privatization, deregulation, revoking social programs) and expressed in the notion that the "market will allocate resources in the best of all possible ways." This media situation justifies the strong opposition that has been voiced by many public interests advocating for an enhancement of the Canadian public-broadcasting system so that it can act as a "vital mirror and exhibitor of national cultures" (Raboy and Taras 2007, 84). Furthermore, it has been noted that during the past few years, private broadcasters have "largely failed to produce programs that link people to their national experience and that address their needs as citizens" (Raboy and Taras 2007, 84). Still, the question remains of whether it is fair to accuse the CBC, as the public broadcaster, of being "distrustful of public taste," as suggested by its adoption of a "paternalistic pattern" (Attallah 2008, 13).

It is my position that the CBC holds an absolute duty to represent all of the Canadian public's ethnic and religious backgrounds. In fact, there are numerous examples of public broadcasting that successfully meets this duty: Vision Television (which features multifaith programming), OMNI1 and OMNI2 TV, the Aboriginal People's Television Network (APTN), Fairchild (for Cantonese and Mandarin programming), Telelatino (for Italian and Spanish programming), and CHIN radio (which airs more than thirty languages), among others. I have argued elsewhere that such media are an absolute enforcement of both the Canadian Multiculturalism Act and the right of *other cultures* to communicate during prime airtime in Canada (Dakroury 2006, 2008). It has been argued that Western nations have reassessed their view regarding the necessity of public broadcasting, coming to believe that it plays a key role in civil engagement within social democracies. As John Ralston Saul puts it, "Everybody who is smart in bureaucracies and government around the Western world now knows that public broadcasting is one of the most important remaining levers that a nation state has to *communicate with itself*" (in Taras 2008, 6, emphasis added). Raboy (1990, xii) maintains that Canadian broadcasting has experienced many conflicting and competitive forces since its early days but has proven that it is "one of the privileged arenas of struggle" in ideological battles. Since its creation in the mid-1930s, the CBC has struggled with competing forces, ideas, and groups. What is important to point out here is that the basic driving force to initiate and create the CBC was the concept of equal access to the Canadian airwaves.[9] Taras (2008, 6) confirms that "the new goal of public broadcasting is to build social capital by 'bridging,' 'bonding,' and 'witnessing,' but most of all by treating audience members as citizens rather than as consumers." The willingness of the CBC to air a primetime sitcom discussing and portraying Canadian Muslims should be applauded on many fronts, notably given that the Canadian "public expectations of the CBC run high" and that the CBC, as the Canadian public broadcaster, "is meant to be all things to all Canadians" (Taras 2008, 5).

Reconstructing Existing Frames: What Is Possible?

That *Little Mosque* is produced, sponsored, and aired in primetime by Canada's national public broadcaster serves to mitigate against some of the criticisms of media representation of Islam and Muslims in Canada. For instance,

Karim (2000) argues that mainstream "cultural workers" in the West (e.g., writers, filmmakers, producers) are creating images that *conform* to the "dominant stereotypes" of Muslims and Islam. Even when an alternative narrative appears, it usually tends, as Karim (2000, 111-17) adds, to be placed in the "back pages." Similarly, Jiwani (2006, 60) asserts that although the efficacy of mainstream media channels in achieving what is desired in media practices "is highly debatable," she depends on alternative media channels and considers such action to be "an urgent matter." Jiwani confirms, moreover, that Canada's regulatory bodies – such as the Canadian Radio-television and Telecommunications Commission (CRTC), the Canadian Association of Broadcasters (CAB), and other media advocates – "support and uphold the principles of objectivity, balance, and impartiality in media organization" (60-61). *Little Mosque* has therefore contributed to developing a new discursive site for the Muslim presence in Canada. And although not all Muslim Canadians unequivocally support the show – many have sharp criticisms, arguing that it reduces Muslims to "mosque-based" communities that are not representative of the diversity of Muslim Canadians – it is by catalyzing these kinds of internal debates that the show further contributes to dialogical encounters inside and outside of the Muslim community. Regardless of the criticisms, *Little Mosque* is an unprecedented intervention that has proven that Muslim experiences are worthy of primetime representation in Canadian television.

In this chapter, I have argued that the CBC (as one of the mainstream cultural industries in Canada) has begun to counter such interpretations by airing an unconventional portrayal of Muslims. This is an initiative that supports public-service advocates who call for a Canadian *self-communicative practice* "from within" society that is inclusive of the voices of groups that are marginalized through underrepresentation or misrepresentation in the media. In fact, Nawaz confirms this argument:

> You know, we were one step removed from 9/11 so that rawness wasn't there in the country. The networks were more willing to take a chance on a subject like this. Also, the network here is the CBC *(the Canadian Broadcasting Corporation)*, which is a publically owned and funded television station. It's a not-for-profit station so they don't have to worry about profit-making as much as representing the diversity and the regionality of the country. ("Little Mosque on the Prairie" 2007)

We can see the difficulties and challenges facing such productions in our age of giant media conglomeration, which favours the consumerist goals of private media. Although this reality may diminish hopes for changing the status quo, the success that the CBC's *Little Mosque* achieved in less than two years and the extent to which private media (in and outside of Canada) showed an interest in airing this sitcom are certainly reasons to be optimistic about television's ability to serve the public interest. It is true that in our post-9/11 society, it is difficult to change the stereotyped construction of the Muslim as "the militant martyr or suicide bomber ... [even] the veiled woman ... depicted as both oppressed by and subjugated under Islam" (Jiwani 2006, 198-99). Yet alternative media productions can possibly reconstruct such images if they are (1) aired in primetime to gain a high viewership, (2) sponsored by a public broadcaster that can lend them credibility, and (3) framed in an attractive genre of writing/production to garner wide audience attention. Such factors explain *Little Mosque*'s success; after all, "laughing is a human nature, not a cultural phenomenon," and by instinct, Muslims are "allowed to laugh" (Dakroury 2008, 43).

NOTES

1 The Arabic word "halal" means "permissible" with respect to Islamic law, in contrast to "haram" (impermissible).
2 Inspired by Zarqa Nawaz, *Little Mosque on the Prairie*'s screenwriter, FUNdamentalist Films is a production company that co-produces the CBC sitcom and that has produced other short films and documentaries with Islamic themes, such as *BBQ Muslims, Fred's Burqa,* and *Random Check*. For more information, see http://fundamentalistfilms.com. Nawaz has been named one of the "ten young visionaries shaping Islam in America" by *Islamica Magazine* and is a recipient of an Outstanding International Achievement Award from Women in Film and Television – Toronto (Zine 2007, 379).
3 For Said (1978, 2-3), Orientalism is "a style of thought based on an ontological and epistemological distinction made between 'the Orient' and (most of the time) 'the Occident.' Thus a very large mass of writers ... poets, novelists, philosophers, political theorists, economists, and imperial administrators, have accepted the basic distinction between East and West as the starting point for elaborate theories, epics, novels, social descriptions, and political accounts concerning the Orient, its people, customs, 'mind,' destiny, and so on."
4 More particularly, according to Said, the West is not the only party responsible for Orientalism. In the Middle East, for example, residents of the region are themselves participating "in [their] own Orientalism" (Said 1978, 325) through their selective consumption of both "material and ideological" American products.

5 Among the many aspects that attract media coverage in this respect is the portrayal of Muslim women as "suppressed, repressed, oppressed, and depressed because of Islam" (Siddiqui 2001). Ramji (2005) adds that Hollywood production "has reinforced this ... stereotype, which is often overwhelmingly negative." Since the 1950s, movies such as *Thief of Damascus* (1952), *Indiana Jones and the Raiders of the Lost Ark* (1981), and *Ishtar* (1987) have propagated the same stereotypical negative images of Muslims. Yet such misrepresentation has become a sensational trend, especially within the Canadian market. Research has shown that after 9/11 Canadian video stores recorded a peak in rentals of movies depicting violent terrorist attacks on Americans, such as *The Siege* (1998) and *True Lies* (1994), which in 1998 were ranked number 3 and 5 respectively on the list of top-selling DVDs in Canada. The plots of these movies usually centre on a "Western" agent battling Islamic terrorist groups, jihadists, fundamentalists, and the like (Ramji 2005). Shaheen, in his *Reel Bad Arabs: How Hollywood Vilifies a People* (2001), presents a longitudinal analysis of more than 1,000 movies produced by Hollywood that portray Arabs (and Muslims) in a negative fashion (see also Shaheen 1984).

6 Nawaz, the "FUNdamentalist," humorously replied to this question by saying, "I don't think Osama is going to be very happy with this show, because I think he'd rather Muslims be fearful of non-Muslims. So, unfortunately, I don't think we'll be getting any funds from his organization" ("Little Mosque on the Prairie" 2007).

7 Bennett (2008, 3) asserts that "the US news media has failed to produce sustained coverage of Islam to challenge the easy assumptions, gross generalizations or untested rhetoric that shape perceptions of Muslims."

8 *Little Mosque*'s high ratings do not alter the fact that there was some dissatisfaction with *Little Mosque* "within" Canadian Islamic organizations. Tarek Fatah, the founder of the Muslim Canadian Congress, criticized the sitcom as "a step backward" (Al Jazeera English 2007).

9 Cook and Ruggles (1992) explain that the concept of balance was introduced by the Aird Royal Commission to "prevent abusive and one-sided comment on religious and political matters" in programming form and content.

REFERENCES

Abu-Laban, B. 1983. The Canadian Muslim community: The need for a new survival strategy. In E.H. Waugh, B. Abu-Laban, and R.B. Qureshi, eds., *The Muslim community in North America*, 75-92. Edmonton, AB: University of Alberta Press.

Akbar, A. 1992. *Postmodernism and Islam: Predicament and promise*. New York, NY: Routledge.

Al Jazeera English. 2007. A little mosque grows. http://english.aljazeera.net/.

Amanullah, Z. 2007. Interview with Nawaz. http://www.altmuslim.com/.

Anderson, B. 1983. *Imagined communities: Reflections on the origin and spread of nationalism*. London: Verso.

Appadurai, A. 1996. *Modernity at large: Cultural dimensions of globalization*. Minneapolis, MN: University of Minnesota Press.

Attallah, P. 2008. What is the public in public broadcasting? In C. Elliott and J. Greenberg, eds., *Communication in question: Competing perspectives on controversial issues in communication studies*, 11-17. Toronto, ON: Thompson-Nelson Canada.

Ausiello, M. 2008. It's official: CW axes Aliens in America. *TV Guide*, May 9. http://www.tvguide.com/.

Babe, R.E. 1995. *Communication and the transformation of economics: Essays in information, public policy, and political economy*. Boulder, CO, and Oxford, UK: Westview.

Barker, C. 1999. *Television, globalization and cultural identities*. Philadelphia, PA: Open University Press.

Barsamian, D. 2003. *Culture and resistance: Conversations with Edward W. Said*. Cambridge: South End Press.

Bennett, P. 2008. *Covering Islam: A challenge for American journalism*. Irvine, CA: Center for the Study of Democracy, University of California.

Bhabha, H. 1998. Culture's in-between. In D. Bennett, ed., *Multicultural states: Rethinking difference and identity*, 29-37. New York, NY: Routledge.

Brawley, E.A. 1983. *Mass media and human services: Getting the message across*. Beverly Hills, CA: Sage.

Canadian Radio-Television and Telecommunications Commission. 2002. *Broadcasting policy monitoring report 2002*. http://www.crtc.gc.ca/.

Cook, G., and M.A. Ruggles. 1992. Balance and freedom of speech: Challenge for Canadian broadcasting. *Canadian Journal of Communication* 17, 1: http://www.cjc-online.ca/.

Dakroury, A. 2006. Pluralism and the right to communicate in Canada. *Media Development: Journal of the World Association for Christian Communication* 53, 1: 36-40.

—. 2008. CBC's *Little Mosque on the Prairie* and the right of "Others" to communicate in Canada. *Media Development: Journal of the World Association for Christian Communication* 3: 42-46.

Department of Justice Canada. 1985. *Canadian multiculturalism act, R.S.C., 1985, c. 24 (4th supp.)*. http://laws.justice.gc.ca/.

Estrin, J. 2006. Sitcom's precarious premise: Being Muslim over here. *New York Times*, December 7. http://www.nytimes.com/.

Fanon, F. 1965. *A dying colonialism*. New York, NY: Grove.

Gillespie, M. 1995. *Television, ethnicity and cultural change*. New York: Routledge.

Hall, S. 1977. Culture, the media and the "ideological effect." In J. Curran, M. Gurevitch, and J. Woollacott, eds., *Mass communication and society*, 315-48. London, UK: Edward Arnold.

—. 1997. The work of representation. In S. Hall, ed., *Representation: Cultural representations and signifying practice*, 13-74. London, UK: Sage.

Harindranath, R. 2000. Ethnicity, national culture(s) and the interpretation of television. In S. Cottle, ed., *Ethnic minorities and the media: Changing cultural boundaries*, 149-63. Buckingham, PA: Open University Press.

Hussain, A. 2006. Review of "Me and the Mosque." *American Journal of Islamic Social Sciences* 23, 2: 124-25.
Intini, J. 2006. Little Mosque on the Prairie: Recreate small-town Canada, then add Muslims – for laughs. *Maclean's Magazine,* December 11, n.p.
Jiwani, Y. 1993. "By omission and commission: Race and representation in Canadian television news." PhD diss., School of Communications, Simon Fraser University.
–. 2006. *Discourses of denial: Mediations of race, gender, and violence.* Vancouver, BC: UBC Press.
Karim, K.H. 2000. *Islamic peril: Media and global violence.* Montreal, QC: Black Rose Books.
–. 2002. Islam in the media: (Mis)using the Muslim lexicon. *Currents* 10, 1: 4-9.
Levant, E. 2007. Censorship in the name of "human rights." *National Post,* December 18. http://www.nationalpost.com/.
Little Mosque on the Prairie. 2007. *Globe and Mail,* January 9. http://www.theglobeandmail.com/.
Lull, J. 2000. *Media, communication, culture: A global approach.* Irvington, NY: Columbia University Press.
Macdonald, G. 2007. Little Mosque steps on the gas. *Globe and Mail,* March 3, n.p.
Marketwire. 2007. Little Mosque on the Prairie producers ink first international distribution deal with French broadcasting giant Canal +. May 8. http://www.marketwire.com/.
Martin, M. 1997. *Communication and mass media: Culture, domination, and opposition.* Scarborough, ON: Prentice Hall and Allyn and Bacon Canada.
Mir-Hosseini, Z. 1999. *Islam and gender: The religious debate in contemporary Iran.* Princeton: NJ: Princeton University Press.
Ogan, C.L. 2002. Communication and culture. In Y.R. Kamalipour, ed., *Global communication,* 207-28. Belmont, CA: Wadsworth.
Ontario Human Rights Commission. 2008. Commission issues statement on decision in Maclean's cases. April 9. http://www.ohrc.on.ca/.
Raboy, M. 1990. *Missed opportunities: The story of Canada's broadcasting policy.* Montreal, QC, and Kingston, ON: McGill-Queen's University Press.
Raboy, M., and D. Taras. 2007. On life support: The CBC and the future of public broadcasting in Canada. In D. Taras, F. Pannekoek, and M. Bakardjieva, eds., *How Canadians communicate II: Media, globalization, and identity,* 83-106. Calgary, AB: University of Calgary Press.
Ramji, R. 2005. From Navy Seals to *The Siege:* Getting to know the Muslim terrorist, Hollywood style. *Journal of Religion and Film* 9, 2: http://www.unomaha.edu/.
Razack, S.H. 1998. *Looking white people in the eye: Gender, race, and culture in courtrooms and classrooms.* Toronto, ON: University of Toronto Press.
Rivers, W., and W. Schramm. 1969. *Responsibility in mass communication.* New York, NY: Harper and Row.
Said, E.W. 1978. *Orientalism.* New York, NY: Vintage.
–. 1993. *Culture and imperialism.* Toronto, ON: Alfred A. Knopf.

Sardar, Z. 2007. Muslims have a sense of humour. *New Statesman,* October 11. http://www.newstatesman.com/.
Sassen, S. 2006. *Territory, authority, rights: From medieval to global assemblages.* Princeton, NJ: Princeton University Press.
Scott, A. 2005. Stand-up Muslim: Azhar Usman brings the halal humour. CBC, January 19. http://www.cbc.ca/.
Shaheen, J.G. 1984. *The TV Arab.* Bowling Green, OH: Bowling Green State University Popular Press.
–. 2001. *Reel bad Arabs: How Hollywood vilifies a people.* Brooklyn, NY: Interlink.
Showbizz.net. 2007. Radio-Canada présentera "La petite mosquée dans la prairie." October 29. http://www.showbizz.net/.
Siddiqui, S. 2001. Status of Muslim women is not well understood. *Winnipeg Free Press,* March 24. http://www.ottawamuslim.net/.
Statistics Canada. 2005. *Study: Canada's visible minority population in 2017.* http://www.statcan.ca/.
Steyn, M. 2002. Battered westerner syndrome inflicted by myopic Muslim defenders. *Jewish World Review,* August 23. http://www.jewishworldreview.com/.
–. 2006. The future belongs to Islam. *Maclean's Magazine,* October 20. http://www.macleans.ca/.
Surette, T. 2008. Fox importing Mosque. *TV.com,* June 10. http://www.tv.com/.
Taras, D. 2008. The CBC and the new wave of public broadcasting. In C. Elliott and J. Greenberg, eds., *Communication in question: Competing perspectives on controversial issues in communication studies,* 4-10. Toronto, ON: Thompson-Nelson Canada.
van Dijk, T.A. 1991. *Racism and the press.* New York, NY: Routledge.
Walt Disney Company. 1992. Disney song lyrics: Arabian nights. http://www.disneyclips.com/.
Zine, J. 2006. Unveiled sentiments: Gendered Islamophobia and experiences of veiling among Muslim girls in a Canadian Islamic school. *Equity and Excellence in Education* 39, 3: 239-52.
–. 2007. An interview with Zarqa Nawaz. *Intercultural Education* 18, 4: 379-82.1.

PART 3

EDUCATION

SCHOOLS are important sites of social and cultural reproduction. Religious schools promote the inculcation of religious beliefs, values, and practice and in so doing reproduce communal norms. For diasporic communities, religious or culturally based schools allow for the preservation of traditional values, language skills, and heritage. For some, this can lead to isolationism; for others, it is a counterbalance to the racism and the demands for conformity with Western cultural codes that they experience in public education. The issue of faith-based schooling has been widely debated in Ontario, where only Catholic schools receive funding to the exclusion of other denominations despite the United Nations ruling that this differential treatment constitutes a violation of the right to religious freedom. Quebec also struggles with maintaining the imperatives of the Quiet Revolution and keeping religion out of schools and child-care centres. The role of religion within education in multicultural societies is a contemporary challenge that exists in a state of tension between goals of multicultural plurality and inclusion, on the one hand, and the insistence that secularism is a universal framework that provides a "neutral" ground, on the other. What is often obscured is how

PART 3 ... the politics of race play into this divide when it is not separate Catholic education that is being debated but rather the push for Islamic schools and Afro-centric schools. The discussion of Islamic education in Canada is framed by these ongoing challenges and contestations.

This section provides both a historical overview of the development of Islamic education in Canada and a sociological analysis of the gendered practices within Islamic schools and the politics of veiling. Nadeem Memon's chapter embarks on a historical journey mapping the development of Islamic educational sites in the Canadian Muslim diaspora from mosques to *madrassas* (religious schools). Memon examines the genesis and development of these religious and educational sites as well as the philosophical, ideological, and discursive formations that shaped them. The chapter delves into how these sites have contributed to the negotiation of faith, education, and citizenship among Muslims in Canada. This historical and discursive overview helps to contextualize Jasmin Zine's chapter, which examines the politics of veiling as they affect the lived experiences of Muslim girls attending a full-time Islamic school in Toronto. In this ethnographic study, narratives of girls attending a gender-segregated Islamic school speak to the challenges they face in society due to their religious identity and dress and describe the limitations and expectations placed on them within their community and schools. This chapter addresses the multiple sites of oppression that Muslim girls and women experience through "gendered Islamophobia" as well as through patriarchal norms within the Muslim community. In this chapter, the issue of the veil, or *hijab*, is discussed in terms of its roots (and contestation) within Islamic doctrine and is explored through the political debates and attempts to ban it in Europe and in Canada. Most important, the voices of young Muslim women guide the analysis of these issues that affect their sense of faith, identity, and citizenship.

From Mosques to *Madrassas*
Civic Engagement and the Pedagogy of Islamic Schools

NADEEM MEMON

Faith, Citizenship, and Education

Faith and citizenship are among the more contested issues in public discourse today. In the Ontario provincial elections of 2007, for example, the Conservative Party's platform to fund faith-based schools arguably made the elections into a single-issue campaign. Some argued that extending public funding to minority, faith-based schools would impede the full integration of newcomers and minorities. Using the same rhetoric of integration, advocates of faith-based schools insist that it is only through faith-centred schools that children from families who esteem faith will be able to integrate with a sense of self.

Civic education is intended "to teach children the virtues of liberal democratic citizenship ... toleration, mutual respect, reciprocity" and how to "respond to differences, especially ... between comprehensive value systems" (MacMullen 2007, 31). Common-school advocates (Gutmann 1999, Macedo 1990) insist that faith-based schools are incapable of teaching civic education for two reasons: first, children in faith-based schools lack exposure to children of other faiths and values; second, children are taught to adhere to a hidden curriculum of rules and structures of authority without the opportunity to challenge the justifications that maintain them. MacMullen (2007) contests this stance, arguing not only that faith-based schools have the potential to teach civic engagement through their formal and informal curricula but also that a liberal democratic state should not deny individual rights in favour of the rights of the collective – for example, by disallowing parents to choose their own schools based on faith. This debate between common-school advocates and those who support the potential of faith-based schooling to embody democratic principles is not novel. Educators, policy makers, and, indeed, concerned parents have grappled with such perspectives since the advent of mass public education. The issue is not whether faith-based schools can, should, or will teach civic education but whether they even aspire to. This is not to say that religious communities are necessarily opposed to civic values but to recognize that within communities there is diversity among the voices that shape the aims of education.

I seek to argue that although faith-based schools have civic-education potential, they vary in the importance they place on civic engagement, responsibility, and the values of a liberal democratic state. In relation to Muslim communities in Canada, for example, the emphasis on civic education varies from one Islamic school to the next based on ideological leanings. Because most Islamic schools in Canada are established by local mosques, if not also housed within the mosque, the aims and objectives of the schools often mirror the values, histories, discourses, and ideologies of the mosque community.

In this chapter, prior to even considering the practice of Islamic schooling in Canada, which is largely in its infancy, I seek to demarcate how the vision of Islamic schooling is complex and complicated even in theory by the Islamic ideological leanings that shape the aims of education. Relying primarily on an analysis of school aims as well as on my own grounding of the vision of Islamic schooling in North America through oral histories, I explain how earlier Canadian Muslim immigrants, most notably those who settled in the 1970s, perceived the aims of faith-based schooling differently.

Resistance, Embrace, and Selective Engagement: A Framework to Understand Mosqued Muslims

Being cognizant that there is great disparity in the levels of commitment to religious practice among Muslims, I focus my analysis on what Zaman (2008, 465) calls "mosqued Muslims," those who attend mosques for religious observances sporadically at the least. To understand how communities of mosqued Muslims have formed around ideology and interpretation, I employ Mattson's (2003) framework, which defines the general political outlooks of Sunni Muslim communities in North America. The three general categories that she has developed are resistance, embrace, and selective engagement. The paradigm is important in differentiating between aspects of Muslim communities that give rise to opposing political outlooks, which in turn inform commitments to civic engagement and the role of civic education in Islamic schools.

The paradigm of resistance is espoused by those who passionately critique Western society as *jahili*, or backward, hedonistic, lawless, and immoral. The approach of such Muslims is to relatively isolate themselves from areas of Canadian society where they might be influenced by such culture. The Tablighi Jamaat and the Salafiyya movements represent two orientations that are explicitly unsupportive of political and civic engagement. Both espouse an apolitical stance toward elections, voting, and teaching about civic responsibility (Johnson 1991). Tabligh Jamaat, an outgrowth of the Darul Uloom Deoband movement of India, comprises largely South Asian Muslim immigrants who aspire to reform Islam from within by bringing lapsed Muslims back to Islam. Sherman Jackson (2005, 81), a scholar of Islam in America, refers to such an approach as "doctrinaire," noting that the emphasis is placed on religious practice and on nurturing leadership for mosques over community organizations.

The Salafiyya movement is exceedingly committed to a doctrinaire agenda that emphasizes the purity of *aqida* (fundamental beliefs) and that aspires to revive the practice of the earliest Muslim community. In Canada, Salafis are generally organized under the Qur'an and Sunnah Society, based out of Vancouver and Toronto. The movement's focus on re-establishing "proper" religious practice and interpretation precludes an emphasis on unity among divergent approaches within Muslim communities or among the disparate values held within the Canadian mosaic.

In her paradigm of embrace, Mattson (2003) describes how some Muslim immigrants who have escaped repressive regimes value the freedom of expression and individuality experienced in North America. They embrace the liberal democratic commitment to not imposing religious values on anyone while at the same time respecting the religious rights of those who choose to practise a religious faith. Those who fall under the category of "embrace" comprise the largest segment of Canadian Muslims. Jackson (2005, 79) refers to this group as "cultural/ethnic Muslims" because they generally mix associations of cultural identity with religious practice and adhere far less stringently to religious tenets.

To extend Mattson's (2003) paradigm of embrace, I argue that there are not only those who are concerned less about religious tenets and more about cultural assimilation, as she describes, but also those who comprise a group that Jackson (2005, 91) calls "Modernized Islam."

Modernized Islam, also referred to as "Traditional Islam" and "Classical Islam" and most commonly adhered to by Sufis, is an approach that relies primarily on the interpretations of the four jurisprudent schools of thought of medieval Islam. These schools of thought, or *madhabs*, allow for intrareligious pluralism and the potential legitimacy of seemingly contradictory discourses. This approach is therefore more willing to accommodate change and difference and to find commonalities with modern Western discourses (Jackson 2005, 85). Although more committed to religious pluralism, this group is as inward-looking as those that fall under the category of resistance. The distinction, however, is that the two groups that fall under the category of embrace are more willing to nurture a sense of civic engagement.

The final paradigm that Mattson (2003) presents is that of selective engagement, where Muslims feel strongly about fulfilling the religious command of addressing wrongs and contributing to societal growth. These Muslims choose active participation in the public sphere through social, political, economic, and environmental activism around issues that affect all citizens.

These Muslim Canadians are largely inheritors of the political-activist ideologies spawned by the Muslim world in the 1960s. Associated most notably with the modern-day Ikwan al Muslimun (Muslim Brotherhood) and Jamaat-i-Islami (Islamic Fellowship) movements, they are most concerned about moving beyond everyday piety and into issues of power and politics. These movements grew out of particular political struggles in the Muslim world coinciding with the major wave of Muslim immigrants to North America. They therefore developed a distinctly Western approach to civic engagement and political action to address social injustices against Islam and Muslims. Jackson (2005, 81) calls these Muslims "folk Muslims," noting that they are generally highly educated, religious, and practitioners of their faith but "not doctrinaire." These are the people who generally comprise the leadership of Muslim organizations in Canada and the United States, such as the Islamic Society of North America (ISNA) and the Islamic Council of North America (ICNA), which are the two eldest and largest Muslim organizations on the continent. They represent the first organizational effort to promote active local citizenship and engagement through participation in the political process. This includes educating Muslims about voting rights, encouraging Muslims to run for office, and mobilizing Muslims toward civic engagement, such as cross-cultural dialogue and community service (Johnson 1991, 111; see also Chapter 3 herein for a discussion of Canadian Muslim women's civic engagement).

Although Mattson's (2003) paradigm makes major generalizations about Muslim communities, it serves as an effective framework to understand the distinctions between Canadian Muslims and their commitments to civic engagement. Resistance, embrace, and selective engagement allow for a deeper understanding of how ideology, not sectarian difference, informs the agendas of religious institutions. For more established religious communities in Canada, such distinctions are more readily understood. A layperson would recognize the difference, for example, between the aims of a Catholic school and Christian fundamentalist school. The former focuses more on conventional academic instruction and the inculcation of basic, relatively uncontroversial religious values, whereas the latter makes a more forthright attempt to integrate the truth and wisdom of the Bible into all educational goals and curricular content (Callen 1999, 163). Such distinctions for faith-based schools within minority communities, however, are not common knowledge. During times of political decision making when issues of religion and schooling meet, as in the Ontario elections of 2007, as mentioned above, there is often an outright sentiment of resistance toward faith-based schooling on the basis of civic education.[1] Islamic schools, like other minority faith-based schools, are viewed as one and the same irrespective of the consideration that many are apt to nurture civic values (Parker-Jenkins, Hartas, and Irvine 2005). In the following, I begin with a brief overview of the establishment of mosques in Canada to contextualize the settlement of substantial Muslim communities in Canada. I then discuss how ideological perspectives shaped the aims of religious preservation through schooling once early mosques were established. Using Mattson's (2003) paradigm, the chapter focuses on four forms of schooling: *madrassas* (traditional religious schools), weekend school programs, full-time Islamic schools, and alternative community-based schools characterized by differing aims of Islamic schooling.

A Brief Historical Overview of Muslims in Canada and the Establishment of Mosques

Prime Minister Pierre Trudeau entrenched Canada's celebrated multicultural policy on October 8, 1971. The policy was a response to the 1969 publication of Book 4 of the report of the Royal Commission on Biculturalism and Bilingualism, entitled *The Cultural Contribution of the Other Ethnic Groups*. It was the commission's validation of Trudeau's commitment to individual identity as the base of a society that legitimated the multicultural policy in 1971. In the early 1980s the policy underwent two major transformations: it began to address race relations, and it became entrenched in the Constitution in 1982 and in the Charter of Rights and Freedoms. Daood

Hamdani argues that the inclusion of religion in the charter was likely the most important development of the multicultural policy (Hamdani 1984, 8). The role of religion in the daily lives of Canadians cannot be overlooked. Simply put, in the words of Biles and Ibrahim (2005, 165), "To Canadians, religion matters." They cite a poll conducted by Ipsos Reid and the *Globe and Mail* in 2002 in which 67 percent of Canadians said that their religious faith was a very important part of their daily lives.

In taking religion seriously, early Muslim immigrants to Canada were no different. Edmonton, where some of the earliest Muslims settled, is also the home of the first Canadian mosque. Al Rashid Mosque opened in 1938. The historic day was inaugurated by local mayors, as well as by Yusuf Ali, a world-renowned translator of the Qur'an (Milo 2004). Since the establishment of Al Rashid, mosques have become commonplace across Canada. Every major city in the country houses a mosque, and larger urban areas like Toronto, Vancouver, and Montreal are home to mosques that represent Islam's cultural and ideological diversity. The Islamic Centre of Québec serves another one of Canada's largest Muslim communities. Established in 1958 by early South Asian immigrants, the mosque and community centre has been rebuilt twice and continues to undergo expansion projects to meet the demands of a burgeoning community (McDonough 1994). Nimer's (2002) study of mosques in Canada shows that there are over 150 and approximately 50 in Ontario alone. However, even small cities in remote parts of the country with growing immigrant populations are now home to mosques. And Yellowknife, Northwest Territories, recently established the first mosque in Canada's North, the "Little Mosque on the Tundra" (White 2007).

For new immigrants in a new land, establishing mosques has not been easy. Many of the earliest mosques began in homes, storefronts, run-down houses, and abandoned churches like Toronto's first mosque. For new immigrants, this situation serves as an awakening to the hybrid nature of life in the West. They come looking for large architectural wonders like they are used to back home (Smith 1999). Makeshift as many of the early mosques may have been, they served as sacred spaces. Metcalf (1996) argues that Muslims in the West use the sacred spaces of mosques to redefine and reappropriate themselves as a community. In new contexts like Canada where immigrants are culturally displaced and in many ways marginalized, mosques serve as spaces for religious observance but also for forging a negotiated identity.

Although most mosques welcome the cultural and linguistic diversity that comprises Canada's Muslim population, many newer mosques have been established not only to serve particular ethnic communities but also to promote specific ideological perspectives. Early mosques and those in remote areas of the country have not had the luxury to distinguish between Muslims based on ideology. However, in urban hubs like Toronto, it is not uncommon today to find mosques espousing particular ideological perspectives. Influenced by what Jackson (2005, 77) calls "Post-Colonial Religion," some early immigrants sought to use mosques as a vehicle to revive and resist, whereas others sought to integrate and to affirm the compatibility of Islam and the West.

The growth of mosques has seen their transformation from solely places of worship to community centres that reinforce particular views. Beyond the conventional religious rites of *salah* (prayers), *janazah* (funeral) prayers, and *nikah* (marriage) ceremonies, the forms of community outreach that each mosque promotes vary based on its commitment to civic engagement. Particular mosques, for example, host public debates with electoral candidates during election times, provide a space for a community service such as a soup kitchen for the needy, and partake in fundraising events around issues of cancer, poverty, or the environment. Other mosques remain more focused on imparting religious knowledge and improving religious practice and are indifferent, if not openly oppositional, to the outreach efforts of the former. Whether engaged in resistance or selective engagement, mosques still comprise only the initial phase of Muslim communities' institution building (Nimer 2002). A study by Nimer (2002) has found that after the establishment of a mosque, most communities aspire for religious education programs that I argue directly reflect the commitments of mosque leadership. Given that the vast majority of Canadian Muslims are immigrants, many would agree that religious and cultural preservation through some form of formal or informal schooling is important, but there is variation in the extent to which the forms of religious schooling replace a public education and its core curriculum of civic education. Thus the trajectory of moving from mosques to madrassas is complex.

From Mosques to Madrassas: The Purpose of Learning Centres in Muslim Communities

The word "madrassa" connotes a place of study, its root-word being *da-ra-sa*, which means "to study." Drawing on its broader usage, I employ this term to refer to the multiple "places of study" that Muslim communities in Canada have established to educate their children and preserve their religious identity.

Historically, a function of mosques has been to provide a space for education. Formal and informal classes are held to teach the Qur'an, to discuss matters of theology and epistemology, and even to study language and literature. In fact, many of the earliest Islamic universities were built adjacent to mosques. Both Al-Azhar in Cairo and Qarawiyin in Fez function to this day as universities that are attached to mosques. And the same is true of elementary schools, or *maktabs* (Khan 1967). The significance of the mosque-madrassa affiliation is essential to an Islamic ethos. These two elements of religiosity and lifelong learning are deeply embedded in an Islamic way of being. The most common support for such a claim is the first verses of the Qur'an, which were revealed to the Prophet Muhammad:

> Read: In the name of your Lord who created;
> Created man from a clinging clot;
> Read! Your Lord is the Most Generous.
> Who taught by the pen.
> Taught man what he did not know.
> (*The Majestic Qur'an*, "Chapter of the Clot," verses 1-5)

A Qur'anic commentary states that these first verses outline a believer's responsibility to seek beneficial knowledge through God (see Tafsir Al Jalalyn online at altafsir.com). The proximity of early schools to mosques and vice versa facilitated this balance between faith and knowledge. With verses like those that were first revealed as well as the emphasis on learning throughout the Qur'an and the Prophetic tradition, Muslim communities have historically had high esteem for the acquisition of knowledge. Commonly quoted statements of the Prophet Muhammad – such as "Learning is from the cradle to the grave" or "Whoever treads a path to seek knowledge, God will facilitate a path for him, a path to paradise" – serve as the reason for educational initiatives. The aims of Islamic education, however, can be interpreted quite diversely.

The term most commonly associated with education in Islam, *tarbiyah*, is translated as "to nurture wholeness." Wholeness, however, is broad in relation to what aspects of life-learning ought to be emphasized. Among Muslims who are more inclined toward inner purification and outward religious practice, tarbiyah implies teaching children the core elements of religion. Schooling in this sense largely comprises memorization of the

Qur'an, aspects of Islamic history, and tenets of faith (belief, prayer, fasting, charity, and pilgrimage). An essential part of tarbiyah is also nurturing moral behaviour and life choices. Islamic schooling, therefore, also aspires to ensure children display a sense of religious and often culturally appropriate behaviour in their *adab* (comportment). This is the more conservative approach to tarbiyah. Based on ideological beliefs and interpretations, Muslim educators also define the term "tarbiyah" in relation to nurturing civic responsibility. Equally reliant on the Qur'an and Prophetic tradition, tarbiyah is also used to encourage teaching of both spiritual and physical wellness, academic achievement, and social consciousness. Recognizing that the aims of education in Islam are diverse and dependent on interpretation and ideology, the following sections outline four unique approaches to schooling among "mosqued Muslims" in Canada. Each of the four approaches serves a community of believers who differ in their aims of education based on sentiments of resistance, embrace, and selective engagement.

Traditional Madrassas in Canada

When the word "madrassa" is mentioned, the images that most often colour our imagination are of young Muslim children (most often boys) sitting on the floor, wearing traditional attire, and rocking back and forth while memorizing the Qur'an. Geertz (1985, xiii) illustrates the conventional perception of traditional Islamic educational methods:

> A simple opposition of an oral tradition and a written one, the first mindless and habitual, the second self-conscious and critical, can hardly survive a man who *first* reduces texts to memory – the Quran, a rhymed grammar, a legal handbook – and *then* starts to employ Arabic as a spoken language. (Emphasis in original)

It is not uncommon to hear similar sentiments even today of Qur'anic schools, or "traditional madrassas," here in Canada where the memorization of the Qur'an is the primary focus. The assumption, however, that such teaching and learning are "mindless" and reductive with respect to the essential message of the Qur'an is overstated. It is fitting, therefore, to begin with the educational experience that first comes to our mind when we hear the term "madrassa."

As discussed above the word "madrassa" broadly implies a place of learning. The notion that the term has come to represent a particular form of learning is not unfounded. Indeed, traditional Muslim societies prize committing the early years of learning to memorization. Memory work at an early age (four to seven years of age especially) expands the intellect and nurtures discipline with respect to dedicated study. In her study of Qur'anic schools in traditional Muslim societies, Boyle (2004) found that memorization is the first step in developing critical understanding.

Given the embedded nature of this model of the Qur'anic school in Muslim societies, it is not surprising that through immigration particular segments among Muslim communities have sought to establish such schools in Canada. In the North American context, however, these schools differ greatly from conventional forms of schooling. The focus of these schools is primarily the preservation of the Qur'an and the Islamic sciences (jurisprudence, Qur'anic exegesis, and interpretation of the Prophetic tradition). Contrasted with Islamic schools or weekend schools whose religious curriculum is intended to nurture an Islamic identity through rites and rituals, madrassas aspire to develop the *imams* (religious leaders), *ulema* (religious scholars), and *hufaz* (those who have memorized the Qur'an) who will serve as religious instructors for coming generations.

Although differing models of the Qur'anic school are prevalent across the Muslim world (i.e., East and West Africa, South Asia, Arabian Peninsula, Malaysia, and Indonesia) (Hefner and Zaman 2007), the model that is most common in Canada remains the "Deobandi" school model, which traces its roots back to the height of Mogul rule in India.[2] The main objective of such madrassas was the preservation and perpetuation of religion and culture to prevent their perceived potential loss (Hashmi 1989). Due to an influx of South Asian (i.e., Pakistani and Indian) Muslim immigrants, the model of the Deobandi madrassa can be found most often on the outskirts of major urban centres.

One such example is Darul Uloom Canada, an organization that comprises three schools: an all-boys boarding school and an all-girls boarding school in Bowmanville, Ontario, and a girls' day school in Toronto, Ontario. Established in 1993, the organization envisages itself as adhering to an "Islamic University model, guided by the Darsi Nizamiyya curriculum."[3] Most madrassas in Canada, therefore, teach a curriculum based on the Islamic sciences that includes *tajweed* and *qiraah* (mastery of Qur'anic recitation, including memorization), *aqeedah* (Islamic doctrine and theology), *usul al fiqh* (principles of Islamic jurisprudence), *usul al hadith* (principles of *hadith*[4] interpretation), *usul al tafsir* (principles of exegesis of the Qur'an), *seerah* (biography of the Prophet Muhammad), and Islamic history. Depending on the program in which a child is enrolled, certain subjects are emphasized over others. For example, for students who commit the Qur'an to memory and become *hufaz*, the majority of the school day, for an average of four years, is focused on memorization. Those who aspire to become *ulema* study many of the subjects listed above in addition to other subjects depending on the school they attend, such as *sarf* (morphology), *nawh* (grammar), and *mantiq* (logic).

Madrassas of this sort are most often located in remote communities yet within proximity to large cities.[5] Boarding therefore allows students to be kept self-contained and in secluded environments that are distant from distractions that would affect their pursuit of knowledge.[6] Based on cultural practice, these schools are also strictly segregated between the sexes for the same reason. As described using Mattson's (2003) framework, the traditional madrassas exhibit a clear sentiment of resistance. Born out of a historical context of resistance to the imposed cultural and religious assimilation under colonial rule in India, these schools similarly seek to protect and preserve religious identity from external, secular influences. The schools should not, however, be misunderstood as anti-Western but rather as utterly committed to preservation. Seeking to purify and protect Islam from within, the madrassa curriculum represents an apolitical, not anti-political, mode of engagement.

Weekend and After-School Religious Education Programs

Whereas Darul Uloom–type madrassas are concerned with the development of Muslim scholars, theologians, and religious leaders, the function of weekend and after-school programs is the exact opposite. Supplemental education programs that are taught outside of the regular public school day are, put simply, for the rest of us. As in any faith, those who aspire (or whose parents aspire for them) to become religious scholars or clergy are few and far between. The majority of adherents of any faith fall under the category of embrace, seeking to understand their religion only at its rudimentary core in order to be able to live by the tenets of faith. Loosely structured evening and weekend religion classes therefore serve this purpose well because children can attend public schools and have the flexibility of dropping in and out of supplementary programs as they wish. For most parents who aspire to nurture a sense of religious affiliation and cursory understanding of religious practice without disrupting their children's full integration into public institutions, these programs allow for varying levels of commitment to Islamic schooling. Although most parents under Mattson's (2003) rubric of "embrace" would never consider enrolling their children in anything more than a supplementary religious education program, these programs are often the precursor to establishing full-time Islamic day schools for students of elementary- and secondary-school age.

Take for example the first mosque in Toronto, Jame' Mosque, established in the west end of the city in 1972. The mosque was established by some of Toronto's early immigrants who in the 1950s and 1960s came to Canada on student scholarships. The mosque was initially established as a communal space for prayer and congregation. The services offered by Jame' Mosque, however, expanded as the needs of the community expanded. M.D. Khalid, an active member of both Jame' Mosque and later its school, said that it was just a matter of time before people in the community started having families and began thinking about schools for their children. "The idea [to open a school] started when Br. Abdalla Idris was here at that time. He was also the imam at Jame Mosque. They started [the school] in the basement of Jame Mosque in 1979. Children were very small so they could be taught in the basement without much facilities."[7] The school began with classes on the weekend and in the evenings before the demand grew and the need for full-time classes arose. In its earliest days, Khalid estimates that the mosque had between fifty and sixty families supporting its evening programs. Families would come from across the city to bring their children for evening classes in Qur'anic recitation and Islamic beliefs. In fact, as the community grew, most of those early immigrants who taught at Jame' Mosque started their own schools, institutions, and informal supplementary programs around the Greater Toronto Area.[8]

Many of the programs like the ones at Jame' Mosque are affiliated with mosques, but in the absence of a mosque or simply out of convenience, such programs can also be found in local community centres, schools, and the homes of individuals. Supplemental programs can also range from almost private tutoring to school-like classrooms with thirty students being taught from a textbook. Since there continues to be no formal structure underpinning these community-based initiatives, there is great variance between them in terms of what is taught and emphasized. Often established ad hoc by concerned community members and elders in response to a request from a few parents, many of these supplementary educational programs are focused on learning to read the Qur'an. Since most immigrant communities consist of elders whose native tongue is not Arabic, what has traditionally been passed down to students is the ability to recite the Qur'an in Arabic but not necessarily to understand the Arabic language.

Other similar programs have emphasized a supplementary religious education in the theological teachings of Islam as a precursor to reciting the Qur'an. These programs emphasize the core Islamic beliefs *(aqida)*, religious observances such as prayer, fasting, and the rites of the hajj, as well as an appreciation of the life of the Prophet Muhammad. The intent of such an approach is to nurture a sense of self in young Muslim children. Children not only learn what Islam is but also begin to understand what it means to be Muslim in their everyday lives. For example, as both an attendee of a weekend school for most of my formative years and recently a teacher at one, I gained an appreciation for the significance of fasting during the month of Ramadan, the benefits of giving charity, and the importance of prayer to one's holistic development. I also learned the values that define Muslims: kindness to others, thankfulness for what we have, and avoiding acts of mischief that would detract from our serving the needs of others. I learned what is *halal* (permissible) and what is *haram* (impermissible). These lessons ingrained in me an appreciation of and responsibility to my parents, family, and community, both local and global.

Today, supplementary programs are blossoming more than ever. Given a growing Muslim presence in Canada and the fact that the vast majority of Muslim children do not attend full-time Islamic schools, either for financial reasons or otherwise, weekend religious education programs are critical. Dr. Seema Imam, active in establishing and administering Islamic school programs since the 1970s, says that weekend programs will always be a more viable option for parents who want their children to have a faith-based upbringing. Simply put, these programs are cheaper and therefore more economically viable for large families. In large cities, Imam says, there are nowhere nearly enough programs to meet the demand. Supplementary programs are popping up everywhere, but securing adequate space and enough volunteer teachers to accommodate student enrolment remains the major concern.[9]

It is for this reason that scholars like Dr. Tariq Ramadan, author of *Western Muslims and the Future of Islam* (2004), feel supplemental programs represent the direction Muslims as a community should be moving toward. A harsh critic of full-time Islamic schools, Ramadan insists that the energy of Muslim communities needs to be directed toward improving the quality of supplementary programs because that is where more than 95 percent of the Muslim community will (and should, he says) place their support. Supplemental programs, he says, allow young Muslims to gain a sense of religious identity while still "integrating" into mainstream schools with children of other religions and ethnicities.

Full-time Islamic Schools

Ramadan's (2004) argument that Islamic schools are sources of "separation" is not uncommon. Nor is his recommendation that we need to support the improvement of our supplementary religious programs statistically unfounded. Whether in Canada, the United States, or the United Kingdom, the exponential growth of full-time Islamic schools over the past ten years still represents the support of only 3 to 5 percent of the Muslim communities. For the advocates of Islamic schools, however, such statistics cannot suffice for the whole story. Islamic school visionaries insist that supplemental programs are raising "schizophrenic, split personality young Muslim children that act one way Monday to Friday and another on the weekend."[10] For supporters, Islamic schools serve as spaces where values nurtured at home can be reinforced by the day school. They serve as educational alternatives to public schools, where subjects are not faith-centred and values are secularized.

In the short history of Islamic schools in Canada, there have been two distinct periods of growth. Following the first wave of Muslim immigration in the 1960s and 1970s and the establishment of mosques in major Canadian cities, the idea of schools as full-time alternatives began brewing in the late 1970s, as was the case with Jame' Mosque. This first wave of Islamic school growth manifested itself only into the early 1980s and was marked by an overall dissatisfaction with the inability and at times unwillingness of public schools to accommodate the religious needs of Muslim students. The pioneering school of this sort was established formally in 1982 in Mississauga, Ontario. The school was initially established through a coalition of parents who were all congregants of Toronto's Jame' Mosque and a decade later came under the auspices of the Islamic Society of North America (ISNA). Many of the early schools around the country share a story similar to that of the ISNA School in Toronto. The BC Muslim School, for example, was established a year later in 1983 by the British Columbia Muslims Association, which has also administered the first BC mosque in Vancouver since 1980. Similarly, the Maritime Muslim Academy continues to be the sole Islamic school in Canada's maritime provinces and yet one of the oldest in Canada. Established originally in 1984 in Dartmouth, Nova Scotia, and relocated to Halifax in 1996, the Maritime Muslim Academy is the third oldest behind only the BC Muslim School and Ontario's ISNA School.

Greater Montreal houses the second largest concentration of Islamic schools after Toronto's fifty schools. Among Montreal's eight schools is Les

Écoles Musulmanes de Montréal, which is Quebec's first Islamic school, established in 1985.[11]

In Ontario, full-time Islamic schools emerged in large numbers after a concerted dissatisfaction with public education was voiced by Muslim parents, largely new immigrants, in the late 1980s. The first push for accommodation came in the form of multicultural education programs in the later 1970s and early 1980s. Immigrant parents advocated for an increased understanding of their religious, cultural, and linguistic backgrounds to meet the educational needs of their children. In response, urban boards, which served the majority of immigrant families, established professional-development sessions that taught cultural sensitivity, facilitated field trips to cultural communities, acknowledged religious observances, and established heritage language classes. But for many parents, these were superficial add-ons to a curriculum that remained at its core secular. The fear that their children were losing religious identity and missing out on spiritual growth remained a founding concern for Muslim parents.

> By the late 1980s, dissatisfied with the fact that there had been few, if any, changes to the Eurocentric curriculum, and that multicultural initiatives were simply a recognition of culture in terms of food, music, and costumes, parents, community members, and some educators advocated for an anti-racism approach to education, whereby the effect of individual and – more importantly – structural racism (e.g., streaming) would be acknowledged. (James 2004, 45)

Full-time Islamic schools that addressed the religious and cultural needs of Muslims while not compromising academic success became an alternative for a small, yet growing, segment of the Canadian Muslim population.

The second major wave of Islamic school growth coincided with the largest influx of Muslim immigrants to Canada. Close to 50 percent of Canada's current Muslim population immigrated between the mid and late 1990s. During this same period, Ontario, the province that is home to the largest concentration of Islamic schools, saw the establishment of close to half of its current fifty Islamic schools.[12] During this period, Muslims globally had a heightened awareness of international affairs that were affecting the *ummah* (global Muslim community). Due to the Bosnian War, Rwandan Genocide, and Somalian civil strife, among other major factors, there was both an influx of refugees and concern over how Muslims were being portrayed by the media. By this period, many of the early mosques and schools had already been well established for over a decade, and the need arose for more schools to meet the growing demand. As a result, most Islamic schools in Canada were established during the mid to late 1990s, like Al-Hijra Islamic School in Winnipeg, Manitoba, in 1997 and Dar Al Iman School in St. Laurent, Quebec, in 2000. Larger Canadian cities like Toronto, Vancouver, and Montreal experienced their greatest growth in Islamic schools during the span of these five years as well.

In most cases, the rise of full-time Islamic schools across Canada has primarily been the result of parents who espouse a sentiment of selective engagement with public institutions in Canada. Muslim parents who are involved either in local mosque projects or in community-building programs are often the driving force in support of these schools. Although studies continue to show that the majority of Muslim parents send their children to public schools, there can be no denying the steady increase in Islamic school alternatives. For their supporters, Islamic schools help to "(1) preserve the culture and customs passed down from generation to generation, and (2) provide Muslim children with a proper identity consonant with one's home environment, thereby ensuring a positive sense of self" (Merry 2005, 374). Many parents support local Islamic schools, hoping that their children will gain a moral and ethical grounding that is absent in public education. As Merry's (2005, 377) research confirms, with the "spectre of secularism and permissiveness looming large, many Muslim parents are eager to shield their children from certain materialist and secular influences by placing them in a comprehensive religious environment in order to foster a highly specific moral orientation." Supporters of full-time Islamic schools most often espouse the need for separate schools in a language couched in sentiments of reaction to prevailing secularism yet aspire to see their children academically competitive in the job market. Contradictory it seems, but these parents refuse to forfeit the rights and opportunities awarded to them by virtue of citizenship at the cost of not preserving religious identity. Unlike the traditional madrassas discussed earlier, which resist mainstream markers of assimilation in dress, leisure, and employment,[13] Islamic schools appeal to parents who generally aspire to political and social mobility for their children.

Alternative Schools
The criticism levelled against full-time Islamic schools is that in trying to selectively engage by resisting outright assimilation while striving for upward

mobility, they end up neither here nor there. They teach about Islam but in reality achieve no more than what a supplementary Sunday school would achieve. And they attempt to teach civic education but can achieve no more than a sprinkling of ad hoc community-service and character-based education similar to that of a conventional public school curriculum (Memon 2009). As a result, selective engagement unwittingly reproduces very standard educational practices. Full-time Islamic schools, for instance, largely strive to meet province-wide curriculum expectations and adhere to the policies and best practices of mainstream public schools to the extent that parents begin to question what really defines the schools as "Islamic" (Merry 2007). Such a critique is most common among second-generation Muslims and Muslim converts.

Among the categories of Mattson's (2003) paradigm that I have yet to discuss is my own extension based on Jackson's (2005, 91) conceptualization of "Modernized Islam." Modernized Islam, as mentioned earlier, redefines Mattson's conceptualization of embrace because it does not seek outright assimilation but searches to find commonalities within traditional Islam that fuse with conventional practices. Such an approach appropriates traditional Islamic principles respecting practices to find common grounds of synthesis. In relation to schooling, many second-generation Muslim parents and converts have begun to question whether earlier approaches are overly concerned with imposing religious practices without nurturing a sense of belonging. Dissatisfied with the inability of public schools to nurture faith consciousness, disappointed with Islamic schools for being pale imitations, and aware that weekend programs are inherently limited due to the lack of contact time, many Muslim parents have begun to seek alternatives that reflect their interpretation of tarbiyah.

Among the alternatives that these parents are seeking out is the option of home schooling. Home schooling networks and supports are numerous but less formally recognized. By and large, they tend to be informal, local community networks of parents who home school within a particular city. Organizations like this exist in many different forms and serve various functions. Some organizations serve as small community-based schools that are not exactly home schools but demand a large commitment by parents to shaping curriculum. In Toronto, for example, there are a number of such organizations: Lote Tree Foundation, Kitab Academy, Dar al-Marifa, and the Toronto Home Schooling Network.

Among the more established initiatives in home/alternative schooling that I have come across is the Muslim Education Foundation (MEF). The

MEF is likely Canada's first home schooling organization that develops curriculum and provides support for other local home schooling families. Based in Edmonton, Alberta, the MEF was begun informally, as are most home schooling networks, by concerned parents. Part of the motivation for home schooling was simple: there are few (if any) Islamic schools that fulfil the definition of an Islamic school. In the words of Iqbal (2005, 12), co-founder of the MEF,

> What makes a school truly Islamic is integrated, holistic educational resources, trained teachers who are themselves rooted in Islam's formidable intellectual and spiritual traditions, and of course an atmosphere permeated by the remembrance of Allah. One would be hard pressed to find an Islamic school with these basic ingredients.

With a dearth of Islamic schools in Edmonton, the MEF has now become an essential educational liaison between concerned Muslim families and educational outlets. In 2007, for example, the MEF formally teamed up with the Argyll Centre, a home- and community-based education-support organization, to develop a program in Islamic education for Muslim home schoolers. Validating the MEF's ability to develop such a program is one of their recent publications, *Concentric Circles: Nurturing Awe and Wonder in Early Childhood Education* (Harder 2006). *Concentric Circles* serves as a handbook for Muslim educators on teaching rooted in the Qur'anic worldview. The book is significant not simply because it helps to define a nuanced Islamic framework of education but also, and more important, because of its contextual relevance to Canadians of faith. The work of the MEF represents both tradition and modernity, with the Qur'an being used as a framework to develop a curriculum that nurtures faith consciousness while also imparting to children a deep sense of civic responsibility toward their country. Many Muslim home schoolers grapple with issues of faith, citizenship, and schooling in new ways. As converts and/or second-generation Muslims who have lived through the public schooling system in Canada and have a renewed sense of faith identity, they aspire for a change in the way they educate their children.

The push for home schooling by a growing number of Muslim parents has its roots in a number of unique, yet parallel and even coincidental, events. One major factor is the coming of age (i.e., adulthood, marriage, and children) of the generation of Muslims whose parents migrated to Canada largely in the 1970s. Having attended public schools and having negotiated a distinct Canadian Muslim identity for themselves, Muslims in this particular segment of the population are better able to find commonalities between their Islamic and Canadian identities. Given their experience of Sunday religious schools, they are also critical of the inability of public schools to nurture faith consciousness. As Gary Knowles (1998) and colleagues have found, the catalyst for concerted home education is often a community's coming of age with the attainment of financial stability, which allows them to confront their feelings of protest. In the case of second-generation Canadian Muslims, this protest is a response to the political backlash from the events of September 11, 2001. In many ways, 9/11 has encouraged greater political participation, social representation, and civic involvement by Muslims attempting to reclaim their Islam. I argue elsewhere that 9/11 has actually produced a deeper sense of civic engagement and what I call critical social consciousness among Muslims (Memon 2009).

Righting the wrongs of Islamophobia generated by 9/11 is a project that has been taken up by many young Muslims who feel the strategies of national Muslim organizations are no longer effective. From elementary and secondary schools to college and university campuses, many young Muslims have become active in addressing the misrepresentation and misunderstanding of Islam. Ukeles (2003, 33) has found that "many young Muslims felt that the 9/11 crisis necessitated new strategies and a clearer message against religious violence." As an immediate response to 9/11, therefore, new local and national organizations were set up to address community needs. Youth groups, leadership training, and mentoring programs now serve internal community needs, and community outreach through new organizations to address, lobby for, and defend civil liberties has become commonplace. Such newfound social activism has created a space for Muslims to step into the public sphere (Ukeles 2003, 33).

The response has created the need for a modernized Islamic discourse of embrace that speaks to the universality of Islam and that exemplifies global responsibility and connection to all, including those whose lives are not God-centred. This discourse insists that the Qur'anic essence of a message and the moral principles of the Prophet Muhammad can be used to direct active global citizenship without having to be oppositional. "Social commitment is a moral commandment, and reform is an obligation of conscience that, in the mind of the Muslim citizen, determines a 'moral responsibility'" (Ramadan 2004, 153).

Canadian Muslims' deeper engagement with tradition and a sense of activism has in many ways bolstered the growth of alternative schools. Supporters of alternative Islamic schools have therefore redefined embrace by actively pursuing the means to teach civic education from within the Islamic tradition. Community-based schools allow concerned parents to develop their own school philosophy, and they place greater emphasis on what it means to be Muslim, supporting a definition that is consistent with civic values.

Faith, Citizenship, and Education Revisited

I began this chapter with a discussion of whether faith-based schools are capable of teaching civic values. I have not tried to answer this question but rather have argued that it is necessary to recognize that some schools do not even aspire to offer what is mandated in public institutions, whereas others have the potential to exceed what is mandated. What I have attempted to outline in this chapter is that forms of Islamic education, as with all forms of religious schooling, are diverse based on their historical influences and more notably their ideological interpretations of civic engagement. This diversity of interpretation, I have argued, is an extension of the ideologies of mosques. As Muslim communities have grown across the country, mosques as sacred spaces for religious practice have equally grown beyond divisions of ethnic and cultural representation to divisions based on ideologies of resistance, embrace, and selective engagement. I have extended Mattson's (2003) paradigm beyond mosques and communities to help describe differences in Islamic schooling. I have tried tactfully not to pass judgment on any form of schooling, as this has not been my aim. Rather, my aim has been to show, first, that Islamic schooling is not monolithic and, second, that faith, citizenship, and education are not inherently antithetical.

NOTES

1 See *Toronto Star* headlines during elections: School issue "not going away": Supporters of PC plan to fund religious schools view election result as a temporary setback, October 11, 2007; Ontario democracy fails faith-based test of maturity, October 7, 2007; PC leader's riding shows split: Divisive issue of funding for faith-based schools is hurting uphill fight against education minister, October 3, 2007; Faith groups still back Tory: Say free vote for funding gives them time to sway public and counteract Liberal "fear-mongering," October 2, 2007.
2 See Hashmi's book *Muslim Response to Western Education* (1989). His chapter on the Darul Uloom Deoband discusses one of the many schools that arose out of a reaction to British colonialism on the subcontinent. Schools such as the Darul

Uloom Deoband began in the mid-nineteenth century to counteract the perceived moral degradation of the Mughal Empire, its downfall, and the establishment of colonial rule. Founded on the Waliullah school of thought and later influenced by the Wahhabi movement's strict definition of Islam, the Darul Uloom Deoband sought political independence from British colonial rule and purification of religious practices to rid them of all forms of perceived internal corruption.

3 Darul Uloom Canada, http://www.darululoom.ca. The "Nizamiyya" curriculum model refers to schools established by the Muslim notable Nizam ul-Mulk in the tenth century in Baghdad. At the height of Islamic civilization at the time, Nizamiyya schools were known for their sophisticated curricula, evaluation systems, and success in producing some of the greatest Muslim thinkers.
4 *Hadith* are reports of sayings or actions of the Prophet Muhammad.
5 Examples include Jaamiah Al Uloom Al Islamiyyah in Ajax, Ontario, and one of the oldest Islamic schools in Canada, Al-Rashid Islamic Institute, in Cornwall, Ontario, which was established in 1984. Another example is the Islamic College of British Columbia Society, in Hope, British Columbia. All of these boarding madrassas are located outside of large cities, namely Toronto and Vancouver.
6 Darul Uloom Canada, http://www.darululoom.ca/.
7 M.D. Khalid, interview with author, September 25, 2007.
8 One example is Abdalla Idris, who administered the ISNA School (discussed later in the text), which grew out of Jame' Mosque. Other examples are Ahmed Kutty, who established the Islamic Institute of Toronto (an Islamic seminary), and Faisal Baksh, who co-ordinates the Ghazali Sunday Schools across the Greater Toronto Area, both of whom were among the early Jame' Mosque teachers.
9 Seema Imam, interview with author, December 18, 2007.
10 Suad Islam, interview with author, November 1, 2007.
11 See http://www.emms.ca.
12 These statistics are online at http://www.edu.gov.on.ca/.
13 Based on religious values and interpretation, such madrassas advocate maintaining traditional attire, refraining from television, and avoiding employment by firms whose practices are deemed unethical because of their basis in usury, such as insurance companies and banks.

REFERENCES

Biles, J., and H. Ibrahim. 2005. Religion and public policy: Immigration, citizenship, and multiculturalism – Guess who's coming to dinner. In P. Bramadat and D. Seljak, eds., *Religion and ethnicity in Canada*, 154-77. Toronto, ON: Pearson Canada.

Boyle, H. 2004. *Quranic schools: Agents of preservation and change*. New York, NY: RoutledgeFarmer.

Callen, E. 1999. *Creating citizens: Political education and liberal democracy*. New York, NY: Clarendon.

Geertz, C. 1985. Foreword. In D.F. Eickelman, *Knowledge and power in Morocco: The education of a twentieth century notable*, xi-xiv. Princeton, NJ: Princeton University Press.

Gutmann, A. 1999. *Democratic education*. Princeton, NJ: Princeton University Press.
Hamdani, D.H. 1984. Muslims in the Canadian mosaic. *Journal of Muslim Minority Affairs* 5, 1: 7-16.
Harder, E. 2006. *Concentric circles: Nurturing awe and wonder in early childhood dducation*. Edmonton, AB: Muslim Education Foundation.
Hashmi, S.M. 1989. *Muslim response to Western education: A study of four pioneer institutions*. New Delhi: Commonwealth.
Hefner, R., and M.Q. Zaman, eds. 2007. *Schooling Islam: The culture and politics of modern Muslim education*. Princeton, NJ: Princeton University Press.
Iqbal, M. 2005. Why Muslim Education Foundation? http://www.mef-ca.org/files/why.pdf.
Jackson, S. 2005. *Islam and the Blackamerican: Looking toward a third resurrection*. New York, NY: Oxford University Press.
James, C.E. 2004. Assimilation to accommodation: Immigrants and the changing patterns of schooling. *Education Canada* 44, 4: 43-45.
Johnson, S. 1991. Political activity of Muslims in America. In Y.Y. Haddad, ed. *The Muslims of America*, 111-23. Toronto, ON: Oxford University Press.
Khan, H. 1967. *History of Muslim education*. Karachi: Academy of Educational Research.
Knowles, J.G. 1998. Home education: Personal histories. In M.L. Fuller and G. Olsen, eds., *Home-school relations*, 302-30. New York, NY: Allyn and Bacon.
Macedo, S. 1990. *Liberal virtues*. New York, NY: Oxford University Press.
MacMullen, I. 2007. *Faith in schools? Autonomy, citizenship, and religious education in the liberal state*. Princeton, NJ, and Oxford, UK: Princeton University Press.
The Majestic Qur'an: An English rendition of its meanings. 2000. Chicago, IL: Nawawi Foundation.
Mattson, I. 2003. How Muslims use Islamic paradigms to define America. In Y. Haddad, J. Smith, and J. Esposito, eds., *Religion and immigration: Christian, Jewish, and Muslim experiences in the United States*, 99-116. Walnut Creek, CA: Rowman and Littlefield.
McDonough, S. 1994. Muslims of Montreal. In Y. Haddad and J. Smith, eds., *Muslim communities in North America*, 317-36. New York, NY: State University of New York Press.
Memon, N. 2009. From protest to praxis: A history of Islamic schooling in North America. PhD diss., Department of Theory and Policy Studies, University of Toronto.
Merry, M. 2005. Advocacy and involvement: The role of parents in Western Islamic schools. *Religious Education Decatur* 100, 4: 374-85.
—. 2007. *Culture, identity, and Islamic schooling: A philosophical approach*. New York, NY: Palgrave MacMillan.
Metcalf, B.D. 1996. Introduction: Sacred words, sanctioned practice, new communities. In B.D. Metcalf, ed., *Making Muslim space in North America and Europe*, 1-30. Berkeley, CA: University of California Press.
Milo, M. 2004. *A new life in a new land*. DVD. Oakville, ON: Magic Lantern.

Nimer, M. 2002. *The North American Muslim resource guide: Muslim community life in the United States and Canada.* New York, NY: Routledge.
Parker-Jenkins, M., D. Hartas, and B. Irvine. 2005. *In good faith: Schools, religion, and public funding.* Aldershot, UK: Ashgate.
Ramadan, T. 2004. *Western Muslims and the future of Islam.* New York, NY: Oxford University Press.
Smith, J. 1999. *Islam in America.* New York, NY: Columbia University Press.
Ukeles, R. 2003. The evolving Muslim community in America: The impact of 9/11. Report for the Mosaica Research Center for Religion, State and Society. http://bjpa.org/.
White, P. "Little mosque on the tundra." *Globe and Mail,* December 6, 2007.
Zaman, S. 2008. From imam to cyber-mufti: Consuming identity in Muslim America. *Muslim World* 98, 4: 465-74.

8

Unveiled Sentiments
Gendered Islamophobia and
Experiences of Veiling among Muslim
Girls in a Canadian Islamic School

JASMIN ZINE

The practice of veiling has made Muslim women subject to dual oppressions: racism and Islamophobia in society at large and patriarchal oppression and sexism from within their communities. In this chapter, which is based on a narrative analysis of the politics of veiling in schools and society, the voices of young Muslim women attending a Canadian Islamic school speak to the contested notion of gender identity in Islam. The narratives situate their various articulations of Islamic womanhood in ways that both affirm and challenge traditional religious notions. At the same time, they are also subject to Orientalist[1] representations of women who wear the *hijab* (headscarf), *niqab* (face veil), or *burqa* (cloak or overcoat) as oppressed and backward. Focusing on ethnographic accounts of veiling among Muslim girls who attended a gender-segregated Islamic high school in Toronto, this discussion allows a deeper understanding of how gendered religious identities are constructed in the schooling experiences of these Muslim youth.

This discussion critically explores ethno-religious oppression encountered by Muslim girls in Toronto, Canada. Focusing on the experiences of Muslim girls attending a gender-segregated Islamic school, the chapter examines how these young women reside at the nexus of dual oppressions, confronting racism and Islamophobia in society at large and at the same time contending with patriarchal forms of religious oppression in their communities. Islamophobia can be defined as "a fear or hatred of Islam and its adherents that translates into individual, ideological and systemic forms of oppression and discrimination" (Zine 2003, 39). For girls who adhere to Islamic dress codes by wearing items such as the hijab that visibly mark them as Muslims, issues of ethno-religious oppression in the form of Islamophobia are particularly salient. These Muslim girls construct their identities in opposition to the stereotypes they encounter in the media and in their public school experiences that portray them as "oppressed," "backward," and uneducated (Zine and Bullock 2002, Haw 1998, McDonough 2003, Rezai-Rashti 1994, Zine 2000, 2002).

Although this study took place prior to the 9/11 attacks, issues of Islamophobia were nonetheless salient and have since been exacerbated by that tragedy. Within this troubling socio-political context, Islamic schools continue to be safe havens where these girls find freedom from racialized and Islamophobic stereotypes (Zine 2003). This discussion allows a deeper understanding of how gendered identities are constructed in the schooling experiences of young Muslim women and examines how the multiple identities that they inhabit as social actors based on race, ethnicity, religion, and gender position them in marginalized sites within the racialized borders of diaspora and nation. This discussion situates the contested notion of veiling and gender identity in Islam and provides an examination of emerging discourses of identity among these young women that both affirm and begin to challenge traditional notions.

Framing the Research: A Brief Overview of Methods

This chapter is drawn from a broader ethnographic study of Islamic schooling that focused on four Islamic schools in the Greater Toronto Area. The study was based on interviews with forty-nine participants, including students, teachers, school administrators, and parents, as well as eighteen months of fieldwork from September 1999 to August 2001, including classroom observations and action research conducted while teaching in an Islamic girls' high school. This chapter focuses on the data gathered among Muslim girls in a gender-segregated high school.

Several themes emerged that help to frame the experiences of these girls, both inside and outside of school. These are discussed through a narrative analysis of accounts by ten female students who attended Al Rajab high school.[2] They ranged in age from sixteen to nineteen and were from South Asian, Arab, and Somali backgrounds. As I am a Muslim scholar and feminist who wore the hijab for fifteen years to mark my faith and identity, the issues explored have both personal and political significance. The discussion that follows examines the politics of veiling within a historical and discursive framework and then examines some of the lived experiences of veiling among the young women in this study.

The Context of Islamic Schools in Ontario

The Ontario Ministry of Education reported 2,240 children attending Islamic schools in 1999, but estimates from the Muslim community suggest that there were as many as 4,000 students enrolled (Scrivener 2001). Students are often added to waiting lists from birth, and some Islamic schools have waiting lists of 650 students or more. In Toronto and the surrounding area, there are over twenty full-time Islamic schools, and across the province of Ontario, there are a total of fifty (see also Chapter 7 for a discussion of the development of Islamic schools and education in Canada). With the exception of one school that belongs to the Shia tradition, all of these schools are part of the Sunni tradition in Islam. These two groups comprise the predominant sects within Islam.

The school featured in this discussion is one of over twenty full-time Islamic schools in the Greater Toronto Area and accommodates students from kindergarten to Grade 12. The school is gender-segregated from Grade 4, and the high school has separate sections of the building designated for girls and boys. Gender segregation and the construction of gendered spaces within Islamic schools, such as separate lunchrooms, classrooms, and prayer areas, are common in Islamic school settings after children reach the age of puberty, when religious codes for modesty in dress and manner and for social distance between the sexes become instituted. In addition to the physical barriers that separate boys and girls socially at this time, the Islamic dress code for girls, which also becomes operative by the age of puberty, is another means of segregation and further marks the shift to womanhood by emphasizing the seclusion of their bodies.

Gendering Islamophobia

Central to the analysis of Muslim women and girls in Western diasporas is the notion I refer to as "gendered Islamophobia." This can be understood as specific forms of ethno-religious and racialized discrimination levelled at Muslim women that proceed from historically contextualized negative stereotypes that inform individual and systemic forms of oppression. Various forms of oppression – for example, racism, sexism, and classism – are rooted within specific ideological/discursive processes and supported through both individual and systemic actions. In the case of gendered

Islamophobia, the discursive roots are historically entrenched within Orientalist representations that cast colonial Muslim women as backward, oppressed victims of misogynist societies (Hoodfar 1993, Said 1979). Such representations served to justify and rationalize imperial domination over colonized Muslims through the emancipatory effect that European hegemony was expected to produce for Muslim women. These stereotypical constructs have maintained currency over time and have marked the borders between the binary spaces of the West (i.e., the progressive and modern) and the East (i.e., the illiberal and premodern) as irreconcilable halves of a world living in renewed relations of conquest and subjugation.

Beyond representational politics, the epistemic violence behind these constructs has material consequences for Muslim girls and women. Studies that highlight the impact of gendered Islamophobia have shown that Muslim women who wear the hijab suffer discrimination in the workplace (Parker-Jenkins 1999). For example, a recent study in Toronto identified significant barriers to veiled Muslim women accessing jobs (Keung 2002, Smith 2002). In this study, twenty-nine of the thirty-two Muslim women surveyed indicated that an employer had made a reference to their hijab when they applied for jobs in the manufacturing, sales, and service sectors. Twenty-one of the participants had been asked whether they could remove their head covers, and one-third had been told at least once that they would have to remove their veils if they wanted a job. Two sets of women were sent "undercover" to apply for the same job bearing relatively identical résumés, ages, and ethnic backgrounds, the only difference being that one of the women wore a hijab. Whereas 62.5 percent of the women without a head cover were asked to fill out a job application, only 12.5 percent of the women wearing a hijab were given the same opportunity. These examples show the nature of gendered Islamophobia as it operates socially, politically, and discursively to deny material advantages to Muslim women.

Banning the Hijab in Public Schools: Case Studies from France and Quebec

In another example of gendered Islamophobia and mounting fears of religious fundamentalism infiltrating secular institutions, Muslim girls in France, Turkey, and Quebec have been exiled from public schools on account of their hijab (a phenomenon the media dubbed "hijabophobia"). The hijab was viewed as an assault on dominant civic values of female liberty and a denial of the dominant national identity (Misbahuddin 1996). These debates emphasize that balancing multicultural pluralism and religious freedom is a fragile act. A case in point is the French controversy known as L'affair du foulard, or the Scarf Affair. The situation first became prominent in 1989 when three Muslim adolescent girls were denied access to public school because they wore the hijab, an act that defies a 1937 French law prohibiting the wearing of conspicuous religious symbols in government-run schools. L'affair du foulard ignited debates over nationalism and the perceived threat of growing ethno-racial and religious diversity. Against this political backdrop, rightwing French politician Jean-Marie Le Pen continued to urge the repatriation of all immigrants who had arrived in France since 1974. Such xenophobic sentiments were echoed in the conservative newspaper *Le Point*, where a provocative headline read, "Should We Let Islam Colonize Our Schools?" (Gutmann 1996, 161).

The debate over secularism and religious freedom that ensued because of this issue divided even the left in France, where some socialists allied themselves with conservatives who were defending the 1937 law. Those on the left who defended the law did so on the grounds that "the veil is a sign of imprisonment that considers women to be sub-humans under the law of Islam" (in Gutmann 1996, 161). Many feminist responses also did not challenge this assertion but instead supported the notion that the hijab is a symbol of gender inequality and therefore incompatible with the ethos and values of French society (El Habti 2004). However, such stereotypes deny the agency of Muslim women who wear the veil and reduce the multiple meanings associated with the veil to a single negative referent. Therefore, in the public debates that took place, L'affair du foulard evoked troubling discourses of fear, aversion, Otherness, and even subhumanness in relation to Muslim girls and the veil that overshadowed the fundamental issue of religious freedom as a human right.

Within the Canadian context, the case of Emilie Ouimet captured national attention in 1994 when twelve-year-old Emilie (a French Canadian convert to Islam) was expelled from her school for not complying with a request to remove her hijab. The largest teacher federation in Quebec supported this move by voting in favour of keeping the hijab out of French schools. The principal at Emilie's school justified his decision by saying that the wearing of a distinctive sign like the hijab or neo-Nazi insignias could polarize the aggressiveness of students, thereby equating the hijab with facism and invoking a discourse of fear and repression. The social, cultural, and political context in which the hijab ban erupted is critical in understanding these debates. In 1977, Bill 101 decreed that all immigrant children in Quebec had to attend French-language schools. This law effectively changed the homogeneous character of French schools and rapidly ushered in a new multicultural dynamic at these schools (Lenk 2000). A backlash of this integration and ethno-racial diversity has been the contestations over religious dress in secular public schools.

Emilie's case also unfolded amid growing French nationalism in Canada, and the veil came to epitomize the challenge of defining a distinctive Quebecois national identity in a changing social and cultural environment. The French and English media were polarized in their representation of the issue and used the forum to further broader contestations over the nature of French society and hegemony in Quebec (Lenk 2000, Todd 1999). The English-language newspapers became the champion of Emilie's cause, citing the need to value individual and human rights. Representing the anglophone minority in Quebec, which is also subject to francophone hegemony, the English-language press capitalized on Emilie's plight as a way to further its own political critique of French society and the failure of Quebec nationalism to conform to the laws of English Canada's discourse (Lenk 2000). So in this political context, the hijab was not only a way to construct the Islamic Other as a threat to liberal civic values but also a way to affirm the polarization of French nationalism and English federalism.

Lenk (2000) reminds us that an important racialized dimension of the debate was the fact that Emilie was a white convert to Islam. She argues that Emilie's Islamization was viewed as racial transgression, making her less sympathetic to the French nationalist constituency. As a result, she became racialized through her refusal to conform to the normative cultural standards by performing the dominant identity. It was seen as a disavowal of her dominant francophone Quebecois identity and thus a threat to the French nationalist goal of developing a "distinct society" with a French character.

Lenk (2000) further points out the critical fact that news media widely excluded the point of view of Emilie herself and failed to include the voices of other Muslim women in the debates. Therefore, that Emilie's control over her body, dress, and ultimately her schooling career was compromised by the ban became almost incidental to the broader social and political issues that framed the debates. This unequal representation was also evidenced by the fact that whereas Muslim women's views were absent from the media and public discourse, a white female reporter received much attention when she decided to put on a hijab and write about her "experience" (Lenk 2000). Throughout the media representation, political analysts and even the school principal who initiated the ban provided the dominant narratives on this issue to the exclusion and appropriation of Muslim women's experiences. In the end, however, Emilie was able to recuperate her agency and her religious rights by appealing to Quebec's Human Rights Commission, which ruled that public schools cannot forbid the wearing of religious headscarves (Khan 2003). These landmark human rights cases represent gendered Islamophobia at play in the negotiation of gendered religious identities in secular educational sites.

A more recent development is the proposed ban on the niqab in Quebec. As discussed in this volume's introduction, if passed, Bill 94 would outlaw the niqab in schools and public spaces. In countries like France and Germany, headscarves have already been banned from schools, and even in Muslim-populated countries like Turkey women who wear the hijab are exiled from schools and other civic sites.[3] The move to have state regulation over Muslim women's bodies in the West has escalated since 9/11 and the ongoing "war on terror." Muslim women's bodies have become part of the battleground on which ideological wars are being waged, and in this context the hijab has become a marker of fundamentalist extremism that is seen as inconsistent with Western values and norms. Yet this narrow and problematic view of the hijab does not take into account the shifting meaning of this sartorial practice within specific historical, social, cultural, political, economic, and religious contexts, which are considered in the discussion that follows.

The Politics of Veiling

Driscoll (1997, 93) argues that "both men's and women's bodies are important sites of cultural and religious inscriptions; yet these markings have particularly devastating consequences for girls and women." Here, she is speaking to the issue of how patriarchal standards of bodily acceptability drive women to self-denial and cosmetic augmentations through the "violence of narcissism" that results in new cultural permutations of the female body that she describes as "the slender or starving body ... the tattooed body, the surgically corrected body ... the self-slashed body" (94), to name a few. In this way, Driscoll articulates a notion of the body as a "cultural medium upon which is inscribed the politics of gender" (94). Indeed, the politics of gender can be mapped on the bodies of women in various ways. For example, Muslim women's dress is one modality that provides a salient form of culturally and religiously encrypting the female body. For example, El Guindi (1999, xvi) notes that as a form of religious dress, the veil is located at the intersection of dress, body, and culture. Through the medium of the veil, therefore, Muslim women's bodies are gender-coded and form a "cultural text" for the expression of social, political, and religious meanings.

Corporeal Inscriptions: Multiple Meanings of Veiling

Hoodfar (2003) argues that dress codes, such as that featuring the Muslim veil, serve significant social, cultural, and political functions, acting as a medium of nonverbal ideological communication. Clarke (2003) describes Islamic dress as a significant means of communicating social and religious values. From these understandings, we can conceive of the body as a site of variable inscriptions that visually mark and code religious, cultural, and gendered norms or, conversely, resist and subvert these norms. Such corporeal inscriptions are meanings silently inscribed on the body that communicate social and political messages through specific forms and styles of dress. Through this process of social communication, meanings are mapped onto the body as it is presented and packaged for public consumption and spectacle. As a form of social communication and bearer of cultural and gendered norms, the Muslim veil is one of the most provocative forms of dress, eliciting as many diverse and conflicting reactions as there are reasons ascribed to its adoption as a distinctive item of the Muslim dress code for women.

Despite the often static representations of veiling, there are multiple meanings associated with the veil that vary historically, culturally, and politically (Bullock 2000, 2002, Hoodfar 1993, Kahf 1999, Zine 2002). Although women's practices of veiling predate the Islamic context, this symbol has entered into the popular imagination in Western societies as the quintessential marker of the Muslim world and as a practice synonymous with religious fundamentalism and extremism. In this conception, the bodies of veiled women operate as cultural signifiers of social difference and social threat and represent fidelity to a patriarchal order, which is a danger to women's autonomy (Bullock 2002, MacMaster and Lewis 1998, Read and Bartkowski 2000). These notions can be traced back to their Orientalist origins, where depictions of veiled Muslim women in the colonial imaginary ranged from oppressed and subjugated women to the highly sexualized and erotic imagery of the sensual, yet inaccessible, harem girl (Alloula 1986, Bullock 2000, 2002, Hoodfar 1993, Kahf 1999, Mabro 1991, MacMaster and Lewis 1998, Said 1979, Yegenoglu 1998, Zine 2002). Therefore, historically, the veiled Muslim woman has been simultaneously constructed as an object of fear and desire. Muslim women's identities are negotiated within the nexus of these ambivalent constructs that mediate between a desire for and a disavowal of their social, racialized, and gendered difference (Khan 2002, Zine 2002).

In some contemporary Muslim societies, the veil has been used as a form of political protest and class-based signification (Bullock 2002, Hoodfar

2003, MacCleod 1991). The veil is also regarded as a means of maintaining the body as a space of "sacred privacy" by keeping it hidden from public view in accordance with religious prescriptions (El Guindi 1999). Remarking on the variability of the veil as a cultural signifier of difference, Todd (1999, 441-42) notes, "Clearly the hijab is no innocent 'signifier' within such a volatile context. It has come to symbolize everything from Islamic fundamentalism, religious expression, women's subordination to women's empowerment and equality." Therefore, as a political and discursive space, Islamic dress represents a mode of gendered communication that is implicated in how the body is narrated, read, and consumed both cross-culturally and within specific religious and cultural frames of reference.

The Veil in Religious Paradigms: The Hermeneutics of Dress

In a scriptural sense, the veil has been interpreted as a divine injunction based on specific verses from the Qur'an and supported by some of the *hadith*,[4] or historical documentation of the words and deeds of the Prophet Muhammad. For example, in the following Qur'anic verses addressing women's clothing, it is stated,

> And say to the believing women that they should avert their gaze and guard their modesty, and they should not display their adornment except what is apparent thereof, and they should throw their veils over their bosoms, and not display their adornment except to their husbands or fathers. (Holy Qur'an 24:31)

> O Prophet, tell your wives and the women of the believers that they should bring some of their cloaks closer/nearer to themselves, that is a minimum [measure] so that they would be recognized as such and hence not molested. (Holy Qur'an 33:59)

During the seventh century in Arabia when these verses were revealed, the customary pre-Islamic practice of women was to wear a long headscarf *(khimar)* that flowed loosely around their shoulders and left their breasts exposed. Some scholars view the verses related here as espousing a corrective to this practice and a means to signify Muslim identity (Abou El Fadl 2001, Hajjaji-Jarrah 2003). Significantly, there are no sanctions in the Qur'an for not covering, and in a survey of relevant hadith literature related to dress, Clarke (2003) notes that only one report in the canonical collections clearly refers to the requirements of women's covering. In this tradition, it is related that the Prophet Muhammad stated that at the age of puberty, women should cover all but their hands and face.

Yet Clarke points out that this part of the hadith is found only in a singular collection and is not considered a strong account since the *isnad*, or chain of transmission, between various historical narrators was broken, meaning the account cannot claim an unqualified validity. Given the complexities of interpretation and the divergence between scholars who invoke literal readings and those who favour historical contextualization, there is no juristic consensus among scholars as to the areas of the body to be covered (Roald 2001). These range from the extreme of covering the entire face in accordance with some of the early Islamic legal schools to covering everything but the hands and face. Still other interpretations note that since the Qur'an does not explicitly state the mandate of covering the hair (rather it refers to drawing the veil over the bosom), this is not a requirement and that maintaining a dress code that is in accordance with the contemporary social and cultural norms of modesty is all that is required (Hajjaji-Jarrah 2003).

Both the Qur'anic verses and references within the hadith narratives have been subject to rigorous re-examination by contemporary scholars who have presented alternative contextualized readings. Some argue that the hijab is a historically specific form of dress that was used during the seventh century as a means to visibly mark Muslim women so that they could be identified as being under the protection of the Muslim clan and therefore avoid being molested or harassed (Abou El Fadl 2001, Hajjaji-Jarrah 2003, Roald 2001). The veil was also the marker of a free woman versus a slave or concubine and set certain social and sexual parameters for the engagement of men with these different social and class-based categories of women (Hajjaji-Jarrah 2003). These interpretations offset other religious views that situate the hijab as a static symbol of religious practice and as a means for the social and legal restriction of women's bodies to private, nonpublic space. This has concerned feminist scholars who rightly see this understanding as contrary and detrimental to the Islamic ethos of equality and justice and as a sociological and ideological factor that has arrested the development of true gender equity within Muslim populations (Ahmed 1992, Mernissi 1987, 1991).

Veiling as Feminist Protest or Fundamentalist Dogma?

As an Islamic feminist construct, the veil represents a means of resisting and subverting dominant Eurocentric norms of femininity and the objectification of the female body and provides a means of protection from the male gaze (Bullock 2000, 2002, Read and Bartkowski 2000). As a sexually politicized referent, the veil has been identified as a symbol of the rejection of "profane, immodest and consumerist cultural customs of the West," making it an anti-imperialist statement marking alternative gendered norms (Read and Bartkowski 2000, 398). These notions construct the practice of veiling as a part of an oppositional political discourse that counters the "tyranny of beauty," a phenomenon that objectifies and commodifies women for the edification of patriarchal capitalist desires. In this way, wearing the veil is viewed by some of its proponents as an empowering move that represents a feminist means of resisting the hegemony of sexualized representations of the female body. Halstead (1991, 274), for example, notes that such rationales have contributed to the saliency of the veil in the British Muslim diaspora:

> The Qur'anic requirement of modesty and decency in dress (Qur'an 24:30-31; 33:59) may be seen not so much as an exemplar of patriarchal domination as a practical attempt to defeat sexual exploitation and harassment, and as such it continues to be upheld by many second generation British Muslim women.

However, rather than placing the onus on men to regulate their behaviour toward women, this notion places the burden of responsibility for avoiding sexual harassment on women, who are expected to regulate their bodies to avoid eliciting the negative sexual attention of men.[5] Therefore, in very reductive ways, narrations of Islamic womanhood, both inside and outside of Muslim ideological and ontological conceptions, have been intrinsically connected to religious attire. On the one hand, conservative Islamic discourses view the veil as a primary determinant of religiosity for women and unequivocally reject other articulations of female identification that do not include the veil as a legitimate constituent of Islamic womanhood. Many secular feminist readings of the veil also use equally reductive paradigms to essentialize the veil as the universal marker of women's oppression, negating veiled women's alternative constructions that locate the practice within spaces of social, sexual, and political empowerment (Lazreg 1988, 1994, Mohanty 1991). Muslim women must therefore navigate between these reductionist and essentialized paradigms to claim their own representation if they are to overcome the discursive practices that determine the way their bodies are narrated, defined, and regulated.

Identifying the locus of the body as a significant site of social control and regulation, Driscoll (1997, 95) argues, "Our bodies are marked by the current cultural forms and norms by which the self, femininity, masculinity and desire are produced, not by way of ideology but by virtue of the manifold ways our bodies are organized and regulated." Therefore, what lies beyond the ideological determinants that underpin the socially constructed notions of gender and faith is the way that corporeal practices, such as dress, are regulated within patriarchal systems of power. Driscoll describes how the mechanics of this regulation operate through the way the "rules and regulations" of culture are written on women's bodies. In a Foucauldian sense, these mechanisms of social control operate to construct "docile bodies" that are subservient to the aims of specific structures of power and cultural authority.

In Islamic societies, Muslim women's bodies are regulated through the vicissitudes of patriarchal social rules, on the one hand, and secularist reforms, on the other. Whether the veil and burqa are mandated items of dress for women, as in Saudi Arabia, Iran, and Afghanistan, or whether they are outlawed in secular public institutions, as in countries like Turkey, the effect is essentially the same: imposed by state authorities, these practices of disciplining and regulating women's bodies challenge the political and spiritual autonomy of Muslim women to make reasoned choices about their bodies. Therefore, the hermeneutics of the veil as an item of an Islamic dress code create a varied discursive terrain where multiple meanings, fears, and desires converge.

Veiling Practices in Public Schools and Islamic Schools

For Muslim women and girls who adopt items of an Islamic dress code, such as the hijab and niqab, and wear an *abaya* (long overcoat), these markers of Islamic identification often lead to social ridicule and ostracism in Western societies (Hamdani 2004). In the day-to-day secular experiences of the girls interviewed, negative stereotypes and discrimination relating to an Islamic dress code were among their most salient concerns. Yet Muslim girls must also contend with how their dress is regulated within the Muslim community. Case studies of Muslim girls attending North American public schools and Islamic schools find similar tensions with respect to their veiling practices. In an ethnographic study of Yemeni school girls in Dearborn, Michigan, who all wore the hijab, Sarroub (2005) describes the complex ways that they negotiate the liminal space between the conservative orientations of home/

community and the dominant mainstream culture of secular public school. Using data from 1997-98, Sarroub documents the cultural interface within one school as these Yemeni students seek accommodations for their dress code in physical education classes and attempt to maintain their traditions of gender-based social distance among members of the opposite sex by avoiding physical contact, such as shaking hands or otherwise "mixing" with boys.

My earlier research examining Muslim students in secular public schools in Canada also examines similar issues of accommodation and negotiation relating to Islamic dress and lifestyle and the resistance strategies employed by students to achieve inclusion (Zine 2000, 2001). The issues of racism and discrimination were also noted in the schooling experiences of these Muslim high school students. In particular, Muslim girls wearing the hijab described how their interactions with teachers were often framed by negative Orientalist assumptions that they were oppressed at home and that Islam did not value education for women (Zine 2001; see also Rezai-Rashti 1994). Such notions were often communicated through the hidden curriculum and through low teacher expectations and streaming practices, with some Muslim girls noting that they were encouraged to avoid academic subjects and stick to lower nonacademic streams.[6]

Whereas Islamic dress was a site of negative attention and challenge in public schools and in Canadian society at large, the hijab was mandatory in Islamic schools. The dress code at the Islamic school involved in this study included a compulsory hijab and burgundy-coloured abaya worn over street clothes. This attire was considered to be the school uniform for the girls, and the dress code was enforced by school authorities. Boys also attended this gender-segregated school but occupied separate areas in the school building. They wore grey pants and white shirts as a school uniform. Male religious head covering in the form of a cap or toque, known as a *kufi*, was optional. The hijab was compulsory for girls due to religious prescriptions regarding modesty, whereas the cap was a sign of Islamic identity for boys and encouraged but not mandated.

Outside of school, the girls were free to dress as they chose or in accordance with family expectations. For many of the girls, wearing the hijab was a choice they made as part of their expression of Islamic identity and modesty and as an act of worship. These girls wore the hijab outside of school as well. Some also wore an abaya over their clothes outside of school, although many wore their hijab with other clothes, such as the South Asian–style *shalwar kameez*[7] or Western-style clothes that conformed to traditional

Islamic dress requirements and were loose-fitting and opaque. None of the girls reported being forced by their families to wear the hijab outside of school, and many chose not to do so, yet some took it up out of their own religious conviction.

In addition to the regulatory practices within the school, where their dress was subject to surveillance by the school authorities, the girls were also confronted with pressures outside of the Muslim community, where the veil has come to represent a marker of backwardness, oppression, and even terrorism (see Zine 1997, 2001). This form of discrimination, Islamophobia, punctuates the experiences of many Muslim girls and women within Canadian mainstream society. The following section draws on ethnographic data to explore Muslim girls' experiences of "gendered Islamophobia" and then examines their experiences contending with the dual oppressions of sexism within their communities and racism and Islamophobia outside.

Unveiled Sentiments: Gendered Islamophobia and Lived Experiences of Veiling

The Muslim girls in this study had to contend with negative stereotypes regarding the hijab outside of school and with the regulation of their dress within the school. Each situation became a challenge to agency and identity. The following narratives explore the experiences of Muslim school girls with respect to instances of gendered Islamophobia outside of school and to the politics of veiling both outside of their schooling experiences as well as within the discursive parameters of religious identification enforced at the school.

Aliyah, Nusaybah, and Zarqa were Grade 11 students at Al Rajab high school. All were sixteen years old and of Pakistani descent, except Aliyah, an Afghani. The topic of Islamic dress entered the conversations often, particularly when we spoke about their experiences outside of school and about why they liked being within an Islamic school environment. During one conversation where we talked about who wore their abaya home and who took it off, experiences of racism, xenophobia, and gendered Islamophobia were revealed as the girls explained the situations they encountered journeying to and from school. Most of the high school girls regularly used the public transit system, and it was there that their encounters with people were often negatively punctuated by racist, xenophobic, and Islamophobic attitudes. In the following exchange, these issues are revealed as the young women speak poignantly about how this discrimination impacted their sense of self and identity:

Aliyah: Truly, I don't wear my abaya home. Honestly, I take it off.

Nusaybah: And I go home with mine on.

Aliyah: Because the thing is, you take your car. I take the TTC,[8] see, and people look at me and they see me, and sometime I'm treated rudely, seriously. Just with the hijab, sometimes I'm treated rudely.

Jasmin: By whom? The passengers or the bus drivers?

Aliyah: The passengers and the bus drivers. Okay, like once this man, a passenger on the subway, called me an illegal immigrant. I think he was drunk. And I told him, "I'm here legally! I didn't come here illegally! I came here legally!" Another time, I was wearing the hijab and I was standing right in front of the bus door, like I made it to the door but the guy [the driver] still shut the door on me and he drove off! And if I hadn't been wearing hijab I think he would have stopped.

Jasmin: Do you notice a difference when you go out without the abaya?

Everyone: [Voices overlapping] Very much, yeah. Very much!

Zarqa: Okay, I was going on the bus one day in Ramadan and I was wearing my hijab and my abaya. I was going to take off my abaya, but then I didn't. And we were going past 5th Street and there was this lady on the bus, right, and there was a little girl and she was really, really cute and I love children, and I was like, "Oh hi, she's so cute!" and her mom, she, like, looked at me and she turns the daughter away from me, and the girl just started crying. It makes you feel so bad!

Aliyah: It makes you feel like, "Oh if I hadn't been wearing this!"

Zarqa: That's exactly what I thought! The minute I saw that, it was in my mind – I should have taken it off! Like, I know I shouldn't, but at the time it made me feel that if I took it off, it'd be different. It'd be like – the girl wouldn't be crying.

Aliyah: It's true. So many people do that. Like, if you look at their kid and you'd be, like, smiling at them, they'll just give you the dirtiest look, like: "Don't look at my kid!" But then when some white lady looks at their kid, they're, like, smiling back at the lady.

Other girls in separate interviews also recounted similar experiences of being called "illegal immigrants" and harassed on buses and subways with comments like "Halloween's over!" Many girls reported the same incident at a bus stop outside the school: the bus driver would often close the door on them and drive off.

As the girls exchanged their stories of lived experiences of racism and Islamophobia, it became clear that these were patterns that they had all encountered as the result of having their bodies marked as Muslims through the practice of veiling. The veil located them as "foreigners" who did not belong to the Canadian social fabric, and the xenophobia they encountered cast them as "illegal immigrants," a tantamount denial of their citizenry.

Being subject to this open hostility created a fragile narrative of "Canadianness" and belonging for these girls that was easily ruptured by the lack of social acceptance they encountered in mainstream society. These were also experiences of social rejection, of being excluded from the simple, banal exchange of smiling at a child and of being treated as "persona non grata" simply because of their religious identity and the negative meanings imposed on the veil. Within these encounters, a specific discourse of "foreignness" and Otherness emerged and framed the way that they came to see their identities as Muslims being socially evaluated and ultimately rejected. This positioning wove its way into their narratives of identity and was implicated in how they located themselves within the racially bordered spaces of nation.

In Canada and other Western societies, the identities of Muslim girls converge on the matrix of race, ethnicity, and religious difference and create a nexus of interlocking oppressions that position them as subaltern subjects (Khan 2000, Zine 2002). In diasporic communities within the broader national narrative, Muslims' identities hinge on the multiple hyphens that demarcate their ethno-racial (e.g., South Asian, Arab, African), religious (i.e., Muslim), and national (i.e., Canadian) identities. Yet these multiple identities also create distance from the dominant society by accentuating specific degrees of racial and religious difference. The white, Eurocentric, secular cultural codes of Canadian society are the standard of measure against which all other identities are judged and positioned and within which all other identities must be disciplined into conformity or face exclusion (Henry and Tator 2005). Therefore, the nonwhite racialness and Islamic Otherness of these young Muslim women meant that the politics of race, ethnicity, and religion were inextricably linked with and woven into their lived experience and often negatively implicated in their encounters within the dominant society.

The girls felt they had to represent Islam everywhere they went and that they needed to be careful of what they said or did since their behaviour would be essentialized as representing all Muslims. These issues emerged in my interviews with Safia, Umbreen, and Sahar. Both Safia and Umbreen were South Asian, being of Pakistani and Indian descent respectively, and Sahar was a Palestinian Arab. The following discussion shows the scrutiny and surveillance to which they were subjected as young Muslim women and how they negotiated the burden of representation and negative essentialism. The discussion is particularly salient in the post-9/11 world because although these interviews took place prior to 9/11, the issue of being collectively labelled "terrorists" was already a strong concern for Muslim youth:

Safia: There's so much pressure, especially for the female Muslims, because if we make one little mistake, the littlest mistake, they'll keep that as a stereotype about us and they'll make us look bad about that. Yet if another girl did that, didn't wear hijab, or wasn't Muslim, it wouldn't be a bad thing for her. Yet for us we're, uh ...

Sahar: Looked at greatly –

Safia: From every single point.

Sahar: Exactly.

Safia: So that's why we have more pressure on us outside in public to act modest and respectfully with everyone. Even if, say, a stranger came up to us and started acting rude, right? If we responded back rudely to them, they would say, "Oh look she's so rude!" this and that, but they wouldn't remember that they started it. So that's why even if someone's rude on the street or whatever, I'll still give them respect just so they can't say, "Oh, Muslims are this and that."

Umbreen: Yeah, but if one Muslim does something, they'll think all Muslims are like that. Everyone is like that. They'll be like, "Oh look at these Muslim people. They don't have any shame, blah, blah, blah." But then when they do it, it's an everyday thing. It's like, "Oh who cares?" Yeah, like if a white man goes and kills someone, they don't go and say all white men killed someone. They don't say, "Oh my God, all white men kill people!"

Sahar: Exactly.

Safia: But if it was ever on the news that a Muslim man killed someone –

Safia: They'd spend years on it!

Safia: It'd be on the news forever.

Umbreen: And then Muslim people feel like more uncomfortable on the streets.

Safia: And you think everyone's looking at you and they're thinking, "Oh my God, this person's going to kill me!"

Sahar: "Oh God, terrorists!"

Jasmin: It's sort of more of a burden because you know your entire community is going to be judged.

Sahar: But here [in Islamic school], you come and they know it's not like that, so you feel more comfortable and more relaxed and freer and more open.

This discussion seemed to foreshadow the burden of collective guilt levelled against the Muslim community worldwide based on the actions of nineteen terrorists during attacks in New York, Philadelphia, and Washington on September 11, 2001. That any actions by Muslims would be held against everyone who shared the same faith (some 1 billion worldwide) was seen as inevitable by these young women. They took proactive measures to ensure their own behaviour would not be negatively essentialized and used to pathologize other Muslims, such as monitoring their actions and consciously avoiding reacting to "rude" behaviour levelled at them by others.[9]

They were acutely aware of the double-standards imposed on them as racialized Muslims and that "white people" did not have to contend with similar stereotypes and essentialized labels based on the actions of individual members of their group. Even without the spectre of September 11 as a reference point, the Oklahoma bombing and the blame initially cast on alleged Arab/Muslim terrorists as the culprits was not far off in the collective memory of the Muslim community, particularly since local mosques, such as the one down the street from Al Rajab high school, had received bomb threats as a result. The Muslim community also noticed that although a white, Christian, American man, Timothy McVeigh, was eventually found guilty of the heinous crime, this had no bearing on how other white, Christian, American men were perceived or treated.

The double-standards were clear evidence that the entitlement of white privilege allowed white Americans to escape unscathed from the actions of their fellow citizens in ways that racialized communities were unable to do. These understandings produced a consciousness of marginality and of the politics of race among these young Muslims.

Negotiating the Discursive Norms of Dress

Muslim girls entering the discursive spaces of Islamic schools are socialized to conform to the prevailing religious orientation within the school and must, therefore, accommodate social and institutional norms that impact the construction of their gendered subjectivities. Therefore, whereas Muslim girls resist the way they are positioned within popular culture and Islamophobic representations, they accommodate the prevailing discourse of "hijab equals piety" within the school and mosque community, thereby exchanging one form of discursive representation and control (i.e., Orientalist) for another (i.e., religious/patriarchal). In turn, they script their identities within and against these competing constructions, at various times resisting or accommodating these discursive positionings. For many, accommodating the gendered norms of the school is very much in sync with their own orientation to their faith and with their religious sensibilities. Reay (2001, 155) refers to this acknowledgment as a process of "discursive recognition" or "feeling a better fit with one discourse than another." Therefore, for many women, the items of an Islamic dress code are taken on as a matter of conscious choice and spiritual freedom.

Without a doubt, some young women in my study did contest the policing of their dress in Islamic school, but they recognized that, apart from being a religious injunction, the dress code was upheld as the basis of the standard school uniform. However, as these young women develop greater political maturity and knowledge and gain the ability to act and engage within the space of Islamic discourse – where such issues are the subject of debate – they may just as legitimately choose to redefine their notions of Islamic identity and identification in alternative ways.

As spiritually centred young women, the majority of those interviewed chose to express their faith within the acceptable norms determined by their Islamic school environment, although these boundaries were often challenged. Nevertheless, their notions of Islamic identity were constructed largely within the prevailing discourse produced by the school and local religious authorities. Among the young Muslim women in this study, this discursive and physical regulation of identity was either validated and upheld or openly contested.

Freedom, Sisterhood, and Articulations of Identity

Interestingly, although these girls attended a gender-segregated Islamic school, they actually reported feeling more "segregated" in public school since the lack of acceptance of their faith-centred lifestyle and religious dress meant they were set apart and more socially isolated from other students. Being in an Islamic school gave them a stronger feeling of freedom to express their religious identities without fear of ridicule or social exclusion (see also Haw 1995).

Not having to conform to standards of dress that are dictated by MTV and the popular styles of youth culture allowed these girls to feel freer to express their identity in a more modest fashion that was in accordance with their faith-centred orientation. Although Islamic school also mandates conformity with a particular form of Islamic dress, this requirement was more congruent with the kind of sensibilities these girls had already developed based on their religious convictions and with the way they articulated styles of dress appropriate to Islam. Without the peer pressure to conform to more popular and less modest forms of clothing, they felt a greater sense of "fitting in" to the school environment. Girls reported that in public school there was a great deal of social pressure to take off their hijab and be like everyone else. Iman, an OAC[10] student of Somali descent, discussed the peer pressure she and her friends encountered while wearing the hijab in public school:

> I was wearing hijab and you know people ask too many questions. They'll be like, "Why do you wear that on your head? Aren't you hot?" You'll feel kind of bad. You'll answer them and they'll be like, "take it off" and stuff like that ... because they want to look like their friends. They don't want to be different. They don't show pride in themselves and the faith that they have.

For Iman, then, the hijab represented pride in her faith and identity as a Muslim woman. She had started wearing the hijab in middle school, and because she did not have many Muslim friends, she felt pressured to take it off. Some friends, she reported, respected that she chose to wear the hijab, and when she later transferred to a school where a higher percentage of Muslims in the school wore the hijab, she felt more comfortable and safe in expressing and living her Islamic identity.

Competing Constructions of Femininity

For the Muslim girls interviewed, deviating from the dominant discourses of sexualized femininity by wearing the hijab and observing a more modest dress code meant situating themselves outside the socially accepted norms of behaviour and dress for girls within mainstream public schools. This was an act of resistance and nonconformity that often resulted in exclusion and social isolation. Peer pressure is another powerful form of social control that levels sanctions against those who transgress the socially constructed norms and expressions of feminine identity. Girls who did not subscribe to the latest fashions and did not wear revealing clothes to attract male attention were operating outside of the dominant discourse that regulated the representation of the female body.

Swimming against the tide in this way was exceptionally difficult given the social conditioning and limited narratives available to the study's young girls in developing their identities. The normative standards of femininity that were made available to these young Muslim girls were already discursively marked and produced within the dominant Eurocentric paradigms. They had either to accommodate these articulations of identity or to challenge and resist the positioning of their bodies in this way. According to Jones (1993, 162),

> Girls perceive (in their wide observations from media, family, everyday life) the positions – including the silences – available to "normal" women, and usually regulate their own desires and behaviours within those parameters. This is not simply false consciousness which can be altered with some feminist education; it is not a choice between being liberated and being oppressed. Rather it is a choice between being "okay" or "normal" and being "weird."

In the same way, the construction of normativity related to Muslim women's identity as articulated within the social and discursive boundaries of the Muslim community was based on conformity to a homogenized religious and social identity that was imbued with the weight of religious authority and divine sanction and was therefore not open to social negotiation in the view of many religious leaders or school authorities. Despite the fact that there are competing viewpoints on the "legitimate" articulations of Muslim women's identity (e.g., see Bullock 2002, Khan 2000), those views that are more challenging to the conservative, status quo interpretations of gender issues in Islam are often marginalized and invalidated by patriarchal religious authorities (Abou El Fadl 2001, Barlas 2002, Wadud 1999).

In Islamic schools, Muslim girls confront more conflicting standards for femininity and womanhood than they encounter in public schools. The ways that the normative standards of hegemonic religious views on gender, faith, and identity circumscribe their choices about how they express their sense of self and womanhood are radically different from the ways that this is done by the secular, although also powerful, discourses of femininity in public schools. However, compared with the prevailing discourses of femininity they encountered in public schools, many girls in my study found the Islamic constructions more consistent with the way they articulated their own sense of religious identity and gender. For example, from a feminist standpoint, they were opposed to the sexualization of women in popular culture and media and felt that this objectification of women detracted from their being taken seriously for their intellect or spirituality. They embraced the veil as a marker of identity and an act of worship but also appreciated the way that it gave them control over the male gaze.

From this standpoint, Muslim women take ownership of the veil as a means of regulating visual access to their bodies and limiting unwanted male sexual attention that they feel detracts from other aspects of their identity and selfhood. However, it can be argued that the emphasis placed on covering the female form in effect limits the construction of women's bodies to a singular sexualized referent. In other words, covering the body as a means of protection from the male gaze also constructs women's bodies as solely sexual objects that need to be guarded and hidden so as not to attract sexual interest or attention.

The extent to which some girls attached their identities so intrinsically to the practice of veiling was disturbing. For example, Zarqa's response to my question regarding what it meant to be a Muslim was an immediate reference to veiling:

> I think it [being a Muslim] means to cover yourself. The main thing is to cover yourself, because um – where did I read it? A woman is a jewel. And when I hear Islam, I think it's the most religious culture ... I never used to see ladies wearing niqab and abayas and hijab and scarves. And now I see them so much. Like, I see them everywhere, like, on buses. And when I see that person, I say "that lady's Muslim." But you can never tell if you're not wearing hijab.

Zarqa highlights the visibility of the hijab as a marker of Islamic identity and applies the rationale often heard in lectures in the mosques for why women wear the hijab: that a woman is like a precious jewel that one conceals because it is so valuable. This notion is further emphasized in the following remark by a Muslim woman who participated in a more recent study of Muslim veiling in North America:

> A woman is not a commodity or an object, but she is like [a] precious pearl. The oyster is the hijab that covers and protects it from the dangers of the

sea. The pearl remains pure and untouched by any corruption. But it is the brutal nature of mankind that strips this treasured gem from its covering and places it for display or sells it for a price. (In McDonough 2003, 110)

Despite arguing powerfully against the commodification of women's bodies in society, this speaker seems oblivious to the fact that she may be trading one discourse of subjugation for another, as her view is rationalized by a similar attempt to regulate women's bodies and sexuality to suit a different set of patriarchal norms and expectations. Whether the intent is to exhibit women's bodies in order to satiate the male gaze or to cover women's bodies in order to inhibit male desires, both realities force women to cater to specific patriarchal demands.

Nevertheless, the veil-as-resistance discourse (Bullock 2000, 2002, El Guindi 1999, Read and Bartkowski 2000) presents a more empowering contrast to a view of the veil that sees women's bodies as causing *fitnah* (discord and chaos) in society and that mandates that their bodies and the sexuality they exude must therefore be disciplined and concealed from the male gaze. Read and Bartkowski (2000), for example, argue that rationalizations of veiling that liken women to jewels and precious objects are rhetorical strategies that invert traditional gender hierarchies that privilege masculine qualities and attributes over feminine ones.

For them, due to this inversion, "women's inherent difference from men is perceived to be a source of esteem rather than denigration" (Read and Bartkowski 2000, 402). Yet both views can be challenged for the ways that they narrowly reduce Muslim women's identities to the practice of veiling.

By limiting the saliency of the veil, these discourses also reduce religion to its extrinsic elements, placing less emphasis on inner spiritual development. There is, for example, no social policing of women's or men's engagement in more vital acts of worship such as regular prayers. Prayer is one of the five pillars of Islam and is viewed as central to Islamic practice, yet maintaining this practice is left to individual regulation and seen as part of a Muslim's private sphere. Women's dress, however, is part of the public sphere since the hijab is worn only in situations where women are in the presence of men outside of their immediate family. Therefore, within this public-private dichotomy, the maintenance of the hijab is subject to greater social control than is the maintenance of prayers, which are of a higher religious significance. There is, therefore, a sad irony in the fact that regulations respecting religious practices are differentially applied within the context of gender.

Challenging Gendered Islamophobia

The Muslim girls in my study consciously and actively challenged some of the stereotypes that governed the way their identities were represented. In my own schooling experience as an undergraduate university student, I recall an anthropology professor who, after I had spoken out forcefully on a particular issue being discussed in class, remarked that he was "surprised" that I spoke so strongly since he expected me to be very "shy and demure." It was obvious that his assumption was based on the way he read my body at the time as that of a veiled Muslim woman and on the negative meanings and connotations with which my body had become discursively inscribed. Muslim women were not "supposed" to be intelligent, forthright, and outspoken, so my speech created a dissonance in the mind of this professor, who saw me from the perspective of dominant stereotypes that rendered me as "oppressed" and without voice or agency.

Some Muslim girls at Al Rajab high school also challenged these negatively essentialized constructions. When I taught at Al Rajab, I arranged for some of my students to make oral presentations to the rest of the school in an assembly. We were examining women and migrancy and the sexual violence and harassment that many female refugees face when they flee their homelands. Rehana, a nineteen-year-old student of Pakistani descent, delivered a powerful speech that addressed issues of rape and gendered violence. As she was preparing, I asked her whether she felt comfortable speaking about these issues since the assembly would include male students and teachers. Rehana reassured me that she did not feel it was problematic for her to raise these issues since she felt strongly that they needed to be addressed and that we could not afford to be shy about it. She reported that her mother had some concerns about the content of her speech, but she argued that the speech was necessary since, as a "niqabi,"[11] she always felt it was necessary for her to engage in ways that challenged people's preconceptions of her:

> My mom said, "Why do you have to talk about this?" And I'm like, no, you have to be open about what you want to say, or else you are just like the stereotype: quiet, you just see two eyes, you don't see anything else. But you have to go against the stereotype!

The type of gendered Islamophobia that Muslim women encounter structures particular counter-responses that openly confront these constructions. Muslim girls face multiple challenges within the constructions of their gendered identities, being subject to patriarchal forms of regulation relating to their body and dress within the Muslim community, on the one hand, and to negative stereotypes and gendered Islamophobia within mainstream society, on the other. Within the competing paradigms that dogmatically attempt to structure their identities, these young women struggle to define a sense of agency, spirituality, and belonging within the discursive parameters of faith, community, and nation. The young women in my study consistently located their strength and resistance within a framework of faith. Creating an alternate space for the articulation of Muslim female identity that resists both patriarchal fundamentalism and secular Islamophobia is a contemporary challenge for Muslim women negotiating the complex epistemological and ontological terrain of race, ethnicity, religion, and gender. By focusing on the voices and struggle of these young Muslim women, we can begin to see them as actors who at times reinforce traditional norms and at other times act in ways that begin to redefine the terrain of gender, faith, and identity.

NOTES

1. "Orientalism" refers to a set of discursive relations and practices that structured colonial relations between Europe and its Muslim colonies. Through Orientalist discourses, "the Orient," comprising the Middle East and Asia, was constructed as a barbaric, anachronistic space outside of the progress and civility of European modernity. These colonial narratives ideologically rationalized and justified European expansion and exploitation within Muslim lands as part of the "white man's burden" of civilizing the savage races. Orientalism still retains currency within the Western imagination, legitimizing more contemporary neo-imperialist practices and maintaining the positional superiority of the West in relation to Islam and Muslim societies.
2. All school names and participant names are identified using pseudonyms to protect the anonymity of the participants.
3. It is interesting to note the ways women have attempted to resist and negotiate these bans. For example, in France school girls took to the streets wearing the French flag as a headscarf in protest of the ban, and in Turkey female university students often wear hats and wigs to maintain their modesty, thereby manoeuvring around the constraints of the ban and the limits it places on their sense of agency and spirituality.
4. The hadith is a record of the sayings of the Prophet Muhammad. Next to the Qur'an, it forms the primary corpus of Islamic knowledge, providing guidance for daily life as well as the moral and ethical basis for Islamic legal codes.
5. The idea of the "dangerous feminine" is evoked in some Islamic discourses that regard women's bodies as sites of temptation that are in need of containment. Mernissi (1987) describes this as resulting from a belief in the passive nature of female sexual-

ity versus the active nature of male sexuality, placing the burden on women to avoid provocation by employing restrictive dress codes and seclusion.
6 Academic "streams" in the Canadian context are the same as "tracks" in American schools.
7 A shalwar kameez is a traditional South Asian form of dress that consists of a long tunic worn over baggy trousers.
8 The term "TTC" is used as an acronym by Torontonians to refer to the public transit system of buses, subways, and streetcars operated by the Toronto Transit Commission.
9 A qualitative study of Muslim schools in Montreal conducted by Kelly Spurles (2003, 58) also echoes these sentiments in the words of a participant who stated, "We know they – the media and the rest of society – are watching us for the slightest proof that we are as bad as they think."
10 "OAC" means "Ontario Academic Credit," which referred to the course work during a fifth year of high school, or "Grade 13," but was phased out after 2003.
11 The term "niqabi" is used among Muslim women to refer to women who adopt the niqab.

REFERENCES

Abou El Fadl, K. 2001. *Speaking in God's name.* Oxford, UK: Oneworld.
Ahmed, L. 1992. *Women and gender in Islam.* New Haven, CT: Yale University Press.
Alloula, M. 1986. *The colonial harem.* Trans. M. Godzich and W. Godzich. Minneapolis, MN: University of Minnesota Press.
Barlas, A. 2002. *"Believing women" in Islam: Unreading patriarchal interpretations of the Qur'an.* Austin, TX: University of Texas Press.
Bullock, K.H. 2000. The gaze and colonial plans for the unveiling of Muslim women. *Studies in Contemporary Islam* 2, 2: 1-20.
–. 2002. *Rethinking Muslim women and the veil: Challenging historical and modern stereotypes.* Herndon, VA: International Institute of Islamic Thought.
Clarke, L. 2003. Hijab according to the hadith: Text and interpretation. In S.S. Alvi, H. Hoodfar, and S. McDonough, eds., *The Muslim veil in North America: Issues and debates,* 214-86. Toronto, ON: Women's Press.
Driscoll, E. 1997. Hunger, representation and the female body. *Journal of Feminist Studies in Religion* 13, 1: 91-104.
El Guindi, F. 1999. *Veil: Modesty, privacy and resistance.* New York, NY: Berg and Oxford International.
El Habti, R. 2004. Laicite, women's rights and the headscarf issue in France. http://www.karamah.org/docs/veil paper.pdf.
Gutmann, A. 1996. Challenges of multiculturalism in democratic education. In R.K. Fullwider, ed., *Public education in a multicultural society: Policy, theory, critique,* 156-79. New York, NY: Cambridge University Press.
Hajjaji-Jarrah, S. 2003. Women's modesty in Qur'anic commentaries: The founding discourse. In S.S. Alvi, H. Hoodfar, and S. McDonough, eds., *The Muslim veil in North America: Issues and debates,* 145-80. Toronto, ON: Women's Press.
Halstead, M. 1991. Radical feminism, Islam and the single sex school debate. *Gender and Education* 3, 3: 263-78.

Hamdani, D. 2004. Triple jeopardy: Muslim women's experiences of discrimination. http://www.ccmw.com/publications/Reports/Triple Jeopardy.pdf.

Haw, K. 1995. Muslim girls' schools – A conflict of interests? *Gender and Education* 6, 1: 63-76.

–. 1998. *Educating Muslim girls: Shifting discourses.* Philadelphia, PA: Open University Press.

Henry, F., and C. Tator. 2005. The colour of democracy: Racism in Canadian society. Toronto, ON: Thompson/Nelson.

Hoodfar, H. 1993. The veil in their minds and on our heads: The persistence of colonial images of Muslim women. *Resources for Feminist Research* 22, 1-2: 5-18.

–. 2003. More than clothing: Veiling as an adaptive strategy. In S.S. Alvi, H. Hoodfar, and S. McDonough, eds., *The Muslim veil in North America: Issues and debates,* 3-40. Toronto, ON: Women's Press.

Jones, A. 1993. Becoming a "girl": Post-structuralist suggestions for educational research. *Gender and Education* 5, 2: 157-66.

Kahf, M. 1999. *Western representations of the Muslim woman: From termagant to odalisque.* Austin, TX: University of Texas Press.

Kelly Spurles, P. 2003. Coding dress: Gender and the articulation of identity in a Canadian Muslim school. In S.S. Alvi, H. Hoodfar, and S. McDonough, eds., *The Muslim veil in North America: Issues and debates,* 41-71. Toronto, ON: Women's Press.

Keung, N. 2002. The hijab and the job hunt. *Toronto Star,* December 18, A27.

Khan, S. 2000. *Muslim women: Crafting a North American identity.* Gainsville, FL: University of Florida Press.

–. 2002. *Aversion and desire: Negotiating Muslim female identity in the diaspora.* Toronto, ON: Women's Press.

–. 2003. Why does a headscarf have us tied up in knots? *Globe and Mail,* September 26, A27.

Lazreg, M. 1988. Feminism and difference: The perils of writing as a woman on women in Algeria. *Feminist Studies* 14, 1: 81-103.

–. 1994. *The eloquence of silence: Algerian women in question.* New York, NY: Routledge.

Lenk, H.M. 2000. The case of Emilie Ouimet: News discourse on hijab and the construction of Québecois national identity. In G.J.S. Dei and A. Calliste, eds., *Anti-racist feminism,* 73-90. Halifax, NS: Fernwood.

Mabro, J. 1991. *Veiled half-truths: Western travellers' perceptions of Middle Eastern women.* London: I.B. Taurus.

MacCleod, A.E. 1991. *Accommodating protest: Working women, the new veiling and change in Cairo.* New York: Columbia University Press.

MacMaster, N., and T. Lewis. 1998. Orientalism: From unveiling to hyperveiling. *Journal of European Studies* 28, 1-2: 121-35.

McDonough, S. 2003. Voices of Muslim women. In S.S. Alvi, H. Hoodfar, and S. McDonough, eds., *The Muslim veil in North America: Issues and debates,* 105-20. Toronto, ON: Women's Press.

Mernissi, F. 1987. *Beyond the veil: Male-female relationships in modern Muslim society.* Bloomington, IN: Indiana State University Press.
—. 1991. *The veil and the male elite: A feminist interpretation of women's rights in Islam.* Trans. M-J. Lakeland. Reading, MA: Addison-Wesley.
Misbahuddin, K. 1996. The lingering hijab question. *Message* 21, 3: 29.
Mohanty, C.T. 1991. Under Western eyes: Feminist scholarship and colonial discourses. In C.T. Mohanty and A. Russo, eds., *Third World women and the politics of feminism,* 51-74. Indianapolis, IN: University of Indiana Press.
Parker-Jenkins, M. 1999. Islam, gender and discrimination in the workplace. Paper presented at the conference "Nationalism, Identity and Minority Rights: Sociological and Political Perspectives," University of Bristol, United Kingdom, September 16.
Read, J.G., and J. Bartkowski. 2000. To veil or not to veil? A case study of identity negotiation among Muslim women in Austin, Texas. *Gender and Society* 14, 3: 395-417.
Reay, D. 2001. Spice girls, nice girls, girlies, and tomboys: Gender discourses, girls' cultures, and femininities in the primary classroom. *Gender and Education* 13, 2: 153-66.
Rezai-Rashti, G. 1994. Islamic identity and racism. *Orbit* 25, 2: 37-38.
Roald, A.S. 2001. *Women in Islam: The Western experience.* New York, NY: Routledge.
Said, E.W. 1979. *Orientalism.* New York, NY: Vintage.
Sarroub, L. 2005. *All American Yemeni girls: Being Muslim in a public school.* Philadelphia, PA: University of Pennsylvania Press.
Scrivener, L. 2001. Islamic schools a "safe space." *Toronto Star,* February 2, D8.
Smith, G. 2002. Muslim garb a liability in job market: Study finds women wearing traditional head scarves turned away by prospective employers. *Globe and Mail,* December 18, A10.
Todd, S. 1999. Veiling the "Other," unveiling ourselves: Reading media images of the hijab psychoanalytically to move beyond tolerance. *Canadian Journal of Education* 23, 4: 438-51.
Wadud, A. 1999. *Qur'an and woman: Rereading the sacred text from a woman's perspective.* 2nd ed. New York, NY: Oxford University Press.
Yegenoglu, M. 1998. *Colonial fantasies: Towards a feminist reading of Orientalism.* London, UK: Cambridge University Press.
Zine, J. 1997. Muslim students in public schools: Education and the politics of religious identity. MA thesis, Department of Sociology and Equity Studies in Education, Ontario Institute for Studies in Education, University of Toronto.
—. 2000. Redefining resistance: Toward an Islamic subculture in schools. *Race, Ethnicity and Education* 31, 2: 293-316.
—. 2001. Muslim youth in Canadian schools: Education and the politics of religious identity. *Anthropology and Education Quarterly* 32, 4: 399-423.
—. 2002. Muslim women and the politics of representation. *American Journal of Islamic Social Sciences* 19, 4: 1-22.

–. 2003. Dealing with September 12: Integrative anti-racism and the challenge of anti-Islamophobia education. *Orbit* 33, 3: 39-41.

Zine, J., and K.H. Bullock. 2002. Editorial. *American Journal of Islamic Social Sciences* 19, 4: i-iii.

PART 4

SECURITY

IN THE POST-9/11 context, domestic-security policies increasingly link the politics of race and immigration to notions of public safety. This practice has resulted in a climate of heightened fear that at the same time serves to justify these policies. The arrests of seventeen Canadian Muslim youth and one Muslim adult in 2006 on terror-related charges galvanized fear of "home-grown" terror cells that could threaten national security and safety. Concerns have arisen not only about how to maintain peace and security but also about how to ensure that civil liberties are not eroded and that entire communities do not bear the brunt of collective punishment through racial and religious profiling based on the actions of a misguided few. The need to maintain a balance between these concerns has not been successful at all times. Anti-Muslim racism, Islamophobia, and hate crimes have been the by-products of the "war on terror" and a draconian domestic-security regime.

In this section, two Canadian security policies are examined: security certificates, which are a part of the Immigration and Refugee Protection Act; and Bill C-36, the Anti-terrorism Act. Both chapters are concerned with the discursive practices that shape these policies and public

PART 4 ... opinion, and both use discourse analysis as a methodology to unpack these policies' racialized dimensions. Jacqueline Flatt's chapter provides a discourse analysis of the *National Post*'s and the *Globe and Mail*'s reporting on the five Muslim men who have been held on security certificates, and Shaista Patel's chapter uses an anti-Orientalist analysis to examine Bill C-36 and the nation-building functions it performs. Both chapters demonstrate the way discursive practices construct the "citizen" and the "outsider" and thereby constitute the nation itself, determining who has rights to belong to the nation and who must be feared, put under surveillance, or exiled. Both chapters provide strong critiques of these policies and of the representational and discursive practices used to justify them.

The Security Certificate Exception
A Media Analysis of Human Rights and Security Discourses in Canada's *Globe and Mail* and *National Post*

JACQUELINE FLATT

> A security certificate,
> It's being a minor at 30 years old
> It's the petty, constipated bureaucrat made inquisitor
> It's the self-satisfied inquisitor with the airs of a torturer
> It's the guilt of being born elsewhere
>
> A security certificate,
> It's big brother at home,
> It's reality TV without the ads,
> It's "Get out, you immigrant!"
> It's shut up and put up. (Excerpts from Charkaoui 2003)

The Security Certificate Debate

The use of security certificates is not a new government policy and practice in Canada. According to *Detention Centres and Security Certificates*, a 2007 report, "The security certificate process, by which non-citizens may be detained and deported based largely on unproven allegations that they pose a risk to the security of Canada, has existed in Canada's immigration law since 1978" (Doyle 2007, 1). The debate surrounding the use of security certificates examines a post-911 world that is centred on negotiating national-security interests while trying to maintain human rights initiatives. From

1991 to 2009, twenty-eight certificates were issued, nineteen of which resulted in deportation and five of which were issued following the events of September 11, 2001 (Doyle 2007, 5). As of 2009, the five men issued security certificates were under strict house arrest and faced ongoing court hearings: Mohamed Zeki Mahjoub from 2000, Mahmoud Jaballah from 2001, Hassan Almrei from 2001, Mohamed Harkat from 2002, and Adil Charkaoui from 2003 (Doyle 2007, Appendix D). In short, the policy of using security certificates denies detainees their human rights because this policy leads to arbitrary arrests, reinforcing systemic racial profiling and stereotypes, criminalizing detainees without actually laying charges, and threatening detainees' lives through deportation measures that could subject them to acts of torture.

To understand the discourses presented in news articles on security certificates, it is essential to identify the debates on policy and law surrounding this issue. This chapter examines the power exercised by government in the use of security certificates when there is a so-called "state of exception" (Agamben 2005) and considers the way that media propaganda supports the "exception" by invoking themes whose language and meaning associate Arabs and Muslims with specific racial markers and make the threat of the "enemy Other" an absolute.

Specifically, the controversy over the use of security certificates has been centred on the Department of Justice's 2001 Immigration and Refugee Protection Act (IRPA). Its articles stipulate immigration policies, refugee regulations, and the terms and conditions of detention and deportation. Under the heading "Certificates and Protection of Information," the IRPA specifies: (1) the rules concerning the process of issuing a security certificate; (2) the conditions under which an individual is seen as a national security threat; (3) the measures to protect undisclosed information in security certificates; (4) the procedures for trials in federal court; and (5) the conditions under which an individual can be deported from Canada (IRPA, Sections 77-85).

In addition, the role of the Canadian Security Intelligence Service (CSIS) has been to gather information and "secret evidence" with which to prosecute alleged "terrorists" who are issued security certificates. However, detainees and their lawyers are not given the case information required to prepare for a fair defence in federal court. Denial of case information to the detainees is a direct violation of Article 14(1) of the International Covenant of Civil and Political Rights, which stipulates the right to a fair and equal trial. This is problematic since the judge in federal court determines whether undisclosed information from CSIS's vague summaries is "admissible" as justification to hold detainees: "The judge may base a decision on information or other evidence even if a summary of that information or other evidence is not provided to the permanent resident or foreign national" (IRPA, Section 83(1)(i)).

In 2007 Norman Doyle, a member of Parliament and chair of the Standing Committee on Citizenship and Immigration, wrote *Detention Centres and Security Certificates* in response to the criticisms of sections of the IRPA. This report specifically highlights and addresses the claims made regarding the unfair treatment of individuals being detained and deported under security certificates. It also presents detainees' letters to the Canadian Border Services Agency, in which they challenge their treatment as *convicted* criminals when they have not been charged as such (Doyle 2007, Appendix E).

In 2008, Bill C-3 was added to modify contested sections of the IRPA. In an attempt to better uphold human rights, Bill C-3 was to provide detainees the use of a special advocate to intervene between a judge in federal court and the detainees and to provide the detainees and their lawyers better access to the undisclosed information being held against them. Within this new policy, the special advocate is to be given the undisclosed information but does not have access to other relevant information, nor can he or she relay any information to the detainee without permission of the judge (Becklumb 2008, 22-23). In turn, this process has been contested, as the use of a special advocate continues to violate detainees' right to a fair and equal trial since they continue to be denied full access to information.

In continuing to unpack this debate, it is essential to include a discussion of articles of the Office of the United Nations High Commissioner for Human Rights' 1966 International Covenant of Civil and Political Rights. This covenant, which was signed and ratified by Canada, is committed to upholding the universal human rights of citizens and noncitizens. The security certificate process is being accused of violating Article 2, which stipulates that everyone has the rights specified in this covenant regardless of race; Article 7, which states, "No one shall be subjected to torture or to cruel, inhuman or degrading treatment or punishment"; Article 9(1), which states, "Everyone has the right to liberty and security of person. No one shall be subjected to arbitrary arrest or detention"; Article 10(2)(a), which states, "Accused persons shall, save in exceptional circumstances, be segregated from convicted persons and shall be subject to separate treatment appropriate to their status as *unconvicted* persons" (emphasis added); and finally, Article 14(1), which states, "All persons shall be equal before the courts and tribunals. In the determination of any criminal charge against him, or of his rights and obligations in a suit at law, everyone shall be entitled to a fair and public hearing by a competent, independent and impartial tribunal established by law."

Similarly, the 1984 Convention against Torture (CAT), which was signed and ratified by Canada, argues for the responsibility of states to uphold the rights of human subjects by preventing any form of torture, cruelty, degrading treatment, or punishment. When examining the abuses of these rights violations taking place under security certificates, it is essential to consider three articles of the CAT: "Each State Party shall take effective legislative, administrative, judicial or other measures to prevent acts of torture in any territory under its jurisdiction" (Article 2(1)); "No *exceptional circumstances* whatsoever, whether a state of war or a threat or war, internal political instability or any other public emergency, may be invoked as a justification of torture" (Article 2(2), emphasis added); and "No State Party shall expel, return ('refouler') or extradite a person to another State where there are substantial grounds for believing that he would be in danger of being subjected to torture" (Article 3(1)).

Covering Muslims: Media Constructions Post-9/11

The powerful influence of news media, which interpret selected coverage for the general public, is due to a system that Chomsky (1989) calls the "propaganda model." According to this model, "the media serve the interests of state and corporate power, which are closely interlinked, framing of state reporting and analysis in a manner supportive of established privilege and limiting debate and discussion accordingly" (Chomsky 1989, 10). Chomsky argues that media coverage employs "vacuous" tactics that consist of "mobilizing community opinion in favor of vapid, empty concepts like ... 'Support our troops'" that imply, "Who can be against that?" (Chomsky 1997, 20).

In mobilizing the community, it is essential that the media create or maintain fear. Chomsky (1997, 22) uses Walter Lippmann's class category of the "bewildered herd" to refer to the mass population receiving coverage:

> The bewildered herd is a problem ... You've got to keep them pretty scared, because unless they're properly scared and frightened of all kinds of devils that are going on to destroy them from outside or inside or somewhere, they may start to think, which is very dangerous, because they're not

competent to think. Therefore it's important to distract them and marginalize them.

Because the news media reinforce fear of the "Other" through the propaganda model, the "war on terror" as well as the security certificate practices of lengthy detention and threats of deportation are seen as legitimate, with government decisions on policy going largely unquestioned. As Chomsky (1989, 165) argues, "the possibility that they [media] are false cannot be raised; it lies beyond the conceivable." Although Chomsky writes on the discourse of the American press, this analysis of selected representation mirrors the context of the Canadian press. According to Henry and Tator (2002, 55), the misrepresentation in news coverage is associated with the lack of minority representation in the workforce of Canadian news media.

The interpretive and selective approach continues to reflect dominant Eurocentric values that exclude certain minority perspectives, framing the "Other" so that the misrepresentation goes unquestioned. The "commonsense" assumptions generated by this approach shaped the discourses of identity formation placed on Muslims in the aftermath reporting of 9/11, reinforcing associations of Muslims with "danger," "mistrust," and "terror" (see also Chapter 4). Karim (2002, 105) argues that rather than focusing on the larger governmental and political implications of their stories, journalists since September 11, 2001, have reinforced government narratives that rely on negative generalizations of Muslims in framing the hunt for "Islamic terrorists." Similarly, Jiwani (2006, 36) argues, "Nonetheless, by collapsing differences between and within groups, by exoticizing and demonizing the Other, the media dehumanize and objectify particular groups, and in so doing, contribute to their marginalization and naturalize inequalities."

In its construction of "the terrorist," media discourse has become a market through which the government "sells" security by creating heightened "risk" and fear. Gillespie (2007, 279) states, "This new conception of risk and an ever-expanding conception of security have served the interests of governments and media, though their disadvantages have by now become apparent. Governments increasingly 'sell' security as a virtual commodity to citizens." In addition, Greer and Jewkes (2005, 21) explain, "The point is that media representations of exceptional offenses construct the 'outsider' status of perpetrators as unequivocal and incontestable ... They are portrayed in terms of their *absolute* Otherness, their utter detachment from the social, moral, and cultural universe of ordinary, decent people – their pure and unadulterated evil" (emphasis in original).

Securitization, Racism, and Muslims in Canada

French (2007, 61) discusses the new security and surveillance measures taken by the Canadian government after 9/11:

> New surveillance is different from traditional forms of social control because of its low visibility, its ubiquity, its decentralization, and its reliance on technical instruments. New surveillance can be conceived of as the mining of data from vast fields of information. Machines collect the information and therefore mediate the process of watching. For Arab and Muslim peoples, the augmentation of this new surveillance by the methods described earlier is striking. The relative absence of the use of these methods in the general population makes their deployment in Muslim and Arab communities the more stigmatizing.

The use of security certificates has, until recently, been largely hidden from the general public. The development of the "war on terror" has produced a dichotomy between security and rights (Banfield and Zekulin 2008) that has compromised human rights in favour of security. Similarly, Aitken (2008, 384) argues that "it is in this language of indefinite detention that the security certificate program certifies and constitutes non-citizens as a racialized threat to national security (effectively securitizing their bodies) and removes from them 'normal' legal and judicial recourse."

The use of security certificates has not only produced human rights abuses but has also been a hidden form of racism. According to Razack (2008, 26), "Security certificates did not begin with the 'war on terror,' but they have become the 'front-line tools' used by Canada to fight terrorism, and their usage is now primarily directed at Arabs and Muslims." Similarly, Arat-Koc (2006, 218) states, "Since 11 September 2001 the category [Arab and Muslim], as a concept of racialization has been raised to the status of 'common sense' in depictions of 'the enemy,' resulting in attacks on many non-Arab and non-Muslim people of South Asian background, who are thought to 'look like Muslims.'" In short, Bell (2006, 65) argues, the security certificate debate is centred on the labelling of "foreignness in the production of danger."

Muslim Citizenship and Belonging

The ideological constructs of citizenship and belonging in Canada determine the inclusion and exclusion of certain individuals. According to

Stasiulis and Ross (2006, 338), governmental power within citizenship exclusion can be understood through the exercise of "flexible sovereignty": "The paradigm of security that is practiced today achieves legitimacy and provides a context in which to further securitize citizenship, rendering it exclusionary and fragmentary and enabling a flexible form of sovereignty to exercise power through and across territorial boundaries." Within the exception allowed for by "flexible sovereignty" practices, Arab and Muslim individuals are placed outside of what is normalized, reinforcing racialized boundaries between who is and who is not seen as a citizen and as belonging to Canada (see also Chapter 1). It is important to understand the larger implications of how security certificate policies in the IRPA have infiltrated the Canadian context and created distinct lines between citizen and noncitizen. Hage (2000, 233) discusses how immigration and migration are seen as "problematic":

> It is immaterial whether the problematisation is aimed at extolling the virtues of multiculturalism and migration or at condemning them as divisive. What is important is the problematisation itself, for it is through it that the Third World–looking migrant is relegated to the position of a national object to be governed by the eternally worried White national subject.

Although Hage is challenging white dominance in a multicultural Australian context, his observations can be applied to a multicultural Canada that associates the "Other" with worry, fear, risk, and danger. In addition, constructing the immigrant or refugee as a "problem" further reinforces "who" and "what" is "Canadian." As Bannerji (2000, 77-78) argues, "By constantly signifying the White population as 'Canadians' and immigrants of color as 'Others,' by constantly stereotyping Third World immigrants as criminals, terrorists, and fundamentalists, the state manages to both manipulate and cancel its alleged dedication to multiculturalism."

In a post-9/11 context, the multicultural agenda facilitates a false sense of belonging because the notion of citizenship is also a part of the national ideology, not just a status bestowed by the state. Similarly, Arat-Koc (2005, 41) states that, "for racialized minorities, the precariousness of belonging creates a disciplinary pressure of having to prove their national loyalty." Thus narratives that construct the "Other" as "foreign," "criminal," "dangerous," "problematic," and "not Canadian" deny racialized immigrants and refugees a sense of belonging to the nation.

Theory: A Framework for the "Exception"

The media messages discussed above contribute to the constructions of security certificate discourse and are evidence of the theoretical "state of exception" considered in this study. The "state of exception," proposed by Agamben (2005), refers to a state's justification of extreme security measures that can compromise certain individuals' human rights. Similarly, Dean (2007, 165) argues that the "exception" can be defined as a form of "ban":

> To be banned is to be placed outside the juridical-political order that defines the normal frame of life of a political community. But in the act of being placed outside this order, who or what is banned is included in the power that places he, she, them or it there. This act gives content and validity to that normal frame. To be abandoned means to be placed in a position where the law has withdrawn and where one is exposed to death.

This function of the "exception" is demonstrated through the process by which the government-supported IRPA sanctions practices in detention, court trials, deportation, and torture that abuse human rights law. Similarly, Foucault (1977, 202) argues that these "panoptic" techniques, within the "seeing/being seen dyad" of observation, surveillance, and control of the "problem population" – in this case, "terrorists" – become an avenue of "exceptional" regulation, as these power tactics subtly infiltrate society. Foucault (1977, 227) states,

> The ideal point of penalty today would be an indefinite discipline: an interrogation without end, an investigation that would be extended without limit to a meticulous and ever more analytical observation, a judgement that would at the same time be the constitution of a file that was never closed, the calculated leniency of a penalty that would be interlaced with the ruthless curiosity of an examination, a procedure that would be at the same time the permanent measure of a gap in relation to an inaccessible norm and the asymptotic movement that strives to meet infinity.

In addition, Foucault (1997, 185) argues that this system of classifying a part of the population as "most dangerous" manifests itself through the form of "a maximum of consequences, a minimum of warning. The most effects and fewest signs." Thus the heightening of "fear" and "risk" allows for the functioning of security certificate practices that equate "danger" with "Arab" and

"Muslim" in the management of the "dangerous terrorist," furthering a discourse that constructs the "Arab/Muslim" as being an innate feature of "terrorism." Security certificates have become a means by which the lines between policy implementation and rights abuses are blurred. According to Agamben (2005, 23),

> In truth, the state of exception is neither external nor internal to juridical order, and the problem of defining it concerns precisely a threshold, or a zone or indifference, where inside and outside do not exclude each other but rather blur with each other. The suspension of the norm does not mean its abolition, and the zone of anomie that it establishes is not (or at least claims not to be) unrelated to the juridical order.

Similarly, Butler (2004) argues that the detainee is no longer perceived as being "worthy" of human rights, for there is no conception of the detainee as "human." This denial of the detainee's humanity reinforces the legitimacy of taking "exceptional" measures to restrict rights. Butler (2004, 77) states,

> If it is the person, or the people, who are deemed dangerous, and no dangerous acts need to be proven to establish this as true, then the state constitutes the detained population unilaterally, taking them out of the jurisdiction of the law, depriving them of the legal protections to which subjects under national and international law are entitled. These are surely populations that are not regarded as subjects, humans who are not conceptualized within the frame of a political culture in which human lives are underwritten by legal entitlements, law, and so humans who are not humans.

Clearly, there is need for a discourse that introduces the media propaganda of the security certificate debate, as news media are a powerful producer and reproducer of dominant knowledge, meaning, and norms in a society where governments justify declarations of "exceptional circumstances."

Methods

The role of the media and media discourse is a reflection of the ownership, knowledge, and power of the state elite. I have already argued that a deconstruction of the media's news coverage can be understood through Chomsky's "propaganda model," which analyzes the "vacuous" tactics employed by government and media elite in their dissemination of meanings and messages. In drawing this discussion toward the need for a discourse analysis of media coverage of government-issued security certificates, Dean (2007, 163) argues, "While what is exceptional cannot be known in advance, and the decision itself is unpredictable, we can analyse how the necessity of the call for decision is made within given forms of knowledge and expertise and in different practices and how the decision is devolved onto various agents."

Discourse Analysis: Language, Meaning, and Theme
This study deconstructs specific themes found in security certificate content presented in the *National Post* and the *Globe and Mail* through a critical discourse analysis. This analysis is being conducted to understand the larger political and racial discourses surrounding the use of government-issued security certificates. These newspapers were selected because they are two of Canada's largest and most politically conservative, the *Globe and Mail* being at the centre or centre-right of the political spectrum and the *National Post* being on the right. In addition, analyzing these two national dailies is important in this study not only because they are influential in determining what is newsworthy for mass public consumption but also because of how they have become influential through the news monopolization within Canadian media (Jiwani 2005, 51).

In discussing critical discourse analysis as a qualitative research method, Ainsworth and Hardy (2004, 236) argue that "text[s] have a[n] ideational function in that they constitute forms of knowledge and beliefs, an interpersonal function in that they help to construct certain forms of self or social identities and a relational function in terms of how they contribute to social relations between different actors." This connection between language and society in discourse analysis is essential to understanding "the relations between discourse, power, dominance, [and] social inequality" (van Dijk 1993, 249).

A content analysis was also performed using NVivo 8, a computer software program, to facilitate qualitative research in themes and word counts, which also provided a quantitative analysis in this study. The sample of news articles was analyzed to determine what themes are represented in each article and the common threads between article themes and words.

Discourse analysis is both an interpretive and a subjective method. Perhaps this subjectivity is a research limitation given that there are always some themes and concepts that are not included in analysis and discussion.

The researcher's standpoint is necessary for readers to consider when implementing the interpretive meanings assigned to the discourse being analyzed. As a researcher, I am a white Canadian female of European and Argentine descent, which is important for readers to understand when they consider how I have approached, deconstructed, and challenged Eurocentric assumptions in the security certificate debate. It is also essential for the researcher not to generalize or conceptualize all Muslims, Arabs, or detainees as having the same needs, wants, and rights. This needs to be recognized in order for the researcher to avoid the reproduction of dominant white cultural assumptions about the "Other."

Sample and Data Collection

In this critical discourse analysis of post-9/11 representations of Muslims in language and text, the *National Post* and the *Globe and Mail* are the two newspapers from which meanings of the political and social constructions of Muslims are drawn. The news articles examined in this study are from January 1, 2004, to December 1, 2008, as the majority of articles on security certificates were published during this time. Within this period, the *National Post* and the *Globe and Mail* printed a combined total of 204 articles under the "security certificate" category. Articles were included in the sample only if the majority of their content is focused on security certificate policy or on the five detainees. In addition, very short articles that highlight what security certificates are or that give short summaries of detainees' cases were excluded.

Findings: Themes and Counts

This section focuses first on the quantitative component of this study. The *Globe and Mail* and the *National Post* produced a number of important and specific news themes related to the security certificate debate that have been counted. In total, from 2004 to 2008, there were 117 such articles from the *Globe and Mail*, and 87 such articles from the *National Post* (see Table 9.1). In the *Globe and Mail*, 99.1 percent of these articles were found in the front "News" section, being the "A" section of the newspaper, with 7.7 percent appearing on the front page. In the *National Post*, 100 percent of these articles were located within the "A" section, with 6.1 percent appearing on the front page and 96.6 percent placed in the "News" section.

The *Globe and Mail* had a small portion of responses in the "Comment" or "Letter to the Editor" sections, with the *National Post* having none. The

Globe and Mail had 9 articles (7.7%) in the "Comment" section and 6 articles (5.1%) in the "Letter to the Editor" section during the five years researched in this study. Thus, in the "Lifestyle" or "Comment" sections of these newspapers, there was a lack of articles focused on the detainees as humans or on the suffering their families had endured. In short, the dominance of "A" worthy news in this study demonstrates the monopoly of propaganda-producing discourses in which alleged terrorist suspects cannot be constructed as human or as participants of an open dialogue within the community.

In the 204 articles in the sample, a number of important themes were reinforced through repetition. "Counts" were based on the number of articles that contained reports or comments associated with these themes. It should be noted that these counts often overlap, as particular words, sentences, or quotations may be associated with more than one theme. The following lists the themes and descriptions that were selected for the NVivo 8 counts conducted for this study:

1. Potential threat: reports/comments that link detainees/terrorist suspects to the "potential threat" of future terrorism (consistent with the discourse of fear and risk to the public).
2. Threat to national security: reports/comments that reference CSIS on security certificate detainees and associate individuals and groups with "terrorism" and with the "threat" to Canadian national security.
3. CSIS rhetoric: reports/comments about the role, actions, or techniques of CSIS in security certificate practices respecting detainees, such as identifying the "threat," information gathering, detention status, house arrest, and CSIS positions/statements as the voice of authority (along with the positions of judges who support these practices).
4. The terrorist: reports/comments that link detainees with extremists such as Osama bin Laden and their groups, with al-Jihad religious fundamentalism, or with violence or participation in acts of terrorism.
5. Mistrust: reports/comments that represent detainees as "liars," mention "fake passports" or other false/forged documents, or question detainees' "credibility" or the legitimacy of their being in Canada.
6. Canadianness: reports/comments that refer to Canadian values (such as being "fair," "liberal," and "democratic," having "balance," or providing "middle-range" solutions when choosing between rights and security) or to Canadian opinions about terrorism, detainees, security certificates, or

security initiatives, including the views of high-profile Canadian backers (such as Pierre Trudeau) and the positions of Canadian political parties.
7 Human rights, policies, and constitutionality: reports/comments on the debate over the constitutionality of the IRPA, of Bill C-3, and of security certificates, on human rights, or on court decisions concerning detention, house arrest, or deportation in the context of the human rights debate.
8 British or US model: reports/comments intended to influence how Canada will fight terrorism by referring to the British model of the "special advocate" as a potential "middle-range" solution for Canada or by referring to American policy and law on terrorism.
9 Not Canadian: reports/comments about the "Other" from Syria, Morocco, or Egypt, "foreigners," "dangerous" immigrants, refugees or newcomers, detainees not being "Canadian," or detainees being a "problem."
10 Deportation: reports/comments that specifically refer to the threat of deportation faced by detainees (but not in the context of the human rights debate).

TABLE 9.1

Count totals by theme for the *Globe and Mail*'s and *National Post*'s coverage of the security certificate debate

Coverage theme	Globe and Mail		National Post	
	Articles	%	Articles	%
Threat themes combined	102	87.2	80	92.0
Potential threat	42	35.9	37	42.5
Threat to national security	60	51.3	43	49.4
CSIS rhetoric	61	52.1	71	81.6
The terrorist	69	59.0	74	85.1
Mistrust	26	22.2	19	21.8
Canadianness	60	51.3	36	41.4
Human rights, policies, and constitutionality	72	61.5	57	65.5
British or US model	19	16.2	8	9.2
Not Canadian	75	64.1	64	73.6
Deportation	65	55.6	47	54.0

Discussion: "Vacuous" Propaganda in the Security Certificate "Exception"

> *Orientalism can be discussed and analyzed as the corporate institution for dealing with the Orient – dealing with it by making statements about it, authorizing views of it, describing it, by teaching it, settling it, ruling over it: in short, Orientalism as a Western style for dominating, restructuring, and having authority over the Orient. (Said 1978, 3)*

As Said (1978) has noted, the discursive power of Orientalism derives from the production of knowledge about the "Eastern Other" as it is continually constructed and reproduced by the "West." Similarly, in the contemporary neo-Orientalist context, the discourse surrounding security certificates has embedded specific values, beliefs, and stereotypes about the "Muslim" and/or "Arab" male. The security certificate discourse has not only centred on the five detainees marked as "terrorists" but has also been extended to include generalizations about the "dangerous" immigrant and refugee. What has supported these characterizations is the ability of CSIS to remain the voice of authority not only on the techniques of surveillance and control measures but also in sustaining the discourse of fear and risk in the news. Thus the "bewildered herd" is influenced through the construction of "who" belongs to "Canada" and who is seen as "innocent," which is based largely on Eurocentric values that reinforce "Canadian" ideologies.

The effectiveness of the propaganda model is evident in its ability to facilitate these constructions of the "Other" and to shape how "we Canadians" view, know, and understand the "war on terror" and the debate on security certificates. It has already been shown that the security certificate discourse is reported mainly within the "A" sections of the newspapers discussed here but remains largely absent from public awareness and discourse. Thus it is clear that reports by newspapers use the propaganda model to limit ideas, beliefs, and attitudes about the "Other" within the security certificate debate.

A "Potential Threat" and a "Threat to National Security"

It is important to build on the different levels of messages that are represented in the security certificate discourse. Therefore, it is essential to begin with the construction of the "threat," which is the umbrella over all other themes discussed in this study. It is through the construction of "threat" that fear is maintained, which assists in facilitating and legitimating the other themes. As the results have indicated, the largest proportions of counts were found within the themes of "potential threat" and "threat to national security." In addition, the combined total for both themes was 87.2 percent of the sample in the *Globe and Mail* and 92 percent in the *National Post*.

As Chomsky's (1989) propaganda model suggests, it is essential that the general population, or the "bewildered herd," remains in a state of fear so that its members cannot question the "common-sense" assumptions repeated and reinforced in security certificate news. This is especially true when the discourse of the "potential threat" continues to reinforce that "terrorists" could be "hiding anywhere" in Canada and that not invoking surveillance measures and immigration policies, such as the security certificate, would be a "risk" to national security.

Thus the policies mandating these tactics are continually written from the position that "secret evidence" measures are both necessary and in the "best interest" of Canadians. The following quotation from the *National Post* is an example of the "threat to national security" theme:

> Mahmoud Jaballah has been accused of orchestrating several bombings in East Africa as a senior member of the Egyptian group al-Jihad. Still wanted by Egyptian authorities, Mr. Jaballah was detained in Canada in August, 2001, after *officials deemed him to be a threat to national security*. Under immigration law, the government is not required to reveal its evidence against him ... During a Federal Court hearing yesterday, lawyers representing the Attorney-General and Immigration Minister argued the *need to protect the security of Canadian residents trumps Mr. Jaballah's right to personal safety*. "Every Canadian citizen, every visitor, every permanent resident has the right to life, liberty and the security of their person and *deserves protection from people like Mr. Jaballah*," lawyer Donald McIntosh said. "They *deserve protection from people who, if left to their own devices, would assist and facilitate the kinds of diabolical acts like those of September 11*." (Cowan 2004, emphasis added)

The message of this article is evident in its definition of "who" has status and the right to know the evidence being held against them. In addition, the "vacuous" association of religious extremism with terrorist activity presumes the guilt of the Muslim detainee. By presenting the argument that trusted and respected CSIS officials and government lawyers have deemed the detainee a security "threat" and by concluding with comments that hypothetically generalize the detainee to include him among the "people" who possess the "potential" to "facilitate the kinds of diabolical acts like those of September 11" in the future, the article leaves no room to even consider an alternative narrative. The "we" is defined as "Canadian," and the "them" is reinforced through the exclusion of those without citizenship status, which can also have larger implications for the Muslim community in terms of its exclusion from the national narrative. The article advocates "fearing the Other" in order to "secure ourselves" and thus reinforces that officials are working in Canadians' "best interests."

Similarly, the "potential threat" is created through the suggestion that the "terrorist" could be "anywhere and anyone." This discourse is used to legitimize the indefinite detention and deportation of security certificate detainees. Consider the following quotation from an article in the *Globe and Mail*:

> *Terrorists will always be terrorists,* and neither time nor prison can temper their probable plots to kill civilians, Canada's spy service says. "Individuals who have attended terrorist training camps or who have independently opted for radical Islam must be considered *threats to Canadian public safety for the indefinite future,*" reads a court-filed CSIS report obtained by the *Globe and Mail*. "It is *highly unlikely that they will cast off their views on jihad* and justification for the use of violence. Given the long planning periods typical of terrorist acts, *extremists can remain 'under the radar' for months or years before engaging in operations,*" the report says ... The spy service says it must always be remembered that *Islamic extremists believe "it is actually moral to commit acts of violence* to fill one's religious obligation and the highest morality is that of a martyr." CSIS says such *suspects will never cease to be a danger.* "Violent beliefs of Islamic extremists will not fade with time, rendering these individuals a *threat to public safety for years to come,*" the report says. It adds: "The service assesses that *extremists will rejoin their network upon release.*" CSIS officials testified this year that the number of their *terrorist targets is "in the triple digits"* – consistent with a CSIS claim a few years earlier that it is *tracking more than 300 potential terrorists.* (Freeze 2005b, emphasis added)

Statements such as "terrorists will always be terrorists" and "violent beliefs of Islamic extremists will not fade with time" produce the notion that the "threat" will never decrease; rather, it is always absolute and is always made absolute through the construction of the "terrorist" as being any "potential" Muslim extremist. This terminology, of course, is never defined by the news but provides it with "easy" references when discussing topics under the umbrella of "terrorism." In addition, although not explicitly stated, it can be suggested that the reports cited in this article generalize the "potential threat" to include by extension any "Muslim" male. By creating suspicion and doubt through undefined repetitious language and statements such as "extremists can remain 'under the radar' for months or years before engaging in operations," "Islamic extremists believe 'it is actually moral to commit acts of violence to fill one's religious obligation,'" and "suspects will never cease to be a danger," this article casts the propagated messages as "fact."

Finally, by reproducing and prioritizing CSIS's statements that "the number of their terrorist targets is 'in the triple digits'" and that they are "tracking more than 300 potential terrorists," this article suggests that there are more than just a few "extremists" and that the "potential" individual could be hiding anywhere in Canada. However, what this also suggests is that the depiction of the "potential threat" implies by extension specific racial assumptions and associations regarding those who are "thought to 'look like Muslims'" (Arat-Koc 2006, 218). Thus the "potential threat" discourse reproduces the notion that alleged "extremists" must be "weeded out" and excluded not only from the rights of the state but also from the notion of belonging in Canada.

As a final example, in such articles the undefined but imminent "threat" is framed in a way that focuses attention on the idea that the "terrorist" could be the "person next door." This "sleeper cell" threat is continually presented alongside references to alleged "potential terrorists." Consider the following statements from the *Globe and Mail:*

> Two weeks ago, Mr. Charkaoui was named as one of two *members of a Canadian sleeper cell* of the Moroccan Islamic Combatant Group, according to the newspaper *Aujourd'hui Le Maroc*. (Ha 2004, emphasis added)

> Mohamed Harkat, an Ottawa man accused of being an *al-Qaeda sleeper agent,* was grilled yesterday about where he got $1,200 (US) to buy the fake passport he used to enter Canada. (Canadian Press 2004, emphasis added)

Even more specifically, these generalized statements that "type" an individual as prone to "terrorism" are extended to include the Muslim community, whose members are continually constructed as a "threat" to Canada. Thus CSIS's strict surveillance of "Muslim" and "Arab" males is legitimated through "vacuous" tactics that leave no room to question the assumptions made. Space is given only to doubting and fearing the intentions of the "Other," cast as a "potential threat" who could be "hiding anywhere."

The strength of the "fear"-based argument, supported by those with the power to speak, convinces the public that this is a "common-sense" procedure that does not actually violate human rights. As Butler (2004, 77) argues, the alleged "terrorists" are represented as "humans who are not humans" and moved outside of normal legal procedure. Butler (2004, 59) also states,

> This act of "deeming" takes place in the context of a declared state of emergency in which the state exercises prerogatory power that involves the suspension of law, including due process for these individuals ... Those who decide on whether someone will be detained, and continue to be detained, are governmental officials, not elected ones, and not members of the judiciary. They are, rather, part of the apparatus of governmentality; their decision, the power they wield to "deem" someone dangerous and constitute them effectively as such, is a sovereign power, a ghostly and forceful resurgence of sovereignty in the midst of governmentality.

"CSIS Rhetoric" and the Construction of "the Terrorist"

The notion of "threat" dominates the discourse, sustained by the relationship between the authority of CSIS and the reinforcement of the "terrorist" narrative, stigmatizing and criminalizing detainees and thus making this link an absolute. The "common-sense" assumptions made credible by the panoptic lens of CSIS, which also influence government lawyers and judges, remain unquestioned by the public because "vacuous" tactics such as the repetition of key terms (e.g., "Osama bin Laden," "al-Jihad," "al-Qaeda") foster Orientalist stereotypes. This also helps to sustain the high level of fear and perception of risk perpetuated by the government and reproduced and propagated in the media. It should be noted again that the coverage for "CSIS rhetoric" and "the terrorist" in the *Globe and Mail* was 52.1 percent and 59 percent of the sample, whereas in the *National Post* the coverage was 81.6 percent and 85.1 percent. In deconstructing the relationship between the authority of CSIS and assumptions about the detainees, this discourse analysis shows that the theme of "mistrust" is also prevalent, making up 22.2 percent of the coverage in the *Globe and Mail* and 21.8 percent in the *National Post*.

The following excerpt is from a report on detainee Mahmoud Jaballah published in the *National Post* that discredits Jaballah by characterizing him through "the terrorist" narrative. It should be noted that the following appears exactly as it is layed out in the newspaper:

> In a summary of secret evidence disclosed to his lawyers, *CSIS contends Mr. Jaballah is a full-fledged member of Al Jihad, playing a role in the group's co-ordinated bombings in 1998 of US embassies in Kenya and Tanzania — attacks that left 200 dead and 5,000 injured ...*
>
> MOHAMED MAHJOUB
>
> *Mr. Mahjoub is Mr. Jaballah's cellmate* at the Kingston Immigration Holding Centre. Both men are among five foreign nationals covered by security certificates in Canada. Mr. Mahjoub, like Mr. Jaballah, *professes his innocence, but CSIS alleges the fellow Egyptian national is a Shura Council member of the Vanguards of Conquest, a cell of Al Jihad.*
>
> MR. JABALLAH'S VERSION Mr. Jaballah testified in the past that if he ever *ran into the likes of Mr. Mahjoub it was probably at mosque*. He said he was never acquainted with him socially. (Hanes 2006b, emphasis added)

Because the article is structured and layed out so that the credibility of the detainees is first undermined by "terrorist" allegations, there is a vacuum of information respecting the detainees that creates doubt, rendering their innocence an impossibility. Jaballah is made guilty by alleged "terrorist" associations determined by vague and undefined CSIS reports. Although Jaballah had been detained for five years at this point, there is no discourse in the article surrounding his indefinite detention; rather, the article gives priority to supporting the statements of CSIS and government officials, reproducing their allegations as "fact." By the time readers reach the section on "Mr. Jaballah's Version," the "vacuous" tactics have already been deployed and readers already doubt there is any chance Jaballah *could* be innocent because he "fits" the profile of the "terrorist" as defined by the "buzz words" of "terrorism." In addition, the article reproduces racial and religious stereotypes reinforcing the "Muslim" as an absolute category associated with "terrorism," and its references to "mosques" depict them as meeting grounds for "terrorist" activity.

In further reinforcing these "terrorist" associations and stereotypes respecting detainees, the following excerpts from the *Globe and Mail* provide a good context for analyzing repetitious messages that support CSIS and the surveillance and judicial techniques used under security certificates:

> Arrested nearly a year ago, Mr. Charkaoui, a 30-year-old immigrant from Morocco, is held on a security certificate and Canadian authorities allege *he is an agent who trained in Afghanistan for Osama bin Laden's al-Qaeda network.* (Ha 2004, emphasis added)

> The Canadian Security Intelligence Service contends *Mr. Harkat is an Islamic extremist and collaborator with Mr. bin Laden's terrorist network.* The spy service, which watched Mr. Harkat for five years before his December, 2002, arrest, also argues that he *supports Afghan, Pakistani and Chechen extremists.* (Jiménez 2006, emphasis added)

It becomes clear that what is considered "reasonable grounds" for surveillance and detention is determined by CSIS and by those with legal and judicial authority. By giving priority to these voices, the media facilitate the repetition of "common-sense" assumptions that cast the "Muslim male" as an absolute in the "terrorist" narrative.

Employing a different strategy, articles in the sample also make references to opinions of CSIS and government judges that further discredit detainees by reinforcing a "mistrust" of them as the "Other." Given that the "Other" is seen as "humans who are not humans," this mistrust makes it easier to convince the public not to have sympathy for detainees and not to participate in fighting for human rights and for the dismantling of the security certificate policy. Consider the following excerpts from both newspapers that emphasize "mistrust" in the "terrorist" narrative:

> But *don't buy the argument that civil liberties are being ground into the dust.* Unlike Maher Arar, *none of these men are citizens of Canada.* They're all *foreign nationals who've lied their way into the country.* All will be able to drag out their cases for years. (Wente 2005, emphasis added)

> Intelligence Officer J.P. told the Federal Court in Toronto that 31-year-old Hassan Almrei *"earned his stripes" in military training camps in Afghanistan, and also forged documents for others with reputed links to al-Qaeda* ... "[He] has *instant credibility with extremists,"* J.P. said. "He has *knowledge of forging documents* ... he'd be quite useful." (D'Andrea 2005, emphasis added)

> Yesterday's decision comes a month after Mr. Jaballah tried to force the removal of Judge MacKay from his case because the *judge said he remains a continuing danger to Canadian security whose credibility "leaves much to be desired."* (Brieger 2006, emphasis added)

These associations of the "terrorist" detainee with "mistrust" are rendered "factual" based on undefined secret evidence gathered by CSIS that is reproduced in the media. Foucault's notion of governmentality is demonstrated here since the authority, power, and voice of the government and CSIS are what determine the ways that security certificates are managed, represented, and understood. Foucault (1991, 102) argues,

> The ensemble formed by the institutions, procedures, analysis, and reflections, the calculations and tactics that allow the exercise of this very specific albeit complex form of power, which has as its target population, as its principle form of knowledge political economy, and as its essential technical means apparatuses of security ... The tendency which, over a long period and throughout the West, has steadily led towards the pre-eminence over all other forms (sovereignty, discipline, etc.) of this type of power which may be termed government, resulting, on the one hand, in the formation of a whole series of specific governmental apparatuses, and, on the other hand, in the development of a whole complex of *saviors* [knowledge].

Thus the "vacuous" tactics used by these articles limit challenges to the security certificates by framing this debate as an "either-or" situation: either you support terrorism by supporting the detainees, or you challenge terrorism that threatens security, freedom, and democracy by denouncing the detainees. In short, this approach echoes US president George W. Bush's rhetoric espousing the idea that "either you are with us or with the terrorists" (Butt, Lukin, and Matthiessen 2004, 275).

As an alternative to these media messages, in June 2009 Adil Charkaoui conducted a cross-Canada speaking tour in association with the Coalition Justice for Adil Charkaoui to talk about his security certificate case and his journey through the legal process. He had been arrested without charge in 2003 and released on strict house arrest in 2005. What became clear from hearing Charkaoui speak on this tour, as I did at the University of Waterloo, and what is evidently lacking in these media reports, is the intelligence, fantastic sense of humour, bravery, and passion this man exhibited in challenging the unfair conditions he had been dealing with for six years without charge. Although CSIS, the government, and the media state that house arrest measures are measures of freedom, Charkaoui (2009) argued, "I don't want to just be free, I want justice." Having been presumed guilty by government and media reports, Charkaoui was fighting not only to promote his innocence by increasing public knowledge of the secret-evidence process but also to eliminate the security certificate policy altogether.[1]

"Canadianness"

These themes and the security certificate discourse also stem from the dominant ideas about what it means to be "Canadian," about "who" is Canadian, and about the privileges of this status. Arat-Koc (2005, 40) states,

> According to Eva Mackey ... Canadian identity is defined by those who position themselves as "ordinary Canadians" or *Canadian*-Canadians – as opposed to "ethnic" or "multicultural Canadians" – both referring to a category of unmarked, "non-ethnic," White Canadians. They are the ones who claim the final authority to define inclusions and exclusions in the nation.

News media reports have presented a substantial amount of material that reflects not only Canadian values and beliefs but also ideas about what and who is included in the conception of the "West" – ideas that contribute to whether one supports or challenges the security certificate policy. The following analysis deconstructs the theme of "Canadianness" as well as the themes of "human rights, policies, and constitutionality" and "British or US model," as these themes also reinforce ideologies and beliefs operative in the construction of the "West." The findings show that the theme of "Canadianness" is represented in 51.3 percent of the *Globe and Mail*'s coverage and in 41.4 percent of the *National Post*'s coverage. It should be noted that some Canadians have spoken out and resisted these anti-terror policies, but in the case of the articles in this study, how they are heard is determined by news media that employ "vacuous" tactics that fail to challenge the problems of the security certificate agenda.

In the security certificate discourse, the following examples from both newspapers depict Canada as "nice," "generous," "open," and "fair" in providing a solution to terrorism and immigration policy, while also emphasizing the importance of Canadian "core values" and "compromise," which in reality trump the rights of the "Other":

Canada's security-certificate law, with its safeguards, its due process, its reliance on designated judges and its sparing use, is *tough but fair ...* The law is, like most compromises, imperfect. But it is the *imperfect compromise* of a rights-respecting, immigrant-respecting society when faced with dangerous newcomers who fight deportation tooth and nail. ("Security Certificate Is an Acceptable Tool" 2006, emphasis added)

Far from being a Draconian attack on non-citizens, *the security-certificate law makes possible the country's generosity and openness ... Canada has relatively open borders.* It is not terribly difficult for foreigners to gain entry. Once here, anyone, whatever crimes they may be suspected of, is entitled to make a refugee claim. The claimant is entitled to the protection of the Charter of Rights. There are no exemptions. ("Liberty and Charkaoui" 2005, emphasis added)

But even though all of them are free to return home at any time, none have done so. Possibly the prospect of a Syrian or Egyptian jail *makes a Canadian jail seem nice.* (Wente 2005, emphasis added)

Supreme Court Justice Louis LeBel was responding to assertions from federal lawyer Bernard Laprade that *national security is a "core value"* that eclipses other constitutional rights because *nothing else matters if Canadians are not safe.* (Tibbetts 2006, emphasis added)

In addition, just as the definition of "us" as "Canadians" is constantly reinforced, so too is the targeting of "them" as the "potential threat" made distinct by comments that place the blame for "terrorism" on the Muslim community. This narrative not only holds "them" responsible but also frames the "problem" of the "Other" as something external to the "Canadian," who is in contrast "nice," "generous," and "rights-respecting." Consider the following example from the *Globe and Mail*, in which the "Canadian" is positioned outside of having a responsibility to challenge security certificate and immigration policy because the Muslim community is constructed as fostering "terrorism" from "within":

Of course, nobody wants to live in a society where secret agents spy on religious gatherings and where freedom of expression – a key element of *our liberal democracies* – is severely curtailed. Still, *something must be done to*

> *prevent radical Islam from spreading,* and this should be the primary *responsibility of the Muslim leaders,* since they are the ones who *have an intimate knowledge* of what's going on *within their community.* It's not enough to denounce terrorism. They must act against it. (Gagnon 2006, emphasis added)

The language and meanings represented in these articles support the idea that *security is freedom* and that heightened draconian security, judicial, and legal initiatives are acceptable and necessary to achieve freedom. This stance is problematic, as it reinforces the need for extreme security measures, embedded in immigration law, and associates the Muslim community with "potential" terrorist threats. As Razack (2008, 26) has argued, heightened security measures such as security certificates have become racialized practices and "front-line tools ... directed at Arabs and Muslims."

These "vacuous" tactics are supported within "state of exception" reasoning by messages of risk and fear that depict who and what is included in the conception of "Canadianness." Citizens find it difficult to challenge heightened security initiatives that are justified as necessary to "freedom" and "human rights," resulting in their inability to oppose and eliminate security certificates. Evidence of this is also found in the articles that treat the theme of "human rights, policies, and constitutionality," which make up 61.5 percent of the sample in the *Globe and Mail* and 65.5 percent in the *National Post*. In the *National Post*, the "rights" debate is constructed through the reinforcement of fear and privilege in the discourse on citizenship status, thereby maintaining what is "Canadian" and who can be included in this category:

> However, Mr. McIntosh [government lawyer] noted the Canadian Charter of Rights and Freedoms specifically limits certain *privileges to citizens.* "Only a Canadian citizen has the right to enter or remain in Canada," he said. (Cowan 2004, emphasis added)

> The 2002 Immigration and Refugee Protection Act (IRPA) enables the Immigration Minister and the Solicitor-General to sign a document called a "security certificate," which declares a person "inadmissible" in Canada on security grounds. The star chamber procedure – it can hardly be called anything else – *has one redeeming feature: The authorities can only use it against non-citizens.* (Jonas 2006, emphasis added)

Interestingly, within the "war on terror," citizenship status and "rights" have begun to shift as security measures and the discourse promoting such initiatives have ceased to distinguish between the citizen and noncitizen "potential" terrorist. Consider, for example, the following front-page article in the *Globe and Mail* giving voice to former minister of justice and attorney general of Canada Irwin Cotler:

> But Mr. Cotler revealed yesterday that he is considering expanding their [security certificates'] use to Canadian citizens, not just non-citizen immigrants ... But adding so-called control measures such as house arrest and electronic ankle bracelets would *expand the arsenal available to deal with terror suspects who are Canadian citizens when there is not enough evidence to convict them of a crime.* "Once we're exploring options in this regard, we ought to explore them for citizens as well as non-citizens alike," Mr. Cotler told reporters yesterday after appearing before a Commons committee reviewing the 2001 law. (Clark 2005, emphasis added)

The "exception" created within the national narrative excludes not only "non-citizen immigrants" but also Muslim males regardless of citizenship. As the need to "explore options" to "deal with terror suspects" has become an undefined, single-minded mission, the discourse has shifted to include fear of "potential" Canadian Muslim "terrorists." Therefore, the security certificate debate has reinforced an association of "rights" with privileged status and has supported their denial to certain members of society.

The articles in the sample also represent the debate over the constitutionality of security certificates and discuss the standards that other "Western" countries, such as Britain and the United States, have applied in comparison to Canada. The theme of the "British or US model" is represented in 16.2 percent of the *Globe and Mail*'s coverage and in 9.2 percent of the *National Post*'s coverage. Consider the following articles from both newspapers:

> IRPA isn't unique. In the wake of 9/11, similar laws have been passed in several Western nations, including the United States (The Patriot Act) and Great Britain (Prevention of Terrorism Bill). (Jonas 2005)

> *The United States used immigration law to round up 762 suspects in the year after Sept. 11, 2001.* A minor violation, such as overstaying a visa, was enough for those suspects, mostly Muslim, to disappear into jails; many had

no access to lawyers for weeks or months. *By comparison, Canada's security certificate is chockablock with safeguards* ... It has been used only five times since 9/11, and only 27 times since 1991. ("Security Certificate Is an Acceptable Tool" 2006, emphasis added)

Drawing on the British system of special advocates for suspected terrorists, a system referred to favourably by the Supreme Court, he [Public Safety Minister Stockwell Day] has *gone further than Britain to allow for fairness* ... Mr. Day said the special advocates will even be able to confer with the suspected terrorists after seeing the secret evidence, though this is not clearly spelled out in the proposed bill. *In Britain, the special advocates are not permitted to talk to the suspects after they see the secret evidence.* ("Detaining Suspects in Security's Name" 2007, emphasis added)

Thus the Eurocentric bias manifests itself within Canada, legitimating its terrorism policies and security initiatives and upholding the consensus that "terrorism" is a fight of "Western allies."

"Not Canadian"

The theme of "not Canadian" represented a significant proportion of newspaper coverage on the security certificate debate. This theme accounted for 64.1 percent of the coverage in the *Globe and Mail* and for 73.6 percent in the *National Post*. Within the repetitious language found in the "not Canadian" theme, which places the noncitizen detainee outside of human rights, the possibility of "deportation" is constructed as a "natural" and "commonsense" outcome. Again, the necessity to direct the "bewildered herd" remains dominant, as the newspaper reports not only continue to include the detainee within the nonrights category of "humans who are not humans," as discussed by Butler (2004, 77), but also begin to problematize all immigrants and refugees, categorizing them as a potential "danger." This in turn has significant consequences for newcomers to Canada, eroding their sense of safety and belonging. Nonetheless, Canada has maintained the position that it has the legal authority to ignore human rights if a person is deemed a "potential threat" or "problem."

By reinforcing who is an "outsider" and placing responsibility for the "dangerous" individual on "foreign" countries, these articles entrench the idea that the detainees do not belong or have any status in Canada. In doing so, they further legitimate the notion that deportation is necessary because these men are not Canada's "problem." The following excerpts from the *National Post* construct the "Other" as belonging to "outsider" countries associated with terrorism, such as Afghanistan, Algeria, Morocco, Egypt, and Syria:

> The Immigration and Refugee Protection Act, which sets out the security-certificate process, allows the government to *detain foreign-born terror* suspects on the strength of secret evidence until they can be deported ... *Five of the men are Arab;* all contend they will be tortured if sent back to the countries they fled. (Duffy 2005, emphasis added)

> Adil Charkaoui, a landed *immigrant from Morocco* who is alleged to be an al-Qaeda agent, was arrested in May, 2003, and released on bail with strict conditions almost two years later; Mohamed Harkat, an *Algerian-born* gas station attendant from Ottawa, was jailed in December, 2002, as an alleged al-Qaeda suspect without any charges being laid against him; Hassan Almrei, a *Syrian-born refugee* and accused al-Qaeda associate, has been detained since October, 2001, mainly in solitary confinement. (Tibbetts 2006, emphasis added)

Note that these examples do not mention where these men live in Canada, how long they have lived in Canada, or that some of their children are Canadian citizens. Although these statements respecting the detainees' citizenship "outside" of Canada can be taken as fact, it is this repetition of the trope of "foreignness" that creates an avenue to legitimate the "weeding-out" of immigrants and the push to deport individuals at the expense of human rights. The following articles from the *Globe and Mail* extend generalizations about the detainees to all immigrants, refugees, and newcomers, including them in the category of those who are "dangerous" and "not Canadian." This in turn facilitates "common-sense" discourse that problematizes and perpetuates fear of the "Other" in a narrative of "paranoid nationalism":

> Chief Justice Beverley McLachlin ... asked whether a newcomer to Canada can expect more in a time of international crisis. (Makin 2006b)

> The security-certificate system gives Ottawa extraordinary powers to *filter out* security risks among the 250,000 *immigrants* a year who reach Canada. ("Detaining Suspects in Security's Name" 2007, emphasis added)

Not only the country's security but its liberal immigration policy (which includes constitutional rights the moment a newcomer sets foot on Canadian soil) depends on a strong security-certificate process. *Imagine if a terrorist were concealed among the 250,000* [immigrants] – not hard to imagine at all. Canadians would quickly insist on *plugging up the flow of immigrants* ... But *democracies don't need to apologize* for insisting on a workable scheme to reject and expel *dangerous newcomers*. ("There's a Good Reason for This Law" 2008, emphasis added)

These examples make the discourse of fear and risk overt through their repetition of the trope of the "dangerous newcomer" and the "dangerous immigrant" who must be thwarted by "common-sense" measures to "filter out" such "foreigners." Coverage of this kind supports the claim by Bell (2006, 65) that these security measures and national narratives perpetuate the focus on "foreignness in the production of danger" and also the definition and regulation of the "terrorist" in terms of what Hage (2000, 242) argues is a preference for "White immigration":

By their very nature, immigration debates and opinion polls are an invitation to judge those who have already immigrated, as well as those who are about to immigrate ... It is in the conditions created by all these discursive effects that a White immigration speak flourishes – a language operating in itself as a technology of problematisation and marginalization: "they should come" and "they shouldn't," "they have contributed" and "they haven't," "there are too many" and "there aren't enough," "they are" and "they aren't," "they will" and "they won't."

In the same way, the "outsider" discourse is used as a propaganda tool when discussing the debate to deport detainees. The theme of "deportation" made up 55.6 percent of the *Globe and Mail*'s coverage and 54 percent of the *National Post*'s coverage. Kruger, Mulder, and Korenic (2004, 77) discuss the process of selecting between "preferred" and "nonpreferred" immigrants as a heightened security measure in the post-9/11 context: "The 11 September attacks in the United States, especially, brought terrorism and related issues of security to the forefront of political attention, indirectly resurrecting past mentalities seeking to classify refugees and immigrants as preferred or nonpreferred based on factors such as race, religion, or country of origin."

Within the context of selecting immigrants and refugees based on race and religion, this discourse presents the push toward deportation as an "exception" in the treatment of those accessing rights based on citizenship status. The following articles from both newspapers are examples of attempts to legitimate the deportation process under security certificates:

> The government is using the process to *try to kick out five alleged extremists: a Syrian, an Algerian, a Moroccan and two Egyptians* ... But Canada's spies, federal ministers and judges have determined *the men are too dangerous* to be allowed to walk free ... The Supreme Court of Canada has ruled that *only "exceptional circumstances" can allow for an immigrant to be sent back to a country known to practice torture.* (Freeze 2005a, emphasis added)

> Accused terrorist Mohamed Harkat, who has been living at his Ottawa home for the past three weeks while on bail, has been *ordered deported to Algeria, despite concerns he will be tortured* ... Mr. Schultz [federal bureaucrat] further decided that the *danger posed by Mr. Harkat outweighed the Algerian-born man's right to be protected* from abuse in his native country. (Duffy 2006, emphasis added)

By allowing the "deportation" debate to be influenced by the discourse of "exceptional circumstances," these articles make the argument that security "outweighs" the possible torture that detainees face if deported since the men are "too dangerous" to be held in Canada. It becomes clear that this discourse centres on perpetuating fear while downplaying the risk that detainees will be tortured. Thus, by reinforcing the legality of deporting non-citizens, these articles create a perception among the "bewildered herd" that the process is legitimate.

From a different perspective, it is interesting to consider the language used in the theme of "deportation" that holds detainees responsible for the indefinite length of detention. For example, the following articles from both newspapers reinforce the notion that detainees are "free to leave Canada at any time":

> The primary principle of immigration law is that the state can in all legitimacy *subject the rights of a non-citizen living on its territory to certain conditions,*" the federal government's defence argues. "This is one of the essential

prerogatives of state sovereignty." Individuals targeted under the process are *free to leave Canada at any time,* the brief says. They have a right to contest their removal, although they may have to *remain detained "to prevent danger to national security or the security of others,"* the Justice Department argues. (Hanes 2006a, emphasis added)

"I don't think the public appreciates how *these people are free to leave,"* Mr. Cotler [justice minister] said in an interview. "They are detained because *they have chosen not to go."* (Makin 2006a, emphasis added)

Thus these individuals are placed "outside" of being "human" and denied equal human rights because the legal and judicial push to "deport" is always present within the discourse of "exceptional circumstances." Former justice minister Irwin Cotler's statement that "these people are free to leave" but "have chosen not to go" reinforces the government's argument that the security certificate process is really only a "prison with three walls" (Coalition Justice for Adil Charkaoui 2008). This notion that detainees can be released if they choose to leave Canada communicates to the public that Canada is "fair" and respectful of human rights. Yet it overshadows the hidden and subtle messages that perpetuate the racialized idea that certain individuals can be "removed" and be subjected to torture since they do not "belong" in Canada. In addition, it places the blame for indefinite detention on the detainees themselves, as the abuse of their human rights is positioned in a blurred area.

Conclusion

In this study, it has become evident that resisting the security certificate policy is very challenging. Mobilization of the "bewildered herd" is limited by use of the propaganda model, which relies on "common-sense" tactics to justify immigration and security policies. As the security certificate debate remains unresolved and the media discourses surrounding it remain largely unquestioned, it is important to challenge the use of this policy measure not only for its problematic contractions that continue to identify Muslims and Arabs as the "hot-bed of terrorism" but also for its failure to move toward a dialogue that seeks more than "middle-range" solutions. Within the security certificate debate, the compromising of human rights should never be part of the "state of exception," as human rights for all should always be an absolute.

NOTE

1 As of October 2009, Adil Charkaoui was finally freed from all security certificate measures, including detention and GPS monitoring; however, he continues to fight attempts by the Canadian government to deport him back to Morocco.

REFERENCES

Agamben, G. 2005. *State of exception*. Chicago, IL: University of Chicago Press.

Ainsworth, S., and C. Hardy. 2004. Critical discourse analysis and identity: Why bother? *Critical Discourse Studies* 1, 2: 225-59.

Aitken, R. 2008. Notes on the Canadian exception: Security certificates in critical context. *Citizenship Studies* 12, 4: 381-96.

Arat-Koc, S. 2005. The disciplinary boundaries of Canadian identity after September 11: Civilizational, identity, multiculturalism, and the challenge of anti-imperialist feminism. *Social Justice* 32, 4: 32-49.

–. 2006. Whose transnationalism? Canada, "Clash of Civilizations" discourse, and Arab and Muslim Canadians. In V. Satzewich and L. Wong, eds., *Transnational identities and practices in Canada*, 216-40. Vancouver: UBC Press.

Banfield, A., and M. Zekulin. 2008. From deference to dialogue: National security and the courts in the post 9/11 era. Paper presented at the Annual Meeting of the Canadian Political Science Association. University of British Columbia, June 4-6.

Bannerji, H. 2000. *The dark side of the nation: Essays on multiculturalism, nationalism and gender*. Toronto, ON: Canadian Scholars' Press.

Becklumb, P. 2008. *Bill C-3: An act to amend the Immigration and Refugee Protection Act (certificates and special advocate) and to make consequential amendment to another act*. Revised. Ottawa, ON: Parliamentary Information and Research Service, July 9.

Bell, C. 2006. Subject to exception: Security certificates, national security and Canada's role in the "war on terror." *Canadian Journal of Law and Society* 21, 1: 63-83.

Brieger, P. 2006. Terror suspect not entitled to protection from deportation: Federal court ruling. *National Post*, March 17, A5.

Butler, J. 2004. *Precarious life: The powers of mourning and violence*. New York, NY: Verso.

Butt, D.G., A. Lukin, and C.M.I.M. Matthiessen. 2004. Grammar – the first covert operation of war. *Discourse and Society* 15, 2-3: 267-90.

Canadian Press. 2004. Terror suspect's trial hears of funds to buy passport. *Globe and Mail*, October 29, A7.

Charkaoui, A. 2003. International Human Rights Day: Poem by Adil Charkaoui. http://www.adilinfo.org/.

–. 2009. Public lecture on cross-Canada speaking tour. University of Waterloo, June 17.

Chomsky, N. 1989. *Necessary illusions: Thought control in democratic societies*. Toronto, ON: House of Anansi.

—. 1997. *Media control: The spectacular achievements of propaganda.* New York, NY: Seven Stories.
Clark, C. 2005. Cotler seeks expanded anti-terror arsenal. *Globe and Mail,* March 24, A1.
Coalition Justice for Adil Charkaoui. 2008. Analysis of C-3. http://www.adilinfo.org/.
Cowan, J. 2004. Return terror suspect to Egypt: Crown: Deportation hearing. *National Post,* August 17, A6.
D'Andrea, A. 2005. CSIS official tells court Syrian could pose threat: Honey vendor "has instant credibility with extremists." *National Post,* July 19, A8.
Dean, M. 2007. *Governing societies: Political perspectives on domestic and international rule.* New York, NY: Open University Press.
Department of Justice. 2001. *Immigration and refugee protection act.* http://laws.justice.gc.ca/.
Detaining suspects in security's name. 2007. Editorial. *Globe and Mail,* October 24, A20.
Doyle, N. 2007. *Detention centres and security certificates: Report of the Standing Committee on Citizenship and Immigration.* Ottawa, ON: Standing Committee on Citizenship and Immigration.
Duffy, A. 2005. Detention still an option despite terror ruling: Issue may move to Supreme Court after recent decision. *National Post,* February 7, A6.
—. 2006. Terrorist suspect ordered deported: Mohamed Harkat. *National Post,* July 18, A8.
Foucault, M. 1977. *Discipline and punish: The birth of the prison.* Toronto, ON: Random House of Canada.
—. 1991. Governmentality. In G. Burchell, C. Gordon, and P. Miller, eds., *The Foucault effect: Studies in governmentality: With two lectures by and an interview with Michel Foucault,* 87-104. Chicago, IL: University of Chicago Press.
—. 1997. About the concept of the "dangerous individual" in nineteenth-century legal psychiatry. In *Power: Essential works of Foucault, 1954-1984,* 176-200. New York, NY: New Press.
Freeze, C. 2005a. Canada criticized on deportations: Ottawa errs in thinking terror suspects no longer tortured, rights group says. *Globe and Mail,* April 15, A16.
—. 2005b. Terrorists are perpetual threat, CSIS says: Prison won't deter extremists dedicated to attacking civilians, report says. *Globe and Mail,* September 10, A12.
French, M. 2007. In the shadow of Canada's camps. *Social and Legal Studies* 16, 1: 49-69.
Gagnon, L. 2006. Taking a community hostage. *Globe and Mail,* June 12, A15.
Gillespie, M. 2007. Security, media and multicultural citizenship: A collaborative ethnography. *European Journal of Cultural Studies* 10, 3: 275-93.
Greer, C., and Y. Jewkes. 2005. Extremes of Otherness: Media images of social exclusion. *Social Justice* 32, 1: 20-31.
Ha, T.T. 2004. Suspect denies naming man, paper says. *Globe and Mail,* April 29, A5.

Hage, G. 2000. *White nation: Fantasies of white supremacy in a multicultural society*. New York, NY: Routledge.
Hanes, A. 2006a. Individual versus state rights: Terror suspect's lawyers to contest the secrecy of security certificates. *National Post*, May 15, A4.
–. 2006b. Suspect explains alleged terror links: Court told of chance encounters, invitations for tea. *National Post*, July 13, A4.
Henry, F., and C. Tator. 2002. *Discourses of domination: Racial bias in the Canadian English-language press*. Toronto, ON: University of Toronto Press.
Jiménez, M. 2006. Terror suspect given bail with strict rules. *Globe and Mail*, May 24, A11.
Jiwani, Y. 2005. The Great White North encounters September 11: Race, gender and nation in Canada's national daily the *Globe and Mail*. *Social Justice* 32, 4: 50-68.
–. 2006. *Discourses of denial: Mediations of race, gender, and violence*. Vancouver, BC: UBC Press.
Jonas, G. 2005. The state's immune system, run amok. *National Post*, March 3, A18.
–. 2006. Ultra-liberal policies beget sub-liberal laws. *National Post*, June 17, A16.
Karim, K.H. 2002. Making sense of the "Islamic Peril": Journalism as cultural practice. In B. Zelizer and S. Allan, eds., *Journalism after September 11*, 101-16. London, UK: Routledge.
Kruger, E., M. Mulder, and B. Korenic. 2004. Canada after 11 September: Security measures and "preferred" immigrants. *Mediterranean Quarterly* 15, 4: 72-87.
Liberty and Charkaoui. 2005. Editorial. *Globe and Mail*, August 26, A14.
Makin, K. 2006a. Rights of detainees goes before top court. *Globe and Mail*, June 12, A1.
–. 2006b. Justices weigh civil rights against security: Certificates violate Constitution, lawyers for terror suspect tell Supreme Court. *Globe and Mail*, June 14, A13.
Office of the United Nations High Commissioner for Human Rights. 1966. *International covenant on civil and political rights*. http://www2.ohchr.org/.
–. 1984. *Convention against torture and other cruel, inhumane or degrading treatment or punishment*. http://www2.ohchr.org/.
Razack, S.H. 2008. *Casting out: The evolution of Muslims from Western law and politics*. Toronto, ON: University of Toronto Press.
Said, E.W. 1978. *Orientalism*. New York, NY: Vintage.
The security certificate is an acceptable tool. 2006. Editorial. *Globe and Mail*, June 14, A20.
Stasiulis, D., and D. Ross. 2006. Security, flexible sovereignty, and the perils of multiple citizenship. *Citizenship Studies* 10, 3: 329-48.
There's a good reason for this law. 2008. Editorial. *Globe and Mail*, February 8, A16.
Tibbetts, J. 2006. Judge questions right of security above all: "Living North Korea": Federal lawyer defends detaining suspects under security certificates. *National Post*, June 15, A16.
van Dijk, T. 1993. Principles of critical discourse analysis. *Discourse and Society* 4, 2: 249-83.
Wente, M. 2005. Dancing the Almrei limbo. *Globe and Mail*, July 21, A15.

10

The Anti-terrorism Act and National Security
Safeguarding the Nation against Uncivilized Muslims

SHAISTA PATEL

In the wake of the terrorist attacks on the World Trade Center and the Pentagon on 11 September 2001, security and fear have become important rationales for implementing various policies in liberal democracies of the West.[1] Many countries, such as the United States, United Kingdom, Australia, and Canada, implemented quick "anti-terrorism" responses in the form of federal acts and statutes. In addition, many countries stood alongside the United States in the violent invasions of Afghanistan and Iraq under the guise of fighting a "war on terror." The hegemonic discourses framing this war have been about the security of the American nation and consequently of all Western nations. This discourse of bringing security and peace to the world was deployed as a moral prop by many Western states for legitimating the massive killings of people of colour overseas and the draconian policies targeting Muslims of colour within the nations of the West.

The political situation in Canada, like in many other countries of the global North, was similar. The government, under the leadership of then prime minister Jean Chrétien, lent military support to the United States in the invasion of Afghanistan, while simultaneously commencing the process of safeguarding Canada from similar terrorist attacks. One of the first legislative responses of the government was to table two bills as part of the federal anti-terrorism policy: Bill C-36, or the Anti-terrorism Act;[2] and Bill C-42, or the Public Safety Act.[3]

Within this heightened rhetoric around security and threat, the presence of the Muslim man within the borders of the nation was deployed by the Canadian state as the most potent "problem" facing the nation. In this discussion, I examine the marginalization of Muslims in post-9/11 Canadian society by arguing that the knowledges produced through Bill C-36, as part of an official post-9/11 "juridical discourse" (Smith 1999, 196) of the state, perform a physical and ideological nation-building role by targeting Muslims of colour as the "enemy within" the physical borders of the white "settler colony."[4]

As dominant discourses[5] of the state, "juridical discourses" provide certain legitimacy to the racist rationalities underpinning the project of making the Canadian nation a white space. Using the three important conceptual tools of race, space, and the law as the state's "juridical discourse," I conduct a critical, anti-Orientalist discourse analysis of Bill C-36 to examine the contemporary nation-building function performed by the bill. In choosing to examine how Orientalist rationalities are expressed discursively[6] through Bill C-36, I employ the bill as a prototype for an entire range of similar Orientalist discursive events targeting Muslims in post-9/11 Canadian society. I begin from the firm belief that the colonial "regime of truth" (Foucault 1980, 131) of these "juridical discourses" is based on a Western/colonial authoritative corpus of knowledge about the East, often accumulated through colonization of land and its indigenous peoples.

In the first part of the discussion, I draw on anti-colonial and anti-racist feminist analyses to map the role of law in the colonialist Canadian nation-building project. Within this discussion, I pay particular attention to the national myths on which the white nation has been founded by Europeans. These historical processes of nation building provide an important framework for discussing the Orientalist representations of Muslim men and women within the "war on terror" and other racialized violences underpinning contemporary empire building.

Despite this marginalization faced by people of colour, Canada is heavily invested in portraying itself to the world as a benevolent multicultural nation. Thus, even though Bill C-36 is racist and exclusionary, it was presented to the public by the Liberal government as a "positionless account" (Smith 1999, 54) written in very matter-of-fact, scientific language and as an instance of depoliticized "juridical discourse." The everyday dominant discourses of the state create numerous "positionless accounts, versions of the world in which subjects are relegated to no place in particular and before which, therefore, all subjects are equal and equally absent" (Smith 1999, 54).

However, these dominant discourses have always been central in reifying the colonial authority of the Canadian state apparatus. In the second section of this chapter, I question the Orientalist nature of the rhetoric of "national security" operating within the Canadian state today. Furthermore, I ask whether the Canadian state sees Muslims of colour as worthy of protection.

In the last part of the discussion, I conduct an anti-Orientalist discourse analysis of Bill C-36. Here, I am not concerned with revealing any "truth" hidden in the bill. Rather, my goal is to examine how certain discourses operate as though they are truthful and what bases of power underpin and benefit from the truth claims of the discourse in question. Therefore, I am interested in exploring how Muslims of colour are relegated to spaces outside the nation by their treatment and representation in the language drawn upon by the Canadian state in Bill C-36.

Colonial Ownership and the Founding Myths of White Canada

The Canadian nation has been imagined in specific ways by bourgeois, white, male society. As Bannerji (2000, 64) argues, Canada is "a construction, a set of representations, embodying certain types of political and cultural communities and their operations." Therefore, a nation is not only a geopolitical and geographic space but also a social and historical construct to which only certain bodies belong and where only certain bodies can "participate in the *idea* of the nation as represented in its national culture" (Hall 1996, 612, emphasis added). As Bannerji (2000, 66) continues, "Living in a nation does not, by definition, provide one with the prerogative to 'imagine' it." The privilege of imagining the nation is not available to those living in the Othered spaces, away from the "imagined community" (Anderson 1983) of the nation. The fictional construct of the nation as homogeneous naturalizes the hegemony of one collectivity and its access to the ideological apparatuses of both state and civil society through conscription of certain "official" discourses within the nation-state. However, the inhabitants of the Othered spaces are not always only people of colour. Although the nation is often portrayed as homogeneous, as "one people," the category of the Other[7] on the peripheries is heterogeneous. This Otherness is a product of interlocking systems of oppression based on race, gender, sexuality, ability, age, and religion.

Each nation is founded on narratives or mythologies that glorify the magnanimity of those belonging within its ideological borders. These national narratives are socially and historically constructed rather than being a consequence of any *natural* or even real course of events. The vocabulary of myths is part of the "imagined community" and is based on those national stories that give its members spaces for imagining themselves as part of a homogeneous community, while simultaneously foreclosing the borders of the nation to the racial Others (see also Chapter 1).[8] One such myth of white Canada has been that of European "discovery" of the land – based on the legal doctrines of *terra nullius* (or empty and uninhabited land requiring "settlement" by the white race) and *terra cognita* (which allowed European sovereigns to claim lands that were "empty"). As Razack (2002, 1-2) observes, the "imagined community" of the Canadian nation cannot be separated from the realm of hegemonic stories of white supremacy:

> As it evolves, a white settler society continues to be structured by a racial hierarchy. In the national mythologies of such societies, it is believed that white people came first and that it is they who principally developed the land; Aboriginal peoples are presumed to be mostly dead or assimilated. European settlers thus *become* the original inhabitants and the group most entitled to the fruits of citizenship. A quintessential feature of white settler mythologies is, therefore, the disavowal of conquest, genocide, slavery, and the exploitation of the labour of peoples of colour. (Emphasis in original)

These foundational myths of the white man's hard labour to develop the land and of Aboriginal communities' barbarity and child-like demeanour prior to contact with the white race are told and retold as part of defining white bodies as the "legitimate" citizens within the nation-state. Consequently, it is those with white bodies who imagine themselves as belonging to the nation and as possessing its spaces. In this powerful account rooted in deliberate amnesia, the Aboriginal peoples as the rightful owners of the land and the immigrants of colour whose labour helped to develop the land are erased from the nation's narratives. The mythology of the land being empty and undeveloped before "settlement" by whites also allows the white race to see itself as "civilizing" the colonized population. This national myth is very powerful, for it allows the settler colony to erase the violent colonization of Aboriginal peoples and instead imagine itself as a white, civilized, and benevolent nation. Moreover, positioning white people as dominant and people of colour as the Other in the discursive construction of the nation has rendered whiteness invisible, stable, and undifferentiated.

A nation, of course, is not only an imagined space. As Ahmed (2000, 98) contends, "An entity can be imagined and real at the same time." A "civilized," white settler colony always has physical spaces where the presence of the racialized Other is seen as threatening the colonial social order. Relegating Others to dark places outside of the city and the nation and policing their bodies seem to be necessary measures for re/legitimizing the nation as white. These spaces of "degeneracy" and "immorality," away from the "imagined community" of the nation, have to exist in order for the spaces of respectability and civilization to exist within a settler colony. As Burman (2007, 179) argues, "internal 'Others,' who become hypervisible when accused of transgressions, are usefully mobilized in political and media discourses as foreign elements, so as to subtly outline the ideal citizen of a particular geopolitical moment." This racialization of space argues for the significance of a sense of belonging to particular spaces. The liminal and primitive spaces within the nation are thus not only metaphorical but also concrete "spaces of removal" occupied by the "*les damnes de la terre*/the wretched of the earth: the geographies of the homeless, the jobless, the incarcerated, the invisible labourers, the underdeveloped, the criminalized, the refugee, the kicked about, the impoverished, the abandoned, the unescaped" (McKittrick and Woods 2007, 2).

The role of law in the production of these "geographies of the wretched of Canada" has been central. In her examination of some key pieces of legislation spanning Canadian history, Backhouse (1999, 15) states:

> Racism is not primarily manifest in isolated, idiosyncratic, and haphazard acts by individual actors, who from time to time, consciously intended to assert racial hierarchy over others. The roots of racialization run far deeper than individualized, intentional activities. Racism resonates through institutions, intellectual theory, popular culture, and law ... Racialized communities were denied the right to maintain their own identities, cultures, and spiritual beliefs.

Throughout Canadian history, the state has used law as an instrument for explaining away racial differences, for reinforcing "common-sense" notions embedded in a dominant colonial cultural system, and for establishing new social constructions of Othered spaces (Backhouse 1999, Mawani 2005, Razack 2002, Thobani 2003, Walker 1997). As Said (2001, 100) notes, "Mythic language is discourse, that is, it cannot be anything but systematic;

one does not really make discourse at will, nor statements in it, without first belonging – in some cases unconsciously, but at any rate involuntarily – to the ideology and the institutions that guarantee its existence."

Law thus becomes an essentially important means for defining who is to be included within the borders of the "imagined community" of the nation and who needs to be excluded from its ideological and physical borders. Razack (2002, 4-5), commenting on the legalized penalties placed on Geneva Convention refugees entering Canada without appropriate documents under the country's Immigration Act, states that "politicians justify the penalty on the grounds that the original inhabitants have a legitimate right to defend themselves from the massive influx of foreign bodies who possess few of the values of honesty, decency, and democracy of their 'hosts.'" In this process of defining the character of the nation, law – as a relation of power – structures race, gender, and class hierarchies in order to distinguish those who can move freely and legitimately within the space of the nation from racialized Others, whose bodies, perceived as a threat, need to be constantly surveilled within the borders. Therefore, "juridical discourses" of the nation often embody the meaning systems produced by the mythologies of the nation.

These racist colonialist and imperialist "juridical discourses" of the Canadian state also embody Orientalist rationalities. The late Edward Said's central concern in *Orientalism* (1978) is with the way that cultural production within the West has effected an ontological and epistemological binary between the Occident/West and the Orient/East, the latter contrived as sometimes romantic and exciting, sometimes dangerous, and usually backward and barbaric. The Orient is not so much a physical space as the idea of everything exotic and Other, and as a result, these Orientalist representations are not "natural" depictions of the Orient but rather constitute a relationship of power, embodied by the hegemony of the Occident. The imaginary geographic divide between the Orient and the Occident constructs Muslims as strangers with whom "Canadians-as-members-of-the-nation"[9] have to live, which simultaneously produces a form of national identity for the latter. As Ahmed (2000, 100) notes:

> The nation becomes imagined and embodied as a space, not simply by being defined against other spaces, but by being defined as close to some others (friends), and further away from Other Others (strangers). In this sense, only strangers within the nation space – that is, the proximity of that

which cannot be assimilated into a national body – is a mechanism for the demarcation of the national body, a way of defining borders within it, rather than just between it and an imagined and exterior Other.

Muslims, like Aboriginals and other people of colour, might share a nationality with white Canadians, but they do not share the national mythologies of European discovery of the land.[10] They cannot claim the space of the nation as their own but rather are forced to remain grateful to the white gatekeepers for allowing them the privilege of setting foot within the physical borders of the nation.

Safeguarding the Nation against "Uncivilized" Muslims

The discourse of the white man's greatness in surviving next to the stranger/Other underpins Said's theories of Orientalism. The imaginary divide between white and coloured bodies remains static in the imagination of the former, even though both share the larger physical space of the nation. This divide also allows Canadians to see themselves as benevolent. This benevolence became part of Canadian legislation in 1971 through Canada's official policy of multiculturalism, adopted under then prime minister Pierre Trudeau. There were four aims of this policy: to support the cultural development of ethno-cultural groups, to support ethno-cultural groups in fully participating in Canadian society, to promote creative encounters and exchanges among all ethno-cultural groups, and to assist new Canadians in acquiring at least one of Canada's official languages.[11]

The notion of "creative encounters" and the aim "to assist new Canadians" operate to give legitimacy to the white Canadian, who allows these encounters to occur in the first place. In fact, as Ahmed (2000, 95) astutely argues, "Multiculturalism is defined, not as providing services for 'specific ethnic groups,' but as a way of imagining the nation itself, a way of 'living' in the nation, and a way of *living with* difference" (emphasis in original). This living with difference not only allows the "imagined community" of the nation to distinguish its space from the liminal and primitive spaces within which the "strangers" are trying to survive but also enables the nation to present itself to the rest of the world as benevolent and as a champion of human rights. As Razack (2004a, 9) rightly notes, "A Canadian today knows herself or himself as someone who comes from the nicest place on earth, as someone from a peacekeeping nation, and as a modest self-deprecating individual who is able to gently teach the Third World Others about civility."

How was it that within a seemingly benevolent nation a draconian policy like Bill C-36 could be released? In popular discourses operating within the Canadian security regime, debates about Bill C-36 have been framed largely in language advocating the security of Canada rather than the civil liberties of Canadians. An important point of contention in this debate has always been whether the bill meets the criteria outlined in the Canadian Charter of Rights and Freedoms. Although the government initially presented Bill C-36 as a necessary compromise of rights in order to ensure security, it later proclaimed that the bill was a necessary measure for safeguarding the security of humanity and thus necessary for human rights themselves. Irwin Cotler (2001, 112), a member of Parliament at the time, urged Canadians to suspend the debate of civil rights versus security and "think outside the box" since, according to him, "The better approach from a conceptual and foundational point of view is to regard the legislation as *human security legislation*, which seeks to protect both national security – or the security of democracy if not democracy itself – and civil liberties" (emphasis added). Bill C-36 was thus championed as necessary not only to the security of Canadians but also to the safeguarding of basic human rights. In turn, the emphasis on "national security" was presented as a natural response to 9/11, instead of as a racialized reaction based on anxieties of the white nation.

Given the debates about national security versus civil liberties of Canadians, the important question at hand is which "Canadians" are seen as worthy of protection? I argue that it is first of all the "Canadians-as-members-of-the-nation," the "normal" and exalted Canadians, who belong to the ideological borders of the nation, to its "imagined community." Given the current geopolitical situation, I contend that the label can also be extended to include other white Canadians outside of this "imagined community," along with other people of colour who are not Muslims, not brown, and not black.

Canadian Muslims and those who "look" like Muslims, regardless of their citizenship status, were constantly called on to demonstrate their loyalty to this country during the Gulf War and again following 9/11. Kashmeri (2000) argues that during Canada's participation in the 1991 Gulf War, the Canadian Security Intelligence Service (CSIS) and the Royal Canadian Mounted Police (RCMP) constantly harassed Arab and Muslim Canadians as though they were all insiders to secrets of the Iraqi government. The Canadian government targeted Arab and Muslim bodies when it launched its very racist national emergency plan in response to a nonexistent terrorism threat in

Canada (Kashmeri 2000, 263). Similarly, today there is little, if any, doubt in the nation's imagination about what a "terrorist" looks like. It is always a Muslim man, construed as belonging somewhere else, most notably to some Arab country, and carrying the hate of the West in his heart.[12] As Said (2002) notes:

> I don't know a single Arab or Muslim American who does not now feel that he or she belongs to the enemy camp, and that being in the United States at this moment provides us with an especially unpleasant experience of alienation and widespread, quite specifically targeted hostility. For despite the occasional official statements saying that Islam and Muslims and Arabs are not enemies of the United States, everything else about the current situation argues the exact opposite ... [A person] with an Arab or Muslim name is usually made to stand aside for special attention during airport security checks.

This racial profiling[13] is justified by the nation's fear of another terrorist attack. These fears reinforce the processes of racialization, such that racial profiling serves a "regime of truth" (Foucault 1980, 131), the purpose of which is to ensure whiteness remains the only legitimate signifier of nationhood (Tator and Henry 2006, 17).

As Fiske (2000) argues, surveillance is a technology of whiteness that racially zones both the physical spaces and the social spaces of the city; these spaces are demarcated by boundaries that whites cannot see and that people of colour cannot cross. Moreover, "surveillance is a technology of normalization that identifies and discourages the cultural expression and behaviour of social formations that differ from those of the dominant, and thus chills any public display of difference" (Fiske 2000, 61). While racialized surveillance normalizes whiteness, it simultaneously renders differences of the Other as abnormal. This pathologizing process is significant if surveillance is to do the work of legitimizing whiteness as the "norm" of Canadian society. However, dominant within the surveillance discourse as it relates to racial profiling is total and pervasive denial that racism exists in the structures and cultures of policing.[14] The minister responsible for introducing Bill C-36, Justice Minister Anne McLellan, has called it an "Act of prevention" (in Department of Justice 2005). In order for national security to take preventive measures, an essentialized and common-sense understanding of the enemy is needed. It then becomes all about being able to "identify the abnormal by what it *looks like* rather than by what it *does:* it needs to abnormalize, or criminalize, by visible social category, not by social behaviour" (Fiske 2000, 61, emphasis in original).

Within contemporary nation-building practices of Canada, this surveillance, or racial profiling, of Muslims of colour has become a regularized practice in order to keep Muslims in their physical and ideological "place." A poll conducted after the London bombings of 2005 revealed that 62 percent of Canadians believed that there would be an attack in this country within the next few years and that stricter security measures should be put in place to safeguard Canada and Canadians (Clark 2005). Even though no reference was made to who these "Canadians" were, it can be critically argued that they did not include the racially profiled Muslim. The intense racial profiling of bodies of Muslim men and women has once again proven that spatial regulation is about membership in the nation. For instance, Mohammed Attiah, an engineer in Ottawa, was fired following 9/11 after being interrogated by CSIS and the RCMP in the parking lot of the plant where he worked. It was feared that he "might" have been making bombs for the terrorists. In May 2004 Shanaka Seneviratne, a South Asian Muslim student at McGill University, was taking photographs at a subway station in Montreal as part of his research work for three urban planning professors when the Montreal police handcuffed him and told him that he was a "threat" to the security of Canada (Tanovich 2006, 28). As Thobani (2004, 597) remarks, "Racial profiling reveals, once again, the fundamental character of liberal democracy as a racialized project."

A 2003 statement by the Canadian Islamic Congress reveals that there has been a shocking 1,600 percent increase in hate crimes against these so-called "Muslim threats." Apparently, so many Muslims were complaining to the Canadian Council on American-Islamic Relations (CAIR-CAN) about being racially profiled that Riad Saloojee, the director of CAIR-CAN, issued more than 30,000 copies of the guide *Know Your Rights* to Muslims and those who "look like" Muslims. Moreover, a 2004 survey by CAIR-CAN, involving 467 respondents, suggested troubling levels of racial profiling of the Arab and Muslim communities (CAIR-CAN 2004). Eight percent of the respondents had been questioned by CSIS. In some cases, the respondents were discouraged from seeking any legal representation and also threatened with arrest under Bill C-36. Eighty-nine percent of those questioned were males between the ages of eighteen and thirty-five, of whom 36 percent were Arabs and 42 percent were South Asians, with the remaining numbers being made up of other racialized groups such as Persians and Africans. Also, 85 percent of those harassed by CSIS were Canadian citizens, and 11 percent were permanent residents.

These statistics remind us again that the figure of the racialized Muslim man has captured the attention of "legitimate" Canadians as the most serious threat facing the nation today. As Mamdani (2004) has noted, Islam has become the next big threat facing the liberal democracies of the West since the end of the Cold War. Therefore, the racialized moral panic and the derogation of Muslims by law enforcement officials and the white nation at large are a consequence not only of the 9/11 attackers being brown Muslim males. I argue that the Orientalist legacies of Muslim men as "barbaric" and "uncivilized" and Muslim women as "oppressed" and "in need of rescue" by the white man have also played a major role in legitimating Bill C-36 and the framing of anti-Muslim discourse as that of national security.

Writing about the alienating treatment of Muslims in Canada, Razack (2004b, 129-30) makes it clear that these Orientalist tropes about Muslims have often been an important constituent of racism levelled against Muslims in the West, especially since 9/11:

> The policing of Muslim communities is ... organized under the logic that there is an irreconcilable culture clash between the West and Islam with the latter bent on the West's destruction. They [Muslims] are tribal and stuck in pre-modernity, the argument goes, possessing neither a commitment to human rights, women's rights nor to democracy. It is the West's obligation to defend itself from these values and to assist Muslims into modernity, by force if necessary, as the wars in Afghanistan and Iraq both underline.

The fear of this "culture clash" has also been mobilized as the "clash of civilizations" (Huntington 1993) by the government and the media alike. Critiquing the racist and Orientalist rationalities underpinning the "war on terror," Thobani (2003, 401) remarks, "President [George W.] Bush was invoking an American 'nation' and its 'enemy' in clearly racialized civilizational terms." One of the questions that the president posed to the American nation was, "Why do they hate us?" In asking this question, he evoked Huntington's (1993) notorious thesis of the "clash of civilizations," which embodies anxieties about the nation by arguing that nations are being replaced by quasi-primordial constructs such as civilizations, which in turn has resulted in a discourse about the Western civilization versus the barbaric, bloodthirsty, irrational, and monocultural ways of Muslim Others.

The post-9/11 discourses on the security of the nation have been carefully designed to designate the "bloodthirsty" Muslim man as the "bad Muslim" (Mamdani 2004) vis-à-vis the seemingly "oppressed" Muslim woman, who is constructed as the "good Muslim" (Mamdani 2004).[15] This ideology underpins the framing and consumption of the Anti-terrorism Act as a policy that includes "good Muslim" women within the Canadian state while simultaneously excluding "bad Muslim" men. As a result, the act is oxymoronic: on the one hand, it is a policy espousing the benevolence of the nation; on the other, it is a draconian act intended to guard the nation's physical and ideological borders.

Muslim women's bodies have also played an integral role in how Orientalist discourses inflict symbolic violences on the bodies and psyches of Muslim men and women.[16] Muslim women's bodies, like the bodies of Aboriginal and other indigenous women in histories of colonial nations, have always been significant in justifying colonial violences as "civilizing missions" (Alloula 1986, Razack 1998, 2004b, Smith 2005, Spivak 1988, Thobani 2003, Zine 2006). The culture of surveillance engulfing Muslims today is often framed in the language of gender equality and is prevalent in the form of a globally organized phenomenon. Muslims are seen as stuck in premodernity, and the "benevolent" West is deemed to be morally obligated to assist Muslims with the transition to modernity or, at least, to rescue their women folk.[17] As Razack (2004b, 130) claims,

> The body of the Muslim woman, a body fixed in the Western imaginary as confined, mutilated, and sometimes murdered in the name of culture, serves to reinforce the threat that the Muslim man is said to pose to the West and is used to justify the extraordinary measures of violence and surveillance required to discipline him and Muslim communities.

This symbolically, and often physically, violent and racialized discourse of "saving" Muslim women strengthens the Orientalist imagining of the Muslim male's body as that of a "barbaric," "irrational" savage who must be disciplined by the white nation. This discipline is achieved through "exclusion, marginalization and denial" (Smith 2002, 68). It is this excuse of "disciplining" the Muslim man and liberating his inherently "oppressed" women that many Western governments have used to legitimate the invasion of Afghanistan, with a hidden agenda of fighting a threat that is part of the heritage of the Cold War (Cloud 2004, Mamdani 2004). The sexualized politics of "saving brown women from brown men" (Spivak 1988, 297) have also been deployed by the state to incite a racialized moral panic about the physical and ideological spaces of the nation being infiltrated by dangerous strangers belonging to an anti-modern civilization.

Within these Orientalist legacies of suspicion and fear of the brown bodies of Muslim men, Bill C-36, with its racist provisions for preventive arrests and investigative hearings and its broad definition of "terrorist activity," has been presented as a *natural* response of the "responsible" "host" nation. In the next section of this chapter, I conduct a more detailed analysis of specific sections of Bill C-36.

Reading for Orientalist Rationalities in the Anti-terrorism Act

Minister of Justice Anne McLellan introduced Bill C-36 in Parliament with the following rationale: "The horrific events of September 11 remind *us* that *we* must continue to work with other nations to confront terrorism and ensure that the full force of Canadian law is brought to bear against those who support, plan and carry out acts of terror – we will cut off *their* money, *find them* and *punish them*" (in Department of Justice 2001, emphasis added). Despite the minister's privileged position as an "authorized spokesperson" (Bourdieu 1991, 77) of the state in making this claim, her statement was presented as dependent on no such position for its legitimacy. The draconian piece of legislation she introduced was presented under the simple rationale that "terrorism is the most significant threat to Canada's national security" (Department of Justice 2001).

I begin by exploring Section 83.01 of Bill C-36, as it is one of the most controversial aspects of the bill since it defines a "terrorist activity" for the first time in the history of Canadian law (Roach 2001, 2003). More important, this definition serves as the lynchpin for most of the offences defined in the bill. Subsection (1)(a) of Section 83.01 defines "terrorist activity" as "an act or omission committed or threatened in or outside Canada that, if committed in Canada, is one of the following offences." It goes on to list ten offences, making reference to several different acts amended by the bill. The Department of Justice (2008) has stated that Section 83.01 of the bill ensures Canada's compliance with ten major United Nations counterterrorism conventions and protocols and that it accomplishes this goal by incorporating into the definition of "terrorist activity" various offences from the UN conventions.

The Canadian Bar Association (2001, 2), comprising 37,000 jurists, including lawyers, notaries, law teachers, and students across Canada, argues in its sixty-seven-page report on the Anti-terrorism Act that no global or universal definition of terrorism exists and that "defining terrorism is not a simple task." In fact, Roach (2001) has repeatedly argued that the Criminal Code of Canada is sufficient to deal with any individuals or groups posing a threat to the wellbeing of the state and its people and that a new act should not have been conceived if indeed the goal was to deal only with the threat or those engaging in harmful activities. In a similar vein, Ligue des droits et libertés (2005, 4) has labelled Bill C-36 "misleading, useless and dangerous." If the only purpose of this "juridical discourse" is to target those posing a threat to the nation, then it is an unnecessary piece of legislation.

The critique of Bill C-36 presented by Dyzenhaus (2001, 28), however, suggests otherwise. Commenting on the definition of "terrorist activity" in the bill, he states,

> The most serious derogation from rule of law in the Bill is inherent in all anti-terrorism statutes. The target is 'terrorism,' an offence which is undefinable since it presupposes that there is an *internal political enemy*, someone so existentially different that we cannot name him in advance in order to deal with him either through the ordinary criminal law, or by relaxing the rule of law to some extent for a definable and clearly supervised period. The Anti-Terrorism Bill is no exception here, nor could it be. Nor will attempts to refine the definitions help, as they will pile definition on to definition, leading to the same vague result. (Emphasis added)

This notion of an "internal political enemy" marks the ideological underpinning that shapes the definition of "terrorist activity" in the bill. This legislative process of labelling a person or a group evil reduces what may be a complex social, political, and economic phenomenon to a simple moral framework of right or wrong, thereby essentializing this wrongdoing as pathological.

Given the post-9/11 geopolitical context framing the release of Bill C-36, the important question is what differentiates "terrorists" from other "criminals" who have been security threats in the past? The ideology of whiteness lies in this unspecified, untested belief that there is an existential difference between "criminals," some of whom are white, and those the state will target as "terrorists" using the law. Therefore, it is obvious that the image of the "terrorist" is unambiguously constructed in the state's anti-terrorism "juridical discourses."

The definition of "terrorist activity" in Section 83.01 also refers to the motives of those suspected of engaging in terrorist activities. The bill states that "terrorist activity" is "[an act or omission, inside or outside of Canada, that is committed] in whole or in part for a *political, religious* or *ideological* purpose, objective, or cause" (emphasis added). Mia (2002, 130) argues that the essential elements of a crime are intent and act and that by injecting the motives clause, Bill C-36 "has moved significantly from the accepted principle that criminal law is designed to prevent and punish socially unacceptable *acts* rather than *motives*" (emphasis in original). This symbolic and material violence of the provision is illustrated by the Coalition of Muslim Organizations (2001) in its report on the subject matter of the bill. The coalition argues that if there were two equally heinous acts of terror, one committed for an ostensible religious purpose and the other for the sake of creating fear itself, the former would be designated a "terrorist" act, whereas the latter would be labelled merely a criminal act.

Many have expressed the fear that efforts to gather proof of motives would lead to religious and political targeting of individuals suspected of engaging in terrorist activities. This fear, of course, as I have argued in the previous section through examples of intense racial profiling of Muslim bodies, is grounded in reality. Although these critiques of the bill's motives clause are important in my analysis, I believe that underlining this motives clause is an intrinsic fear of the "roots of Muslim rage" (Lewis 1990) in Canada. As a result, Christianity as a motive for protesting in the streets would not be deemed abnormal, whereas Muslims protesting against the "war on terror" can be arrested under the motives provision. Since the definition of "terrorist activity" includes acts or omissions committed outside of Canada, foreign governments have become increasingly dangerous actors in collecting information about individuals' motives. It is clear that most of the suspects whose information is obtained by Canada from foreign governments are people of colour. This implies that many Geneva Convention refugees who have managed to escape persecution by their government for their political activities can be labelled terrorists and deported back to those same repressive regimes.[18] Therefore, the highly racialized nature of citizenship and of any other legal status for people of colour within the white Canadian nation is obvious here.

The anxieties of the white nation about the presence of Muslim Others are clearly embodied by two of the most draconian provisions of Bill C-36, found in Sections 83.3 and 83.28.[19] Section 83.3, which allows for "preventive arrests," has been euphemistically labelled the "Recognizance with Conditions" provision. It allows for "preventive arrest" without a warrant and without a charge being laid for several days if the officer believes that a person *may* commit an offence. The Canadian Bar Association (2001, 35) has argued that "preventive arrest should only be possible where a police officer believes that the terrorist activity will be carried out imminently. We should not countenance detention without warrant on mere suspicion that an offence will at some future time be carried out." Detention without charge indicates that the officer is acting on a prejudicial hunch and without sufficient evidence to confirm the existence of a particular offence.

The person suspected of carrying out terrorist activity is then to be taken to the provincial judge, who will "order that the person enter into a recognizance to keep the peace and be of *good behaviour* for any period that does not exceed twelve months and to comply with any other reasonable conditions prescribed in the recognizance" (emphasis added). The term "good behaviour" indicates that the bodies of those who are held without charges, those who are the subjects of this racialized violence of the bill, need to be contained and detained until they learn the "Canadian" values and become "civilized" enough to be let free among the public. Any sign of contrary behaviour would result in incarceration under the suspicions of the state. The Orientalist trope of disciplining the bodies of the racialized Other is obvious here. The containment of the Othered bodies is constructed and carried out for the safety and security of the physical and social spaces of the white nation.

Moreover, that a Canadian citizen can now be arrested without a warrant erases the difference between racialized citizens and racialized immigrants and refugees in Canada (see also Chapter 9). Under Canada's Immigration and Refugee Protection Act (IRPA),[20] only noncitizens deemed to pose a threat to the nation can be arrested without a warrant on the basis of a security certificate.[21] However, under Bill C-36, even Canadian citizens can be arrested without a warrant, thus erasing the difference between charter rights offered to citizens and noncitizens within the nation. Thobani (2007, 104) is right when she asserts that Canada's official policy of multiculturalism has led to an "ideological erasure of the legal distinctions between the 'immigrant' and 'citizen' status of racial minorities." This erasure of status of racialized groups is extremely clear in this case. In fact, no legal status within Canada can safeguard the civil rights of Muslims living within the Othered spaces of the "wretched of the earth" in Canada.

Section 83.28 of Bill C-36 is titled "Investigative Hearings." Under this provision, "a peace officer may, for the purposes of an investigation for a terrorism offence, apply *ex-parte* to a judge for an order for the gathering of evidence." The basis of this request must be "that there are *reasonable* grounds to believe that (i) a terrorism offence has been committed, and (ii) [there exists] information concerning the offence, or information that may reveal the whereabouts of a person suspected by the peace officer of having committed the offence" (emphasis added). Section 83.28 employs the evasive language of "reasonable grounds" to justify ordering the suspected individual to appear before the judge.

These two provisions violate various fundamental rights guaranteed to legitimate Canadian citizens. As Mia (2002) outlines, under Section 9 of the Canadian Charter of Rights and Freedoms, warrantless arrests can be made only on the grounds that the commission of the offence is imminent. In contrast, under Bill C-36, only the suspicion of the officer is required to permit an arrest. As the former vice-president of the BC Civil Liberties Association, John Russell (2001), states in his critique of the bill and of these provisions in particular,

> When we make Canadian citizens subject to preventive detention on a reasonable suspicion but not on probable grounds of a threat of wrong-doing, when we compel them to testify when no charges have been laid against anyone, when we permit elected partisan figures to exclude possible exculpatory evidence from criminal trials or to order covert surveillance of Canadian citizens, we come perilously close to being ruled by men and women and not by law.

It is significant to acknowledge here that these charter rights are not available to racialized groups within the white nation. The references to "Canadians" in popular discourses of national security have been about "legitimate" Canadians only. As a result, the logic of colonial violence in removing people of colour at the will of the colonizer is very much at play in this infringement of rights of Muslims and those who "look like" Muslims.

The surveillance of Othered spaces is also illustrated in section 83.05 of Bill C-36, which allows for a "list of entities"[22] to be created. Under this provision, the solicitor general has the authority respecting a government's "list of terrorists" to permit the inclusion of any entity whom he or she has reasonable grounds to believe has carried out, participated in, or facilitated a terrorist activity. There are no procedural safeguards to challenge such a decision, and in fact the bill includes a provision stating that if the solicitor general does not respond within sixty days to a challenge concerning a group's placement on a list, the group is to remain a listed entity.

This has led to a growing fear among Canadian religious and humanitarian nongovernmental organizations (NGOs) that humanitarian assistance could be discouraged from reaching those areas of conflict where it is often impossible for personnel to avoid relating to all involved combatants in the process of delivering assistance to those in need.[23] As Mia (2003, 93) observes, this list may be used in three ways:

> First, those on the list are subject to scrutiny by the state and private parties. Second, the list serves as foundation of evidence for a variety of serious offences under the *ATA* [Anti-terrorism Act], such as the facilitation of terrorist activity or participation in terrorist activity. Third, the list is significant to a regime of private enforcement, which may result in social ostracism. The fact of being "listed" is sufficient evidence that an individual or organization is a terrorist entity, which conclusion then becomes the basis for prosecution of that entity or anyone associated with it.

That being listed is considered sufficient proof that an individual or organization is engaged in terrorist activities has serious repercussions for those whose survival depends on these organizations. For instance, sending aid to countries on the watch list of Canadian officials, or even sponsoring a Muslim relative who has any sort of criminal record in his or her country, can lead to an individual's being put on this list. An example of a person whose life has been drastically affected by this provision is Liban Hussein, a Somali Canadian, who discovered that both he and his money-transfer company with a branch in Ottawa were black-listed and that his accounts were frozen. Hussein remained in an utter state of panic and fear of the unknown for six months before the Canadian government admitted in 2002 that there had been a "mistake." Within six weeks of this admission, Hussein's name was removed from the list, and he received compensation from the government (Tanovich 2006, 9).

When such a "mistake" becomes institutionalized, however, it is little wonder that bodies of colour are the ones usually misrecognized by police and other law enforcement authorities of the state. In fact, as Bahdi (2003) notes, the Office of the Superintendent of Financial Institutions (OSFI)[24] has advised several financial institutions in Canada to regard with suspicion not only the people whose names are actually on the list but also anyone whose name *resembles* the name of a listed person. Therefore, it seems that "doing business while Muslim" has become criminalized in Canada. Being perceived and/or labelled a terrorist or a potential terrorist, the "criminal Other" is essentialized as the rightfully surveilled Other. As a result, Bill C-36 has been carefully designed so that only the bodies of those who are not part of the "imagined community" of the nation become its targets.

Employing the notion of discourse as a powerful social practice means taking into account the social, political, and historical factors that allow certain discourses to circulate as "official" discourses within the nation, as well as the political practices that these discourses have affected. Thus I turn my attention to a recent case that explores the contestation over the truths produced by Bill C-36.

In June 2006, in a dramatic and spectacular predawn raid, 400 police officers arrested seventeen men, and an eighteenth was detained two months later. These Canadian Muslim men of colour, five of whom were of minor age and had their identities protected by Canada's Youth Criminal Justice Act, were arrested under the Anti-terrorism Act. The police claimed that they had disrupted a major terrorist plot to storm Parliament and behead the prime minister. In popular discourses of various state institutions such as the media, there was no critical investigation of the situation. Instead, the suspects were labelled terrorists even before any of them appeared for a trial.[25] On June 12, 2006, *CBC News*, in an article titled "Indepth: Toronto Bomb Plot – Profiles of the Suspects," released caricatures of the mug shots of these men, along with their names, age, and the provisions of the act under which they were arrested. Some of the information made available to the public included when the suspect immigrated to Canada, even though in most cases it had been over twenty years prior. In fact, many of the suspects were born in Canada. In one case, while listing information about the suspect's educational credentials, the report made a point of stating that his *father* (not the suspect himself) had immigrated to Canada from Trinidad and Tobago over forty years prior. I argue that this information was disclosed because these men were not seen as Canadians but as belonging "somewhere else," to some primitive and anti-modern civilization bent on destroying the Canadian values of freedom and tolerance. Moreover, the Western credentials of these alleged suspects were included (such as which school they attended and what they studied) in order to argue that no matter what, these barbaric Muslim men were just not *capable* of learning the Western values upheld by the act.

The dramatic nature of these arrests, along with the discursive strategies framing them, continues to reify the significance of Bill C-36, despite the arguments made by many that it is an unnecessary piece of legislation. The dramatic arrests were important in consoling the nation that law-enforcement officials, through the bill, were constantly working to keep the national space "safe" and "secure."

Conclusion

The rhetoric of "national security" has always been about maintaining Canada as a predominantly white nation with a Judeo-Christian ethos, for national security is not only about keeping the physical borders of the nation safe but also about keeping its ideological borders as "morally clean" as possible. As a result, national security becomes naturalized as a "norm" that "Canadians-as-members-of-the-nation" live and consume every day. Many of these legitimate Canadians have no experiential basis to be critical of the regime of national security. As Kinsman, Buse, and Steedman (2000, 283) argue, "These processes of 'inclusion' and 'exclusion' from human and civil rights become key to the maintenance of the hegemony of the national security regime discourse and practice." An individual's inclusion in the category of those whose lives are worth protecting means that his or her life is "grievable" (Butler 2004). As the derogatory Bill C-36 and the treatment of Muslim men and women illustrate, Muslims of colour are not included in the category of those with grievable lives.

My findings here strongly suggest that the Anti-terrorism Act is built on very specific rationalities of Orientalism and on very particular racialized notions of who constitutes the "enemy insider/terrorist." I agree with all of the critiques of the act outlined above, and I have powerfully demonstrated that in formulating the act, the state had a preconceived idea of who would be suspected of "terrorism" in Canada. The definition of "terrorist activity" is not at all ambiguous in the imaginations of those who produced these knowledges regarding anti-terrorism measures. I have also argued that charter rights are specifically reserved for "Canadians-as-members-of-the-nation," whereas those constructed as the "wretched of the earth" in Canada occupy the underside of democracy and, in doing so, live in vulnerable spaces of removal far from the "imagined community" of the nation. My analysis also reveals how the act constructs certain truths about "terrorists" and how these truths are then applied to vilify Muslim men, as in the above example of the eighteen arrests.

Linda Tuhiwai Smith (2002, 26) writes that "the struggle to assert and claim humanity has been a consistent thread of anti-colonial discourses on colonialism and oppression." It is as a small part of this struggle to assert and claim my humanity as a Canadian Muslim woman of colour that I have written an anti-Orientalist analysis of the Anti-terrorism Act. However, the question that still needs much consideration is how to claim humanity as Muslims of colour in a nation built on colonial and racialized violences.

NOTES

1 Throughout this chapter, I use the term "West" to refer to rich, industrialized, predominantly white, Judeo-Christian countries that have hegemony in the global community and that exercise omnipresent colonial domination worldwide. However, I also understand the term to refer to a racialized, mythical construct defined in relation to "the Rest" – that is, to nonwhite, often colonized nations. For a detailed discussion of this term, as employed here, see Hall (2007, 56-60).
2 Anti-terrorism Act, R.S.C. 2001, c. 41.
3 Public Safety Act, S.C. 2001, c. 15. Bill C-42 was withdrawn and replaced by other bills with similar provisions for security measures, and the Public Safety Act did not receive royal assent until 2004 (McMenemy 2006, 310). Because of internal dissent, Bill C-42 was withdrawn on April 24, 2002, and replaced by other modified versions, such as Bill C-55 and later Bill C-17, also titled the Public Safety Act, which received royal assent in 2002. Bill C-17 amends twenty-three different acts.
4 I use the term "settler colony" here to refer to nations established by white European colonizers through the violent colonization of indigenous populations. See Razack (2002) for a detailed discussion on the formation of these white settler colonies.
5 Henry and Tator (2002, 26) define "dominant discourse" as the collection of expectations we take for granted; it is also distinguished by "its power to interpret major social, political, and economic issues and events" and rarely includes the perspective of the Other. However, I caution the reader against regarding the dominant discourse as monolithic or static. This discourse is constantly evolving and is formed by a multiplicity of other discourses.
6 I use the term "discursively" here as a general term to refer to "any approach in which meaning, representation and culture are considered to be constitutive" (Henry and Tator 2002, 26). In this sense, discursive practices are exercises in power and control, for they make it difficult for individuals to think outside of them.
7 I use the term "Other" – based on Edward Said's *Orientalism* (1978) – to refer to those who have been historically dehumanized because of their race. These Others have usually been colonized and exterminated based on colonial rationalities for civilizing the native Other and bringing them into modernity by force. See Said (1978) for further discussion of this term.
8 In highlighting race as the primary criterion for inclusion in or exclusion from the nation's "imagined community," I do not intend to assert that other social constructs of gender, sexuality, ability, and so forth have not played a role in who has been

included in or excluded from the space demarcated by the nation's ideological borders.

9   I have borrowed the phrase "Canadians-as-members-of-the-nation" from Thobani (2000, 2003). She uses this term to refer to the white settlers in Canada, who, through violent histories of colonization and inequalities inherent in the social structure of society, continue to imagine themselves as the rightful owners of the land. In doing so, they reinforce the concept of pre-invasion *terra nullius*, or "empty land." Within this context, the presence of bodies of colour is constructed as a burden on the white nation, such that nonwhites can never become part of the national imaginary and hence remain outside the legitimate, or "official," spaces of the nation.

10 I am definitely not asserting here that the struggles of Muslims or any other group of immigrants within Canada have been the same as those of Aboriginals. The violences visited on bodies of Aboriginals have been different and have occurred alongside their ongoing struggles against colonization and for title to their lands. Immigrants of colour share no such prior relationship to this land, and therefore their struggles in this country have a different socio-historical specificity. However, for the purpose of my arguments in this chapter respecting the Othering of bodies of colour, it is helpful to place the Orientalist construction of Muslim bodies on a continuum that includes the racialized imagery of Aboriginal peoples in Canada.

11 Pierre Trudeau, in *House of Commons Debates,* October 8, 1971: 8545-6.

12 For instance, see Coyne (2001).

13 Tanovich (2006, 13) defines racial profiling as occurring when "law enforcement or security officials, consciously or unconsciously, subject individuals at any location to heightened scrutiny based solely or in part on race, ethnicity, Aboriginality, place of origin, ancestry or religion or on stereotypes associated with any of these factors rather than on objectively reasonable grounds to suspect that the individual is implicated in criminal activity."

14 For instance, one week after the 9/11 attacks, the RCMP issued a profile of the terrorists that specifically identified them as "men who flew the planes," without ever referring explicitly to their ethnic and religious characteristics. See Commission of Inquiry into the Actions of Canadian Officials in Relation to Maher Arar (2005).

15 However, the categories of "good Muslims" and "bad Muslims" are not homogeneous in terms of gender. The Canadian state does not perceive all Muslim women as "good Muslims." A classic example of this is the vilification and denigration of Sunera Thobani, a professor in the Women's Studies Department at the University of British Columbia, who, in a speech given to 500 feminists in Ottawa in October 2001, opposed US foreign policies, colonialism, imperialism, and the war in Afghanistan, for which the Bush government was preparing at the time. Her speech created havoc in the media, and she was vehemently criticized for being "anti-American," which somehow translated into anti-Canadian, and therefore labelled a "bad Muslim." Margaret Wente of the *Globe and Mail* rejected her (not just her speech) as "stupid and morally bankrupt" and further argued that Thobani's ability to deliver such a speech and not be killed was proof enough of her freedom in Canada. Wente not only invokes Thobani's Otherness by stating that Thobani should be thankful that

she was permitted to deliver an anti-national speech in Canada (to which she can never belong regardless of her citizenship status), seen here as the land of freedom, but also constructs herself as the good white subject who tolerates the putative Other because of her (white) benevolence and goodness.

16 Here, I do not mean to assert that this symbolic violence is not often tied intimately to material violences as well. However, the state as benefactor of the "imperilled" Muslim woman does limit the capacity of Muslim women to speak for themselves and, in doing so, is a significant source of symbolic violence.

17 I do not mean here to deny that many parts of the Muslim world are continually exploited for economic reasons. I am merely stating the popular view that today frames discourse on the Muslim East and the Christian West.

18 This possibility is exemplified by the case of Maher Arar, a Syrian Canadian who had lived in Canada for almost twenty years. In 2003 he was accused by the United States and Canada of planning a terrorist attack and was deported back to Syria, where he was brutally tortured for months before his wife's political activism to free her husband, along with public support, forced the government to bring him back to Canada. In 2006 he was exonerated of all charges, and the government issued a formal apology.

19 These two sections were subject to a sunset clause. A sunset clause is a "statutory provision for a law to expire at a given time, subject to its re-enactment" (McMenemy 2006, 375). Even though these two clauses have expired and have not been renewed since March 1, 2007, my concern here is with what is "sayable" in the nation and by whom. That these two provisions were drafted in the first place and were allowed to remain as part of the national legislation, despite appeals from minority groups, is significant proof of how Bill C-36 targets racialized minorities within the nation.

20 Immigration and Refugee Protection Act, S.C. 2001, c. 27.

21 The Supreme Court ruled against the use of security certificates in 2007.

22 As Mia (2002, 134) notes, the government amended Bill C-36 prior to its passage to introduce more palatable language, changing "list of terrorists" to "list of entities."

23 See International Civil Liberties Monitoring Group (2003, 7).

24 Under the Criminal Code (as amended by Bill C-36), the provisions relating to terrorist financing fall to the OSFI in so far as the OSFI issues a consolidated list that includes both names and organizations suspected of engaging in or supporting terrorist activities.

25 See Kutty (2006).

REFERENCES

Ahmed, S. 2000. *Strange encounters: Embodied Others in postcoloniality*. New York, NY: Routledge.

Alloula, M. 1986. *The colonial harem*. Trans. M. Godzich and W. Godzich. Minneapolis, MN: University of Minneapolis Press.

Anderson, B. 1983. *Imagined communities: Reflections on the origin and spread of nationalism*. New York, NY: Verso.

Backhouse, C. 1999. *Colour-coded: A legal history of racism in Canada, 1900-1950*. Toronto, ON: University of Toronto Press.

Bahdi, R. 2003. No exit: Racial profiling and Canada's war against terrorism. *Osgoode Hall Law Journal* 41, 2-3: 293-316.
Bannerji, H. 2000. Geography lessons: On being an insider/outsider to the Canadian nation. In H. Bannerji, ed., *The dark side of nation: Essays on multiculturalism, nationalism, and gender*, 63-86. Toronto, ON: Canadian Scholars' Press.
Bourdieu, P. 1991. *Language and symbolic power*. Cambridge, MA: Harvard University Press.
Burman, J. 2007. Deportable or admissible? Black women and the space of "removal." In K. McKittrick and C. Woods, eds., *Black geographies and the politics of place*, 177-92. Toronto, ON: Between the Lines.
Butler, J. 2004. *Precarious life: The powers of mourning and violence*. New York, NY: Verso.
CAIR-CAN. 2004. Presumption of guilt: A national survey on security visitations of Canadian Muslims. http://www.caircan.ca/downloads/POG-08062005.pdf.
Canadian Bar Association. 2001. Submission on Bill C-36: Anti-terrorism Act. October. http://www.cba.org/pdf/submission.pdf.
CBC News. 2006. Indepth: Toronto bomb plot – Profiles of the suspects. June 12. http://www.cbc.ca/.
Clark, C. 2005. Canadians want strict scrutiny, poll finds. *Globe and Mail*, 11 August, AI.
Cloud, D.L. 2004. "To veil the threat of terror": Afghan Women and the "Clash of Civilizations" in the imagery of the U.S. war on terrorism. *Quarterly Journal of Speech* 90, 3: 285-306.
Coalition of Muslim Organizations. 2001. Special senate committee on the subject matter of Bill C-36. December 5. http://www.Muslimlaw.org.
Commission of Inquiry into the Actions of Canadian Officials in Relation to Maher Arar. 2005. *Transcripts of proceedings, 30 June 2005, 8184-86 and 8187, II.3-8*. http://www.stenotran.com/commission/maherarar/2005-06-30%2033.pdf.
Cotler, I. 2001. Thinking outside the box: Foundational principle for a counter-terrorism law and policy. In R.J. Daniels, P. Macklem, and K. Roach, eds., *The security of freedom: Essays on Canada's Anti-terrorism Bill*, 111-30. Toronto, ON: University of Toronto Press.
Coyne, A. 2001. We have no choice but to confront evil. *Regina Leader Post*, September 15, A14.
Department of Justice. 2001. Government of Canada introduces Anti-terrorism Act. October 15. http://www.canada.justice.gc.ca/.
–. 2005. Joint statement by the Hon. Anne McLellan, deputy prime minister and minister of public safety and emergency preparedness and the Hon. Irwin Cotler, minister of justice and attorney general of Canada. November 14. http://www.justice.gc.ca/.
–. 2008. The Anti-terrorism Act: Definition of terrorist activity on Feb 7, 2007 (updated). http://www.justice.gc.ca/.
Dyzenhaus, D. 2001. The permenance of the temporary: Can emergency powers be normalized? In R.J. Daniels, P. Macklem, and K. Roach, eds., *The security*

of freedom: Essays on Canada's Anti-terrorism Bill, 21-38. Toronto, ON: University of Toronto Press.

Fiske, J. 2000. White watch. In S. Cottle, ed., *Ethnic minorities and the media: Changing cultural boundaries*, 50-66. Philadelphia, PA: Open University Press.

Foucault, M. 1980. *Power/knowledge: Selected interviews and other writings, 1972-1977*. New York, NY: Pantheon.

Hall, S. 1996. The question of cultural identity. In S. Hall, D. Held, D. Hubert, and K. Thompson, eds., *Modernity: An introduction to modern societies*, 595-634. Malden, MA: Blackwell.

–. 2007. The West and the rest: Discourse and power. In T.D. Gupta, C.E. James, R.C.A. Maaka, G. Galabuzi, and C. Andersen, eds., *Race and racialization: Essential readings*, 56-60. Toronto, ON: Canadian Scholars' Press.

Henry, F., and C. Tator. 2002. *Discourses of domination: Racial bias in the Canadian English-language Press*. Toronto, ON: University of Toronto Press.

Huntington, S. 1993. The clash of civilizations. *Foreign Affairs* (Summer). http://www.foreignaffairs/.

International Civil Liberties Monitoring Group. 2003. In the shadow of the law. http://www.waronterrorismwatch.ca/In_the_shadow_of_the_law.pdf.

Kashmeri, Z. 2000. When CSIS calls: Canadian Arabs, racism, and the Gulf War. In G. Kinsman, D.K. Buse, and M. Steedman, eds., *Whose national security? Canadian state and the creation of enemies*, 256-66. Toronto, ON: Between the Lines.

Kinsman, G., D.K. Buse, and M. Steedman. 2000. How the centre holds: National security as an ideological practice. In G. Kinsman, D.K. Buse, and M. Steedman, eds., *Whose national security? Canadian state and the creation of enemies*, 278-86. Toronto, ON: Between the Lines.

Kutty, F. 2006. Canada calling – Toronto arrests spark debate about Muslim extremism. http://faisalkutty.com/.

Lewis, B. 1990. The roots of Muslim rage. *Atlantic Monthly*, September. http://www.theatlantic.com/.

Ligue des droits et libertés. 2005. The *Anti-terrorism Act*, 2001: A misleading, useless and ... dangerous law. May 9. http://www.liguedesdroits.ca/.

Mamdani, M. 2004. *Good Muslim, bad Muslim: America, the Cold War and the roots of terror*. Toronto, ON: Random House of Canada.

Mawani, R. 2005. Genealogies of the land: Aboriginality, law, and territory in Vancouver's Stanley Park. *Social and Legal Studies* 14, 3: 315-39.

McKittrick, K., and C. Woods. 2007. No one knows the mysteries at the bottom of the ocean. In K. McKittrick and C. Woods, eds., *Black geographies and the politics of place*, 1-13. Toronto, ON: Between the Lines.

McMenemy, J. 2006. *The language of Canadian politics: A guide to important terms and concepts*. 4th ed. Waterloo, ON: Wilfrid Laurier University Press.

Mia, Z. 2002. Terrorizing the rule of law: Implications of the Anti-terrorism Act. *National Journal of Constitutional Law* 14, 1: 125-52.

–. 2003. *The end of law: Canada's national security legislation and the principle of shared humanity*. Toronto, ON: University of Toronto Press.

Razack, S.H. 1998. *Looking white people in the eye: Gender, race, and culture in courtrooms and classrooms.* Toronto, ON: University of Toronto Press.
—. 2002. When place becomes race. In S.H. Razack, ed., *Race, space and the law: Unmapping a white settler society,* 1-20. Toronto, ON: Between the Lines.
—. 2004a. *Dark threats and white knights: The Somalia affair, peacekeeping, and the new imperialism.* Toronto, ON: University of Toronto Press.
—. 2004b. Imperilled Muslim women, dangerous Muslim men and civilised Europeans: Legal and social responses to forced marriages. *Feminist Legal Studies* 12, 2: 129-74.
Roach, K. 2001. The new terrorism offences and the criminal law. In R.J. Daniels, P. Macklem, and K. Roach, eds., *The security of freedom: Essays on Canada's anti-terrorism bill,* 131-50. Toronto, ON: University of Toronto Press.
—. 2003. *September 11: Consequences for Canada.* Montreal, QC, and Kingston, ON: McGill-Queen's University Press.
Russell, J. 2001. Speaking notes in federal anti-terrorism proposals, Bill C-36. http://www.bccla.org/.
Said, E. 1978. *Orientalism.* New York, NY: Vintage.
—. 2001. Shattered myths. In A.L. Macfie, ed., *Orientalism: A reader,* 89-103. New York, NY: New York University Press.
—. 2002. Thoughts about America. *Al-Ahram Weekly,* 28 February–6 March. http://www.bintjbeil.com/.
Smith, A. 2005. *Conquest: Sexual violence and American Indian genocide.* Cambridge, MA: South End.
Smith, D.E. 1999. *Writing the social: Critique, theory and investigations.* Toronto, ON: University of Toronto Press.
Smith, L.T. 2002. *Decolonizing methodologies: Research and indigenous peoples.* New York, NY: Palgrave and St. Martin's.
Spivak, G. 1988. Can the subaltern speak? In C. Nelson and L. Grossberg, eds., *Marxism and the interpretation of culture,* 271-316. Urbana, IL: University of Illinois Press.
Tanovich, D.M. 2006. *The colour of justice: Policing race in Canada.* Toronto, ON: Irwin Law.
Tator, C., and F. Henry. 2006. *Racial profiling in Canada: Challenging the myth of "a few bad apples."* Toronto, ON: University of Toronto Press.
Thobani, S. 2000. Nationalizing Canadians: Bordering immigrant women in the late twentieth century in Canada. *Canadian Journal of Women and the Law* 12, 2: 279-312.
—. 2003. War and the politics of truth-making in Canada. *Qualitative Studies in Education* 16, 3: 399-414.
—. 2004. Exception as rule: Profile of exclusion. *Signs: Journal of Women in Culture and Society* 29, 2: 597-99.
—. 2007. Imperial longings, feminist responses: Print media and the imagining of Canadian nationhood after 9/11. In D.E. Chunn, S.B. Boyd, and H. Lessard, eds., *Reaction and resistance: Feminism, law and social change,* 98-124. Vancouver, BC: UBC Press.

Walker, J. 1997. *"Race," rights and the law in the Supreme Court of Canada: Historical case studies.* Waterloo, ON: Osgoode Society for Canadian Legal History and Wilfrid Laurier University Press.

Zine, J. 2006. Between Orientalism and fundamentalism: The politics of Muslim women's feminist engagement. *Muslim World Journal of Human Rights* 3, 1 (5): 1-24.

Contributors

Katherine Bullock completed her doctorate in political science at the University of Toronto in 1999. She has taught and lectured on Islamic civilization and Middle East politics in California and Toronto. Her most recent appointment is with the University of Toronto, where she has been teaching a course entitled "The Politics of Islam" since 2002. Currently, she is president of the Tessellate Institute, a nonprofit research institute, and also of Compass Books, a newly founded publishing company. She was the editor of the *American Journal of Islamic Social Sciences* from 2003 to 2008 and the vice-president of the Association of Muslim Social Scientists (North America) from 2006 to 2009.

Her publications include *Muslim Women Activists in North America: Speaking for Ourselves* (2005) and *Rethinking Muslim Women and the Veil: Challenging Historical and Modern Stereotypes* (2002), which has been translated into Arabic, French, and Turkish. She is a community activist and lectures frequently, both to Muslim and non-Muslim groups. Originally from Australia, she lives in Canada with her husband and children. She embraced Islam in 1994.

Aliaa Dakroury is an assistant professor replacement in the Department of Communication, University of Ottawa. Dr. Dakroury is the managing editor of the *American Journal of Islamic Social Sciences*. She is the author of *Communication and Human Rights* (2009), editor of *The Right to*

Communicate: Historical Hopes, Global Debates, and Future Premises (2009), editor of *The Right to Communicate*, a special issue of *Global Media Journal – American Edition* (Fall 2008), and co-editor of *Introduction to Communication and Media Studies* (2008). She is the winner of the Canadian Communication Association's 2005 Van Horne Award and has been nominated as an honorary expert by the Islamic Resource Bank (IRB), a joint project of the Minaret of Freedom Institute, the Association of Muslim Social Scientists, and the International Institute of Islamic Thought. Her publications appear in various journals, including the *Journal of International Communication, Media Development: Journal of the World Association for Christian Communication*, the *American Journal of Islamic Social Sciences, Reconstruction: Studies in Contemporary Culture*, the *Journal of InterGroup Relations*, the *American Journal of Islamic Social Sciences*, the *Global Media Journal – American Edition*, and the *Journal of Culture, Language, and Representation*. Her work examines communication and human rights, and her research interests include the right to communicate, media policy, international communication, diaspora and globalization, media representations, and Islam.

Jacqueline Flatt has a master's degree in sociology from Wilfrid Laurier University. Her contribution to this volume is the first published chapter from her master's thesis, and she is looking forward to continuing her research interests in media discourse, securitization and citizenship policies, and race/ethnic migration studies.

Yasmin Jiwani is an associate professor in the Department of Communication Studies at Concordia University, Montreal. Her doctorate in communication studies at Simon Fraser University examines issues of race and representation in Canadian television news. Her recent publications include *Discourses of Denial: Mediations of Race, Gender and Violence* (2006) and an edited collection with Candice Steenbergen and Claudia Mitchell titled *Girlhood: Redefining the Limits* (2006). Her work has appeared in *Social Justice, Violence against Women, Canadian Journal of Communication, Journal of Popular Film and Television, Topia, International Journal of Media and Cultural Politics*, and numerous anthologies. Prior to her move to Concordia, Dr. Jiwani was the executive co-ordinator and principal researcher at the BC/Yukon FREDA Centre for Research on Violence against Women and Children. Her previous work has focused on gendered narratives of war.

Her most recent research, funded by the Social Sciences and Humanities Research Council of Canada (SSHRC), focuses on a comparative examination of femicide reporting in the press.

Nadeem Memon is the director of the Islamic Teacher Education Program (ITEP), a collaboration between Razi Education and the Ontario Institute for Studies in Education, University of Toronto (OISE/UT). He also teaches courses in equity and education, alternative pedagogies in education, and Muslim studies at a number of universities in Ontario. Nadeem completed a doctorate in theory and policy studies in education at OISE/UT in 2009 with a research focus on faith-based schooling in North America and a particular emphasis on Islamic schooling. He is currently completing a co-edited book entitled *Discipline, Devotion, and Dissent: The Promise and Problems in Jewish, Catholic, and Islamic Schooling*.

Shaista Patel is a doctoral student at the Ontario Institute for Studies in Education, University of Toronto. Her doctoral work explores the relationship between people of colour and First Nations people on the northern half of Turtle Island. She is interested in examining how immigrants of colour build solidarity with people of the Native nations and whether this relationship of people of colour to the territory called Canada is colonial and one of conquest. She has taught courses in women's studies and sociology at the University of Toronto.

Meena Sharify-Funk is an assistant professor in the Religion and Culture Department and the co-ordinator of the Muslim Studies Option Program at Wilfrid Laurier University. Dr. Sharify-Funk specializes in Islamic studies with a focus on contemporary Muslim thought and identity. She has written and presented a number of articles and papers on women and Islam, Islamic hermeneutics, and the role of cultural and religious factors in peacemaking. Her book *Encountering the Transnational: Women, Islam and the Politics of Interpretation* (2008) is about the impact of transnational networking on Muslim women's identity, thought, and activism. She has also co-edited two books, *Cultural Diversity and Islam* (2003) and *Contemporary Islam: Dynamic, Not Static* (2006).

Itrath Syed is a doctoral student in the School of Communication at Simon Fraser University. This follows her completion of a master's degree in women's studies at the Centre for Women's and Gender Studies, University of British Columbia. Her master's work explores the gendered and racialized construction of the Muslim community in the media discourse surrounding the "shar'ia" debate in Ontario. She has been an instructor at Langara College, Centennial College, and Simon Fraser University, teaching courses in women's studies, popular culture, and Canadian politics and a course entitled "Contemporary Debates in Muslim Women's Feminisms."

She received her undergraduate degree from Simon Fraser University, where she completed a major in Middle East history and minors in political science and women's studies. During the years between her undergraduate and graduate degrees, she worked in the anti-violence field at a rape crisis centre and then at transition houses for battered women and their children. She is a social justice activist involved in the local anti-war movement, in anti-occupation solidarity work, and in resisting the erosion of civil rights and the racial profiling of members of the Muslim, Arab, and South Asian communities in Canada. In the 2004 federal election, she ran as a candidate for the New Democratic Party in her home riding of Delta-Richmond East, British Columbia. She has been interviewed for several documentaries and is a frequent presenter on a wide array of political and social issues.

Jasmin Zine is an associate professor of sociology and Muslim studies at Wilfrid Laurier University, where she teaches courses on critical race and ethnic studies, race and postcolonial studies, education and social justice, Muslim cultural politics in Canada, and race, gender, and imperialism. She has produced numerous publications in the field of Muslim studies and Muslim women's studies, including a chapter in the book *War Stories and Camouflage Politics: (En)Gendering the War on Terror* (2006), republished in the *Muslim World Journal of Human Rights* (2006), that examines Muslim women's responses to the "war on terror." Her book *Canadian Islamic Schools: Unraveling the Politics of Faith, Gender, Knowledge and Identity* (2008) presents the first ethnographic study of Islamic schools in North America. She has also produced numerous journal articles and book chapters that examine the politics of race, religion, gender, and identity within education and within anti-racist and Islamic feminism.

As a scholar-activist, Dr. Zine has also worked in community-based research from an anti-racism and anti-oppression framework, conducting research on homelessness among Latin Americans and Muslims in Toronto and developing anti-oppression programs, workshops, and policies for community organizations. She has also developed curriculum resources for anti-Islamophobia education that have received awards and international recognition. She is presently co-editing a book that deals with the cultural, literary, and cinematic representations of Muslim women and the pedagogical possibilities for anti-colonial readings of these cultural texts. In 2009 Dr. Zine received a research grant from the Social Sciences and Humanities Research Council of Canada (SSHRC) to pursue a Canada-wide study of Muslim youth and the politics of empire, citizenship, and belonging post-9/11. She has spoken internationally on these topics in several academic forums. She was also part of an expert group working on an international project with UNESCO, the Council of Europe, and the Organization for Security and Cooperation in Europe to combat discrimination against Muslims.

Index

Abdel-Fatah, Nawal, 123
Aboriginal communities, 3, 21, 275, 294n10
Abou El Fadl, Khaled, 147
Abu-Laban, Baha, 5
Abu-Laban, Yasmeen, 93, 96, 107
activism: categories of activity, 106-7; defined, 95, 98-99; delegitimization of activists, 67; negative views of, 100-1; social movements, 101, 102-3. *See also* political Islam
Adams, Michael, 7, 8-9, 34n1
L'affair du foulard, 212
Afghan Women's Counselling and Integration Community Support Organization, 107
Afghanistan, 134n5
African National Congress (ANC), 79
Agamben, Georgio, 14, 246, 247
Agathangelou, Anna M., 134n3
Agnew, Vijay, 93
Ahmed, Leila, 53, 69-70, 71
Ahmed, Mahmoud, 130
Ahmed, Naema, 10
Ahmed, Sara, 276, 277, 278

Ainsworth, Susan, 248
Aitken, Rob, 244
Al-Hijra Islamic School, 200
al-Islamiyya, 103
al-Jama'a, 103
Al Jazeera Network, 170-71
al-Qaeda: backlash and recruitment, 129; and *Little Mosque on the Prairie*, 170; newspaper coverage of, 127-29
Al Rajab high school, 209, 221, 231
Al Rashid Mosque, 190
Al-Yassini, Ayman, 25
Aladdin (Disney film), 168
Alberta, 4, 190
Ali, Syed Mumtaz, 61, 68
Ali, Yusef, 190
Allender, Sarah, 127-29
Almrei, Hassan, 240, 258, 265
alternative dispute resolution. *See* faith-based arbitration
American Journal of Islamic and Social Sciences, 149
Amnesty International, 11
ANC. *See* African National Congress

Anderson, Benedict, 12, 68, 165
anti-citizen, 7, 53
anti-Semitism, 127
Anti-terrorism Act (Canada). *See* Bill C-36 (Canada)
AQSAzine, 35n7, 102
Arabic language, 196
Arar, Maher: comparison to, 258; detention of, 16, 295n18; wife of (Dr. Monia Mazigh), 109n17, 295n18
Arat-Koc, Sedef, 46, 244, 245, 260
Arbitration Act of Ontario: history of, 81; IICJ's application to, 57n5, 61, 62-64, 68, 82n1; and Ismaili Muslim community, 82n1; "original" intentions of, 68. *See also* faith-based arbitration
Argyll Centre, 202
Arjomand, Homa, 63, 73, 108n6
the Asper family, 117
Attiah, Mohammed, 281
Atwood, Margaret, 123
Azizah Magazine, 107

Babe, Robert E., 174
Backhouse, Constance, 276
backlash: against Muslim women, 125; and home schooling, 203; increase in hate crimes, 281; legitimization of violence, 128-31. *See also* Islamophobia; racism
Bahdi, Reem, 289
Baksh, Faisal, 205n8
Bannerji, Himani, 57n4, 245, 274
barbarism. *See* civilization
Barlas, Asma, 149
Bartkowski, John P., 230
BBC, 172
BC Muslim School, 198
BCE Globe Media, 117
Bell, Colleen, 244, 266
Bell Canada, 133n1
Bennett, Philip, 171-72, 178n7
Beshir, Ekram, 106, 109n19

bewildered herd, 242-43, 252, 253-54
Bhabha, Homi, 161
Bhabha, Mariam, 107
Biles, John, 190
Bill 94 (Quebec), 9-15, 214
Bill 101 (Quebec), 212-13
Bill C-3 (Canada), 241
Bill C-17 (Canada), 293n3
Bill C-36 (Canada): about, 283-91; Canadian Charter of Rights and Freedoms, 279; definition of "terrorist activity," 284-86, 291; denial of racism in, 280; ideological framing of, 282-83; investigative hearings, 287-88; legal criticisms of, 284-85; list of entities, 288-89, 295n22; preventive arrests, 286-87; rhetoric of, 291; security justifications for, 272-73, 279; sunset clause, 295n19; and terrorist financing, 284, 295n24. *See also* security; terrorism
Bill C-42 (Canada), 272, 293n3
Bill C-55 (Canada), 293n3
bin Laden, Osama: and *Little Mosque on the Prairie*, 170, 178n6; and media, 127-28
binaries: faith-based arbitration debate, 61; gendered Islamophobia, 211; use by newspapers, 120-23, 126. *See also* categorization
Bird, S. Elizabeth, 133n2
Black, Conrad, 117
Blair, Cherie, 134n5
boarding schools. *See* madrassas
Bouchard, Gérard, 23-25
Bouchard-Taylor Commission, 23-25, 55-56
Bouyeri, Mohammed, 158-59n10
Boyd, Marion, 48, 66-67
Boyd Commission, 79, 83n6
Boyle, Helen N., 194
Brawley, Edward Allan, 163
British Columbia, 198
Brown, Wendy, 20-21

Bullock, Katherine, 106
burka. *See* niqab
Burman, Jenny, 276
Buruma, Ian, 159*n*14
Buse, Dieter K., 291
Bush, George W., 259, 282
Bush, Laura, 134*n*5
Bush family connections, 132-33
Butler, Judith, 247, 253-56, 256, 264

CAIR-CAN (Canadian Council on American-Muslim Relations), 79, 281
CampusWatch, 131
Canada: anti-American sentiment, 122-23; "Canadians-as-members-of-the-nation," 277, 291, 293-94*n*9; demographics of, 161; elected Muslim women, 105, 108*n*1, 109*n*16; minority representation in Parliament, 108*n*2; pride of Canadian Muslims in, 8. *See also* names of specific bills, under "Bill x"
Canadian Bar Association, 284, 287
Canadian Border Services Agency, 241
Canadian Broadcasting Corporation (CBC): *CBC News*, 290; *Counterspin*, 78-79; and Multiculturalism Act of 1985 (Canada), 173-77; reasons for, 175, 178*n*9. *See also Little Mosque on the Prairie*; public broadcasting; television
Canadian Charter of Rights and Freedoms, 288
Canadian Council on American-Muslim Relations. *See* CAIR-CAN
Canadian Council of Muslim Women (CCMW): awareness of women's issues, 35*n*7; on Bill 94, 14; on *Counterspin*, 78-79; and Lila Fahlman, 109*n*17; objectives of, 102; position statement on Muslim family law, 78-79; and school curriculum, 97; on vulnerability of Muslim women, 73; WERF conference, 63-64
Canadian identity. *See* identity (Canadianness)
Canadian Islamic Congress, 164, 281
Canadian Muslims for Peace and Justice, 107
Canadian Race Relations Foundation (CRRF), 25
Canadian Security Intelligence Service (CSIS): harassment of Muslims by, 282; reasonable grounds for surveillance standards, 258; and security certificates, 240-41, 252, 254-58
Canwest Corporation, 116-17
The Cash Nexus (Ferguson), 121
categorization: bewildered herd, 242-43; of crime by motive, 285-86; distancing and, 141; framing of events by media, 115-16; in media, 165-66; of Muslim women, 71-76; of Muslims, 131, 282-83, 294*n*15; by newspapers, 117-20, 129-30; and Orientalism, 167-68; of population segment as dangerous, 246-47; surveillance measures, 244, 254-55. *See also* binaries; identity (Muslim); political outlooks; stereotypes
categorization (specific labels): cultural/ethnic Muslims, 187; ex-Muslims, 141; folk Muslims, 188; Islamists, 131; Manji's self-categorization, 159*n*13; Moderate Muslims, 144, 148-50, 158*nn*7-8, 159*n*14; modern Muslims, 150; Modernized Islam, 187-88, 201; mosqued Muslims, 186; Muslim refusenik, 141; as terrorists, 223-25, 254-55, 257-58
CBC. *See* Canadian Broadcasting Corporation (CBC)
CBC News, 290

CCMW. *See* Canadian Council of
    Muslim Women (CCMW)
Center for the Study of Islam and
    Democracy (CSID), 159n14
Central Committee for Ex-Muslims,
    158n7
Central Committee of Muslims, 158n7
Charest, Jean, and Bill 94, 15
Charkaoui, Adil, 240, 258, 259-60, 265,
    269n1
Chesler, Phyllis, 19
Chomsky, Noam, 242-43, 247-48, 253
Christianity: fundamentalism in, 132;
    separation of church and state, 74
Citizen's Code. *See* Hérouxville, Quebec
citizenship: civic education, 96; construction of anti-citizen, 7, 53; *Discover Canada* publication, 18; faith-based arbitration debate, 65; inclusion and exclusion of individuals, 3-4, 16-17, 57n4, 244-45; minorities becoming worthy of, 18; of Muslims, 17, 71; national imaginary, 68-69; niqab ban in Quebec, 12; and public broadcasting, 175; rights of, 262-63; subaltern citizenship, 16, 20, 43-45, 57n2. *See also* identity (Canadianness)
civic engagement: and education, 96, 185-86; Muslim political involvement as, 102-3; as springboard to politics, 105; and *tarbiyah*, 192-93; visibility as criterion, 104. *See also* non-governmental organizations; politics
civilization: activism to prove status, 101; Canadian citizenship guide, 18; clash of civilizations, 71, 282; governmentality of tolerance, 20-21; Islamic contributions to, 147; minorities as uncivilized, 67-68; threat of multiculturalism, 52; versus barbarism, 18, 120-21, 126; white settler societies, 275-76

Clarke, Linda, 215, 216-17
classification. *See* categorization
clothing, 205n13. *See also* veiling
Coalition of Muslim Organizations,
    286
comedy. *See Little Mosque on the
    Prairie*
Communication and Mass Media
    (Martin), 163
Concentric Circles (Harder), 202
Conservative Party (Ontario), 185
Consultation Commission on Accommodation Practices Related to Cultural Differences. *See* Bouchard-Taylor Commission
Convention against Torture, 242
Cook, Peter G., 178n9
Cotler, Irwin, 263, 268, 279
counter-narratives, 114. *See also Little
    Mosque on the Prairie;* Muslim
    dissident literature; stereotypes
Counterspin, 78-79
covering. *See* veiling
Coyne, Andrew, 122
credentials (foreign), 8
Criminal Code (Canada), 295n24
critical discourse analysis, 248
CRRF. *See* Canadian Race Relations
    Foundation (CRRF)
CSID. *See* Center for the Study of Islam
    and Democracy
CSIS. *See* Canadian Security Intelligence
    Service (CSIS)
CTV, 133n1
*The Cultural Contribution of the Other
    Ethnic Groups*, 189
culture: change over time, 3-4; civilization versus barbarism, 120-21; common-sense notions, 276; contamination of, 43-44, 50-51; cultural imperialism and media, 166-67; cultural terrorism, 21; cultural/ethnic Muslims, 187; death of culture, 52-56; ethnic media, 173; immigration policies,

43, 54-55; interculturalism, 24-25; and Islamic reform, 148, 151-52; and media, 163; national narrative formation, 22; and Orientalism, 167-68; peer pressure in schools, 227-28. *See also* identity (majority culture); multiculturalism; Muslim community; veiling; Western values

culture (French Canadian). *See* identity (French Canadian)

curriculum: madrassas, 194-95, 205n3; public schools, 97, 107

CW Network, 171

dangerous feminine, 232-33n5
Dar Al Iman School, 200
Dardenne, Robert W., 133n2
Darsi Nizamiyya curriculum, 194
Dartmouth, Nova Scotia, 198
Darul Uloom Canada, 194, 205n3
Darul Uloom Deoband movement, 187, 205n2
Day, Stockwell, 264
Dean, Mitchell, 246, 248
Debating Modern Islam, 149
Deobandi school model, 194
deportation, 5, 16, 251, 264-65, 266-68, 295n18
Detention Centres and Security Certificates (Doyle), 239, 241
diaspora (term), 3
Direly, Becky, 129
Discover Canada (Kenney), 18
discrimination: concerns of Canadian Muslims about, 8; within Muslim community, 72-74; in public schools, 220; on public transit, 221-23; workplace discrimination, 8-9, 98, 211. *See also* Islamophobia

Disney. *See* Walt Disney Corporation
dissent: to anti-terror policies, 260; newspaper attacks on, 124, 134n4; political Islam, 99-101. *See also* Muslim dissident literature

distancing, 121-22, 141
divorce, 79-80
domestic violence: awareness of actual issues, 35n7; death by culture, 48-52, 75-76; as foreign import, 18-20; honour killings, 19, 49-51; racism, 39-40, 49-50, 75-76. *See also* gender; women

dominant discourse, 293n5
Doyle, Nathan, 241
dress. *See* veiling
Driscoll, Ellen, 214, 219
Dyzenhaus, David, 285

Les Écoles Musulmanes de Montréal, 198-99
Edmonton, Alberta, 190, 201-2
education (faith-based schools): and civic engagement, 185-86; functions of, 183; and Ontario elections, 185, 189, 204-5n1; variations between schools, 189

education (Islamic): curriculum of, 194; Deobandi school model, 194; and education, 192; and Ekram Beshir, 109n19; gender segregation in, 194, 195, 210; history of full-time schools, 198-200; home schooling, 201-3; Islamic American University, 109n19; Islamic reform and, 144; memorization in, 193, 194-95; Muslim Education Foundation (MEF), 201-2; and Olivia Monem, 107; in Ontario, 210; in Pakistan, 127; paradigm of selective engagement, 200-1; purpose of Islamic schools, 200; as source of separation from society, 198; *tarbiyah*, 192-93; veiling in, 220-21, 226-27; weekend and evening classes, 195-97, 198. *See also* madrassas

education (public): curriculum development, 97, 107; dissatisfaction of Muslims with, 199; experiences with veiling in, 219-20, 226-27; expulsion for refusal to remove niqab, 10; hijab ban in public schools, 44, 211-14, 232n3; information tables at malls, 97; need for immigrant education, 55; parent involvement in, 98, 106-7, 109n19; purpose of civil education, 96, 185
educational achievement: and employment status, 8; of Muslim women in Canada, 94, 159n17; of Muslims in Canada, 8
Egypt, 103
Eickelman, Dale, 99-100
El Guindi, Fadwa, 214
Elmasry, Mohamed, 130, 132
embrace (paradigm of): about, 187; and Modernized Islam, 201; supplementary religious education, 195-97
Enloe, Cynthia, 17, 45
Europe: European media, 172-73; immigration policies, 43, 54. See also names of specific countries
ex-Muslims: Central Committee for Ex-Muslims, 158n7; distancing by, 141
extremists: distancing of, 141; Islamic reform and, 144-45, 150; and Muslim dissident literature, 138, 156, 157n2; niqab as marker of, 13; and Qur'an, 144; as threat, 149, 253-55. See also Islamists

face veil. See niqab
Fahlman, Lila, 109n17
Faith without Fear, 151, 158-59n10
faith-based arbitration: benefits for women, 79-80; fiqh (term), 47; Islamophobia, 47-48; media on, 64; moral panic from, 69, 81; non-Muslim communities, 47, 61; opposition to, 62-64, 67-68, 83n6; private negotiations as option to, 80; rejection of the Other, 71; threat to national imaginary, 61-62. See also Arbitration Act of Ontario; family law; Islamic Institute for Civil Justice (IICJ); Islamic law
family law: as being public, 80; Muslim Personal Law (MPL) debate, 79. See also faith-based arbitration
Fanon, Frantz, 166
Fatah, Tarek: case against niqab, 34n4; on Little Mosque on the Prairie, 178n8; on Marion Boyd, 66. See also Muslim Canadian Congress (MCC)
Fédération Internationale de Football Association (FIFA), 51
Federation of Muslim Women (FMW): and information tables, 97; and Mariam Bhabha, 107; objectives of, 102; and Sharon Hoosein, 106
female genital mutilation, 18-19
feminism and feminists: Canadian Islam, 2; faith-based arbitration, 48, 57-58n6, 62-64, 75, 79-80; Muslim feminists, 76, 77-78, 79; niqab ban in Quebec, 12-13, 14; sexualization of women, 229-30; on veiling, 212, 217-18; woman as term, 108n4
Ferguson, Niall, 121
FIFA. See Fédération Internationale de Football Association
Fiorito, Joe, 130
fiqh, 47, 77
Fiske, John, 280
flexible sovereignty, 245
FMW. See Federation of Muslim Women (FMW)
folk Muslims, 188

foreign credentials, 8
Foucault, Michel, 246, 259
France, 14, 44, 211-13, 232n3
Free Medical Clinic (name), 109n14
French, Martin, 244
French language television, 171
FUNdamentalist Films (production company), 177n2
"The Future Belongs to Islam" (Steyn), 164

Gagnon-Tremblay, Monique, 65
Gee, Marcus, 120, 123
Geertz, Clifford, 193
gender: Canadian citizenship guide, 18; Canadian Islam, 2; faith-based arbitration, 62-64, 71-76; gendered coverage in newspapers, 123-27, 131-32; gendered Islamophobia, 74-75, 210-11, 213-14, 231-32; hypermasculinity, 123, 134n3; politics of, 214; rationalizations of veiling, 229-30; segregation in schools, 194, 195, 210. *See also* domestic violence; men (Muslim); women
Germany: categorization of Muslims, 158n7; hijab ban in public schools, 14, 214; immigration policies, 43, 54
Ghazali Sunday Schools, 205n8
Gidengil, Elisabeth, 92
Gillespie, Marie, 165
Gitlin, Todd, 116
Globe and Mail: on Afghan women, 125; on backlash against Muslims, 128-31; binaries in, 120; coverage of 9/11, 116, 124-25, 132-33; coverage of bin Laden and al-Qaeda, 127; faith-based arbitration, 64; headline use by, 118-20; on Islam, 132; justification for war in, 122, 129; and Muslim men, 126; and Muslim women, 125; ownership of, 117, 133n1; on Palestinian reaction to 9/11, 120, 123-24; quotes from Muslims, 123, 125, 126, 132; readership of, 117; religious poll by, 190; on security certificates, 248, 249-51, 254-55, 256, 257-58, 260-66; on "shar'ia" debate, 64-65; on Sunera Thobani, 294n15; on Western values and West, 121-22
Goldberg, David Theo, 54
Goldberg, Jeffrey, 127
good and bad Muslims. *See* categorization
governmentality (concept), 259
Gramsci, Antonio, 117
Greer, Chris, 243

Haddad, Yvonne Yazbeck, 104-5
hadith: about, 232n4; defined, 34n5, 108n10; use in activism, 102; and veiling, 216-17. *See also* Muhammad (Prophet); Qur'an
Hafez, Mohammed, 99
Haffajee, Khadija, 107, 109n15
Hage, Ghassan: defining nationalism, 44; on feeling secure within nation, 26; on immigration and migration, 245, 266; on multiculturalism as offer of tolerance, 22-23; and national belonging, 42; on nationalists, 17, 45, 54
halal (defined), 177n1
Halifax, Nova Scotia, 198
Hall, Stuart, 117-18, 163
Halstead, Mark, 218
Hamdani, Daood, 4, 94, 189-90
haram (defined), 177n1
Harder, Elma, 202
Hardy, Cynthia, 248
Harkat, Mohamed, 240, 255, 258, 265, 267
Harper, Stephen, 9, 15
Hashmi, Syed Masroor, 205n2

Index

Hassan, Farzana, 19
head covering. *See* veiling
headlines (newspaper), 118-20, 204-5n1
Henry, Frances, 243, 293n4
herd mentality: bewildered herd, 242-43, 252, 253-54; fear of minorities, 10; and Islamic reform, 148
Hérouxville, Quebec: Citizen's Code, 52-56; demographics of, 41, 52-53, 58n8; Muslim women's visit to, 58n9; secularism and, 24; Town Charter, 41-42. *See also* identity (French Canadian); Quebec
hijab: ban in public schools, 211-13, 232n3; ban in soccer leagues, 51; experiences in public schools, 219-20; hijabophobia, 211; honour killings, 49-50; in Islamic schools, 220-21, 226-27; on public transit, 221-23; symbolism of, 216; as visual marker of Islamic identity, 229; workplace discrimination, 8-9, 98, 211
Hirsi Ali, Ayaan, 138, 159n13
Hogben, Alia, 78-79
Holland, 43, 54
home schooling, 201-3
honour killings, 19, 49-51
Hoodfar, Homa, 215
Hoosein, Sharon, 106
Houda-Pepin, Fatima, 67, 109n16
humanitarianism: and Bill C-36, 288-89; imperialism as, 121
Huntington, Samuel, 71, 282
Hussein, Liban, 289
hypermasculinity, 123, 134n3

Ibrahim, Humera, 190
ICNA. *See* Islamic Council of North America (ICNA)
identity (Canadianness): after 9/11, 46; of Canadian Muslims, 7; "Canadians-as-members-of-the-nation," 277, 291, 293-94n9; citizenship, 43-45; death of culture, 54-55; exalted subjects, 45; faith-based arbitration, 48; gender equality, 64-65; history of Canadian identity, 141-42, 274-79; immigration and, 142; multiculturalism, 45-46; newspapers, 116, 133n2; niqab ban in Quebec, 12; "not Canadian" theme in media, 264-68; performance of, 42-43; public broadcasting, 174-75; security certificate coverage, 250-51, 252, 260-64; veiling and, 44. *See also* citizenship; nation and nationalism; Western values
identity (French Canadian): ban on hijabs, 51-52, 213; death of culture, 52-56; French language television, 171; interculturalism, 56; secularism in, 23-24. *See also* Hérouxville, Quebec; Quebec
identity (majority culture): interculturalism, 24-25; negotiation with Muslim-minority community, 139-43; terminology of negotiation with, 158n5. *See also* culture
identity (Muslim): Bill 94, 9-15; claiming of rights as citizens, 17; common-sense assumptions of majority, 243; competing cultural standards for women and girls, 50, 209, 223, 227-28, 229; and education, 194; identity negotiation with majority culture, 139-43, 158n5; Muslim dissident literature and, 142; national pride of Canadian Muslims, 7; negotiations on, 141; politics of, 96-97; pressure to be perfect, 223-25, 233n9; state control of, 44-45; traditional male clothing, 18; and veiling, 219-20, 226-27. *See also* categorization; Muslim community; women (Muslim)

ideology: and Bill C-36, 282-83; and categorization, 117-20; and media, 165, 174; and mosques, 191; political Islam as, 99
Idris, Abdalla, 196, 205*n*4
IICJ. *See* Islamic Institute for Civil Justice (IICJ)
ijtihad, 143
Ikwan al Muslimun movement, 188
"illegal immigrant" accusation, 223-24
Imam, Seema, 197
immigration: adoption of Western values, 6-7, 34*n*1; bad immigrant archetype, 42, 57*n*1; Canadian citizenship guide, 18-19; Canadian identity and, 142, 275, 277-78; Canadian Muslim diaspora, 3-6; cultural gate-keeping, 43, 54-55; deportation, 5, 16, 251, 264-65, 266-68, 295*n*18; diversification of culture, 23; "illegal immigrant" accusation, 223-24; immigrants as dangerous, 252; immigrants as Other, 277-78; informal power structures, 45-46; and *Little Mosque on the Prairie*, 171; migrants as problem, 245; Muslim history in Canada, 4-6; Quebec government and, 26, 55-56, 65-66; race and religion as selection criteria, 266-67; reactions against, 41-42; and secularism, 24; xenophobic responses to, 26, 43-44, 212. *See also* minority communities; Muslim community
Immigration and Refugee Protection Act (IRPA), 240, 241, 265; and arrests without warrants, 287; practices sanctioned by, 246; use against non-citizens, 262-63. *See also* security certificates
imperialism: cultural imperialism and media, 166-67; as humanitarianism, 121
India, 205*n*2

individuality, 151
Infidel (Hirsi Ali), 138
INIG. *See* International Nurses Interest Group
Inside the Gender Jihad (Wadud), 147
interculturalism, 24-25, 56
International Covenant of Civil and Political Rights, 240, 241-42
International Nurses Interest Group (INIG), 106
investigative hearings, 287
Iqbal, Muzaffar, 202
IRPA. *See* Immigration and Refugee Protection Act (IRPA)
Is Multiculturalism Bad for Women? (Moller Okin), 51-52
Islam: Canadian Islam, 2; "Islamic activism" defined, 95, 98-99; majority culture reaction to white converts, 213; Modernized Islam, 187-88; newspaper analyses of, 131-32; regulation of prayer, 230; separation of church and state, 74; veiling and, 44-45; and Western values, 141. *See also* mosques; peace (religion of)
Islamic American University, 109*n*19
Islamic Centre of Québec, 190
Islamic Council of North America (ICNA), leadership of, 188
Islamic education. *See* education (Islamic)
Islamic Fellowship movement, 188
Islamic Institute for Civil Justice (IICJ): actual wording of application, 68; application for arbitration standing, 57*n*5, 61, 82*n*1; on Islamic law as closed system, 76; on Muslim rejecting faith-based arbitration, 57-58*n*6; reaction to application of, 62-64. *See also* faith-based arbitration
Islamic Institute of Toronto, 205*n*8
Islamic law: diverse nature of, 77-78; *fiqh*, 47, 77; *ijtihad*, 143; Muslim

Personal Law (MPL), 79; as static, 61, 76-79; as tool for reform, 79. *See also* faith-based arbitration

Islamic reform: appeal of, 140-41; on beliefs and doctrines, 145-48; criticism of Islam, 144-45, 158-59n10; and culture, 148; hijacking by radicals, 144-45; *ijtihad*, 143; on interpretation and practice, 145-48; Moderate Muslims and, 144; Modernized Islam, 187-88, 201; presuppositions of, 150; as reaction to 9/11, 143; Western values and, 150-53; women's emancipation in, 154-55. *See also* Muslim dissident literature

Islamic Social Services Association, 107

Islamic Society of North America (ISNA): ISNA school, 198, 205n8; leadership of, 188; women in, 104, 107, 109n15. *See also* Jame' Mosque

Islamists, 67, 101, 131. *See also* extremists

Islamophobia: after 9/11, 203; being called "illegal immigrant," 223-24; defined, 208-9; distancing and, 141; faith-based arbitration, 47-48; gendered Islamophobia, 74-75, 210-11, 213-14, 231-32; hijabophobia, 211; honour killings, 49-50; in media, 164; media tactics to prove innocence, 130; niqabophobia, 10. *See also* backlash; discrimination; racism

Ismaili Muslim community: and Arbitration act, 82n1; constructed as Western, 83n8; women in political office, 109n16

ISNA. *See* Islamic Society of North America (ISNA)

Israel: anti-Semitism, 127; in newspapers, 121, 122; as representative of attacked nation, 123-24, 132

Jaballah, Mahmoud, 240, 253, 256-57, 259

Jackson, Sherman: on bringing lapsed Muslims back to Islam, 187; on cultural/ethnic Muslims, 187; on folk Muslims, 188; and Modernized Islam, 187, 201; and post-colonial religion, 191

Jaffer, Mobina, 109n16

Jamaat-i-Islami movement, 188

Jame' Mosque, 196, 198. *See also* Islamic Society of North America (ISNA), ISNA school

James, Yolande, 55

Jewkes, Yvonne, 243

Jews. *See* Israel

Jhappan, Radha, 19-20

Jimenez, Marina, 123

Jiwani, Yasmin, 56, 176, 243

Johnson, Gilbert, 4

Jones, Alison, 228

journalists: control of, 117. *See also names of specific journalists*

Joya Jafri, Gul, 107

juridical discourses: and Bill C-36, 273; as tool to define inclusion, 277-78

Kahf, Mohja, 51

Karim, Karim H., 168-69, 173, 176, 243

Kashmeri, Zuhair, 279

Kenney, Jason, 18

Kepel, Gilles, 159n14

Khalid, M.D., 196

Khan, Sheema, 9-10, 15

Kibria, Shaila, 109n17

Kinsman, Gary, 291

Know Your Rights, 281

Knowles, Gary, 203

Knox, Paul, 127

Korenic, Bojan, 266

Kruger, Erin, 266

Kumar, Deepa, 125

Kutty, Ahmed, 205n8

Laprade, Bernard, 260
law. *See* juridical discourses
Le Pen, Jean-Marie, 212
LeBel, Louis, 260
Legal Education and Action Fund (West Coast LEAF), 63
Lenk, Helle-Mai, 213
liberalism: controls on Islamic dress, 12-13; governmentality of tolerance, 20-21; Islamic reform and, 150-53
Ligue des droits et libertés, 285
Ling, L.H.M., 134n3
Lippmann, Walter, 242-43
list of entities, 288-89, 295n22
Little Mosque on the Prairie: and Al Qaida, 170; and CBC, 173, 175, 176; content of, 169-70; and cultural resistance, 167, 170; international reaction to, 170-72; and national consciousness, 2; and Osama bin Laden, 170, 178n6; and public broadcasting, 162; reactions to, 177, 178n8; translation to French, 171. *See also* Canadian Broadcasting Corporation (CBC); media; mosques
Lorenz, Andrea, 4, 5
Louw, Eric, 129
Love, Agnes, 4
Love, James, 4
Lukas, Salome, 9, 36
Lull, James, 163

MacKay, Andrew, 259
Mackey, Eva, 260
Maclean's magazine, 164
MacMullen, Ian, 185
Macpherson, Don, 58n8
madrassas: in Canada, 194, 205n4; curriculum of, 194-95, 205n3; history of model for, 194, 205n2; and paradigm of resistance, 195, 200, 205n13; public perceptions of, 193; use of term, 191-92, 193-94. *See also* education (Islamic); mosques
Mahjoub, Mohamed Zeki, 240, 257
Mamdani, Mahmood, 130, 282, 283
Mandaville, Peter, 100
Manitoba, 200
Manji, Irshad: about, 142, 155; criticism of, 147, 156; and criticism of Islam, 144-47, 158-59n10; *Faith without Fear*, 151, 158-59n10; as freelance Muslim commentator, 143; honorary positions held by, 157-58n3; on Judeo-Christian secular synthesis, 153; on moderate Muslims, 150; and reform, 142, 147-48, 152, 154-55; on religion of peace argument, 146-47; self-labelling of, 150, 158n8, 159n13; and tolerance of Muslims, 153; and Western values, 150-51, 153; on women's emancipation, 154-55. *See also* Raza, Raheel; *The Trouble with Islam Today* (Manji)
Mann, Bonnie, 123
Mansour, Asmahan, 51
Maritime Muslim Academy, 198
marriage contracts, 79
Martin, Michèle, 163
Masmoudi, Radwan, 159n14
Mattson, Ingrid: explanation of framework of, 186-87; and Islamic Society of North America (ISNA), 104; and "Modernized Islam," 201; paradigm of embrace, 187, 195-96; paradigm of resistance, 187, 195; paradigm of selective engagement, 188; use of framework, 189, 204
Mazigh, Monia, 109n17, 295n18
MCC. *See* Muslim Canadian Congress (MCC)
McGuinty, Dalton: establishment of Boyd Commission, 83n6; and termination of faith-based arbitration, 48, 81

McIntosh, Donald, 253, 262
McLachlin, Beverley, 265
McLellan, Anne, 280, 284
McLuhan, Marshall, 162
McPhedran, Marilou, 73
McVeigh, Timothy, 130, 132, 225
Me and the Mosque, 169-70
media: American media, 171-72, 178*n*7, 242-43; British media, 172-73; categorization in, 165-66; control of journalists, 117; cultural imperialism and, 166-67; ethnic media, 173; European media, 172; faith-based arbitration, 47-48, 78-79; framing of events by, 115-16, 152; on honour killings, 49-51; and ideology, 174; ignoring of Muslim women's viewpoints, 213; importance of, 161; Islamophobia and, 1, 164; Muslim women involved with, 107; "not Canadian" theme in, 264-68; ownership of, 116-17, 133*n*1; perceptions of Muslims in, 178*n*7; propaganda model, 242-43, 247-48, 250, 252, 253; public broadcasting, 173-75; radio programs, 17-18; role and function of, 113-14, 162-64; stereotypes in, 165-66, 168-69, 176-77, 178*n*5; terrorism arrests in Canada, 290; on veiling, 50. *See also Little Mosque on the Prairie;* newspapers
medical clinics, 109*n*14
MEF. *See* Muslim Education Foundation (MEF)
memorization, 193, 194-95
men: control over male gaze, 218, 229-30, 232-33*n*5; hypermasculinity, 123, 134*n*3
men (Muslim): inside North America, 125, 127, 130; outside North America, 124, 126, 127; and oppression of women, 71-76; presence in Canada as threat, 273; responsibility for control of sexual attention, 218, 232-33*n*5; security certificates and, 263; terrorist narratives, 257, 258; as threat, 254-55. *See also* gender
Mernissi, Fatima, 232-33*n*5
Merry, Michael S., 200
Metcalf, Barbara Daly, 190
Mia, Ziyaad E., 286, 289, 295*n*22
militant Islam. *See* extremists
Milton-Edwards, Beverly, 99
minority communities: demographics of, 161; domestic violence, 49-50; ethnic media, 173; political involvement of, 92-93, 108*n*2. *See also* immigration; Muslim community
Mississauga, Ontario, 198
mob mentality. *See* herd mentality
Moderate Muslims: appeal of label, 148; categorization, 148-50, 158*nn*7-8, 159*n*14; Islamic reform and, 144, 148
modern Muslims, 150
Modernized Islam, 201
Moghissi, Haideh, 3
Moller Okin, Susan, 51-52
Monem, Olivia, 107
Montreal, Quebec: Islamic schools in, 198-99; requests for accommodation in, 11. *See also* Quebec
Montreal Gazette, 55
Moore, Kathleen, 104-5
mosques: awareness of women's issues from, 357; civic engagement and, 191; distribution in Canada, 190; and education, 192; ideology in, 191; importance of, 169, 190; Jame' Mosque, 196, 198; mosqued Muslims, 186; stereotypes of, 170; terrorist activity, 257. *See also* Islam; *Little Mosque on the Prairie;* madrassas; religion
motive (criminal), 285-86
movies, 165-66, 168, 178*n*5
MPL. *See* Muslim Personal Law

Muhammad (Prophet): on learning, 192; on veiling, 216-17. *See also* hadith

Mulder, Marlene, 266

multiculturalism: Aboriginal populations, 3; Canadian identity, 45-46; Canadian image as benevolent, 26, 273, 278, 294n15; CBC and government policy, 173-77; death by culture, 48-52; disciplining culture, 47-48; and education, 199; failure of, 4; faith-based arbitration, 68; false sense of belonging, 245; goals of, 173, 278; historical overview of policy, 21-22, 57n3, 189-90; inclusion of religion, 190; informal power structures, 45-46; measures of success for, 23; minorities proving themselves worthy, 18; Multiculturalism Act of 1985 (Canada), 173-77, 279; as offer of tolerance, 22-23; reasonable accommodation, 56; role of religion in education, 183-84; as source of pride, 7. *See also* culture

multiculturalism (backlash against): arrest of Toronto 18, 23; as bad for minority women, 18-19, 51-52; concerns over integration, 6-7; difference as disruptive, 24, 46; hijab ban in public schools, 211-14, 232n3; interculturalism, 24-25, 56; media and, 164; minorities as threat, 67; Muslim dissident literature and, 140, 151. *See also* tolerance

multiple critique, 152-53

Muslim (defined), 95-96

Muslim Association of Canada, 102

Muslim Brotherhood movement, 188

Muslim Canadian Congress (MCC): case against niqab, 34n4; on honour killings, 19; niqab ban, 13. *See also* Fatah, Tarek

Muslim community: Canadian Islam, 2; claiming rights as citizens, 17; discrimination as concern of, 8; divisions within, 6; faith-based arbitration, 65, 82n3; feelings on Canada, 7; history of, 3-6; increasing importance of, 1; Mattson's framework of community outlooks, 186-89; as outsiders, 71; political involvement of women, 109n15; private negotiations within, 80; public debates, 1; questions of loyalty of, 17-18; responsibility to stop terrorism, 261-62; sexism within, 72-74; subaltern citizenship, 16, 43-45; surveillance of, 244; as threat, 1; veiling and, 219-20. *See also* culture; identity (Muslim); immigration; minority communities; *names of specific debates*

Muslim Community Association of the San Francisco Bay Area, 109n14

Muslim Council of Montreal, 11

Muslim dissident literature: about, 137-39, 157n1; audience of, 138; and radical Muslims, 138, 156, 157n2; reactions to, 140, 155-56, 158n6; role in identity negotiation, 139-40, 142. *See also* dissent; Islamic reform

Muslim Education Foundation (MEF), 201-2

Muslim identity. *See* identity (Muslim)

Muslim men. *See* men (Muslim)

Muslim organizations: about, 188. *See also names of specific Muslim organizations*; politics

Muslim Personal Law (MPL), 79

Muslim Politics (Eickelman and Piscatori), 99-100

Muslim Response to Western Education (Hashmi), 205n2

Muslim women. *See* women (Muslim)

Muslim Women Activists in North America (Bullock), 106

Muslim Women in America (Haddad, Smith and Moore), 105
Muslim women's groups: objectives of, 102. *See also names of specific groups*
Muslims: erasure of victims of war on terror, 115; "Muslim" defined, 95-96; Muslim politics, 101-3; Muslim refusenik, 141, 150, 158n8. *See also* categorization; Palestinians
Muslims (radical). *See* extremists
Mustapha, Nadira, 107
Mutawakkil, Wakil Ahmed, 127

9/11: Canadianness after, 46; coverage of, 116, 124-25, 132-33, 134n5; Islamic reform as reaction to, 143; Islamophobia after, 203; Palestinian reaction to, 120, 123-24; racism after, 46; reaction of Canadian Muslims to, 143; women's reactions to, 129. *See also* terrorism; Twin Towers attack; war on terror
Narayan, Uma, 75
nation and nationalism: in context of security risks, 16; exclusion of Others, 17, 274; feeling secure within nation, 26; multiculturalism as national narrative, 22, 26, 273, 278, 294n15; nation defined, 17; national belonging, 42; national imaginary, 56, 61-62, 68-69; nationalism defined, 44; nationalists and, 17, 45, 54; position within nation, 44, 57n4; pride of Canadian Muslims, 7; Thobani on, 45, 293-94n9; white settler nation, 291. *See also* identity (Canadianness)
National Post: on Aqsa Parvez, 49-50; on backlash against Muslims, 128-31; and Canadian women, 125-26; chronology of terrorist incidents in, 120; coverage of 9/11, 116, 124-25, 132-33, 134n5; coverage of bin Laden and al-Qaeda, 127-28; differences between editions, 129-30; headline use by, 118-20; on Islam, 131-32; justification for war in, 122, 126, 129; and Muslim men, 127; and Muslim sources, 123, 125, 126, 130; and Muslim women, 125; ownership of, 117; on Palestinian reaction to 9/11, 120-21, 123, 124; readership of, 117; on security certificates, 248, 249-51, 253-54, 256-57, 260, 262, 263-64, 266; on "shar'ia" debate, 64-65; support for US in, 121, 122-23
nationalism. *See* nation and nationalism
Nawaz, Zarqa, 169-70, 172, 176, 177n2, 178n6
New Democratic Party, 109n17
New York Times, 124
newspapers: analyses of Islam, 131-32; attacks on dissent in, 124, 134n4; categorization of information by, 117-20; faith-based arbitration, 64, 72; gendered coverage in, 123-27, 131-32; Orientalism in, 116, 168-69; Osama bin Laden, 127-28; overview of coverage, 132-33; ownership of, 133n1; role and function of, 116, 133n2; security certificate content in, 248, 249-51, 253-58, 256-59; use of distancing by, 121-22; use of headlines by, 118-20, 204-5n1, 212. *See also* media; *names of specific newspapers*
Nimer, Mohamed, 190, 191
niqab: as election issue, 9-10; gendered Islamophobia and, 231; "niqabi" defined, 34n2, 233n11; niqabophobia, 10; Quebec ban of (Bill 94), 9-15, 214; statistics on wear in Quebec, 11; Stephen Harper on

niqab ban, 9, 15; support for Bill 94, 15
Nizam ul-Mulk, 205*n*3
Nizamiyya curriculum model, 194, 205*n*3
non-governmental organizations: as "informal sector," 96; list of entities, 288-89; Muslim involvement in, 102-3, 105-7. *See also* civic engagement
Northwest Territories, 190
Nova Scotia, 198
NVivo 8, 248, 250

Office of the Superintendant of Financial Institutions (OSFI), 289, 295*n*24
"On Life Support" (Raboy and Taras), 173
Ontario: Conservative Party platform, 185; faith-based schools, 183, 185, 189, 204-5*n*1; history of Muslims in, 4; Islamic schools in, 210; mosques in, 190, 196, 198
Ontario Human Rights Commission, 164
Orientalism (concept): and Bill C-36, 273-74, 291; and bin Laden, 128; defined, 177*n*3, 232*n*1; and European culture, 167-68; faith-based arbitration, 47-48; gendered Islamophobia, 211; Hérouxville Citizen's Code, 53-54; immigrants and, 277-78; and Manji, 147; and media, 168-69; Middle Eastern participation in, 177*n*4; and newspapers, 116, 168-69; niqab and, 13; power of, 252; in public schools, 220; and racism, 282; subaltern citizenship, 43. *See also* the Other, Otherness; stereotypes
Orientalism (Said), 277, 293*n*3
OSFI. *See* Office of the Superintendant of Financial Institutions

the Other, Otherness: anti-citizen, 7, 53; Bill C-36, 291; cultural/ethnic Muslims, 187; dissent and, 134*n*4; excluded from creation of national identity, 17, 274; as external to Canadian, 57*n*4, 260-61; faith-based arbitration, 63-64, 71; foreign as dangerous, 26, 69-71, 244; and Hérouxville Town Charter, 41-42; "not Canadian" theme in media, 264-68; Palestinians as, 124; power of Orientalism and, 252; as problem, 245; propaganda model, 243; security certificate coverage, 251, 254-56, 258; television programming and, 172-73; use of term, 293*n*7; veiling and, 51, 212-13, 223. *See also* Orientalism (concept); Western values
Ouimet, Emilie, 212-14

Pakistan, 127
Palestinians: gendered coverage of, 123-27, 131-32; newspaper articles on, 120-21. *See also* Muslims
panoptic techniques, 246
Parvez, Aqsa, 49-51
Patriot Act (United States), 263
peace (religion of): Islamic reform and, 144-45, 146-48, 156; statements by Muslim men, 130; stereotype of Islam as violent, 146. *See also* Islam
Pearl Harbor, 118-19
Pearson, Patricia, 117
peer pressure, 227-28
Persad, Judy Vashti, 9
Philps, Alan, 132
Pilger, John, 115
Pipes, Daniel, 34*n*4, 131
Piscatori, James, 99-100
Le Point, 212
political Islam: contrast with Muslim politics, 101-3; defined, 98-99; and

integration, 101; as protest, 99, 100; variances in, 99-100
political outlooks: overview of Mattson's framework, 186-89; paradigm of embrace, 187, 195-97; paradigm of resistance, 187, 195, 200, 205n13, 217-18; paradigm of selective engagement, 188, 200-1. *See also* categorization
politics: Islamists, 131; minority representation in Parliament, 108n2; "political engagement" defined, 95-96, 96-98; public broadcasting, 174; of veiling, 9-10, 214; war on terror, 70-71, 272. *See also* civic engagement; Muslim organizations
politics (female involvement): assertion of identity, 96-97, 107; elected Muslim women, 105, 108n1, 109n16; formal involvement in government, 92, 93; informal sector involvement, 92, 101-3, 105-7; Muslim associations, 104, 109n15; Muslim candidates, 105, 109n17; political advocacy, 107; public education, 97-98; workplace discrimination, 98
Post. *See National Post*
prayer, 230
Prevention of Terrorism Bill (United Kingdom), 263
preventive arrests, 286-87
Progressive Muslim Union of North America, 152
propaganda model, 242-43, 247-48, 250, 252, 353
Prophet Muhammad. *See* Muhammad (Prophet)
public broadcasting, 162, 173-75. *See also* Canadian Broadcasting Corporation (CBC)
Public Safety Act (Canada), 272, 293n3
public transit, 221-23
Pushtuns, 128

QSF. *See* Québec Soccer Federation (QSF)
Quebec: Bill 94, 9-15, 14, 214; Bill 101, 212-13; hijab bans, 51, 211, 212-14; immigration policies, 26, 55-56, 65-66; interculturalism, 24-25; Islamic schools in, 198-99; multiculturalism policy and, 21; niqab ban, 214; racism survey, 25; reasonable accommodation, 23-24, 56; religion and schools, 183; statistics on niqab wear in, 11; use of veiling as election issue, 9-10. *See also* Hérouxville, Quebec; identity (French Canadian); Montreal, Quebec
Quebec Council for the Status of Women, 14
Québec Soccer Federation (QSF), 51
Québecor, 133n1
Queen's University Muslim Students Association (QUMSA), 107
Quiet Revolution, 24
Qur'an: and extremists, 144; and Islamic reform, 144-46, 148; supplementary religious education, 196-97; use in activism, 102; and veiling, 216-17. *See also* hadith
Qur'an and Sunnah Society, 187
Qur'anic schools. *See* madrassas

Raboy, Marc, 173-74
racism: activism, 101-2; after 9/11, 46; Bill 94, 9-15; Bill C-36, 295n19; border racism, 16; Canadian citizenship guide, 18; categorization of Muslims as terrorists, 223-25; citizenship categories, 57n4, 245; crisis of whiteness, 22; domestic violence, 39-40, 49-50, 75-76; and education, 199; immigrant integration, 3-4; informal power structures, 45-46; interculturalism, 25; juridical discourses and, 273;

minorities as threat, 67; Orientalism and, 282; racial profiling, 279-80, 294n13; racial securitization defined, 34-35n6; reasonable accommodation, 23-24; rhetoric of security, 25-26, 291; selection of immigrants, 266-67; subaltern citizenship, 43-45; surveillance of Arabs and Muslims, 244, 246-47, 279; survey in Quebec, 25; white converts to Islam, 213; white settler societies, 4, 276-77. *See also* backlash; Islamophobia

radical Muslims. *See* extremists

radio, 17-18

Rahman, Mona, 107

Ramadan, Tariq, 17, 197-98

Ramji, Rubina, 166, 168, 178n5

Ratansi, Yasmin, 109n16

Raza, Raheel: about, 142, 155; condemnation of militants by, 144, 145, 146, 158-59n10; as freelance Muslim commentator, 143; on Judeo-Christian secular synthesis, 153; on misunderstanding of Islam, 144; and multiple critique, 152-53; on Muslims in society, 153; perceptions of, 149-50; position of, 142-44, 156; on reform, 148; self-identification of, 148; threats to, 157n2; and Western values, 150, 152-53; on women's emancipation, 154. *See also* Manji, Irshad; *Their Jihad ... Not My Jihad!* (Raza)

Razack, Sherene: on the body of the Muslim woman, 283; on categorization, 83n9; on cultural reductionist arguments, 75; on imagined community of the Canadian nation, 275; on penalties on Geneva Convention refugees, 277; on security measures, 244, 262; on self-image of Canadians, 278; on state of exception, 46; on treatment of Muslims, 282; on violence in immigrant communities, 49; on Western media, 164

RCMP (Royal Canadian Mounted Police), 294n14

Read, Jen'Nan Ghazal, 230

reality shows, 172

reasonable accommodation, 23-24, 56

Reay, Diane, 226

Reel Bad Arabs (Shaheen), 178n5

reform. *See* Islamic reform

Registered Nurses Association of Ontario (RNAO), 106

regulatory bodies (Canadian television), 176

religion: government controls on, 10-11, 212; importance to Canadians, 190; in media, 165-66; paradigm of embrace, 187; religious divorces, 79; and secularism, 151; separation of church and state, 74; teaching of, 144; veiling and, 44-45. *See also* faith-based arbitration; mosques; secularism

rescue of women. *See* women (Muslim) (as victim)

resistance (paradigm of): about, 187; and madrassas, 195, 200, 205n13; and media, 166-67; and veiling, 217-18, 227-28

Rivers, William, 162

RNAO. *See* Registered Nurses Association of Ontario

Roach, Kent, 284

Rodgers, Jayne, 124

Rogers Communication, 133n1

Rose, Alexander, 131-32

Ross, Darryl, 245

Royal Commission on Biculturalism and Bilingualism, 189

Ruggles, Myles A., 178n9

Russell, John, 288

Said, Edward: central concern of *Orientalism,* 277; and culture,

166-67; on Islamic identity, 96; on media, 167; on mythic language, 277; on Orientalism, 167-68, 177nn3-4, 252; on racial profiling of Arabs and Muslim Americans, 280; references to, 162, 293n7

Salafiyya movement, 187

Saloojee, Riad, 281

Salutin, Rick, 122

San Francisco Bay Area, 109n14

Santa Clara, California, 109n14

Sardar, Ziauddin, 172

Sarroub, Loukia K., 219-20

Saskatchewan, 4

Sassen, Saskia, 164-65

Saul, John Ralston, 175

Saunders, Doug, 129

the scarf affair, 212

Schramm, Wilbur, 162

Schultz (federal bureaucrat), 267

Section 83 (Bill C-36), 284-85, 286, 288

secularism: education and, 183-84; Islamic reform and, 150-53; in Quebec, 23-24; veiling and, 44-45. *See also* religion

security: border racism, 16; citizenship as category, 245; deemed as necessary, 16; as freedom, 262; as government commodity, 243; governmentality (concept), 259; niqab as threat to, 14-15; Orientalist nature of rhetoric, 274; Patriot Act, 263; Prevention of Terrorism Bill, 263; racial secularization defined, 34-35n6; racism rationalized by, 25-26; as rationale for government policy, 70-71, 272; security-industrial complex, 34-35n6; state of exception, 14, 46; white settler nation, 291. *See also* Bill C-36 (Canada); surveillance; war on terror

security certificates: Adil Charkaoui's speaking tour, 259-60; Bill C-3, 241; Canadian Security Intelligence Service (CSIS), 240-41, 252, 254-58; certificates issued to, 240; content of, 248, 249-51; debate on, 239-42; detainees as free to leave, 267-68; *Detention Centres and Security Certificates*, 239, 241; hidden nature of, 244; International Covenant of Civil and Political Rights, 240, 241-42; and IRPA (Immigration and Refugee Protection Act), 240, 241, 262-63, 265; newspaper coverage, 248, 249-51, 253-58, 260-66; state of exception, 246-47, 262-63; Supreme Court ruling on, 295n21; terrorist narrative construction, 256-60; threat theme in coverage, 252-56. *See also* Immigration and Refugee Protection Act (IRPA); terrorism

selective engagement (paradigm of): about, 188; and Islamic schools, 200-1

seminaries, 205n8. *See also* madrassas

Senate (Canadian), 109n16

Šeneviratne, Shanaka, 281

sexualized feminine, 227-28

Sha'aban, Salim, 4-5

Shaben, Larry, 4

Shaheen, Jack G., 178n5

Shamma, Freda, 104

shar'ia: in Middle East, 66-67, 101; usage of term, 76-77

shar'ia debate. *See* faith-based arbitration

Shar'ia Street, 172

Sharify-Funk, Meena, 24-25

Siddiqui, Samana, 107

Siddiqui, Shahina, 107

The Siege, 166

Smith, Jane I., 104-5

Smith, Linda Tuhiwai, 292

soccer, 51

social activism. *See* activism

social movements, 101, 102-3

social services: free medical clinics, 109n14; Islamic Social Services Association, 107; Muslim involvement in, 102, 107; reduction of state expenditures on, 108n13
Sokoloff, Yitzhak, 120
Sound Vision, 102, 107
South Africa, 79
Spector, Norman, 122, 123-24
Spivak, Gayatri, 12-13, 48, 283
Sprinzak, Ehud, 132
Spurles, Kelly, 233n9
St. Laurent, Quebec, 200
St-Pierre, Christine, 12
Stabile, Carol, 125
Stasiulis, Daiva, 245
state of exception, 14, 46, 240, 246-47, 262-63
Steedman, Mercedes, 291
stereotypes: activism related to, 101; curriculum development, 97; gendering Islamophobia, 210-11; of immigrants, 42, 57n1, 245; individual struggles with, 98; Islam as violent, 146; Islamic reformist protest of, 152-53; in media, 165-66, 176-77, 178n5; of mosques, 170; of Muslim women, 231-32; need to be perfect, 223-25, 233n9; in public schools, 220; terrorist narratives, 254-55, 257-58. *See also* categorization; counter-narratives; Orientalism (concept); women (Muslim)(as victim)
Steyn, Mark, 120-21, 163
strangulation, 51
Students for International Peace and Justice, 107
subaltern citizenship, 43-45
Sun newspaper chain, 133n1
sunnah (defined), 108n5
Sunni Muslim communities: Mattson's framework, 186-89
sunset clause, 295n17
Supreme Court (Canada), 295n21

surveillance: harassment by CSIS, 281; increased surveillance measures, 244, 246, 253, 255; list of entities, 288-89; racial profiling of Muslims, 70-71, 279, 280-81; reasonable grounds for, 258; within Muslim communities, 261-62. *See also* security
Syed, Amjed, 130
Syed, Itrath, 44, 62-64, 63-64
symbols: symbolic annihilation, 115; symbolism of hijab, 216
Sympatico, 133n1

Tablighi Jamaat movement, 187
Taliban, 125
Tanovich, David, 294n13
Taras, David, 173-74, 175
tarbiyah, 192-93
Tator, Carol, 243, 293n4
Taylor, Charles, 23-25
Taylor, Tayyibah, 107
television: Al Jazeera Network, 170-71; *Aliens in America*, 171-72; Canadian regulatory bodies, 176; *Shar'ia Street*, 172. *See also* Canadian Broadcasting Corporation (CBC)
terrorism: Canadian arrests, 1, 6, 52, 290; cultural terrorism, 21; definition of, 284, 291; as ever-present threat, 254-55; and ignorance, 130; as irrational, 121, 126; Islamic reform and, 144-45; movies about, 178n5; newspapers on, 121; niqab as marker for, 13; published chronology of, 120; "terrorist" as collective label for all Muslims, 223-25. *See also* 9/11; Bill C-36 (Canada); security certificates; Twin Towers attack; war on terror
Their Jihad ... Not My Jihad! (Raza): author's analysis of, 139. *See also* Raza, Raheel
thematic categories. *See* categorization

Thobani, Sunera: attacks on, 134n4; and bad immigrant archetype, 57n1; and "Canadians-as-members-of-the-nation," 293-94n9; on crisis of whiteness, 21-22; criticisms of, 294n15; on erasure of status of minority groups, 287; on national subjects, 45; on racial profiling, 281; on war on terror, 282

Todd, Sharon, 216

tolerance: governmentality of, 20-21; Manji on, 153; multiculturalism as offer of, 22-23. *See also* multiculturalism (backlash against)

Toronto, Ontario: civic involvement of Muslims, 102; home schooling networks, 201; Islamic schools in, 210; Jame' Mosque, 196, 198

Toronto Star: ownership of, 133n1; on "shar'ia" debate, 64-65; use of headlines by, 204-5n1

Torstar Corporation, 133n1

torture, 242, 246

The Trouble with Islam Today (Manji): author's analysis of, 139; effect of book, 138; and multiculturalism, 140; purpose of writing of, 156; title changes to, 158n9. *See also* Manji, Irshad

Trudeau, Pierre, 189

Tuchman, Gaye, 115

Turkey, 14, 211, 214, 232n3

Twin Towers attack: benevolence of women, 126; categorization of headlines about, 118-20; gendered coverage, 123-27, 131-32; use of binary descriptions, 120-23. *See also* 9/11; terrorism

Ukeles, Raquel, 203

ul-Haq, Sami, 127

ululating (defined), 124

United Kingdom: BBC programming, 172-73; Prevention of Terrorism Bill as model, 263

United Nations: Convention against Torture, 242; counterterrorism conventions and protocols, 284; International Covenant of Civil and Political Rights, 240, 241-42

United States: Canadian anti-American sentiment, 122-23; clash of civilizations, 282; free medical clinics, 109n14; Muslims in media, 171-72, 178n7; Patriot Act as model, 263; portrayed as attacked, 118-19, 121-22; propaganda model in media, 242-43; as scapegoat, 152-53; support for, 121; visibility of Muslim women in, 105

university student associations, 107

van Dijk, Teun A., 118, 165

van Gogh, Theo, 158-59n10

veiling: ban of niqab, 9-15, 214; control of, 10, 44-45, 215, 219; as election issue, 9-10; gendered Islamophobia and, 231-32; and Hérouxville Town Charter, 41-42; hijabophobia, 211; historical representation of Muslim women, 51; honour killings, 49-50; identity construction, 219-20, 227-29; in Islamic schools, 220-21, 226-27; as marker of Otherness, 13, 223; media on, 50; multiple meanings of, 215-16; and national identity, 44; niqabophobia, 10; politics of, 214; as protest, 215, 232n4; in public schools, 211-13, 219-20, 232n3; on public transit, 221-23; in religious paradigms, 216-17; responsibility for control of sexual attention, 218, 232-33n5; support for Bill 94, 15; workplace discrimination, 8-9, 98, 211. *See also* culture; women (Muslim)

Vincent, Isabel, 127-28

Volpp, Leti, 130

Wadud, Amina, 147

Wahhabi movement, 205n2
Waliullah school of thought, 205n2
Walt Disney Corporation, 168
war on terror: erasure of Muslim victims, 115; exclusions of Muslims, 43; media justifications for, 121-23; propaganda model and, 243; protection of women, 125-26, 134n5; security certificate coverage, 252; security justifications for, 272; state of exception, 46. *See also* 9/11; security; terrorism
Weinstock, Daniel, 55-56
Wente, Margaret: inclusion of statements by Muslims, 131; on Muslim men, 126; on Sunera Thobani, 294n15; on use of Arbitration Act by Jewish community, 74; use of binaries by, 120
WERF. *See* Women's Equality and Religious Freedom Conference
the West: Canadianness in context of, 260; and Orientalism, 167-68; as scapegoat, 152-53, 293n1; selective consumption of Western products, 153, 177n4; as term, 82n2, 159n11
West Coast Legal Education and Action Fund (West Coast LEAF), 63, 82n4
Western Muslims and the Future of Islam (Ramadan), 197
Western values: construction of anti-citizen, 53; embrace of, 187; faith-based arbitration, 48; *Globe and Mail* on, 121-22; immigrant adoption of, 6-7, 34n1; Islamic reform and, 150-53; rejection of, 187; relationship with Islam, 141; security certificate coverage, 250-51; "Western" as term, 82n2. *See also* culture; identity (Canadianness); the Other, Otherness
White immigration, 266

white settler societies, 275-76, 291, 293n4
Wiktorowicz, Quintan: definition of "Islamic" activism, 95, 98-99; and the evaluation of women's involvement, 103; use of Islamic symbols, 101
Winch, Samuel, 128
Winnipeg, Manitoba, 200
Winter, James, 117, 133n1
women: benevolence of, 126; dangerous feminine, 232-33n5; female body as sexual object, 229-30; protection of, 125-26; reactions to 9/11, 129; use as term, 108n4; women's groups, 106, 107. *See also* domestic violence; gender; *names of specific women's groups*
women (Muslim): backlash against, 125; Canadian demographics of, 94, 108n3; controversies involving, 42; faith-based arbitration, 62-63, 79-80; ignoring of opinions of, 13-14, 63-64, 213; in media, 123, 125, 131; Muslim feminists, 76, 77-78, 79; right to choose to veil or not, 13-14, 213, 215; stereotypes about, 231-32; university education of, 94, 159n17. *See also* veiling
women (Muslim)(as victim): Afghan women, 125, 134n5; awareness of actual issues, 35n7; Canadian citizenship guide, 18; death by culture, 48-52; faith-based arbitration, 48, 63-64, 71-76; honour killings, 19, 49-51; Islamic law and, 77-78; Islamic reform and, 154-55; limits on agency, 39-40; niqab ban in Quebec, 12-13; Orientalist legacy of, 282; surveillance of Muslims, 282; symbolic violence against, 294n16; veiling, 212. *See also* domestic violence; stereotypes

Women's Equality and Religious Freedom (WERF) Conference, 63-64, 67-68, 82n4, 82-83n4
workplace discrimination, 8-9, 98, 211
World War I, 5
World War II, 118-19, 122

Yellowknife, Northwest Territories, 190

Zaman, Saminaz, 186
Zine, Jasmin: on gendered Islamophobia, 74-75; performance of national identity by, 42-43

Printed and bound in Canada by Friesens

Set in Futura Condensed and Warnock by Artegraphica Design Co. Ltd.

Copy editor: Robert Lewis

Proofreader: Lana Okerlund

Indexer: Natalie Boon